Access and SQL Server Developer's Handbook

John L. Viescas

Mike Gunderloy

Mary Chipman

Access® and SQL Server® Developer's Handbook™

John L. Viescas

Mike Gunderloy

Mary Chipman

SYBEX®

SAN FRANCISCO • PARIS • DÜSSELDORF • SOEST

Associate Publisher: Amy Romanoff
Acquisitions Manager: Kristine Plachy
Developmental Editor: Melanie Spiller
Editors: Anamary Ehlen, Christa Anderson
Project Editor: Shelby Zimmerman
Technical Editor: Bruce Loehle-Conger
Book Designer: Suzanne Albertson
Graphic Illustrators: Kelly Jonick, Catalin Dulfu
Desktop Publisher: Alissa Feinberg
Production Coordinator: Alexa Riggs
Proofreader: John Selawsky
Indexer: Ted Laux
Cover Designer: Design Site
Cover Illustrator: Gregory MacNicol

Library of Congress Card Number: 95-73267

ISBN: 0-7821-1804-6

Manufactured in the United States of America

10 9 8 7 6 5 4 3 2

Acknowledgments

This book has benefitted greatly from the efforts of our editors, Christa Anderson and Anamary Ehlen, and from the efforts of our project editor, Shelby Zimmerman. They all kept us moving and were instrumental in ensuring a quality product. Bruce Loehle-Conger, our technical editor, contributed his knowledge and insight; Michael Kaplan provided valuable assistance with Chapters 3 and 4. We would like to thank both of them for their help. We would also like to thank all the folks at SYBEX who worked hard behind the scenes to make this book come to life.

CONTENTS AT A GLANCE

TABLE OF CONTENTS

Introduction

Computing professionals have been talking about the benefits of client/server applications for at least a dozen years. Many have actually stepped into the fray and built successful applications that support multiple users sharing a single data source over a network. The tools for building client/server applications have been getting better and better, but building and implementing a successful application using this architecture still requires a lot of hard work.

The introduction of Access in 1992 represented the first standardized support for easily linking the desktop to server data via Open Database Connectivity (ODBC). Access also provides a simple yet robust facility for developing client application interfaces for the Windows environment. A key feature in Access is its ability to build a form that is "bound" to a source table or query—the programmer doesn't have to worry about moving the data from the data source to the screen display and back. With ODBC, the source table or query can be a table or view in a true server database such as SQL Server.

For certain high-performance applications, the programmer may still have to get "behind the scenes" to write queries in the application directly to the server, using the ODBC Application Programming Interface (API) or the server's own native API. In some cases, the application designer may have to turn to more robust tools, such as Visual Basic or C, to create efficient client facilities. But for many applications, Access for the client and SQL Server for the server will fill the bill quite nicely. With the rapid development tools in Access, you can quickly build a working client/server application. If you encounter any performance problems, you can then concentrate on adjusting those particular areas using lower-level tools.

About This Book

Application designers and programmers can find many books that help them to get the most out of Access, or that show how to set up and tune SQL Server for different types of applications. The purpose of this book is to bring the two products together and specifically discuss the techniques you should use—and those that you should avoid—to build a successful client/server application using Access and SQL Server.

Who Can Use This Book?

MIS directors will find this book useful as a guide to what techniques should and should not be used to implement any client/server application. Although the book covers many technical topics in great detail, it also provides background material about the technologies available and how they should be employed to create successful applications using Access and SQL Server.

Anyone charged with designing and implementing a client/server application using Access and SQL Server should find this book invaluable. We assume you already have a good working knowledge of both Access and SQL Server; for example, you should already know how to build queries, forms, and reports in Microsoft Access. We also assume that you understand the basics of creating tables and views in SQL Server. This book takes you beyond the basics, with dozens of concrete examples showing you how to leverage the technology. We also included a large assortment of sample databases and code on the CD-ROM bound in the back of this book.

A Word about Versions

This book was written with Access for Windows 95, version 7.0, and SQL Server, version 6.0. We'll just call these products "Access" and "SQL Server" from this point on. New versions of both Access and SQL Server are scheduled to be released while this book is on the shelf. Although the code in this book hasn't been tested on these new versions, it should run with a minimum of difficulty, as the basic concepts of writing client/server applications in a mixed Access and SQL Server environment have been stable through several versions of each product.

What's in This Book?

This book is divided into ten chapters covering an assortment of intermediate to advanced topics about using Access and SQL Server together to create applications. For someone new to client/server, reading the chapters in sequence may be most appropriate, beginning with design issues, continuing with in-depth analysis of various technical capabilities, and winding up with discussions about securing, installing, and maintaining a client/server application. A more advanced user may want to jump in to one of the chapters that covers a particular technology of interest.

The chapters are as follows:

- Chapter 1 provides an overview of client/server architectures, a discussion of the reasons for implementing an application in such an architecture, and a review of some of the technologies that make client/server easier to implement.

- Chapter 2 discusses relational database design and specifically covers special considerations for operating in a client/server environment.

- Chapter 3 covers application design techniques for client/server applications, with emphasis on the advantages and limitations of both Access and SQL Server.

- Chapter 4 provides an overview of techniques to use and avoid when building queries that must run efficiently across a network to access data on SQL Server.

- Chapter 5 shows you techniques you can use to enhance performance by directly calling the Open Database Connectivity (ODBC) Application Programming Interface (API) from your Access client code. The chapter also covers the technical details of using Remote Data Objects (RDO), an OLE technology wrapper around ODBC, from Access.

- Chapter 6 covers the "upsizing" tools available to help convert a stand-alone Access application to SQL Server. The chapter also discusses common problems and additional steps you should take to optimize your application after you upsize.

- Chapter 7 shows you how to manage your SQL Server from Access using the Distributed Management Object (DMO) model.

- Chapter 8 provides a thorough discussion of the replication features you can find in both Access and SQL Server and how to use them together.

- Chapter 9 discusses the security features in Access, SQL Server, and Windows NT and how you can use them together to secure your application and data.

- Chapter 10 covers installation tools and techniques for managing your client/server application after you have deployed it.

The appendices include a glossary of key SQL Server concepts to help developers with an Access background come up to speed with the server terminology. Also included is a guide to the contents of the companion CD-ROM, including instructions for installing and using the samples.

Conventions Used in This Book

Provided that you are running Access for Windows 95 or later, and SQL Server Version 6.0 or later, you should be able to copy and use all of the code samples shown in this book exactly as shown. In a few cases, we indicate information you should supply (such as the name of your table or column name) in italics. Wherever a line of code is too long to fit on one line within the book, we have liberally used the Visual Basic line continuation character (space, underscore, carriage return, line feed) to make the lines readable and accurate. Within SQL Server, Transact-SQL allows more free-form entry, so there's no problem with line lengths.

CHAPTER

ONE

Client/Server Architectures

- Defining client/server architectures

- Components of client/server applications

- Using Access and SQL Server

- The role of SQL and ODBC

In one form or another, client/server architectures have become commonplace for implementing computer applications. Anyone who dials in to an online information system is using a client/server architecture. When you use an ATM (Automated Teller Machine), have your purchases scanned at a store checkout counter, or pay for your purchases with a credit card, you're most likely interacting with a client/server computing system.

Client/Server Defined

There are probably as many different perspectives about what constitutes a "client/server" application as there are sites on the World Wide Web. One of the main goals of a client/server architecture is to achieve improved efficiency by breaking the task at hand into smaller pieces and distributing the work across two or more available computer processors. Necessarily, some of the tasks are in control of major processes but require additional work to be done by other processes in the system. These controlling tasks can be thought of as "clients" or "requesters," and the subservient tasks are "responders" or "servers."

Using this rather liberal definition, one could argue that even the Microsoft Windows NT operating system, when executing on a multiprocessor computer, is a client/server application. The architecture of Windows NT promotes the creation of many small tasks that request work from each other via messages sent from client tasks to server tasks to gain most efficient use of the available processors. In fact, state-of-the-art database management systems (like Microsoft SQL Server version 6.0) take advantage of this type of architecture to spawn many server tasks that can execute on different processors to quickly solve complex query problems.

When building application software (as opposed to system software), we need a more rigorous litmus test for what constitutes a true client/server application. In this context, a client/server application may be defined as an application architected with *significant* portions of the application executing on different computing systems. Furthermore, a true client/server application is constructed so that processes reside where the work specific to each process can be most efficiently performed. Note that this second definition is more rigorous but still subject to interpretation of the meaning of "significant" portions of the application.

For discussion purposes throughout the remainder of this chapter, we will be using both the more liberal as well as the more rigorous definitions when characterizing client/server applications. You'll notice that we adhere to the more rigorous definition in later chapters regarding accepted client/server application and database design techniques.

Client/Server: Benefits and Challenges

Information-processing professionals today recognize that implementing a computer application with a client/server architecture is an intelligent way to best use available computing resources. A client/server architecture provides several distinct advantages:

- Workload is naturally spread across multiple computers.
- Data can be easily shared between users.
- Sensitive data can be reliably secured in a central location.

- Smaller computers dedicated to specific tasks are more cost-effective.

However, a client/server architecture also presents interesting design and administration challenges:

- The designer must decide which tasks should execute on the client or the server.
- The designer must select appropriate hardware for each type of task.
- Client software upgrades must be carefully managed.
- Server database design changes may impact all clients.
- Network topology is often much more complex.
- Monitoring performance and making necessary adjustments can be more difficult than a centralized architecture.

This chapter introduces several ways to implement a client/server architecture using Microsoft Access 95 and Microsoft SQL Server. The advantages, pitfalls, and limitations of each are discussed as well as an overview of some of the database technology that makes creating a client/server architecture with these products possible.

Client/Server Components

One key to a successful client/server implementation is achieving a balance across the various components. On one end of the spectrum, you can implement a very simple and inexpensive architecture that may adequately serve a small number of users and/or a simple application. If you must support a large number of users or a very complex application, your architecture must necessarily be more robust.

The key to implementing a computer application with a client/server architecture is understanding the various layers that normally exist within the application. Figure 1.1 shows you some of the potential layers in any computer application. On the far left, the Application User is the ultimate client in this architecture—the requester of services from the application. As you move from left to right in the diagram, each layer on the left can be viewed as a client of the server composed of the layers to the right. So, the application user works through the user interface to request the execution of application tasks. Application tasks might include, for example, setting up a new customer, entering an order, or printing an invoice.

FIGURE 1.1:

Typical computer application layers

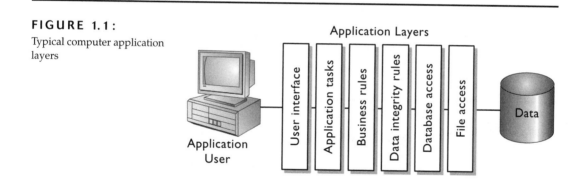

Application tasks must interact with and adhere to business rules (a customer can't place an order for more than the customer's established credit limit) which in turn are subject to data integrity rules (an order can be entered only for an existing customer; an order amount must be a number with two decimal places). At the far right, data retrieval is usually handled by a database engine which in turn often uses a file access engine provided by the computer operating system.

Separating Client from Server

When all layers of the application execute on a single computer, you have a single-user application. To create a client/server architecture, you must separate the client side from the server side at any logical application layer boundary. You can obtain the simplest client/server separation by choosing a boundary close to either end of the architecture.

Performing Most Work on the Server

One simple way to separate client work from server work is to place only user interface processing on the client and the remainder on the server as shown in Figure 1.2. Only the part of the application responsible for displaying output and accepting keyboard or mouse input resides on the application user's system. The remainder of the application executes on a large, shared computer system.

FIGURE 1.2:

Allocating most tasks to the server

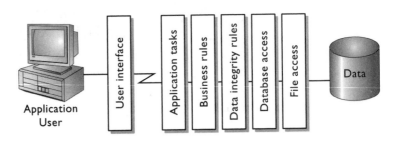

Sometimes the client computer is no more than a "smart" data terminal. You can often find this type of architecture in legacy mainframe systems. Even when the user works with this type of application through a personal computer, the PC may be doing no more than terminal emulation or providing a "graphical" look and feel to an older character-based system. At most, the client portion of the application is also handling simple data type validation.

This architecture is also similar to that found on most online service systems. The user's computer runs the communication and display software (such as a Web browser), but the computers on the network to which the user connects do most of the work. The X-Windows system under UNIX is another example. In these cases, although the client side is still handling only data presentation and flow, the client computer must be powerful enough to rapidly handle complex graphic data streams coming from the server.

Most computing professionals today would agree that this sort of simple split *does not* constitute a true client/server application. Even so, if the software on the client computer or workstation is performing significant work to present an enhanced graphical interface to the user while sending requests to the server using a simple character data stream, then this sort of application adheres to the spirit of client/server computing.

One of the key advantages to this architecture is that all data and most application logic is centralized in a single location. Any changes or upgrades to the application generally need only be made at the central server. One disadvantage is the central server must be very large if the application needs to allow simultaneous access by dozens of users. Also, since the link between client and server may need to handle high volumes of graphical information, obtaining good response times may require a very expensive, high-speed network between the clients and the server.

Performing Most Work on the Client

On the other end of the client/server spectrum is an application split so that the server acts only as a simple data repository or file server (see Figure 1.3). All of the data presentation and application logic reside on the client machine.

FIGURE 1.3:

Allocating most tasks to the client

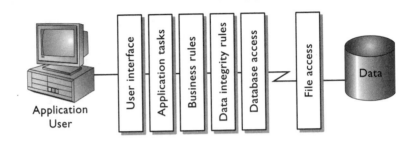

As you'll see later in this chapter, this is the architecture most often implemented when you use a desktop database product like Microsoft Access for Windows 95 for the entire application. Although it's easy to move the data tables to a server and attach links to multiple copies of the application database, everything except base-level file access executes on the client machines.

The primary advantage of this architecture is its simplicity. To get the basic benefits of client/server data sharing, you need only move the data files to a file management server. However, this type of architecture requires relatively sophisticated computer hardware on the client side. Also, since most file servers implement primary data sharing at the file level, this architecture can handle only light data access loads or a relatively small number of concurrent users. Even when the software on the client side is sophisticated enough to use server locking mechanisms that allow block-level sharing (Access does this), a large number of users can quickly exceed the resources of even the most robust servers, unless the application is designed to request only the minimum data required to handle a specific task.

Note that taking an Access application initially designed for a single user and moving its data tables to a shared file server *does not* necessarily constitute a true client/server implementation. A typical single-user Access application generally assumes all data is local, so most presentation and handling of data is designed to work with all the available data. To work efficiently in a client/server architecture, the client side of the application must be designed specifically to be a "good data citizen" and request only the information required to solve the specific task at hand. As you'll see later, an Access-only application designed in this manner "upsizes" easily to utilize a true database server. When the application is not designed in this way, it can never be efficiently implemented as a client/server application regardless of how much work you push to the server.

Achieving a Balance

To gain the full benefit of a client/server architecture, you must design the application system to balance the workload equitably across the client and server computer systems. The first step in this direction is to implement a true database server rather than a file server. With a database server, the client can make very specific requests for the data needed to accomplish any particular task. The database server performs any work necessary to satisfy requests by accessing the data storage devices directly. Only the data required for a specific task need be returned over the network (often the slowest component in a client/ server architecture).

Also, the database server can centrally implement all of the data integrity and security rules. There is no dependence on the integrity of *all* clients to ensure the integrity of the application data. Furthermore, sophisticated database servers (like Microsoft SQL Server) can be programmed to enforce higher level business rules that cannot be violated, regardless of tasks attempted by clients (see Figure 1.4).

FIGURE 1.4:

Balancing workload equally between client and server

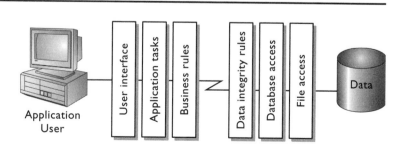

Implementing a balanced architecture requires more work and planning, but pays dividends in higher data integrity and the ability to handle larger and more complex workloads. The drawback is that neither the client nor the server is a simple implementation.

The following sections explore some of the implications of using these architectures when building a client/server application with Microsoft Access and Microsoft SQL Server. Chapters 2 and 3 explore design issues in detail.

Architectures Using Access and SQL Server

Because Access is a complete desktop database application product, it is virtually impossible to use it as a display management front-end tool connected to an application server. When you include Access in the mix, you can build either a full application client with a file server (see Figure 1.3), or a balanced client/server application in conjunction with a true database server such as SQL Server (see Figure 1.4). The following sections explore these possibilities.

Using Only Access for a Client/Server Application

Many developers successfully use Access for Windows 95 to implement client/server applications. Access includes not only user interface and application coding tools but also an efficient database management engine that supports the SQL standard. More on the importance of SQL is discussed later in this chapter.

Access works very well as a single-user database application system. You can use its forms design tools to create a very usable client interface, Visual Basic for Applications (VBA) to create the application task code, facilities in both VBA and the database engine to implement business rules and data integrity rules, and the highly efficient database engine to store and manage the application data.

To convert an Access stand-alone application to client/server, you only need move the data tables into a separate database file to be shared from a file server by many copies of the application code. When you do this, however, you are creating a client/server architecture similar to that shown earlier in Figure 1.3. In other words, everything but the low level file access and management is encapsulated in the Access product that runs on the client. There is actually no portion of Access that operates on the server to help balance the load. Figure 1.5 shows you the specifics.

Advantages

Some of the advantages to using Access alone to create a client/server application are:

- The mechanics of converting a single-user application into client/server are simple.
- You use a single, integrated product to create your application.
- The wide popularity of Access makes obtaining expertise in this product relatively easy.
- Simple applications require little to no coding.
- The code required to build more complex applications uses Visual Basic for Applications, which is shared across multiple Microsoft products.

- It's relatively easy to build moderately complex applications to support up to twenty users.

- You can build a client/server application using more inexpensive peer networking technology.

Microsoft Access client/server architecture

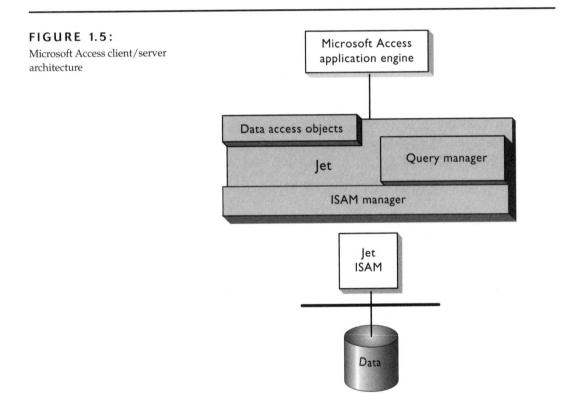

Disadvantages

Some of the disadvantages to using Access by itself to build a client/server application are:

- File server technology is more prone to data loss in the event of a system failure.

- Business rules must all be enforced on the client. A sophisticated user can gain access outside the client application and bypass rule enforcement.

- Even when carefully designed, accessing a file server typically generates more network traffic than using a true database server.

- More careful attention must be paid to database and query design to eliminate full data scans over the network.

- The Access file server architecture is not conducive to managing large volumes (over one gigabyte) of data on the server.

- This architecture will not support hundreds of simultaneous users.

Upsizing to a Back Office Server

When you use a full-fledged database management system like Microsoft SQL Server in a client/server architecture, you automatically create a more balanced workload by moving more of the work to the server. Instead of sending low-level file access commands to the server, the client can send more specific database requests over the network.

Note that we said can send more specific requests. A single-user system that may work just fine reading all the rows from a small local table can be disastrously slow when upsized to client/server, regardless of whether the server is a file server or a database server. However, a carefully planned client/server application using Access on the client and SQL Server on the server can handle large volumes of data and many users.

Advantages

Some of the advantages to using Access with SQL Server to create a client/server application are:

- SQL Server running on Microsoft Windows NT is more impervious to system outages.
- A database server can handle much larger volumes of data than can a file server.
- Data can be secured more effectively on a database server.
- Data integrity and many business rules can be enforced on the server and can't be bypassed from any client.
- The server can be programmed with efficient update and editing procedures that can be triggered from the client.
- If carefully designed, a database server can handle hundreds of simultaneous users.

Disadvantages

Some of the disadvantages to using Access with SQL Server to build a client/server application are:

- A poorly designed database server application may run more slowly than a well-designed file server application.
- You have to learn an additional variant of SQL (see the sections below on SQL and ODBC) to create the most efficient applications.
- Database server applications tend to be more complex.
- Database server implementations force the designer to plan security and integrity on the server.
- It may be better to build a database server application from scratch than to try to upsize a file server application.

When to Make the Move

If you have already developed a client/server application using only Access, you should consider moving up to database server technology when any of the following are true:

- You need to support more than twenty simultaneous users.
- The database has grown larger than 500 megabytes.
- Even though infrequent, crashes on the file server are causing too much application downtime.
- Users are becoming more vocal about slow response times.
- The application has expanded to include either high-volume on-line transaction processing or many complex query searches.
- Security or data integrity requirements have increased beyond what can be supported with a file server.

Naturally, you should consider a database server implementation from the start for a brand new application if any of the above points are true.

The Role of SQL and Open Database Connectivity (ODBC)

Two key technologies make linking Access to SQL Server possible:

1. The SQL relational database language standard
2. Open Database Connectivity (ODBC)

Application developers today take for granted the existence of a "standard" language for managing data in any database management system (DBMS). Furthermore, ODBC in the Microsoft Windows environment is the glue that can tie any client application system speaking a common variant of SQL with virtually any DBMS that supports SQL.

A Brief History of SQL

As little as a decade ago (although ten years is an exceedingly long time given the rapid advance of computer technology), application developers had fairly cumbersome tools to deal with the problems of data management and storage. On mainframes, some complex systems used exotic and rigid database management systems to handle data. Without going into great and gory detail, suffice it to say that it often took years to get a database design right, months to implement a system that was obsolete the day it went live, and an act of god to make changes to the database design to try to cope with changing business needs. The writers of this book can fondly remember many a lost holiday weekend dedicated to the dreaded "database conversion."

As a result, most applications written for any type of computer used one of the many popular "flat file" data storage systems. On mainframes, this meant something called VSAM or RMS. On the desktop, one of the xBASE products was often used. The main problem with either an old-style database or a flat file was that the application programs had to be discretely tied to the data structure. Insert a new field or change an index, and you could impact hundreds of programs. The only advantage to large system database management systems was that they enforced a level of data integrity and security. Flat file systems offered little or no integrity (beyond what the application programmer coded) at all.

Computer vendors recognized the problems inherent in existing database or other file storage mechanisms. Some, including IBM, had been working on the problem for a long time. In fact, as far back as 1970, IBM made major investments in research dedicated to finding a new and more flexible data storage management technology. Out of this research came the Relational Data Model proposed by Dr. Edgar Codd, who is recognized as the "father" of today's modern relational database technology. To implement this model, IBM created a series of research database management systems (often referred to collectively as "System R") and a language called Structured English Query Language (SEQUEL) to handle access to the data.

The concept of the relational model is elegant: provide all the flexibility of a flat file system, the data integrity of a rigid DBMS, and a powerful access language that hides the complexity of the underlying structure and allows for changes in the structure without impacting application code. Most of today's "relational" database management systems do just that.

But the history of the development of today's standard relational DBMS language, SQL, is long and spotty. Long before any of the standards bodies got serious about creating a standard data language for the relational model, dozens of vendors had created their own implementation of "sequel." As most vendors are wont to do, each created unique extensions to the base language to give their product a competitive edge in the marketplace. Although the SQL standard was first published in 1986 and updated in 1989 and 1992, many implementations of SQL existed long before any standards.

Naturally, SQL and "relational" caught on quickly among Fortune 500 companies. However, large companies need to build database and application systems that operate across many different platforms. As you might suspect, the "best" SQL implementation on a mainframe computer is not necessarily from the same vendor as the "best" DBMS on a departmental minicomputer or on the desktop. In response to pressure from these large customers, more than 30 vendors formed the SQL Access group in 1990 to create a Common Language Interface (CLI) that they would all agree to understand when communicating across platforms.

ODBC Architecture

Having a CLI standard was a big step in the right direction. However, a standard is meaningless without the system software to support it. As one of the key members of the SQL Access group, Microsoft saw the need to produce not only standards but also the Application Programming Interfaces (APIs) built into their operating systems for desktop and server computers. ODBC is the software implementation of the SQL Access CLI for Microsoft Windows operating systems.

As it turns out, Microsoft Access version 1.0 was the first commercial implementation of the SQL Access CLI using ODBC. Microsoft also produced the initial support for the SQL Server product, jointly developed with Sybase. Since then, dozens of database vendors have jumped on the bandwagon and developed ODBC-compliant drivers for their relational database products. It's interesting to note that even though the SQL Access CLI defines a "common subset" of standard SQL to be understood by all clients and servers adhering to the standard, it also defines a "passthrough" mode to allow clients to bypass the translation layers of ODBC to take advantage of specific DBMS server added-value features.

Figure 1.6 shows you the architecture of ODBC as implemented through the Microsoft Access Jet database engine. This architecture allows Access or Visual Basic applications to have relatively transparent access to data stored not only in Access database files but also in xBASE, Btrieve, spreadsheet, text, or any ODBC-compliant database format. Note that Visual Basic applications can also call the ODBC driver manager directly.

Benefits and Limitations

Using standard SQL can limit access to additional functionality provided by a particular server. Also, if the client application supports

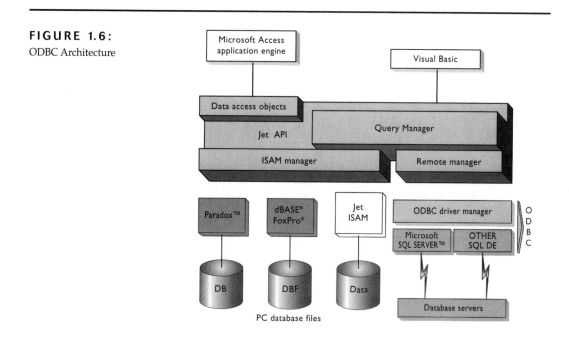

FIGURE 1.6:
ODBC Architecture

SQL, it may have its own extensions that aren't supported by a particular server. One way to bypass these limitations is to selectively use passthrough mode to take advantage of features on a specific database server that aren't defined in the base SQL Access CLI. Later chapters in this book specifically address when to take care using extended features of Access SQL and when to use passthrough mode to take advantage of additional SQL Server features.

The benefits are clear. Once you learn at least one major variant of SQL, you have skills that are portable across many database platforms. In addition, you can take advantage of many of the promises of the relational model, regardless of platform. Finally, technologies like ODBC give you the flexibility to link any compliant desktop application development tool with virtually any relational DBMS. This lets you pick the right tool for the right job.

What's Next

The next two chapters discuss in detail the issues surrounding the design of database and applications for Access and SQL Server. Later chapters cover the technical details of designing queries for client/server, using the ODBC API, leveraging the upsizing tools, and managing SQL Server databases.

CHAPTER

TWO

Designing Databases
for Client/Server

- Normalizing data

- When to denormalize

- Transaction-based database design

- Information processing database design

- Implementing databases in SQL Server

.

Anyone who's ever been even half-way serious about building a database application will tell you, "If you don't get the database design right, you might as well not start." Even for single-user database applications, spending time on the database design up front will save tons of time down the road. As you might imagine, building a correct database design is even more important for a client/server application than for a single-user desktop application.

In this chapter, you'll find a short review of the fundamentals of relational database design using a process called "normalization." Although there is a mathematically rigorous theory underlying normalization, we'll consider it on a more operational level, as for most databases, an understanding of the goals and techniques of normalization is sufficient. For very large and complex databases, you will want to investigate normalization theory more deeply, or bring in a normalization expert to review your database design.

As with most books that tackle this subject from a business perspective, we'll be using an order-entry system as the model. Why order-entry? If you think realistically about the business problems you'll solve with a database application, you'll realize that the vast majority of them will be based on the "sell some product to some buyer" model. If you schedule students in classes, prescribe medications for patients, assign editors to book projects, or sell products to grocery stores (as in the ubiquitous Northwind Traders sample database used in Microsoft Access), your database table structure will have some or all of the attributes of a classic order-entry database.

We'll also discuss considerations for designing a "production" database to fulfill particular requirements in a client/server environment.

For transaction-oriented applications, you'll need to consider additional tables that capture the status of each "order" as it moves through the system. For information processing applications, we discuss considerations for deciding on the level of detail and the time scope of the data saved in your database. In both cases, we'll cover several examples where denormalizing the data structure is necessary either to enhance performance or to maintain the integrity of data saved over time.

We'll also cover the basics of implementing a database on SQL Server. You're probably already familiar with the graphical object design tools used in Access, but you may never have worked with the more SQL-oriented tools used in SQL Server. We'll cover both the "traditional" SQL methods and the newer, graphical SQL Enterprise Manager interface.

Normalization Review

If you've been building applications with relational databases for a while, you're probably already familiar with the fundamentals of creating a "normalized" table structure for your data. You may want to skip over this section, but you should, at a minimum, review the summary of rules to obtain Third Normal Form shown in Sidebar 2.1. Understanding normalization and knowing when to use it is fundamental to creating databases that will function well in any environment, not just a client/server one.

The examples that follow are based on a hypothetical company that repairs and services machines. The company also sells parts over the counter and maintains an extensive parts inventory. If you look in the sample "Parts and Services" Microsoft Access database included on the companion disk, you'll find the final table structure along with some sample data in some of the tables.

<table>
<tr><td>NOTE</td><td>You can apply the rules of normalization to any database, whether it's stored in Access, SQL Server, or some other system entirely. We've chosen Access to present our normalization discussion, as the graphical relationship window it provides is ideal for understanding the relations between tables.</td></tr>
</table>

Problems with Unnormalized Data

When you begin to build a database application to automate a particular business function, you'll most likely begin by examining the current way the company performs the task. For our "parts and services" example, you might begin by examining the data required to assemble a customer work order and provide a bill for the customer to pay. If you were to create a flat file solution to store the data required for these tasks, it might look something like Table 2.1. A *flat file* database just stores all the information in one big table, using individual columns to hold individual pieces of data.

For a small business just beginning to take advantage of personal computers, it's a great temptation to drop this data structure into a spreadsheet program to calculate and print customer work orders. If you convert this simple flat structure to a single database table or spreadsheet, however, you'll run into many problems, including:

- The customer information must be repeated for each work order. If you want to track business by customer, you may find that the information for any one customer varies from work order to work order—perhaps due to data entry errors or simply because different abbreviations were used in the different records (3rd Avenue, Third Ave.). If you do a lot of repeat business, you'll require extra storage space for this repeated information.

TABLE 2.1: An unnormalized view of a parts and services work order

Field Name	Description
Customer Name	Name of the customer
Customer Address	Street, city, state, and zip
Work Order Date	Date the customer asked for service
Service Rep	Service representative who took the order
Problem	A description of the problem
Work Done	A description of the work performed
Technician 1	Name of first technician who worked on this order
Tech Hours 1	Hours spent by first technician
Tech Rate 1	Hourly rate charged for first technician
Tech Amount 1	Extended hours times rate
Technician 2	Name of second technician who worked on this order
Tech Hours 2	Hours spent by second technician
Tech Rate 2	Hourly rate charged for second technician
Tech Amount 2	Extended hours times rate
Technician 3	Name of third technician who worked on this order
Tech Hours 3	Hours spent by third technician
Tech Rate 3	Hourly rate charged for third technician
Tech Amount 3	Extended hours times rate
Subtotal Labor	Sum of Tech Amount 1, Tech Amount 2, Tech Amount 3
Part Number 1	Part number used in repair or service
Part Description 1	Description of part used in repair or service
Part Price 1	Price charged customer for this part
Part Quantity 1	Quantity of this part used
Part Amount 1	Extended cost (Price times Quantity)
Part Number 2	Part number used in repair or service
Part Description 2	Description of part used in repair or service
Part Price 2	Price charged customer for this part
Part Quantity 2	Quantity of this part used
Part Amount 2	Extended cost (Price times Quantity)

TABLE 2.1: An unnormalized view of a parts and services work order (continued)

Field Name	Description
Part Number *n*	Part number used in repair or service
Part Description *n*	Description of part used in repair or service
Part Price *n*	Price charged customer for this part
Part Quantity *n*	Quantity of this part used
Part Amount *n*	Extended cost (Price times Quantity)
Sub Total Parts	Sum of all Part Amount fields
Sub Total Parts and Labor	Sum of Sub Total Parts and Sub Total Labor
Shop Overhead	Miscellaneous materials charge (3% of Subtotal Parts and Labor)
Freight	Freight charge for custom parts orders
Subcontract Amount	Amounts for work done by outside subcontractors
Sales Tax	Sales tax on parts, labor, and overhead
Work Order Total	Total amount owed

- Because the customer address information is all in one field, it's impossible to sort data by street, city, or zip code without performing tedious and time-consuming calculations on each record.

- The structure allows for only three technicians to work on an order. If only one technician works on the order, you've wasted space in your database. If a fourth technician needs to work on the order, you have nowhere to enter the information.

- There's a similar problem with the repeated fields allocated for parts used in the order. At a minimum, you waste space, and at worst, you run out of slots to store the data.

- Multiple slots for technicians or parts makes it difficult to search and add up hours by technician or sales by part.

- The structure is full of calculated values, requiring updating sub-total and total fields whenever you change the information on which those fields are based. If this is a manual process, the chances are high that the totals will get "out of sync" with the de-tails as changes are made. If it's a programmed process, someone will have to maintain the programming.

- This structure doesn't track parts kept in inventory, which ven-dors supply what parts, or current part prices.

The way to solve these problems in a relational database management model is to apply a process called *normalization* to your data. As you apply the rules of normalization, you will take your data table design through increasing levels of clarity, called Normal Forms. Most experts agree that you have a reasonably workable database design if you achieve at least Third Normal Form.

NOTE   If you undertake serious study of normalization, you'll find references to normal forms beyond those that we consider here. The classic reference is C.J. Date's *An Introduction to Database Systems*, now in its sixth edition. If you're faced with an exceptionally difficult or complex database design problem, this book is a necessity.

Achieving Third Normal Form

As you refine your database design, you will apply a series of rules to achieve each level of normalization. The higher normal forms are a superset of the lower ones, so it's natural to learn them in order. That is, any database in Third Normal Form is also in First and Second Nor-mal Form, but the reverse is not necessarily true. For First Normal Form, you need apply only one rule: Each data field must be *atomic*, meaning that each field must contain a single data element, and any particular data element must not be repeated within a table. The sample structure for the unnormalized parts and services data violates first normal form in two ways. First, storing Address, City, and Zip information in the same field violates the principle that a single field should only contain one type of data. Second, the repeating columns for techs and parts place the same data in multiple fields. By correcting both of these deficiencies, we can place the table into First Normal Form.

First Normal Form

To accomplish First Normal Form for the data proposed earlier in Table 2.1, you would need to store the separate parts of the customer address as individual fields. You also must split the repeating technician hours and parts information into separate tables to eliminate the repeating fields. Your result might look something like the structure presented in Table 2.2.

TABLE 2.2: A view of a parts and services work order in First (and Second) Normal Form

Table Name	Field Name	Description
WorkOrder	WorkOrderID (Primary Key)	A unique ID for each work order
	CustomerName	Name of the customer
	CustomerAddress	Customer street address
	CustomerCity	Customer city
	CustomerState	Customer 2-digit state code
	CustomerZip	Customer zip code
	WorkOrderDate	Date the customer asked for service
	ServiceRep	Service representative who took the order
	Problem	A description of the problem

TABLE 2.2: A view of a parts and services work order in First (and Second) Normal Form (continued)

Table Name	Field Name	Description
	WorkDone	A description of the work performed
	SubtotalLabor	Sum of Tech Amount 1, Tech Amount 2, Tech Amount 3
	SubTotalParts	Sum of all Part Amount fields
	SubTotalParts and Labor	Sum of Sub Total Parts and Sub Total Labor
	ShopOverhead	Miscellaneous materials charge (3% of Sub Total Parts and Labor)
	Freight	Freight charge for custom parts orders
	SubcontractAmount	Amounts for work done by outside subcontractors (see attached invoices)
	SalesTax	Sales tax on parts, labor, and overhead
	WorkOrderTotal	Total amount owed
WorkOrder-Parts	WorkOrderID (Primary Key 1)	Matches field in WorkOrder table
	WorkOrderPartLineNo (Primary Key 2)	A line number for each entry
	PartNumber	Part number used in repair or service
	PartDescription	Description of part used in repair or service
	PartPrice	Price charged customer for this part
	PartQuantity	Quantity of this part used
	PartAmount	Extended cost (Price times Quantity)
WorkOrder-Labor	WorkOrderID (Primary Key 1)	Matches field in WorkOrder table
	Technician (Primary Key 2)	Name of technician who worked on this order
	TechHours	Hours spent by this technician
	TechRate	Hourly rate charged for this technician
	TechAmount	Extended hours times rate

As you can see, the changes have not only solved the problem of searching for customer data by state or zip code, but have also allowed us to separately record the hours for any number of technicians and sell an unlimited number of different parts on any work order. Problems still exist, however, with redundant data (the customer name must be entered for every work order; the part description must be entered for every part in each work order) and with calculated data. To eliminate these problems, we'll have to revise the tables into a higher Normal Form.

Second Normal Form

As it turns out the design in Table 2.2 also follows the rules to achieve Second Normal Form, specifically:

- Each table must contain data about one subject.
- Each table must have one or more fields that form the unique identifier (Primary Key) for each row in the table.
- All non-key fields must be defined by the complete unique identifier of the table.

The last point can be particularly confusing. When a table has a single field as its identifier, or *Primary Key*, it's easy to see when a non-key field doesn't belong. For example, each row in the WorkOrder table is about a particular work order, and all the data fields in that table relate specifically to a particular work order. Although we didn't include part vendor information in this example, it would be clearly wrong to include vendor name in the WorkOrder table, because fields such as vendor name and address are not specifically related to an individual work order.

When a table has multiple fields that make up the Primary Key, it becomes much easier to mistakenly include fields that violate Second Normal Form. For example, you could easily make the mistake of including the customer information in the WorkOrderParts table and eliminating the WorkOrder table altogether. Customer information relates directly only to each work order, not to work order *and* part line number. To be in Second Normal Form, a non-key field must relate directly to the *entire* primary key, not just part of the key.

Even though the structure in Table 2.2 is in Second Normal Form, it's not well normalized. We still have to do something about the redundant data and the calculated data.

Third Normal Form

Finally, you achieve Third Normal Form by applying one additional rule: All non-key fields must be mutually independent. In other words, you must be able to change the value in any non-key field without having to change the value in any other field in the database. This clearly eliminates any fields that are the result of a calculation on one or more other fields. It also helps eliminate data which is repeated from record to record (achieving First Normal Form eliminates data that repeats from field to field). Table 2.3 shows you the data in Third Normal Form.

TABLE 2.3: A view of a parts and services work order in Third Normal Form

Table Name	Field Name	Description
WorkOrder	WorkOrderID (Primary Key)	A unique ID for each work order
	CustomerID (Foreign Key)	The ID of the customer for this work order
	WorkOrderDate	Date the customer asked for service
	ServiceRepID (Foreign Key)	Employee ID of the Service Rep who took the order
	Problem	A description of the problem
	WorkDone	A description of the work performed
	Freight	Freight charge for custom parts orders
	SubcontractAmount	Amounts for work done by outside subcontractors

TABLE 2.3: A view of a parts and services work order in Third Normal Form (continued)

Table Name	Field Name	Description
Customers	CustomerID (Primary Key)	The unique ID for this customer
	CustomerName	Name of the customer
	CustomerAddress	Customer street address
	CustomerCity	Customer city
	CustomerState	Customer 2-digit state code
	CustomerZip	Customer zip code
Employees	EmployeeID (Primary Key)	Unique ID for this employee
	EmployeeName	Name of the employee
	EmployeeJob	Service Rep, Technician, etc.
	BillingRate	Usual hourly billing rate
WorkOrderParts	WorkOrderID (Primary Key 1)	Matches field in WorkOrder table
	WorkOrderPartLineNo (Primary Key 2)	A line number for each entry
	PartNumber (Foreign Key)	Part number used in repair or service
	PartPrice	Price charged on this work order
	PartQuantity	Quantity of this part used
WorkOrderLabor	WorkOrderID (Primary Key 1)	Matches field in WorkOrder table
	TechnicianID (Primary Key 2, Foreign Key)	Employee ID of a technician who worked on this order
	TechHours	Hours spent by this technician
	TechRate	Hourly rate charged for this technician on this work order
Parts	PartNumber (Primary Key)	Unique part number
	PartDescription	Description of part
	PartPrice	Current price charged for this part

All of the extended cost fields in the example in Table 2.2 violate Third Normal Form. As you'll see a bit later in this chapter, you may want to consciously include some calculated fields to improve performance, but you must then also take care to include procedures to automatically maintain these "unnormalized" data fields. Triggers and stored procedures in SQL Server make this relatively easy to accomplish.

The rule for Third Normal Form helps you identify groups of data that are actually about another subject in your database. For example, although you do need complete customer information to complete a work order, the customer name and address fields are clearly part of another subject altogether. You can verify this by applying the independence rule for Third Normal Form. If, for example, you need to correct the address for a customer, you can't change it in only one place, as every outstanding work order for that customer would be affected. Moving the customer information to its own table solves this problem. You can use the referential integrity features of either Access or SQL Server to maintain the proper connections between these multiple tables. Figure 2.1 shows the relationships between the tables presented in this example within Access.

Beyond Normal Forms

Once you achieve Third Normal Form, you're only partly done. Although your data may be in the most efficient form for storage, it may still not function correctly in the business context. If you study the example in Table 2.3 carefully, you'll notice some apparent redundancies in the table designs. For example, there's a "PartPrice" field in both the WorkOrderParts table and the Parts table. These sorts of apparent anomalies will begin to appear as you examine how the business actually functions, and you subsequently apply business rules to the design of both your data tables and the application itself. In this example, we assume that the price of parts can vary over time, but we must capture

FIGURE 2.1:

Normalized data within Access

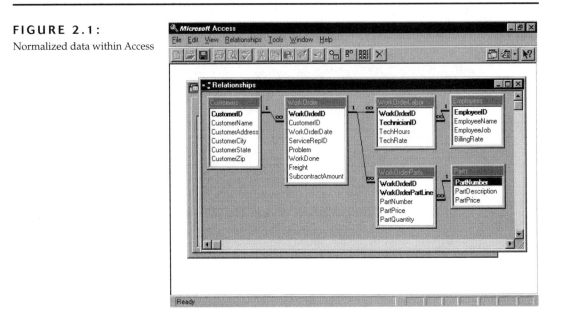

the actual price of the part at the time the work is performed. We made a similar assumption about the technician billing rate. So the two "PartPrice" fields aren't really the same information: one is the current price of the part on the shelf, and the other is the price that the part had at the time it was used on a particular order.

In practice, you may decide that when the price of a part changes, you assign an entirely new part number. If this is true, then you won't need the apparently redundant price field in the WorkOrderParts table. On the other hand, you may decide to create a separate Parts-PriceHistory table that saves the price of the part as it changes over time. One advantage to this approach is that you can keep a complete record of all price changes and even enter upcoming price fluctuations before they actually become effective. Again, you won't need the price in the WorkOrderParts table, but you may need to create some rather complex queries to retrieve the "current" price based on the date of the work order.

Rules for Third Normal Form

Apply the following rules to create a table structure for your data that is in Third Normal Form.

1. Fields must store data in the simplest form required by the application. For example, create separate fields for City, State, and Zip Code rather than a single field containing all three.

2. A table must not contain multiple fields that each contain data from the same domain. That is, a table cannot contain any *repeating groups of data*.

3. Each table must contain data about a single subject.

4. Each row in a table must have one or more fields whose value is unique in each row (called *a row identifier* or *Primary Key*).

5. Each field in a table must be *functionally dependent* on the Primary Key. In other words, all fields in a table must be related to the particular subject defined by the Primary Key in each row.

6. Any field other than a field in the Primary Key must be *mutually independent* of every other field in the database. In other words, you must be able to change the value of each non-key field without impacting any other field in the database.

Figure 2.2 shows you part of the expanded data model you'll find in the sample "Parts and Services" Access database we supplied on the companion disk. Note that we've added a table to track the actual customer "unit" (a car, washing machine, etc.) on which the service was performed. Tables also exist to track the invoices and payments. For most service businesses, the work order can also serve as the invoice. However, if your service business works on large projects that are progress-billed on a weekly or monthly basis, you'll need the extra Invoice table to track the interim bills.

FIGURE 2.2:

These tables in the Parts and Services database handle work orders and customer billing.

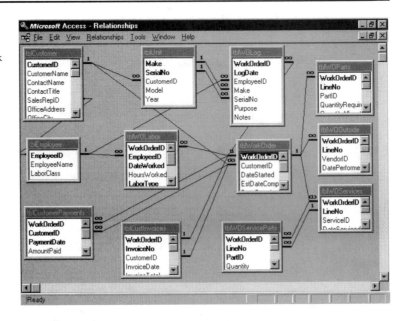

> **NOTE**
>
> The relationship views in this section are designed to show you how the tables relate to one another. The individual tables have been condensed so that we can fit more of this view in a single figure. You'll find the complete definitions of each table within Parts and Services.MDB. If you want to view the tables in context, just open the Relationships Window to get the big picture, right-click on any table, and choose "Design Table" to see the details for that table.

The design has also been further enhanced to allow each technician to record both regular and overtime hours on a daily basis. The Work-OrderLog table allows the technicians to make discrete entries about the work in progress. The design includes other tables to track services sold as a package (30,000-mile tune-up, for example) and the parts normally used to perform those services. We've also added a table to record any work that was performed by a third party.

You might ask, "Where's the Parts table?" It's there, but the relationship diagram is too complex to display in a single figure, so Figure 2.3 shows you additional supporting tables for Work Orders. Here, you can see the "master" tables that store the Parts and Services data. Note that the Work Order has companion tables to store the actual usage of parts or performance of a service for a particular work order. These are "point-in-time" tables that we'll discuss in more detail later in this chapter.

Another group of tables supports inventory and ordering activities. Figure 2.4 shows you all the tables that support tracking Inventory and ordering parts from vendors. The Parts table is the "master" table that describes all the parts available. One or more vendors may supply any given part, so the VendorParts table provides that linking information along with the last quoted price from any particular vendor and an indication of the relative priority of each vendor (the VendorSeq field) when ordering a particular part. To keep track of vendor prices over time, you would need to add a price history table to the mix.

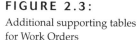

FIGURE 2.3:

Additional supporting tables for Work Orders

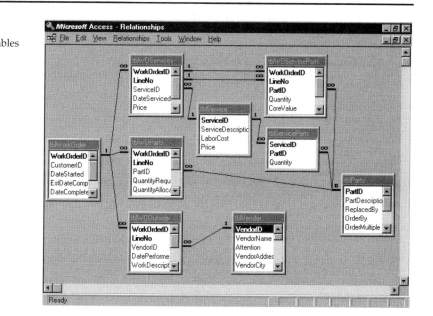

The Inventory and Stock tables are where the system actually records the current stock of any part. The Stock table contains a record of every shipment of any part received from a vendor. The application also uses this table to keep track of parts used in Work Orders and contains a calculated field (in conscious violation of Third Normal Form) to indicate parts left to sell. The Inventory table is a place-holder for any part ever ordered for inventory, and it notes where in the warehouse this part is normally stored. The remaining fields in this table are all calculated values (again, in conscious violation of Third Normal Form). We'll discuss some of the reasons for storing calculated fields later in this chapter.

FIGURE 2.4:

These tables track inventories, purchase orders, and vendor invoices.

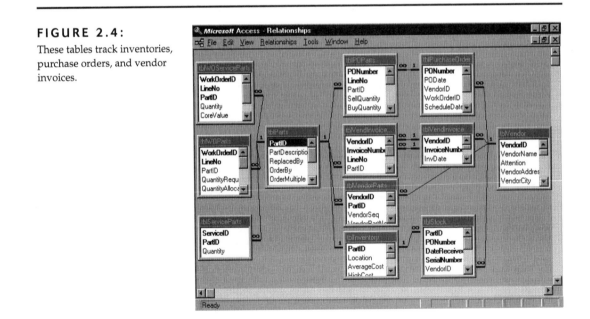

Finally, this design includes tables to track purchase orders issued to vendors, the parts ordered in each purchase order, and the matching invoices from the vendors when parts are shipped. Some businesses may need to add additional tables to track partial shipments.

The bottom line is that Third Normal Form is a great place to start, but you will need to enrich the design you get from normalization with your knowledge of how the business actually runs. You must think of your database design as a computerized model of the business you are trying to automate in your application. The model presented here is quite robust, but by no means complete for every order entry system. It's easy, for example, to see how this model can be extended from Purchase Orders, Vendor Invoices, Customer Invoices, and Customer Payments into a complete accounting system.

When to Denormalize

Denormalization is the process of deliberately violating the rules of Third Normal Form. The only legitimate reason to denormalize a relational database design is to improve performance of the final application. You should be aware that every time you make a decision to violate normalization rules, you will have to write code somewhere to keep the data intact. You should also carefully document your decision so that other programmers who later work on your design are fully aware of the choice you made and the way you chose to overcome this deliberate deficiency.

There are some obvious examples of denormalization in our parts and services sample database. For example, take a look at the Inventory and Stock tables. The QuantityRemaining field in the Stock table is Quantity (amount received in a shipment from a vendor) minus the sum of QuantityAllocated (parts set aside for a work order but not actually sold yet) and QuantitySold (parts sold in an invoiced work order). In truth, this value could easily be calculated in queries, and storing the data in the table may provide only a modest performance gain. Fortunately, SQL Server provides tools (described later in this chapter) that make it simple to maintain this sort of calculated field.

Clearly, the AverageCost, HighCost, QuantityInStock (quantity physically in inventory, some of which may be allocated to incomplete work orders), and QuantityOnHand (actual quantity available to sell) are all calculated fields. The AverageCost field is there to assist in calculating a current value for inventory. This business likes to sell all its parts based on a markup of the highest price paid, so HighCost is of real value and saves searching all the Stock records. Likewise, QuantityIn-Stock and QuantityOnHand provide large performance gains when you need to decide whether you can sell from stock or must place an order. Especially after thousands of rows accumulate in the Stock table, calculating these values in real time could require a large amount of time and computer resources.

Price in the Inventory table is a more subtle example of a calculated field. The application may provide an automatic calculation of a standard markup whenever the high cost changes. The parts manager may also have the ability to set the value directly in the Inventory table (subject, perhaps, to a rule that the price can't be less than the cost).

Other subtle examples of calculated fields are the HazDisposalFee, MiscMaterials, and Tax fields in the customer invoices table. These are probably all based on some percentage of the total of all parts, labor, and services for the work order. It's most likely much more efficient to write code to calculate these values one time whenever a new invoice record is generated rather than search all the subordinate tables to calculate subtotals and percentages every time you examine invoices. Once again, denormalization provides a speed benefit, while increasing the amount of code that you need to write in the application to keep things working.

Keep these points in mind when deciding to violate normalization rules:

- Make a conscious decision to denormalize.
- Violate normalization rules only when doing so achieves significant performance benefits in your application.
- Write and fully test application code to maintain data dependencies.
- Fully document your decision.

Designing for a Transaction-Based Application

A *transaction-based application* is any application that is designed to control, record, and support day-to-day business transactions. The sample schema shown earlier in this chapter forms the foundation for a transaction-based application. When you design a database for this type of application that you intend to implement in a Client/Server architecture, you may find a need for two types of specialized tables:

- Point-in-Time tables
- Transaction logs

In addition, when you design an application for client/server use, you need to carefully consider which tables should be kept on the client and which ones should be kept on the server.

Point-in-Time Data

All transaction-based application systems contain tables that record data as of a particular point in time. When you include this type of table in an application database, it may appear on the surface that you have stored redundant data in your tables. For example, you may have a "Price" field for a part in inventory, a "Price" from the Vendor's catalog, and a "Price" charged to a particular customer on a work order.

None of these are duplicates because each records the "price" at a different point in time. The VendorParts table may show the last known "price" charged by a vendor, the Parts or Inventory table may record the "price" of the part based on the cost of a physical part in inventory, and the WorkOrderParts table is a point-in-time table that notes the actual "price" charged to the customer.

Other point-in-time data in your system may be a bit more subtle. For example, the PurchaseOrderParts table shows quantities of parts that are on order *until* a particular record is marked with a received date. Once received, those parts may be sitting on a loading dock awaiting filing into inventory. When finally marked Posted, the part should have a companion record in the Stock table indicating that the part is now in inventory and available for sale.

Transaction Logs

Another type of table you may want to include in a business system is a *transaction log*, or a table that records individual state-changes in the business system. Many systems require more than one transaction log to track different sorts of information. In the sample schema presented here, there's no way to track from order to sale, for example, a particular part received on a certain date from a given vendor. The record in the Stock table does note the original purchase order number, but it's not clear what part may be chosen from stock for sale in a particular work order.

If each part has a serial number, then that solves the problem as long as the serial number follows the part through the system. Most parts won't have a serial number, however, so to track this you would either need to copy the original purchase order number into the WorkOrder-Parts table or add one or more transaction log tables that note each time some quantity of a part "moves" through the system.

For certain types of transaction systems, log tables are absolutely essential. For example, most banking systems require transaction logs that allow auditors to reconstruct all changes to the database. When designed correctly, transaction tables can act as a secondary backup system that allows you to roll back or roll forward any changes to the database; however, you will have to write additional application code to implement any roll-back or roll-forward functionality.

NOTE

Although you will generally need to write application-specific code to implement roll-back and roll-forward, some database management systems include this functionality without such code. SQL Server does offer these capabilities automatically. If you're only using transaction tables to get this functionality, you may dispense with them if your DBMS is SQL Server. See Chapter 10 for more information on SQL Server's native transaction-logging capabilities.

One note of caution: Transaction log files can easily consume several times the space of your basic application tables because each time you change data in your application tables, you must also add a log record. Also, you must be sure to take advantage of transaction protection so that the log stays synchronized with your application tables. That is, any time you're writing to the transaction log tables and the application tables, you should wrap both changes in a single Begin-Trans/CommitTrans pair in order to ensure that either both changes are committed or neither is.

If your application uses a Microsoft Access shared database in file/server mode, rather than a true client/server database, you should use log tables only when absolutely necessary because of their typically large space requirements. For applications that require log tables for most transactions, you should take advantage of the more robust data management capabilities of SQL Server. In either case, when you may need to depend on the log to reconstruct events, you should place your log tables in a separate database on a physical disk drive remote from the base application tables.

Placing Data on the Client or Server

One way to enhance the performance of a client/server application is to place certain key tables local to the user. If you place a table on the client machine, then records read from that table don't have to travel across the slow network connection back to the server. As we'll see, though, there are tradeoffs in this approach when data in the local tables needs to be updated for all clients.

Infrequently Updated Tables

Tables that are infrequently updated are candidates for placement of duplicate copies on the client machine. For example, a Parts catalog may change only once a month or once a quarter. You may add new vendors very infrequently. In some businesses, it may even be possible to copy basic customer information to the client machines.

When you place selected tables locally, you can improve the user interface, improve performance, or both. For example, it's not usually a good idea to provide a combo or list box to set a foreign key (perhaps the CustomerID on a new Work Order) when the source data exceeds several thousand rows—particularly when the source data is on a remote server. Although Access is particularly good at caching the rows needed to populate this sort of list, performance can suffer greatly, not only for the local user trying to search to the bottom of the list, but also for other users on the network because of the additional data being retrieved over the network. If, for example, you can provide a local copy of the valid parts list, you can certainly improve the speed of individual probes to validate entered part numbers, and you may be able to take advantage of list controls to completely automate the process for the user.

If you choose to include local copies of data in your database design, you must also provide the mechanisms to periodically synchronize the copies with a master copy stored on the server. In some cases, you may be able to take advantage of replication features built into Access or SQL Server to handle this synchronization automatically (see Chapter 8 for details on replication).

Lookup Tables

When your tables contain any code fields whose valid values derive from a static list that's more than a few values, you may want to put the list of values in a table to make data validation easier. The most common example of such a lookup table is a list of the valid 2-character state codes in the United States. Another common use for data entry applications is a list of U.S. Post Office zip codes and their related cities and states—if you've ever wondered why some telephone-order companies ask you for your zip code before verifying your city and state, they're most likely using a zip code lookup table. Other examples of places where a lookup table might be appropriate in the sample used in this chapter are the Make and Model fields in the Unit table, the LaborClass field in the Employee table, and OrderBy (each, pound, foot, case, etc.) and SellBy (each, ounce, inch, etc.) fields in the Parts table.

Lookup tables are also useful to store data values used by your application code. For example, a lookup table might store the current parts or labor markup percentages or the current "standard" rate to charge for work by a certain class of technician (regardless of the pay scale of the individual who did the work). A lookup table for state or zip codes might also include the current sales tax rate for that geographic area.

You should decide where to place your lookup tables depending on usage. For static but frequently referenced lookup tables (such as state or zip codes), copies on each client machine will give you the best performance with little worry about data integrity. Of course, you should still provide a mechanism to update these tables on all client stations should any values change. For example, an Access application might download a fresh copy of the lookup tables from the server each time the user enters the application.

When a lookup table provides application run-time constants that may vary from day to day, placing it on the server is often the best choice. The client application should contain procedures to load the current values either into local tables or global variables when the application starts. When any value changes in the master copy on the server, you can instruct each client user to simply restart the application to obtain the latest values. You can also include procedures in the client application that periodically check and refresh values based on date or clock values.

Local User Option Tables

The last type of table we will discuss for transaction-based applications is a table to store run-time options chosen by the local client machine user. You may design a particularly complex application to allow the user to customize how they use the application. For example, some users may always want to see certain reports in print preview while others may want to always send reports directly to the printer. Some users may be interested in only certain geographic areas.

If you include ways for the user to customize how they work with the application, you should also design in local option tables to allow the application to "remember" the last setting of any particular option. When multiple users work at the same client machine, you may also want to store options by user ID.

Designing for an Information Processing Application

Most businesses today recognize that the data stored in their application databases is not only useful for running the day-to-day business of the company but also valuable for later analysis, to help make decisions about how to more efficiently run the business in the future. After a large amount of data accumulates in a transaction-oriented database, you may need to provide ways to purge or archive old information.

Rather than throw such data away, many companies carefully summarize and collect the data to help spot both short and long-term trends.

You may even design features into a transaction-based application to take advantage of historical data. For example, you might give the parts manager some tools to examine sales history so that replenishment orders can be placed just before a new stock is needed, rather than waiting until you run out. If you decide to archive data, the business managers may also ask for tools to analyze this saved data. The following sections discuss some of the considerations for designing tables to capture historical data.

Denormalization Is the Rule

In transaction-based business systems, you must take great care to create a normalized table design and provide mechanisms to avoid anomalies when you denormalize for performance reasons. In information processing systems, denormalization is the rule rather than the exception.

The main reason for denormalization is the sheer volume of the data that would have to be captured and summarized to enable a multi-year view of the data. In large businesses, saving the original data in normalized form for even one year can involve *tera*bytes of information. Even when raw data storage is not a problem, the time required to search this amount of data can far exceed the amount of time available to solve a particular problem or answer a question.

The most common technique in information database design is to store only summaries of data. You save a lot of space, for example, by storing the total sales by part and by month rather than retaining each individual sale. Even if you also store summaries by customer and month, you save a large amount of storage. However, you must make some effort predicting the types of questions (there's no way you can predict *all* of the questions) that management may want answered. Given only the two summaries noted here, for example, you won't be able to show which customers ordered what parts in any given month.

Another common type of summary involves rolling totals up into a table that looks more like a spreadsheet than a normalized table. For example, a table might have one row per part number, and each row containing a field for recording sales by month. This certainly violates the rules for even First Normal Form, but it's a very efficient way to store data for an entire year.

Choosing Summary Levels

When designing tables to store information-processing data, perhaps the most difficult problem to solve is how to decide on the level of summarization. The most common way, of course, is to summarize over periods of time. One rule of thumb is that detailed data becomes less and less valuable over time, so you may need to capture daily summaries for the most recent six months, monthly summaries for up to three years, and quarterly summaries beyond that.

If you use this time-based technique, you may want to always create the monthly summaries at month end (even though you still keep the daily information for a while) and the quarterly summaries at quarter end. Doing this makes the summaries immediately available for high-level analysis and avoids extra work creating the summaries before you purge the aged detail data. The trade-off of using an immediate roll-up technique is that you consume somewhat more disk space by storing the quarterly summaries for the latest three years and the monthly summaries for the latest six months.

Another, more sophisticated, way to deal with levels of summary is to decide what constitutes a "significant" change from a base line of activity and record only the points of change. This technique assumes that you maintain a certain number of records for the baseline and that you also keep a sufficient amount of recent detail data to be able to perform the analysis.

Dealing with "Old" Data

Even when you have successfully summarized and saved relevant data, you can't save all data forever. At some point in time the value of old data falls below the cost to save it in an online database. For most businesses, saving historical data beyond three to five years is of little value.

Even so, you can most likely make the purging of old data a year-end process rather than trying to "age" data each day, week, or month. Before you finally delete data from any business system, you should always make an offline copy of both the data and the schema for the data.

Taking Advantage of SQL Server Features

When you use SQL Server as the data repository for your client/server application, you can take advantage of many of the advanced features in SQL Server to make implementation of your application easier. Many of the features allow you to go beyond simple table definition to enforce data integrity or to offload some of the application coding and execution to the server. We'll discuss the specific mechanics of implementing these features later in the chapter. But first, let's get an overview of some of the important data management features that SQL Server offers:

- Views
- Constraints
- Triggers

Views

You can use CREATE VIEW in SQL Server to represent the results of a complex SQL Server SELECT statement as a virtual table. This table can be subsequently linked to your Access database. One of the most common uses of a view in SQL Server is to define a restricted set of rows from a table, then grant certain users access to the view but not to the underlying table(s). (See Chapter 9 for further details on SQL Server security.) You can also gain a performance advantage by saving a complex join as a single view. SQL Server compiles and stores the plan when you create the view. You can attach this view as a table in your Access database, and Access will generate simple select statements against the pre-compiled view when you need to retrieve data. You could also define the join in Access, but Access will send the complex join statement to SQL Server for compilation and execution at runtime.

One drawback to using views in SQL Server as linked tables in Access is that you most probably won't have the same flexibility to update a view as you might have if you built the query on linked base tables in Access, as you must include one or more columns from the underlying tables that form a unique value for each row in the view, then inform Access which columns are unique when you link the table. For example, suppose you define the following view in the sample Pubs database in SQL Server:

```
CREATE VIEW TitlePub AS
Select pub_name, titles.*
From titles, publishers
Where publishers.pub_id = titles.pub_id
```

When you link this view as a table in Access, Access recognizes that it can't determine the unique fields without your assistance. When you pick a view, Access shows you a dialog box similar to Figure 2.5 that asks you to identify what fields define a unique key for each row in the view.

FIGURE 2.5:

Specifying the unique fields for the TitlePub View

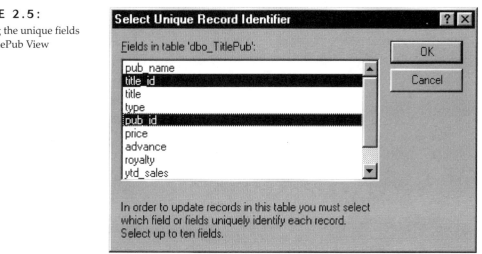

Note that Access does not verify that you have made the right choice. Access will include a WHERE clause using these fields for any UP-DATE statement it sends to SQL Server using the view. Note also that you can update the data in a SQL Server view that joins data from multiple tables only if the resulting UPDATE statement affects a single row in the *first* table listed in the FROM clause of the view. This is a SQL

Server limitation that is much more restrictive than the Access rules for updating fields in dynasets. In the TitlePub view shown above, you can update any field in the Titles table, but you can't update the pub_name from the Publishers table. In contrast, if you were to link the two tables separately to Access and create a joined query similar to the view, Access would allow you to update any field on either side of the join.

Constraints

When you create a table in SQL Server, you can include various constraints in the CREATE TABLE statement to ask SQL Server to enforce various data integrity rules automatically on data in your table. If you "upsize" an Access database (see Chapter 6), the Upsizing Wizard propagates many of the Access data integrity rules to their SQL Server equivalents. This section summarizes the constraints available in SQL Server. For specific details, see your Transact-SQL Reference Manual.

NOT NULL

You can require that a column in a new row must always contain a value by specifying a NOT NULL constraint on a column definition. This is identical to setting the Required property of a field in an Access table to Yes. You can avoid errors on rows inserted via views that do not contain a NOT NULL column by specifying a non-null DEFAULT constraint on the column (see the later section on DEFAULT).

PRIMARY KEY

A Primary Key is identical in concept and implementation in both Access and SQL Server. Both database management systems enforce the Primary Key by constructing a unique index on the field(s) that make up the key. If you have created a normalized database design, you will have one or more fields that make up the Primary Key in each table. You should use the PRIMARY KEY constraint in SQL Server to enforce the uniqueness of the identifier for each row. Both Access and SQL Server disallow null fields in the Primary Key.

UNIQUE

You can also ask either Access or SQL Server to enforce a unique value in a field across all rows in the table. In SQL Server, you apply the UNIQUE constraint to the field(s) you want to be unique (these are in addition to the Primary Key). SQL Server prohibits duplicates in a UNIQUE field by building a unique index on the specified field(s).

FOREIGN KEY

SQL Server Version 6.0 has the ability to define referential integrity constraints between tables. You do this in SQL Server by defining a FOREIGN KEY constraint on the field(s) in a table that forms a reference to the Primary Key in the parent table. Unlike Access, you cannot define automatic cascade of updates or deletes via a FOREIGN KEY constraint. If you want SQL Server to automatically cascade an update to a Primary Key or cascade delete all child rows on the delete of a parent row, you must define a trigger and not include a FOREIGN KEY constraint. Triggers are discussed in more detail later in this chapter.

DEFAULT

You can define a default value for a column in a SQL Server table by applying a DEFAULT constraint to the column definition. This works similarly to setting the Default Value property for a field in an Access table. SQL Server also lets you set the default value of a column to NULL.

CHECK

You can define a CHECK expression on a column that must be true for any data that you insert or update in the column. This type of constraint is similar to the Validation Rule property in Access. The expression can reference other columns in the table, but cannot contain a subquery, and must evaluate to a Boolean True or False.

Triggers

One of the biggest strengths of SQL Server is its robust Transact-SQL command language. Transact-SQL not only supports the typical SELECT, UPDATE, INSERT, and DELETE data manipulation statements but also declaration and manipulation of local variables, a robust library of built-in functions, and an extensive control-of-flow language that lets you "program" actions that you want to occur when certain events take place.

From the perspective of database design and definition of integrity constraints, triggers provide a powerful mechanism to validate and manipulate data whenever a row is inserted, deleted, or updated in the database. Specifically, triggers allow you to:

- Validate changes in one table based on data values in other tables
- Propagate (cascade) changes made to a Primary Key value into child tables
- Cascade a delete in a parent table to all related child records
- Automatically maintain calculated values whenever one of the source values changes
- Place many other business rules directly on the server

As you'll learn in Chapter 6, the Upsizing Wizard version 1.0 propagates referential integrity constraints that you define for your Access tables to update and delete triggers in SQL Server when you convert your tables from Access to SQL Server. If you design your tables in SQL Server, you can also implement triggers to calculate dependent fields that you may have included in a denormalized design to improve performance.

Inside a trigger, SQL Server makes available special temporary tables, named "inserted" and "deleted," that contain copies of the affected rows. When you delete one or more rows, "deleted" contains copies of the rows about to be deleted. When you update rows, "deleted" contains copies of the rows before they are updated. When you insert rows, "inserted" contains copies of the new rows about to be added. When you're updating, "inserted" contains copies of the rows as they will exist after the update. You can't change rows in "inserted" or "deleted" but you can inspect them and choose whether to update rows in the base tables.

From the preceding Parts and Services example, you might recall that the Stock table contains a calculated QuantityRemaining field that is the result of a calculation using the Quantity, QuantityAllocated, and QuantitySold fields in that same table. Here's an update trigger that you could define in SQL Server to ensure that this value is always calculated correctly:

```
CREATE TRIGGER stock_qty_update
ON tblStock
FOR INSERT, UPDATE
AS
IF UPDATE (QuantityAllocated) OR UPDATE(QuantitySold) OR
UPDATE(Quantity)
UPDATE tblStock
SET tblStock.QuantityRemaining = tblStock.Quantity -
(tblStock.QuantityAllocated + tblStock.QuantitySold)
FROM tblStock, inserted
WHERE tblStock.PartID = inserted.PartID
AND tblStock.PONumber = inserted.PONumber
AND tblStock.DateReceived = inserted.DateReceived
AND tblStock.SerialNumber = inserted.SerialNumber
```

As you might imagine, you can use a similar technique to maintain the calculated values in the Inventory table that are affected by changes in the Stock table. This facility is much more powerful than what you have available in Access because it is enforced directly by the database engine. Any change to a table from any source is monitored and handled appropriately. Within Access, you must hook this sort of integrity update to a form event and must make sure that all updates occur only through that specially programmed form. You have no control of updates made from outside your form.

> **NOTE** Appendix A contains more information about the basic SQL Server object types and their differences from the analogous objects in Access.

Implementing SQL Server Databases

If you're new to SQL Server, you may have never tried to design a SQL Server database from scratch. When you do, you're likely to be a bit perplexed at the lack of graphical design tools. Like most server databases, SQL Server implements a wide range of Data Definition Language (DDL) features in its SQL, so that you can create new objects using queries. SQL Server 6.0 also includes SQL Enterprise Manager, which does include graphical tools that were not present in earlier versions.

SQL Server also includes tools for loading data in from other databases. We'll look at some of these tools in this section as well.

> **NOTE** In this section, we'll assume that someone has already set up SQL Server and installed the client utilities on your computer. Chapter 10 has a guide to installing and configuring SQL Server that you can refer to if this hasn't been done yet.

Using SQL Server Utilities for Database Design

SQL Server includes two utilities that can help you design databases and the objects that they contain: ISQL/W and SQL Enterprise Manager. ISQL/W (an abbreviation for Interactive Structured Query Language/ Windows) is available in both SQL Server 4.21 and SQL Server 6.0. It offers a way to execute queries directly on the server without having to build a dedicated front-end application. SQL Enterprise Manager is a newer tool, available only in SQL Server 6.0, and provides a graphical view of the server, using the Distributed Management Objects discussed in Chapter 7. We'll show you how to use either of these tools to build a database, so you can work with any version of SQL Server.

ISQL/W

ISQL/W is a tool designed to let you submit queries to a server and see the results onscreen. You can run it on any Windows 95 or Windows NT computer on your network, and connect to any SQL Server on the same network. When you start ISQL/W, you'll see the login dialog box shown in Figure 2.6.

FIGURE 2.6:

Logging in to a server with ISQL/W

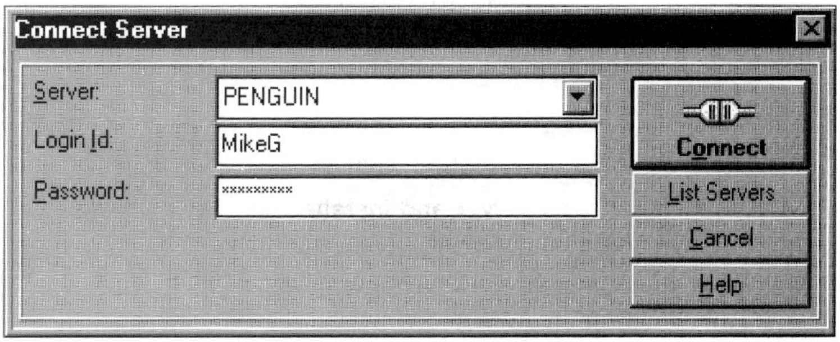

To log in to the server, fill in a valid server name, user name, and password here and then click the Connect button. If you're unsure about the server name, you can click on the List Servers button to obtain a list of servers that are currently broadcasting on your network.

After you've logged in, you'll see the main ISQL/W window shown in Figure 2.7. This window has four tabs for four different types of information:

- **Query:** Type in any Transact-SQL query here that you want to have executed on the server.

- **Results:** Displays results of the most recent query.

- **Statistics I/O:** If you turn on the Display Statistics I/O option, this tab will contain information on the query's execution.

- **Showplan:** If you turn on the Display Showplan option, this tab will show you the plan that the server used to execute your query.

FIGURE 2.7:

The main ISQL/W window

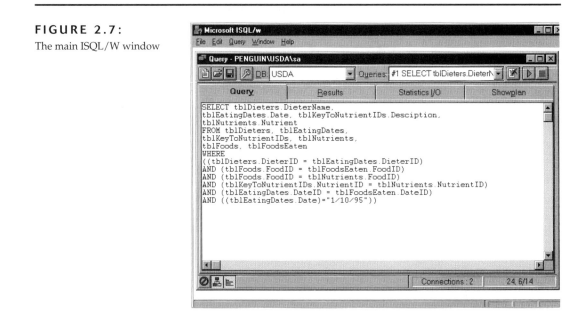

The ISQL/W toolbar contains a number of controls to allow you to manage multiple queries. From left to right, these are:

- **New Query:** Clear the query tab, but store the previous contents so you can return to them later in the session if you wish.

- **Open Query:** Load a query that was previously saved as a SQL script.

- **Save Query:** Save the current contents of the query tab as a SQL script.

- **Query Options:** Selects the format for the Results tab, and also allows you to specify some SQL Server options, such as a limit on the number of rows returned.

- **Select Database:** Choose the database on the server to process your queries. (To choose a different server, you must use File ➤ Connect.)

- **Select Query Set:** Choose a previous query in the same session to return to.

- **Remove Query Set:** Discard the current contents of the query tab.

- **Execute:** Send the query to the server and show the results.

- **Cancel:** Cancel processing of a currently executing query.

Note that you may group multiple queries together by typing them on the query tab and separating them by the GO keyword. For example, this set of Transact-SQL statements is perfectly valid in ISQL/W:

```
SELECT * FROM tblDieters
GO
SELECT * FROM tblKeyToNutrientIDs
GO
```

This ability to group statements into a single script allows you to save groups of SQL Server statements to be executed as a batch. When you execute the above statements with ISQL/W, you'll get both result sets successively, as shown in Figure 2.8.

FIGURE 2.8:

Multiple result sets from a single query set

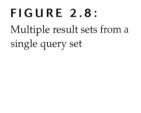

The status bar of ISQL/W has three more toolbar buttons which allow you to set query options. From left to right, these are:

- **No Execute:** Analyze the query, but don't actually run it. This causes the server to store a compiled execution plan.

- **Display Showplan:** Fill in the Showplan tab when the query is executed.

- **Display Statistics I/O:** Fill in the Statistics I/O tab when the query is executed.

Showplan and Statistics I/O let you analyze the way in which the server is executing your query. Figure 2.9 shows the Statistics I/O graph from the query in Figure 2.7. In this particular case, we can see that the server scanned tblKeyToNutrientIDs many times, suggesting that better indexing on this table might help speed up the query.

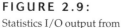

FIGURE 2.9:

Statistics I/O output from ISQL/W

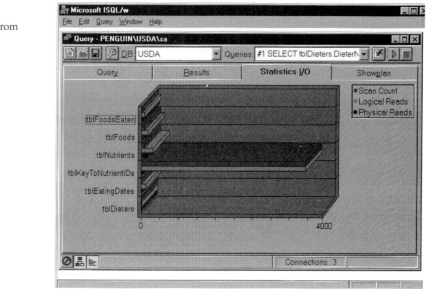

Showplan output (a portion of which is shown in Figure 2.10) gives you another way to see what the server is doing. SQL Server's cost-based optimizer chose to begin the process of evaluating this query by first scanning the tblEatingDates table, and then joining the results to a scan of the tblDieters table and an indexed search of the tblFoods-Eaten table. (There are more steps to this query. The USDA database is included on the CD-ROM if you'd like to see the rest of the output yourself.) If you think the optimizer is doing things wrong, you can experiment with the SET FORCEPLAN ON Transact-SQL statement. This forces tables to be used in the order that they appear in the FROM clause of your query, without regard to what the optimizer thinks.

You can execute any SQL query with ISQL/W. The example query here is a Data Manipulation Language (or DML) query. You can also use ISQL/W to send Data Definition Language (or DDL) queries to the

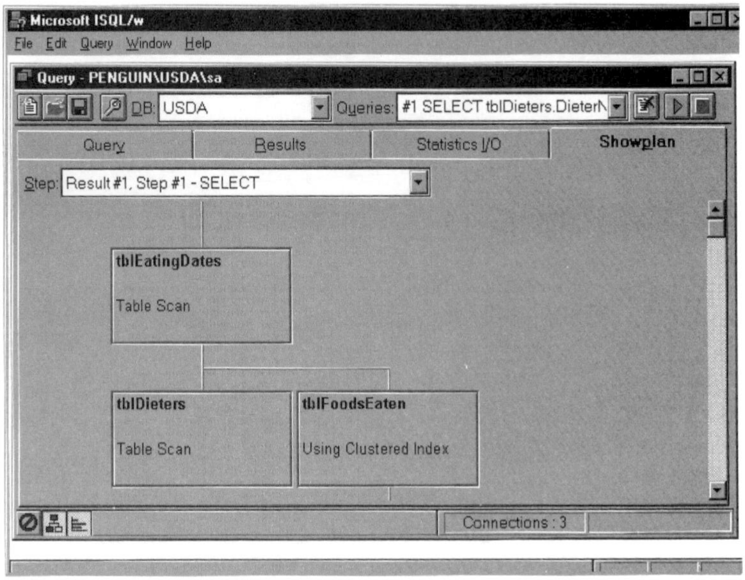

FIGURE 2.10:

A portion of Showplan output
from the sample query

server to build objects. We'll cover the syntax for some simple DDL
queries later in this chapter.

SQL Enterprise Manager

Although ISQL/W is functional, it's not very flashy, and it can't present an overall view of the activity of a SQL Server. With SQL 6.0, Microsoft has included a new utility named "SQL Enterprise Manager"
which remedies these faults. Like ISQL/W, SQL Enterprise Manager
runs on both Windows 95 and Windows NT. It uses the new SQL-DMO
OLE object layer to control and represent SQL Servers. Figure 2.11 shows
a SQL Enterprise Manager view of some objects on a SQL Server.

As you can see, SQL Enterprise Manager organizes database objects
into a hierarchy, even across servers (here, JEDDAK and PENGUIN) if
necessary. With this one tool you can view and change objects on multiple

FIGURE 2.11:

SQL Enterprise Manager

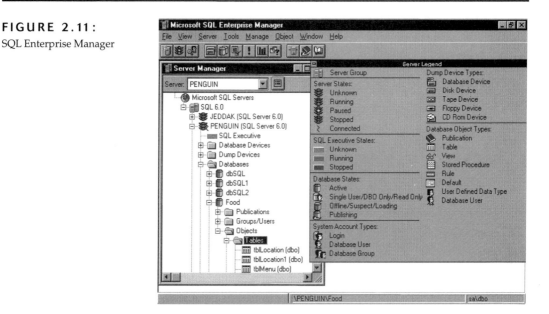

servers. In addition, each object has a right-click context menu that presents operations specific to that object. We'll refer to these menus later when we discuss how to perform DDL operations with SQL Enterprise Manager.

> **NOTE**
>
> A full tour of SQL Enterprise Manager is beyond the scope of this book. You'll find an introduction in the *SQL Server Administrator's Companion*, but SQL Enterprise Manager's own help file has the most complete and current information.

Creating SQL Server Objects

There are at least two ways to create any SQL Server object: either using a query through ISQL/W, or via the dedicated user interface in SQL Enterprise Manager. We'll explain both of these ways for the following common SQL Server objects:

- Devices
- Databases
- Tables
- Views
- Triggers

By knowing both ways, you'll be able to manage databases in both SQL Server 4.21 and SQL Server 6.0. In addition, once you understand the syntax of SQL DDL statements, you may find the interactive query mechanism more natural than the more graphical SQL Enterprise Manager tools.

Devices

To create a new database device, use the DISK INIT statement as follows:

```
DISK INIT
  NAME = devicename,
  PHYSNAME = diskfilename,
  VDEVNO = number,
  SIZE = numberofblocks,
  [VSTART = address]
```

NOTE   In Transact-SQL syntax diagrams, capital letters are used for keywords that you must type exactly. Italics represent arguments that you must supply. Square brackets delimit optional parts of the SQL statement. Curly brackets surround alternatives—you can use one or the other of the alternative arguments. An ellipsis indicates arguments that may be repeated. The exact arrangement of the statement in the query window doesn't matter, so you can add as many tabs, spaces, and carriage returns as you like to make it easy for you to read.

Table 2.4. shows the arguments to DISK INIT. A typical DISK INIT statement might look like this:

```
DISK INIT
 NAME = 'customers',
 PHYSNAME = 'd:\sql60\data\cust.dat',
 VDEVNO = 17,
 SIZE = 1000,
```

This will create a two-megabyte device named "customers." If there's already a device number 17, you'll get an error.

TIP

If you'd like to see the device numbers that have already been assigned on your system, you can execute the sp_helpdevice stored procedure. (You can execute stored procedures simply by typing their names into an ISQL/W window and clicking the Execute button.) If you scroll the results to the right, beyond the extremely wide description column, you'll find a column that contains all of the device numbers that have already been assigned on your server.

TABLE 2.4: Arguments for DISK INIT

Argument	Purpose
DEVICENAME	Name to use within SQL Server for this device, enclosed in single quotes.
PHYSNAME	Disk file to store the device. This must include the drive and path, and must be enclosed in single quotes.
VDEVNO	Unique device number between 1 and 255.
SIZE	Number of 2K blocks with which to begin the database. The minimum size is 1MB, or 500 blocks.
VSTART	Offset of the first database to be stored in the device. Let this default to zero unless you're rebuilding a damaged device.

To create a new device using SQL Enterprise Manager, right-click on Database Devices in the treeview and select New Device from the context menu to open the dialog box shown in Figure 2.12. This dialog box offers several improvements over using DISK INIT directly:

- SQL Server will automatically assign the next available device number.
- You can specify mirroring options when you create the device.
- You can see graphically how much of your system's free space will be allocated to this device.

Databases

Once you've created a device, you can place databases on it using the CREATE DATABASE statement as follows:

```
CREATE DATABASE dbname
 [ON {DEFAULT ¦ devname} [= size]
 [, devname [= size]]... ]
 [LOG ON devname [= size]
 [, devname [= size]]... ]
 [FOR LOAD]
```

Here *devname* is the name of a database device, and *size* is the number of megabytes to allocate to this database on the device. The new database will be named *dbname*. As you can see, you can also spread a database over multiple devices, and choose to create a log for the database at the same time.

At its simplest, you can just let SQL Server take care of the details. You can just execute a simple statement and let SQL Server take care of the rest, as shown here.

```
CREATE DATABASE cust
```

If you do this, SQL Server will create a database called "cust" on the *master* device with a default size of 2MB. If you want something different, you'll

FIGURE 2.12:

Creating a new device with
SQL Enterprise Manager

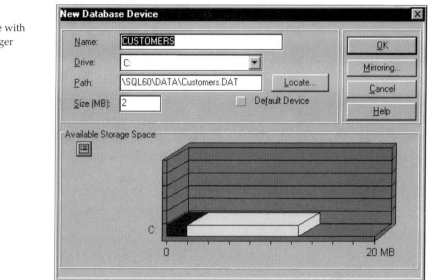

need a more complex statement. For example, to create a database and
a log on two different devices, you could use this statement:

```
CREATE DATABASE cust
  ON customers = 1000
  LOG ON custLog = 500
```

The FOR LOAD option reserves the database for reloading a previous
database backup. If you specify FOR LOAD, no one can accidentally
(or deliberately) write to the database between the time that it's created
and the time that the LOAD statement is executed. (For more information on backing up and restoring databases, see Chapter 10.)

To create a new database using SQL Enterprise Manager, right-click on
Databases in the treeview and select New Database from the context
menu. This will bring up the dialog box shown in Figure 2.13.

This dialog box includes all of the options that CREATE DATABASE
provides, as well as a graphical view of free space on all of your database devices.

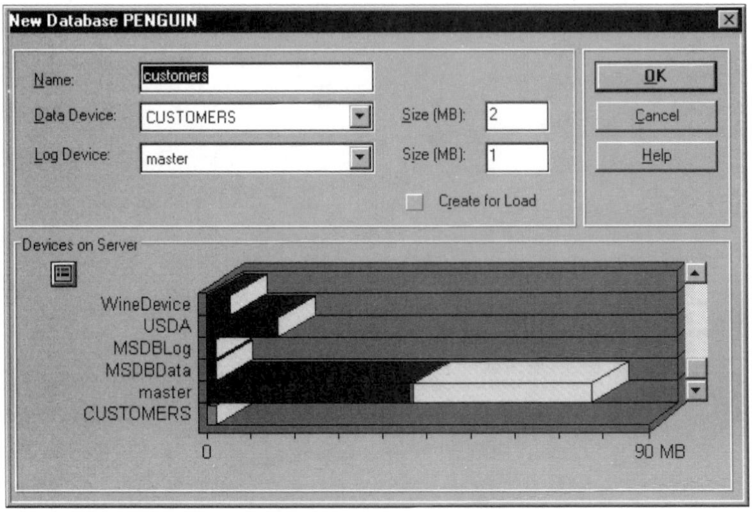

FIGURE 2.13:

Creating a new database with
SQL Enterprise Manager

Tables

The CREATE TABLE statement is one of the more complex Transact-SQL
statements. It has many options, as it has to be able to build up the entire
schema of a table. The basic outline of CREATE TABLE is shown here:

```
CREATE TABLE [database.[owner].]tablename
({colname datatype [NULL | NOT NULL |
IDENTITY[(seed, increment)]]
[constraint [constraint [...constraint]]]
| [[,]constraint]}
[[,] {nextcolumn | nextconstraint}...]
) [ON segment]
```

Table 2.5 provides an overview of the arguments for CREATE TABLE.

When you create a new table, you specify all of the column names and
datatypes in the table as well. (You can use the ALTER TABLE statement later to add new columns, but not to delete columns or change

TABLE 2.5: Arguments for CREATE TABLE

Argument	Purpose
database	Database name to contain the table. If omitted, defaults to the last database set with a USE statement.
owner	Owner of the new table. If omitted, defaults to the user who runs the statement.
tablename	Name of the new table. This must conform to the SQL Server rules for identifiers.
colname	Column name in the table. This must conform to the SQL Server rules for identifiers.
datatype	A valid SQL Server data type. This can be either one of the built-in datatypes or a user-defined datatype.
seed	Starting value for an identity column.
increment	Difference between successive values in an identity column.
constraint	Table-level or column-level constraint to implement.
segment	Segment name on which to create the table.

the datatypes of existing columns.) For example, here's a statement to create a new table with four columns:

```
CREATE TABLE customers
 (cust_id smallint IDENTITY(1,1),
 cust_name varchar(50) NOT NULL,
 cust_address varchar(100) NOT NULL,
 cust_balance money)
```

This definition makes use of two of the possible constraints on columns:

- IDENTITY specifies that SQL Server should automatically assign a value to this column when a new record is inserted (a function similar to that of the Access AutoNumber datatype).

- NOT NULL specifies that this column must have a value in each new record. This is the default. If you want to allow nulls, you must specify NULL for the column.

Each column must be assigned a datatype when you create it. Table 2.6 shows the built-in datatypes that SQL Server supports. You can also create your own datatypes by using the sp_addtype system stored procedure.

Names of both tables and columns must conform to the SQL Server rules for identifiers:

- The names must be 1–30 characters long.
- The first character must be a letter, _, @, or #. Identifiers starting with @ are reserved for local variables, and identifiers starting with # are reserved for temporary objects.
- The remaining characters may be letters, digits, or #, _, or $.
- Embedded spaces are not allowed.
- Table names must be unique for tables with the same owner in the same database.
- Column names must be unique within the same table.

You may also specify constraints for either tables or columns. There are five types of constraints allowed:

- Primary Key (table)
- Unique (table)
- Foreign Key (table)
- Default (column)
- Check (column)

SQL Server makes sure that values within a primary key are unique, and can use primary keys in Declarative Referential Integrity (DRI) operations. To create a primary key for a table, include a PRIMARY KEY constraint:

```
[CONSTRAINT constraintname
 PRIMARY KEY [CLUSTERED ¦ NONCLUSTERED]
 (colname1 [,colname2 [... , colname16]])
 [ON segment]
```

TABLE 2.6: SQL Server datatypes

Datatype	Comments
binary(n)	Binary data exactly n bits in length. Does not allow nulls.
varbinary(n)	Binary data up to n bits in length. Can allow nulls.
char(n)	Character data exactly n characters in length. Does not allow nulls.
varchar(n)	Character data up to n characters in length. Can allow nulls.
Datetime	Date between January 1, 1753 and December 31, 9999 with an accuracy of 3.33 milliseconds.
Smalldatetime	Date between January 1, 1900 and June 6, 2079 with an accuracy of one minute.
decimal(p,s)	Exact decimal number up to p total digits, with up to s total digits to the right of the decimal point. P must be less than or equal to 38 and s must be less than or equal to p.
numeric(p,s)	Exact decimal number up to p total digits, with up to s total digits to the right of the decimal point. P must be less than or equal to 38 and s must be less than or equal to p.
float(n)	Possibly rounded floating point data with b digits of binary precision. The maximum value for b is 15, which accomodates values up to 10 to the 308th power.
real	Possibly rounded floating point data with up to 7 digits of binary precision.
int	Integer between -2,147,483,648 and 2,147,483,647 (the equivalent of the Jet long datatype).
smallint	Integer between -32,768 and 32,767 (the equivalent of the Jet integer datatype).
tinyint	Integer between 0 and 255 (the equivalent of the Jet byte datatype).
money	Non-rounded floating point number from -922,337,203,685,477.5808 to 922,337,203,685,477.5897.
smallmoney	Non-rounded floating point number from -214,748.3648 to 214,748.3647.
bit	1 or 0. Multiple bit fields in the same table will be collected into bytes for a storage savings.
timestamp	A unique value generated by SQL Server every time the record is modified. A table may only have a single timestamp column.
text	Long character data (up to 2 billion bytes).
image	Long binary data (up to 2 billion bytes).

A primary key can index up to 16 columns within the table. A *clustered* primary key determines the actual physical order of rows within the table, while a *nonclustered* primary key allows SQL Server to keep rows in the fashion it thinks is most efficient. Clustered indexes can increase the chance of lock contention within a database.

SQL Server uses UNIQUE constraints to enforce uniqueness on values in a particular column or set of columns. To create a unique constraint, you use the UNIQUE keyword:

```
[CONSTRAINT constraintname]
 UNIQUE [CLUSTERED ¦ NONCLUSTERED]
 (colname1 [, colname2 [... , colname16]])
 [ON segment]
```

As with primary keys, Unique constraints can be either clustered or nonclustered. Of course, you can only have one clustered constraint on a single table.

A Foreign Key constraint forces values in a table to be drawn from values in another table. The syntax used to create a Foreign Key constraint specifies the referenced table but is included when defining the referencing table, as shown here:

```
[CONSTRAINT constraintname]
 [FOREIGN KEY (colname1 [, colname2 [... , colname16]])]
 REFERENCES [owner.]reftable
 [refcolumn1 [, refcolumn2 [... , refcolumn16]])]
```

A *default constraint* is the equivalent of an Access default. To create a default constraint, you specify the default value, as shown below.

```
[CONSTRAINT constraintname]
 DEFAULT {constantexpression ¦ NULL}
 [FOR colname]
```

You need to supply the FOR clause when you implement a default constraint as a separate clause within the CREATE TABLE statement, but not if it's contained within one of the column definitions for the table.

Finally, you can create a CHECK constraint. As shown here, this constraint allows you to provide an expression to check when inserting a new value in a column, similar to the action of an Access validation rule.

```
[CONSTRAINT constraintname]
 CHECK [NOT FOR REPLICATION] expression
```

The NOT FOR REPLICATION clause lets you specify that this constraint should be ignored when a table is being replicated (see Chapter 8 for more on replication).

SQL Enterprise Manager also supplies a user interface for defining tables, as shown in Figure 2.14. When you're defining a table, you can simply type in column names and select datatypes for each column. The table definition dialog box includes an Advanced Features toolbar button which provides access to primary keys, foreign keys, and other constraints. All CREATE TABLE options (except the ability to specify the segment for a particular table or index) are implemented in this dialog box.

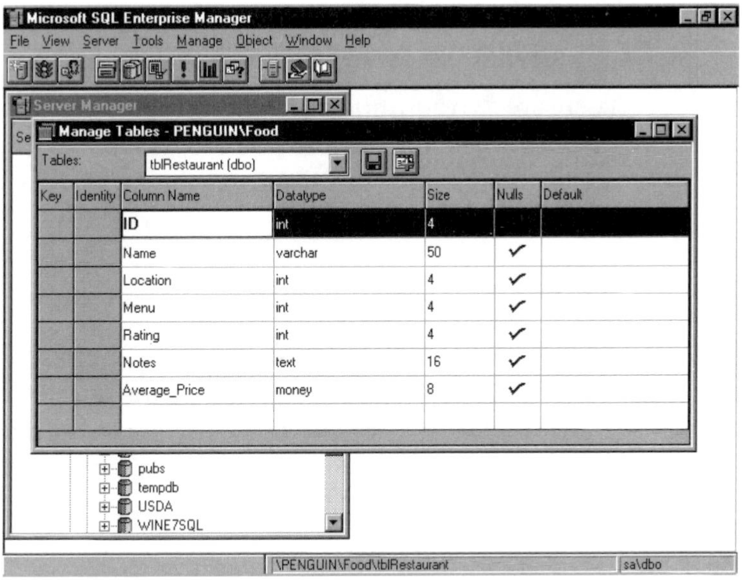

FIGURE 2.14:

The SQL Enterprise Manager table definition dialog box

If you're accustomed to Access, you may find the SQL Enterprise Manager table tools somewhat annoying. Remember, it's SQL Server itself that does not allow you to delete a column or change its datatype. This is not a limit imposed by the user interface.

Views

You can create new SQL Server views with the CREATE VIEW statement. As you can see here, this statement has a much simpler syntax than CREATE TABLE does.

```
CREATE VIEW [owner.]viewname
 [(colname1 [,colname2] ... )]
 [WITH ENCRYPTION]
 AS selectstatement [WITH CHECK OPTION]
```

The view draws its columns from the *selectstatement* argument, which must be a valid SELECT query. You can use the *colname* arguments to rename columns for purposes of this view. For example, this SQL statement will create a view that uses proper case for columns named with lower case:

```
CREATE VIEW custview
 (FirstName, LastName)
 AS SELECT firstname, lastname FROM customers
```

There are two additional clauses that you can add to a CREATE VIEW statement. The WITH ENCRYPTION clause provides some security to prevent users from determining where the view obtains its columns. You won't generally need this option. The WITH CHECK OPTION clause checks all operations performed on rows in the view to make sure that they won't cause the row to vanish from the view.

Although SQL Enterprise Manager does provide a user interface for views, in this case it doesn't really add much to ISQL/W. Figure 2.15 shows the Manage Views window, which is just a dialog box that allows you to enter and execute CREATE VIEW Transact-SQL statements.

The SQL Enterprise Manager
CREATE VIEW interface

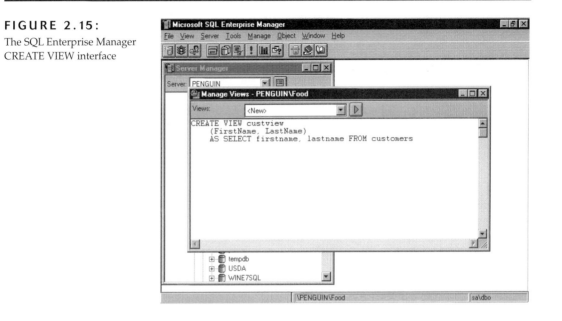

Triggers

Triggers can be created with the CREATE TRIGGER statement as
follows:

```
CREATE TRIGGER [owner].triggername
 ON [owner].tablename
 FOR {INSERT, UPDATE, DELETE}
 WITH ENCRYPTION
 AS sqlstatements
```

Here *triggername* is the name of the trigger, and *tablename* is the name
of the table with which it is associated. A trigger can be run when new
rows are inserted, when existing rows are updated, when existing rows
are deleted, or under any combination of these circumstances, and can
consist of any set of valid Transact-SQL statements. As with views, the
definition of a trigger can be encrypted so that others cannot see the
SQL statements that it invokes.

A simple trigger like this one might prevent the user from deleting rows from a particular table:

```
CREATE TRIGGER nodelete
 ON keytable
 FOR DELETE
 AS RAISERROR(50001, 16, 10)
 ROLLBACK TRANSACTION
```

Here error 50001 is a user-defined error that would have to be added to the system tables with the sp_addmessage stored procedure. You can do nearly anything within a trigger, so they are ideal for enforcing business rules that depend on data changes. For example, when a new row is added to your sales table, you could check inventory levels and place an order for the product if necessary.

To manage triggers in SQL Enterprise Manager, right-click on the table that you want to see the triggers for and choose Triggers from the context menu. As you'll see in Figure 2.16, though, this interface is just a wrapper for the same CREATE TRIGGER Transact-SQL statements that you could write in ISQL/W.

Loading SQL Server Data

If you're moving an existing database from Access to SQL Server, you have several choices for moving the data. You can simply export the Access table to SQL Server (see Appendix A), or use the Upsizing Tools (see Chapter 6) to export the table. You can write an update query or use a pair of recordsets to move the data. You can also take advantage of SQL Server's own BCP tool to load data that's been written to a disk file. Let's look at two of these alternatives, recordsets and BCP, in more detail here.

Using RecordSets

If you're used to working within Access, you may find Access Basic code is the easiest way to move data from an Access database to a new

FIGURE 2.16:

SQL Enterprise Manager showing a trigger

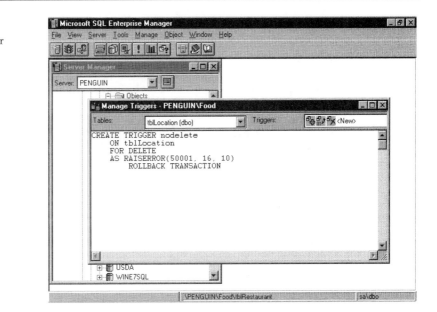

server. SQLTransfer.MDB, on the companion disk, includes a general-purpose procedure (shown here) to move records from a client table to a server table with the same structure as the client table.

```
Function TransferToServer(strLocalTable As String, _
 strServerTable As String)
' Move the contents of a local table to the server.
' The two tables must have fields with the same names.
' The server table must already be attached.
Dim rstLocal As Recordset
Dim rstServer As Recordset
Dim lngCount As Long
Dim varRet As Variant
Dim i As Integer
Set rstLocal = CurrentDb.OpenRecordset(strLocalTable)
Set rstServer = CurrentDb.OpenRecordset(strServerTable, _
dbOpenDynaset, dbAppendOnly)
lngCount = 1
Do Until rstLocal.EOF
varRet = SysCmd(acSysCmdSetStatus, _
  "Moving record " & lngCount)
```

```
rstServer.AddNew
 For i = 0 To rstLocal.Fields.Count - 1
 rstServer.Fields(rstLocal.Fields(i).Name) = _
  rstLocal.Fields(i)
 Next i
rstServer.UPDATE
rstLocal.MoveNext
lngCount = lngCount + 1
Loop
varRet = SysCmd(acSysCmdClearStatus)
End Function
```

This function works by opening a pair of recordsets and copying data between fields of the same name. It also updates the status bar so that you can keep track of the progress of the copy.

You may find that this approach is far too slow for large amounts of data. One problem is that every operation on a recordset is logged in the SQL Server transaction log, and this takes time. You can work around this by using the SQL Server BCP utility.

Using BCP

SQL Server ships with a command-line utility called Bulk Copy Program, or BCP. BCP can take a tab-delimited file and import it directly to a SQL Server table. As Access can export to tab-delimited files, this gives you a fast path between the two databases.

To move data from an Access table to a SQL Server table with the same fields, follow these steps:

1. Select the table within your Access database, and select File ➤ Save As/Export.

2. Choose the option to export the table to an external file.

3. Select Text Files as the type of file to use, and click Export. This will load the Text Export Wizard.

4. Choose to use a delimited file, and click Next.

5. Choose tabs as your text delimited, and no text qualifier, as shown in Figure 2.17.

6. Name the disk file and finish the export.

7. On the server, set the Select Into/Bulk Copy option to True. You can do this with the sp_dboption stored procedure.

8. Drop the indexes on the table, to prevent them from being rebuilt for each record. You can do this by right-clicking on the table in SQL Enterprise Manager and choosing Indexes from the context menu.

9. Copy the text export file to the server.

FIGURE 2.17:

Options for exporting a table in BCP format

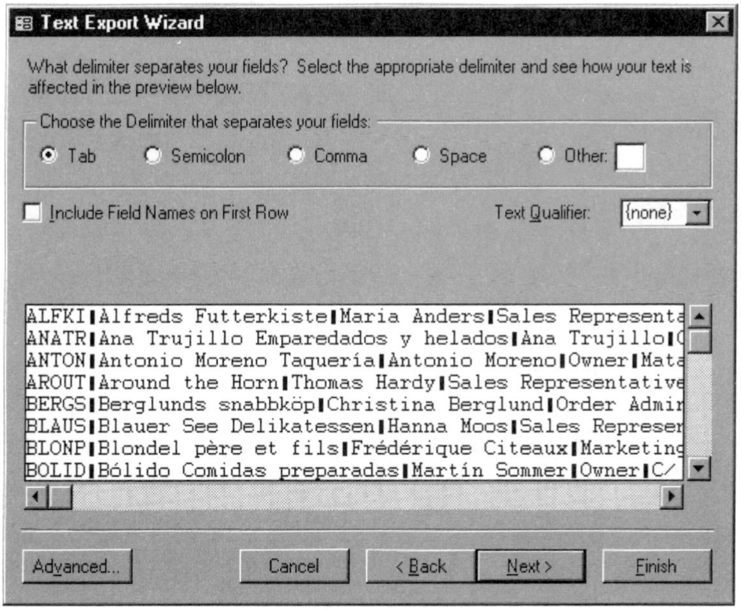

10. Use the BCP utility to copy the data. The command line will be similar to this:

```
bcp dbSQL.dbo.Customers in cust.txt /C /U Mike /P wallaby
```

In this command line, after specifying the table, the direction of copying, and the disk file, the /C parameter tells BCP that this is a character mode file, and the /U and /P parameters supply a username and password.

11. Return the indexes to the table.

12. Revoke the Select Into/Bulk Copy permission.

13. Back up the database (otherwise, you can't recover, as BCP is a non-logged operation).

You can use BCP to move data either in or out of your database with the same syntax—just substitute "out" for "in" as the second argument to move data out. Also note that you can specify a drive letter (for example, b:) to copy data to a series of diskettes. BCP will prompt for new diskettes as it needs them, although it won't format them for you.

Summary

Paying in-depth attention to the design of your database can save you an incalculable amount of time when you build the code and user interface on the client side of your application. When you use a robust product like Microsoft SQL Server to manage the data, you can take advantage of many features to ensure the continued integrity of data stored within your database design. In the next chapter, we'll cover some of the key points to consider as you build the client side of your client/server application.

CHAPTER

THREE

Designing Applications for Client/Server

- Thinking client/server

- Optimizing a file server application for client/server

- Dealing with performance issues

- Specific guidelines for Access

- Client/Server architecture and Access

If you have any experience at all in building desktop database applications, you can use many of the available tools to easily "upsize" your application. In fact, we dedicated an entire chapter (Chapter 6) to a discussion of how using these tools can help you out. As that chapter explains, many of the little details that you need to do when you move up to SQL Server are taken care of by the Upsizing Wizard. But will your application be successful when you set it up to be used in a client/ server environment? Unless your application deals with small amounts of data and/or only a few users, the answer is probably "No," or at least, "Not right away."

Why? The reason is that you must go through the process of making sure that your application is optimized for the client/server environment, and an application that has just been upsized or *converted* has not yet completed this process (sometimes referred to as *porting* an application, which implies that you have not only made it work in a new environment but that you made it work well). In this chapter we will be looking at many of the optimizations and problems to look out for that can make this process go more smoothly. In addition, you will want to keep these issues in mind when you start applications in Access 95 that *might* be upsized at some later date—you may find that some careful planning now can save you days, weeks, and perhaps even months of work when porting your application later.

This chapter gives you a thorough overview of the key issues you must address as you design an application to be used in a client/server environment. First, we explain why the simple act of moving your data to a shared remote server can cause you so much pain (and make it seem initially as though upsizing makes your application worse instead of better). Next, we discuss ways in which you might change your application design to achieve acceptable performance over a network in the client/server environment, which is very different than the file/server environment. Then, we walk you through a number of "good, bad, and ugly" examples of what to do—and what *not* to do— to build a successful client/server application using Access for your client interface. Finally, we present some examples of the types of independent forms you can create to control how much processing takes place on the client and on the server. Although the real specifics of getting data from SQL Server are discussed in Chapter 4, this chapter will give you a clearer picture of the mindset that you must adopt to create successful client/server solutions.

Thinking "Client/Server"

When you build any database application on a reasonably robust desktop computer, it's very easy to create an application that will be anywhere from disappointing to downright unusable when you deploy it in a client/server environment. This does not mean your application is somehow faulty, it's just that an application designed for optimal performance in one environment may be woefully unprepared for another. Rather than looking at these items as mistakes, you should view them as methods that may have worked for you in the file/server environment but just don't translate well to client/server. (To help you adopt the right mindset, you should avoid using them in the file/server arena as well, especially when you work on applications that may eventually be upsized.) Some of the more common design flaws are:

- Testing on a large memory machine (or more accurately, testing on a machine with more memory than those on which the application will run).

- Testing with a small amount of sample data (that is, small when compared with the amount of data the application is meant to support).

- Testing with sample data that is not representative of the real data that will appear in the application (for example, copying the same hundred rows over and over).

- Not testing over a network or testing over a network whose performance is significantly different from the target network.

- Ignoring future contention from multiple users and new features that will be added.

If you commit any or all of these sins, it's far too easy to build forms that don't reflect reality: they edit data that always open on a recordset containing all the rows from the target table, access over the network combo or list boxes that will ultimately be populated by thousands of rows, or leave out simple error detection and recovery for locking errors. Even when you test with a moderately large number of rows in sample tables, but do so only on your local machine, you avoid dealing with many of the data retrieval overhead issues inherent in a networked client/server environment. Keep in mind that every minute you save now by avoiding these issues can come back to haunt you later, so it's best to consider them in the initial design stages.

Mistake #1: Testing on a Large Memory Machine

If you're serious about using a 32-bit operating system like Windows 95 or Windows NT and you are developing applications using a 32-bit version of Access, you probably have a workstation running with 32MB or more of memory. The Jet Engine takes advantage of every scrap of memory to speed up access to data. For example, let's say you're working with reasonable 150-byte rows from your data tables. On a 32MB machine, it's quite possible for Access to load 50,000 or more rows into memory without breathing hard. You probably won't notice any performance degradation, particularly if you also make the mistake of testing with local data (noted next).

The solution is not to develop your applications on slower machines, but rather to make sure that you do a significant amount of your testing in the environment in which the application will run. If your client machines have 16MB of RAM, then you have no idea what performance degradation, or even outright errors (due to timing problems), you may unintentionally cause by working on a faster machine than that of your users.

Mistake #2: Testing with Local Data

Next, let's suppose that you've generated a reasonable amount of test data—perhaps as much as 200,000 rows—and that you have not simply copied the same few rows over and over, thus making sure that your test data corresponds to reality. Assuming 150-byte maximum length rows, Access can store anywhere from a dozen to perhaps more than fifty rows per logical page on your hard drive. The Jet Engine can do an excellent job of trying to "read ahead" pages of data, particularly when it finds them on the hard disk in the same sequence as it requests them. This happens even more often with Jet 3.0 than with Jet 2.x, as every time you compact a Jet 3.0 database it rewrites the records in primary key order, which can give some of the same benefits as the clustered indexes you find on SQL Server. It also uses background threads to continue to retrieve pointers to data after it has brought enough data into memory to satisfy the immediate needs of your edit form. This asynchronous capability keeps working while you do your work. It can be very helpful when you are dealing with Access by itself but it can also be very misleading as an indicator of performance in the client/server environment. The reason for this is that when you are getting data off the network, this process is significantly slower.

So, for example, the time to open a form that can edit 200,000 rows of data is probably less than two seconds. In fact, Access will probably spend more time loading the form definition and any VBA code than it will loading the data from a local drive. Even if you immediately ask the form to scroll to the last row, Access will show you the last row in ten seconds or less. If it had to read all the data from your hard drive, it might actually take a bit longer (see Table 3.1). However, in most cases Access retrieves only *pointers* to the intervening rows, or the primary keys of the table. As a primary key uniquely defines its row, Jet knows that it can get the whole row any time it needs to simply by keeping track of that primary key value.

The problem with all this is that it's tremendously faster to access data from a hard drive and memory than from most typical networks. Trying to estimate network performance based on local performance is nearly impossible—you can almost never tell how your application will perform over the network until you test it there. In addition, problems related to timing errors may also turn up when using the network, and the only way to trap them is to test for them in the right environment.

If you look at Table 3.1, you may begin to understand why testing over a network is so important. You should be aware that the numbers presented in this table are worst case. That is, we derived the numbers

TABLE 3.1: Relative speeds to access 200,000 150-byte rows

Medium	Speed (worst case)	Elapsed Time
Memory	70 nanoseconds per byte	2.1 seconds
Local Disk	15 milliseconds per track, 63 512-byte sectors per track, 12 rows per logical page + memory time	20 seconds
Local-Area Network Disk	2 megabits per second overhead + local disk time	170 seconds (2.8 minutes)
Wide-Area (dial-in) Network Disk	28,000 bits per second + local disk time	9,400 seconds (2.6 hours)

assuming that the machine would be fetching data from memory one byte at a time (a true 32-bit computer handles at least four bytes in one "chunk"), using a relatively slow hard drive, reading full, uncompressed rows, and using a relatively slow 10Base2 Ethernet network. The point of the table is to show that getting data from a hard drive is at least an order of magnitude drop in performance from accessing data in memory. Likewise, moving your data out to a network can cause an order of magnitude or more drop in performance compared to a local disk.

The most extreme case in this table is that of performance over a phone line. Perhaps unfortunately, one of the most common reasons for upsizing is the desire to link multiple sites together via a common server. As you may have guessed, the phone connection makes the network connection look incredibly fast by comparison. If you ever consider extending your applications over a wide-area network, you will definitely need to consider the architecture of your front end and how it requests data. This will make the information in this chapter and in Chapter 4 crucial in your application design.

Mistake #3: Testing on the Right Network

Ideally, you want to test in network conditions that are as close to the target network as possible. In practice, it is nearly impossible to duplicate the number of PCs, the amount of network traffic, the network protocol(s) used, the type and speed of the network, and all the other variables that come into play.

Despite this, you should do the best that you reasonably can to duplicate conditions on the target network, which means you need to learn what those conditions are and change the testing protocols of your application to match them when possible.

Mistake #4: Ignoring Shared User Contention

In most cases, it may be difficult, if not impossible, to give your database application a thorough "shakedown" with multiple users sharing the data. You should, however, make some effort to predict how much individual users may get in each other's way. This is a little more complicated then simply deploying your application on a network and having multiple programs request data from the server and processing it. Although this would make a good generic testing suite for your application, if the programs are not created to mimic the types of actions your users will be doing, the information provided may not give you an accurate picture of how your application will perform.

The 3.0 version of the Jet Engine has actually addressed some of the problems that occur when many people are accessing the same application. By increasing performance and eliminating contention for the "new" record (a huge problem in Jet 2.x wherein a user might lock the data page that contains the new record for a table and thus keep everyone else from being able to add records to that table), it is better able to deal with some of the problems that multiple users can cause.

But no matter how many enhancements have been made, you're still running multiple copies of the engine on different computers. Thus, there is no way to take advantage of the fact that one user has loaded certain records that you needed on another client machine; your copy of the engine will have to load them all over again. For an information-processing application using a true database server like SQL Server, however, performance may actually improve when multiple users request the same or similar data. Why? If the server has sufficient memory to retain the most recently requested rows in memory, it can respond to additional requests from memory, not from disk.

Most business applications, however, must support multiple users randomly updating or inserting data. If the level of activity is relatively low across a very large database, chances are low that two users will ever "collide" with one another. If, on the other hand, update activity is high—even on a large database—your application must be ready to gracefully deal with a variety of conflicts. You must think carefully about how you want to handle issues such as record locking and bulletproof error trapping for any multi-user application, but it's absolutely essential when multiple users attempt to update the same data at the same time. Chapter 4 has some further details on trapping and analyzing data errors from both Jet and SQL Server.

Dealing with Performance Issues

If you understand the potential huge drop in performance by moving data to a server, you may be wondering why you want to make the switch at all. You may have had this very thought if you've upsized an Access application in the past and watched acceptable performance become truly awful after the upsizing was complete. But after seeing some of the issues involved, it should be obvious that the way to gain acceptable performance is to absolutely minimize the amount of data that your application moves over the network. After all, the advantage of a client/server architecture is to have clients and servers who can *both* perform tasks. Because of this, the only way to ensure good performance is to make sure that you give the correct job to each and minimize the amount of traffic that flows between them. In the following sections, we discuss various strategies you can employ in your application design to accomplish this.

Using Local Data

Because accessing data on the local client machine is measurably faster than getting it from the server, you should place as much data as possible locally. The strategy you use depends on how frequently (if ever) the data changes: in most cases, lookup tables that never change (such as a table of zip codes and cities) or seldom change (such as a price or product list) can often be kept locally and updated only as needed. The benefits to your application can be tremendous, especially for data that is accessed frequently. We discuss some specific examples next.

Code Tables

A common way to minimize the amount of storage that applications require is to use short codes in place of longer descriptive phrases. For example, a "Cash customer" might be represented by the numeric code value "1," "Bank card credit customer" by a "2," "Company credit" by a "3," and so on. Another, more common, example is the recognized list of two-character abbreviations that the U.S. Postal Service uses in place of state names. Sometimes such abbreviations will be in common use by a client before you even install an application, and your users might insist on these "shortcuts."

Once you establish the relationship between codes and their descriptive meanings, they rarely, if ever, change in meaning. If the code list is short, you can take advantage of the Value List option in combo and list boxes in Access. By doing this, you store the list within the definition of the form itself. If the list is longer than a half-dozen or so entries, however, it can be easier and more efficient to design a data table to hold the codes and their descriptions.

To gain best performance when using code tables in your application, the tables should almost always be local Access tables on each client machine. We say "almost always" because it is still reasonable to load small table lists over the network if the list changes at all and you would otherwise be faced with updating hundreds or thousands of client copies of the table every time an entry in the list changed. When this is the case, it is often a good idea to think about keeping local copies of remote data, as discussed in the following section.

Local Copies of Remote Data

Even when you know that data changes occur in tables, you may decide to keep a "master" copy of the data on the server, but still use local copies of the data at each client. You can use this technique effectively if any of the following are true:

- Changes to the master copy occur at infrequent and predictable intervals, and you can provide automated procedures on the client machines to refresh the local copy after each update.

- Changes to the master copy occur at infrequent and unpredictable times, but the client application can be programmed to probe the master copy and reload a changed copy when needed.

- Changes to the master occur fairly frequently (perhaps several times a day), but the application is not impacted as long as each client can obtain a new copy at a regular interval (perhaps once a day).

- Changes to the master table occur frequently, but the part of the table you need for a selection list in the client changes infrequently or not at all.

You should particularly examine how you use certain key tables in your application. For example, the tables containing your customer, vendor, or parts information may not change often enough to warrant always reading the data over the network. Periodically refreshing the data on the client machines to get added or changed data may do the trick.

Even when a server table changes quite frequently, the part of the table you use for your list (for example, to set the Customer ID foreign key in a new work order) may not change at all. You can use a local table that contains the latest list of customer IDs and names for your list, refreshing it perhaps only at the beginning of each day when the application starts.

If you choose to do this, you may want to consider adding code to your "not in list" event to probe the server for a customer that has been added to the master copy but doesn't yet exist in the local copy. The necessity of this type of addition depends heavily on the "business rules" of the application. For example, in an order entry system, if a customer calls to check on an order but they do not exist in the local table, the customer will certainly know whether they have called before. This type of tradeoff, which gives you excellent performance when the data happens to be available locally and a performance hit for these "searches" is often the best way to improve the apparent speed of your application. Most users will readily accept the difference between data that they have on hand versus data that has to be retrieved from the home office.

Avoiding Opening Unfiltered Recordsets

When you build a desktop database application for a single user, it's convenient and quite acceptable to build forms to edit and insert data that use a record source containing all the rows from the underlying table. Even when you don't base a form on an entire table, it is all too easy to choose queries that can return too large of a recordset. Although you may not notice a big hit in performance when the application is small and the table is local, you can move this table to a server (either as an Access table or one "upsized" to SQL Server), and performance will suddenly become unacceptable—particularly when the underlying tables contain thousands of rows. This is in fact the main villain causing the initial fear the first time you upsize, when you see your application performance decline rather than improve.

To avoid this in a true client/server application, you'll find yourself building many "intermediate" unbound forms that let the users specify what data they want to edit. Think about it—users almost never want to see *all* the data anyway. If the user wants to see customers in a particular zip code or orders containing a particular type of part, give them a way to specify the restriction and then either change the underlying recordset of the form to include the filter or apply the filter as you open the form. It is important to filter the data before you request it rather than after, because if your table initially does open against a huge recordset, your users will complain about the long load time and not notice how fast things are when they start specifying criteria for a filter.

Another often overlooked technique is to ask the user if they want to add new records or edit existing ones. When they want to add data, open a form specifically designed for data entry that does not allow the user to edit any pre-existing records. A data-entry form can also include various combo or list boxes to help the user choose related foreign key values for new rows. When the user wants to edit, ask for a filter (and perhaps even reject the request if they supply no filter) and then open a form that uses joins in the underlying query to display related parent data rather than separate list or combo boxes.

Once again, the actions your users need to take can often help you decide the best way to apply filters. If you have users who (for example) often need to look at data from only the last week, you might want to base your form on just that recent chunk of data and perhaps even give them separate ways (with different filters) to open the same form. Generally, you *must* let the needs of the user dictate what filters you supply—it's useless to give them many options if the key ones that they need to help the application's performance are not available.

Performing Updates in Batches

In the previous section, we mentioned the technique of opening a form specifically designed for data entry when users only want to add new rows. An even more efficient technique is to open a data entry form on a local "transaction" table that collects and validates new data they eventually want to add to master tables on the server. This method, using a temporary table that is then appended to the server's data, can give you substantial performance gains. A good example is an application in which a specific group of users is responsible for entering new orders. If they need to have the ability to enter data quickly, such as when the user is talking directly with the customer on the phone and rapid response times are critical, this technique can be the ideal way to boost performance. ("Uh, excuse me while I wait for my computer to find the part you want to order," doesn't make for very happy customers.)

Two different users are unlikely to be working on the same order at the same time, so conflicts are rare. The major exception would be in an application where one user transfers a customer to a second user and that second user needs to pull up the customer's account. In those cases you would need to provide some way to quickly save the data so that it is available to the second user. You might want to automate the process somewhat with a button that will immediately send this information back to the server. One other alternative to consider if the other user is on the same local network is to directly connect to the server via Jet to give them the single record. Although not strictly in line with the client/server model, this type of operation may sometimes ideally fit in with the application. Your application must also provide mechanisms to allow a user to save rows into a local transaction table, then send the results in a single batch to the server when the user is finished. Depending on the immediate need for this information by other users, you can design the process to send a batch of inserts at the end of each order or collect several orders before updating the server. You may also want to take advantage of some of Jet 3.0's asynchronous processing abilities, writing data to the server independently of entering it in the local table.

Taking Advantage of Transactions

Access and SQL Server work well together to make sure that either all of the changes in a "batch" arrive safely at the server or none do. In fact, you can initiate a transaction that protects the batch on both the client and on the server, called an *explicit transaction*. You can start a transaction in Access, send the changes to the server, clear the local tables, then commit the transaction. If something fails, you will still have the changes in the local table to try again. If the changes go to the server successfully, they won't "commit" there until the client has also successfully deleted the local copies.

In code form, the process looks something like this:

```
Dim db As Database
Dim wrk As Workspace

' Get a copy of the current database object
Set db = CurrentDb
' Point to the current workspace
Set wrk = DBEngine.Workspaces(0
' Start an explicit transaction
wrk.BeginTrans
' Insert parent rows on the server
db.Execute "qappLocalOrders"
' Insert child rows on the server
db.Execute "qappLocalOrderParts"
' Delete the local orders
' —assumes orders cascade delete to parts
db.Execute "Delete * From tblLocalOrders;"
' Commit all updates on server and client
wrk.CommitTrans
```

Before you decide to use explicit transactions in all cases, however, you should keep in mind that some of the enhancements to Jet 3.0, namely support for asynchronous ODBC queries, asynchronous updates, and

implicit transactions, can sometimes decrease performance by lump-
ing actions into transactions in this way. Sometimes it can take careful
benchmarking to determine whether a situation is better suited to explicit or implicit transactions.

Specific Guidelines for Access

Although ODBC provides a generic interface that allows you to use
similar syntax to connect Access to different back ends, there are many
advantages to knowing both your front end and back end very well so
that you know how to integrate the features of each. This section will
discuss many of the specific issues to keep in mind as you consider the
upsizing process.

If you have been using the Seek method of a table type recordset, you
will need to deal with one of the most important specific changes in
your code that is not really a high-level design issue (but which does
have some relevance): the Seek method is not supported for ODBC
sources such as SQL Server. Although this feature gives optimal performance under Access and some of the databases that it connects to it
via ISAM drivers, it is not available for SQL Server databases. Unfortunately, the only methods that you can "plug in" to sections that use
Seek are the FindFirst, FindNext, etc., methods, which have substantially worse performance than Seek. Although this is not a major issue
in client/server architecture, it is an important point to keep in mind,
and a perfect example of why trying to quickly jump from an Access
database to an Access/SQL Server one without giving thought to the
architecure of each can lead to major problems.

To help you better understand some of the application design approaches
we have recommended, we constructed a few queries and forms in the
sample "Parts and Services" database that illustrate both right and
wrong ways to approach building a client/server application. We discuss

these techniques in the following sections, and the various forms include comments that discuss some of the good and bad points of these different forms.

If you see familiar features in the forms that we have labeled as "bad," don't panic! We're not saying that your application is bad; we're merely saying that although performance may be fine right now, upsizing will almost certainly be a painful experience and you might be unhappy with performance in a client/server environment. These guidelines can help you to understand some of the issues that we have discussed here. The examples will also naturally lead you to wonder **how** you are supposed to get data from SQL Server, and this is exactly what Chapter 4 will cover.

If you copy the sample "Parts and Services" database to a local hard drive and run the samples from there, you will see some of the performance impact of "right" versus "wrong" ways. To see a bigger difference, copy the database file to a network file server and open the database over your local area network. For the most dramatic impact, use the Upsizing Wizard described in Chapter 6 to move tblVendor, tblVendorParts, tblParts, tblInventory, and tblStock to SQL Server. We have included both the "Access only" and the upsized versions of this database on the CD-ROM that accompanies the book; see Appendix A for more information on how to load the SQL Server back end, or if you like you can run this application for practice through the Upsizing Wizard. For what it's worth, this is a somewhat idyllic sample to work with, as the upsizing process for it is fairly painless and we have gone to great lengths to make sure to point out ahead of time which parts will perform well and which won't. But it's worth the time to review the differences between the good forms and the bad ones, because you will face the same issues when you develop and upsize your own applications.

Doing It Wrong

Access is a great desktop database product. It provides tools that make it incredibly easy to build small applications with very little code. Because it also does a lot of the grunt work of managing the mapping of data to forms in the user interface, it's a good product to use as the foundation for the client half of a client/server application. All this flexibility comes with a price, however: Access doesn't warn you when you're doing something in a sub-optimal way. For example, in doing its best to get the data to you, it doesn't warn you if you attach a 100,000 row table over a network line, or any number of other problems. Therefore, if you go about building client forms using the simplest techniques in Access, you'll probably commit these cardinal sins:

- Your forms will always open unfiltered, even if you add the filters later on.

- You'll use the same form to both add and edit records, without specifying any built-in constants to open it for "adding only" or "editing only."

- You'll use combo or list boxes bound directly to server data—even when the ControlSource query returns thousands of rows to help users enter foreign key values.

- You'll create forms with multiple open subforms all bound to unfiltered server data, requiring a separate query to be sent to the server for each subform.

Open the "Parts and Services" Access database you'll find on the sample disk. The upsized version's front end is identical to the Access-only version; in both cases, you'll see the main "switchboard" form open, as shown in Figure 3.1.

Click on the Parts and Inventory button to see the dialog box shown in Figure 3.2. As you can see, we've given you some clues on the command buttons about which ones give you "OK" or "Bad" examples.

FIGURE 3.1:
The main form in the Parts
and Services sample database

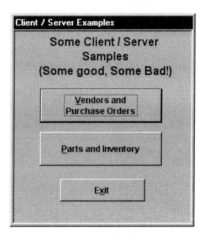

FIGURE 3.2:
This dialog box gives you
options to edit parts and
inventory entries.

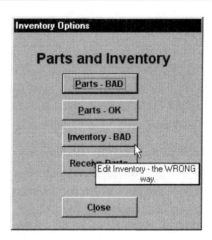

Click on the "Inventory - BAD" button to see a typical Access form that
someone might design for a desktop database, as shown in Figure 3.3.
If you open it locally on a Pentium machine with lots of memory, it
should take two to three seconds to open. If you move the MDB file to
a network file server, it may take as long as five to ten seconds.

FIGURE 3.3:

An editing Inventory form done the wrong way

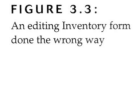

As noted within the dialog box itself, this particular form violates almost all the rules. It opens the entire Inventory table. Even though it's for editing existing rows, it has a combo box for the Part ID that has to fetch another 3,300 or so rows from the database. A combo box in the subform shows which vendors supply the current part—this combo gets re-filtered as you move from row to row in the outer form, even though it would be far better to make such a list available only when the user indicates a need to enter a new stock adjustment row.

This is a pretty extreme example and it might seem a little farfetched. But in many instances, especially in applications that constantly have features added to them, it is easy to add a combo box here and a subform there and a few more records returned somewhere else, and before you know it, you may be looking at a form just like this. And although you may have saved some time when you added all the features by cutting those corners, you can load the upsized version of the database to see whether or not it was really worth it (it wasn't).

When It's OK to Cheat

In the sample Parts and Services database, the Vendors table is a candidate for violating some of the rules because it contains only a few (29) rows. Figure 3.4 shows you the edit form for Vendors that opens to edit all the rows in the sample. Obviously the hit for 29 rows is not that much, and it simply isn't worth the overhead of creating complex filters in such cases.

FIGURE 3.4:

The Vendors edit form

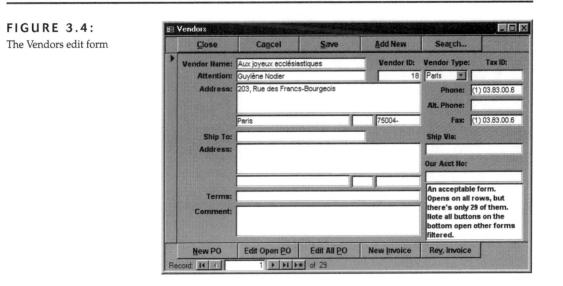

If you look behind the scenes of this form, however, you'll find that the command buttons across the bottom that let you get to related data for vendors all filter the resulting recordset, at least based on the current vendor. The idea is that it's acceptable to let the user browse the relatively short list of vendors directly from the server, but we revert to good client/server design techniques when the user wants to work with a larger set of related data. This is a compromise that you will often have to make, as few users want their data served up just one row at a time.

Because the vendor list is short, it's also acceptable to use the vendor table directly on any form where we need a Vendor ID to fill a foreign key in the edited record source. For example, the Purchase Order form shown in Figure 3.5 uses the Vendor table directly in a combo box that sets the Vendor ID foreign key in the Purchase Order table.

FIGURE 3.5:

The form to edit purchase orders

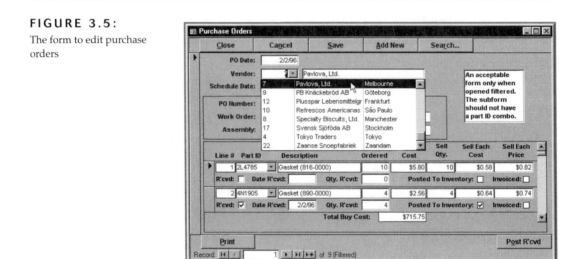

However, this form is still poorly designed. When you're editing an existing purchase order, you shouldn't need the vendor list at all. In fact, there's code in the form to lock the Vendor ID when you aren't on a new row, so the Vendor ID combo box is pointless for most editing. This type of extra "feature" added to a form is very common, as it is easy to add when a client asks for it. In most cases, one of the biggest challenges is stripping all those "features" away to improve performance in the client/server environment.

So why show you a bad example? If you're converting an existing desktop-only application to client/server, this is an acceptable shortcut to take if the amount of underlying data allows you to. Be aware, however, that you may have to come back to forms like this later and redesign them if the amount of data in the underlying table increases significantly. (Because of this, you should limit it to data that will *not* increase significantly.) If you are starting from scratch, a better approach would be to provide an entirely separate data entry form that perhaps takes advantage of a local vendor list table to make data entry easy. In most cases, the main edit form shouldn't have a combo box at all.

Getting It Right

Once you get into the habit of building separate forms to edit or insert data, you're on your way to building efficient client/server applications. For your main transaction tables, always insert a layer that asks the user for criteria. The first one will be a bit tedious to build, but they're well worth the effort. Even if you leave the door open for the user to (in theory) ask for hundreds of rows at a time, you'll find your users taking advantage of your filtering forms to focus on the task at hand and get a quick response. The key to making sure they take advantage of this is to give them the ability to filter on the data that they consider important. As we mentioned before, it is pointless to allow users to filter on six criteria that they care about if the one or two most important to them are ignored.

You can find one good example in the sample database of using separate forms and a filter form for editing Parts. Click on Parts and Inventory from the main form (shown in Figure 3.1), then choose the Parts - OK button in the form you saw in Figure 3.2. You'll see the dialog box in Figure 3.6.

When you make the selections shown in Figure 3.6, the application responds with the two rows that solve your request, as shown in Figure 3.7. Generally, this is the way you want to design your interface: your feedback should be quick and precise, as should your requests for information—the key is to minimize the amount of data you request from the server.

FIGURE 3.6:

Requiring criteria to edit server data

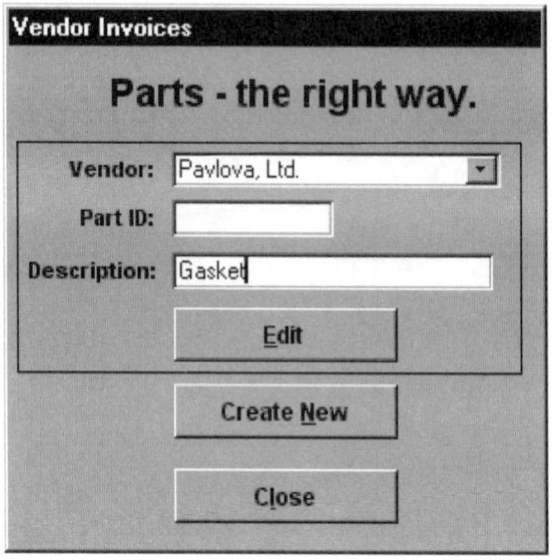

FIGURE 3.7:

The result of making a specific search in a client/server application

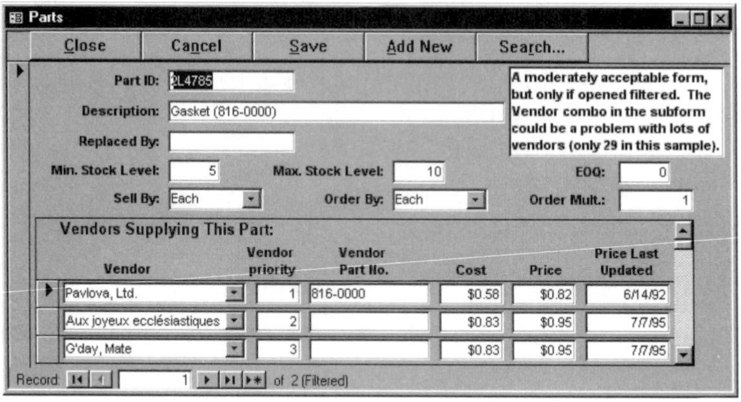

The code to create an efficient request from the data entered in an unbound "query by form" form is somewhat tedious to build but relatively straightforward. (Some people prefer a simpler model such as the one shown a little later in the chapter that filters by a single criteria that uniquely idenfities a record.) The code behind the Edit button on the form shown in Figure 3.6 is:

```
Private Sub cmdEdit_Click()
  Dim strSQL As String
```

```
' Check for a vendor ID
If Not IsNothing(Me!cboVendor) Then
strSQL = "([PartID] In (Select [PartID] From " & _
"tblVendorParts Where [VendorID] = " & _
Me!cboVendor & "))"
End If
' Check for a Part ID
If Not IsNull(Me!txtPartID) Then
If Len(strSQL) <> 0 Then
strSQL = strSQL & " AND ([PartID] = """ & _
Me!txtPartID & """)"
Else
strSQL = "([PartID] = """ & Me!txtPartID & """)"
End If
End If
' Check for a Description
If Not IsNull(Me!txtPartDesc) Then
' Slap an "*" on the end for LIKE
If Right(Me!txtPartDesc, 1) <> "*" Then
Me!txtPartDesc = Me!txtPartDesc & "*"
End IF
If Len(strSQL) <> 0 Then
strSQL = strSQL & _
" AND ([PartDescription] Like """ & _
Me!txtPartDesc & """)"
Else
strSQL = "([PartDescription] Like """ & _
Me!txtPartDesc & """)"
End If
End If
If IsNull(strSQL) Then
MsgBox "You must specify criteria to edit a part.", 16
Exit Sub
End If
' Open the form with a filter, hidden
DoCmd.OpenForm "frmParts", acNormal, , strSQL, _
acEdit, acHidden
' Check to see if we got any results
If Forms!frmParts.RecordsetClone.RecordCount = 0 Then
MsgBox "No parts match your criteria.", vbCritical, "Edit Error"
DoCmd.Close acForm, "frmParts"
Exit Sub
End If
```

```
DoCmd.Close acForm, Me.Name
Forms!frmParts.Visible = True
End Sub
```

If you check behind the Create New button on the dialog box in Figure 3.6, you'll find that it opens an entirely separate form that's designed only for data entry. Sometimes this is the best answer, especially when the functionality for adding versus editing is different. Many times, however, you will use the same form for different operations such as adding and editing, but with some of the built-in features of Access when you open it up to make sure that you limit the functionality to what's needed for that specific task.

More on Client/Server Architecture and Access

The discussion of using unbound forms rather than bound forms is a little more fundamental then we have presented here so far. We have looked at the idea of using unbound forms and then batching the updates as a way of helping performance for those operations, but we have not discussed getting data from the server in this manner. Although much of this is discussed in the next chapter, which also discusses more specifically the different ways that you access data, this section will discuss some of the architectural issues that apply to getting data in the client/server environment.

A typical "ideal" unbound form will contain a control (such as a combo box) with a local source. This source could be a customer list or a product list. There should be some easy way to refresh it regularly, perhaps with code such as the following (in this case in the OnClick event of a button on the form):

```
Private Sub cmdRefreshProducts_Click()
  'Delete all the old records from the local table
  CurrentDb().Execute "DELETE * FROM tblProducts_Local;"
  'Use a stored procedure to fill up the local table
  CurrentDb().Execute "INSERT INTO tblProducts_Local " & _
```

```
"SELECT * FROM qryPstProducts"
'Requery the combo box
Me!cboProducts.Requery
End Sub
```

This is basically the same idea as we discussed earlier in this chapter: keeping the data locally and providing a mechanism for updating it from the server. This model would be extended further in a completely unbound form; you would then write code that would request that one record from the server once the user selected one of the products from the combo box. The following code, for example, builds a string that uses a stored procedure spFindProduct and passes it to the server, filling up the form with the data when it is returned:

```
Sub cboProducts_AfterUpdate()
 Dim qdf as QueryDef
 Dim rst as Recordset
 Dim fld as Field
 Dim strProcedure as String

 'Build the call to the stored procedure
 strProcedure = "spFindProduct '" & Me![cboProducts] & "'"
 'Build the pass-through query
 Set qdf = CurrentDb().CreateQueryDef("")
 qdf.Connect = "ODBC;DSN=Catalog on Kermit;UID=;PWD=;" & _
 "DATABASE=Catalog"
 qdf.SQL = strProcedure
 'Create the recordset from the pass-through query
 Set rst = qdf.OpenRecordset(dbOpenSnapshot)
 'Put the data into the fields on the form
 If NOT rst.EOF Then
 For Each fld in rst.Fields
 Me("ctl" & fld.Name) = fld
 Next fld
 End If
End Sub
```

This particular procedure is made easier by the fact that all the control names and the field names are the same except for the "ctl" prefix, allowing the easy use the For Each...Next construct. In any case, this is a good example of how you could populate an unbound form. Such a stored procedure would be run completely on the server, as discussed in much more detail in Chapter 4. The only thing you would need to do from here is construct another function that would update the server data—if this is a form that allows changes. In any case, the twofold goal here is clear: to minimize the traffic on the network, and to give both the client (Access) and the server (SQL Server) specific tasks to perform based on their relative strengths.

The use of stored procedures and pass-through queries relates the discussion in Chapter 2 with that in Chapter 4 in an important way: the best way to upsize is to make sure to take advantage of the abilites of the server. By making practical use of the native abilities of SQL Server (such as stored procedures, triggers, views, defaults, rules, and other features), you can design your applications to take the best advantage of both environments, regardless of whether they are connected over a network, via a phone line, down the street, or halfway across the country.

Summary

You learned in Chapter 2 that designing tables correctly is critical to supporting the tasks in your application. That chapter also discussed many of the important features of SQL Server and how to handle its administration and maintenance features. In this chapter, you've learned some of the key design considerations for setting up your application forms to execute in a client/server environment. In Chapter 4, you'll extend what was presented in this chapter and learn how to create more efficient queries, so as to optimally use the back end and front end.

CHAPTER

FOUR

Building Efficient Queries for Client/Server

- Deciding where to store the data

- Using passthrough queries

- Optimizing queries for the Jet Engine

- Handling SQL Server errors from Access 95

- Mapping datatypes from SQL Server to Access

In Chapter 3, we focused on application design. Once you have the right design, however, you need to focus on how to use queries to get data into your application. Although some of these issues came up during the design stage in Chapter 3 (for example, avoiding combo boxes with a remote table as a ControlSource), many of them will be brand new, and the question is very important. It's crucial to remember that if you design your client/server queries incorrectly, the application's performance will be far worse than anything you could imagine in a desktop-only file/server application. This chapter will focus on some of the issues you will need to keep in mind when designing the queries your application will use.

Where is the Data Kept?

The first and most important point has already been dealt with in the design stage: you need to decide where to put what data. Some data will need to be stored in SQL Server, while other information will be stored in local Access tables. As a rule, it is easier and faster to access local data, so it's often worth keeping data that does not change often locally. For example, in an order-entry application, the price list is kept locally and periodically updated from the server.

Other, more changeable, data will obviously need to be kept on the server, and here is where things can get tricky. It can be hard to decide exactly how best to get the data from the server to the client. There are many ways to access the data, including:

- Keeping remote data in Access tables locally and refreshing it periodically, where you can open it directly without a performance hit
- Linking to SQL Server tables and treating them like Access tables once the link is made
- Directly accessing the server data programatically
- Using passthrough queries

We'll look at each of these options in turn throughout the rest of the chapter. In addition to the direct access techniques discussed here, you can use the programmatic interface to server datasources (the ODBC API) directly, as discussed further in Chapter 5.

Keeping Remote Data on the Client

If you are accustomed to using Access by itself, it's easiest to envision keeping data on the client and at regular intervals simply copying the contents of a table from the server to the client. The interval at which you update the data depends on how often it changes—this might be done at the beginning of each day, once a month, or perhaps only when the data changes. For data that stays relatively constant and for which it is not critical to keep track of changes at the moment they happen, this option can help performance tremendously. However, in most applications that require client/server this option is only practical for a few kinds of tables.

In many cases, the easiest way to update local data is to create a simple delete query to clear out the old data and an append query to copy the data from the SQL Server table to the local table (this method keeps the structure, relationships, indexes, and properties on the local table intact). The client can access SQL Server data either by linking directly to the table on the server or by using a passthrough query.

For example, if you have a server table called Products and a local copy of it called Products_Local, you would generally first run a delete query like this one to delete all the data from Products_Local:

```
DELETE Products_Local.* From Products_Local
```

and then use an append query as shown here to add all the data from the server table to the local table:

```
INSERT INTO Products_Local.*
SELECT Products.* FROM Products;
```

This coding assumes that you have previously created a linked table in Access. You can enhance this method in some additional ways: you can, for example, also make the query that gets the data from the server a passthrough query. Another enhancement would be to not pull down all the data; by adding a WHERE clause that filters the data so that only certain products end up in the local table, you can reduce the performance hit that occurs when bringing large amounts of data to the client.

Linking Directly to SQL Server Tables

You also have the option of linking (attaching) client tables directly to SQL Server tables. If you are accustomed to using Access by itself, you will find this option very attractive. By letting the Jet Engine transparently handle all communication with the SQL Server tables, you can (in theory) treat every table as if it were a local table. Access will then store information on the remote table so that it does not need to retrieve it each time, such as field attributes and the existence of indexes.

Making the Link

Linking to a SQL Server table is relatively straightforward. From the menu, choose File ➤ Get External ➤ Link Tables. In the Files of Type combo box in the Windows Open File dialog box, choose ODBC Database. The SQL Data Sources dialog box, shown in Figure 4.1, will appear.

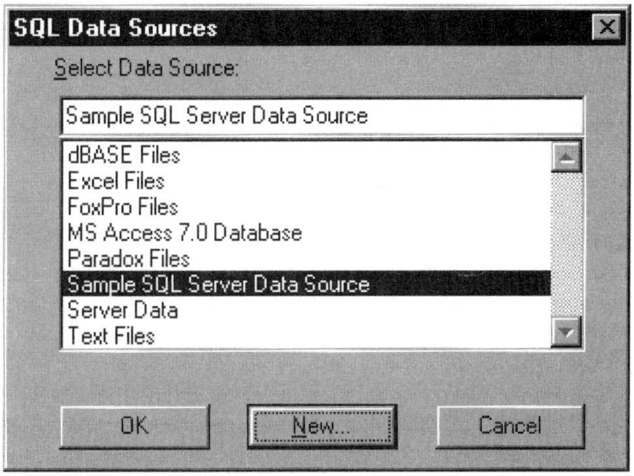

FIGURE 4.1:

The SQL Data Sources
selection dialog box

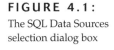

You can then choose the data source you wish (or create a new one if you need to) and click OK.

You can also create the linked TableDef from code by specifying the ODBC Connect string for the TableDef. The following code will create a linked table in the Access database container from the Customers server table.

```
Function ConnectCustomers() as Boolean
On Error Goto ConnectCustomer_Err
 Dim db as Database
 Dim tdf as Tabledef

 Set db = CurrentDb()
 Set tdf = db.CreateTableDef(Customers)
 tdf.Connect = "ODBC;DATABASE=Orders;UID=mk;PWD=;DSN=Order"
 db.Tabledefs.Append tdf
 ConnectCustomers = True

ConnectCustomers_Exit:
 Exit Function
```

```
ConnectCustomers_Err:
 MsgBox Err.Number & Err.Descripton, vbCritical, "Error!"
 ConnectCustomers = False
 Resume ConnectCustomers_Exit

Exit Function
```

Using SQL Server Views

You can also link to SQL Server views as if they were tables without indexes. The only restriction is that you must create an index specification if you want the view to be updateable, as Access needs to have a field or fields that uniquely identifies each record (in a normal table this is the primary key, but in a view Access cannot directly decide which field or fields to use). For example, you might have a SQL view called ImportedProductsView that returns a subset of the Products table on the server. You can then link to this view from the client and name the link ImportedProducts. When you link to a view in SQL Server, Access detects no primary key and prompts you to identify the key fields, as discussed in Chapter 2. If you fail to identify the primary key when you link the view, you can still add one later with a SQL command. For example, as ProductID (the primary key for the Products table) is a unique value, you can use the statement

```
CREATE UNIQUE INDEX FauxKey ON ImportedProducts (ProductID)
```

to define ProductID as the unique field that it can use to allow you to update records.

This statement will not create an index on the server, but will let Access/Jet know that ProductID is a unique key that it can use to update this view as needed.

Linked Tables Are Not Always the Answer

In theory, linked tables are the ideal solution for accessing data from the server, both in terms of making use of existing Access knowledge and in combining local and remote data. In practice, however, this method contains many pitfalls to avoid. Although you may be tempted to simply use this method for all your connections (and thus significantly shorten the learning curve for a client/server database), as we'll discuss a little later in this chapter there are many performance issues that make linking tables a less-than-perfect solution.

Directly Accessing the Server Data Programmatically

Many people who use Access take advantage of Data Access Objects (DAO), using the OpenDatabase method to open up their Access DATA.MDB directly. By supplying an ODBC connection string, you can do the same thing with data on SQL Server to create a dynamic connection in your client code any time you need it. Because you are creating the link dynamically, however, all of the information that Jet stores when you use linked tables (such as fields, indexes, the capabilities of the server, and the location of the table) must be retrieved each time, which can substantially affect performance.

On the other hand, there are times when it can be useful to make such a programmatic connection in code so that your application chooses when to make the connection to the server's data. You might particularly decide to do this in an information-processing application designed to connect dynamically to one of several different sources of data in the same format (last year's summary, a summary from three years ago, etc.). Ordinarily, this dynamic link would take place when you first opened up a form or report based on data from the server, but a procedure that makes a connection will cause Access to cache the connection information. The DoConnect() function below shows a typical way to do this:

```
Function DoConnect(strUser as String, strPwd as String) as
Boolean
On Error Goto DoConnect_Error
```

```
Dim wrk as Workspace
Dim db as Database
Dim strConnection as String

strConnect = "ODBC;DSN=ServerName;DATABASE=DBName;" & _
"UID=" & strUser & ";PWD=" & strPwd & ";"
Set wrk = DBEngine.Workspaces(0)
Set db = wrk.OpenDatabase("", False, False, strConnect)
db.Close
DoConnect = True

DoConnect_Exit:
 Exit Function

DoConnect_Error:
 DoConnect = False
 Resume DoConnect_Exit
End Function
```

When you use the Close method, this function will close the database but it will not disconnect you from the server, so when you go to use the connection again Access will already have saved the connection information and won't have to retrieve it again for another data source on the same server. This cached connection information is also used by passthrough queries on this data source. (We'll discuss passthrough queries in the next section.)

Using Passthrough Queries

One of the most powerful weapons in the client/server arsenal is the *passthrough query*, or essentially any arbitrary string passed directly to SQL Server with no processing or compiling done by the Jet Engine. This approach has many advantages:

- You don't have to worry about what parts of the query will be run on the server versus the client because all of it will be run on the server.

- You can take advantage of stored procedures, security commands, SQL Server administration, and other functions that are only supported on the server.

- You can log any information that the server returns (such as statistics, warnings, and error messages) that Jet might ignore or not make available.

However, all of this flexibiliy (in addition to the performance boost you get in skipping over the Jet query optimizer) does not come without a price. First, passthrough queries cannot be updated—they always return a snapshot. Second, as Jet does not compile the query the syntax must be correct, and you therefore must know the exact syntax that the server supports. You are also limited in that you cannot call Access-specific or user-defined functions in passthrough queries. (Although you would usually want to avoid this anyway, with passthrough queries you don't have the option.)

Creating a Passthrough Query

To create a passthrough query in the user interface, simply create a new query, and then choose Query ➤ SQL Specific ➤ Passthrough. The ODBCConnectStr property (seen in the query's property sheet in Figure 4.2) will change to "ODBC" (you can specify a full Connect string, but the user will simply be prompted for any information you do not provide).

You can also choose whether this query will return records or not (for example, data definition queries and some stored procedures would not), and whether or not to log messages from the server. Figure 4.3 shows an example of a passthrough query in the SQL passthrough window.

Of course, you can also create passthrough queries in code by creating a QueryDef in DAO and setting the Connect property to an ODBC

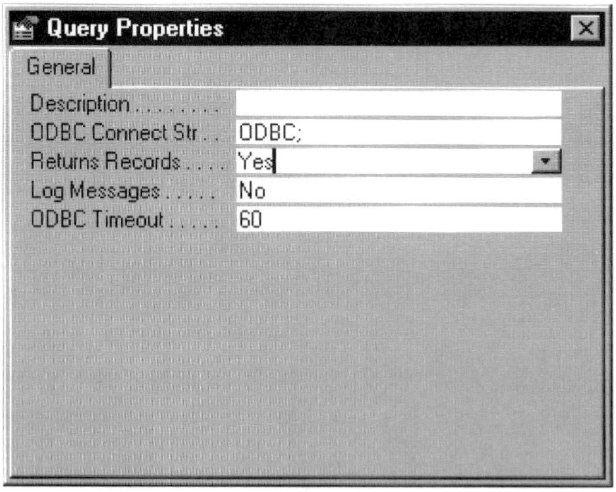

FIGURE 4.2:

The property sheet of a
passthrough query

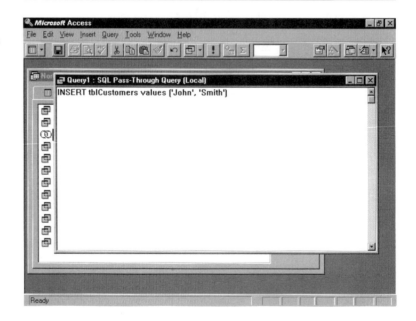

FIGURE 4.3:

The Access SQL passthrough
window

source. For example, the following function creates a passthrough query that adds a record to the customers table (tblCustomers):

```
Function NewCustomer(strFirst as String, strLast as String)
as Boolean
On Error Goto NewCustomer_Error

 Dim db as Database
 Dim qdf as Querydef

 Set db = CurrentDb()
 Set qdf = db.CreateQueryDef("")
 With qdf
 .Connect = _
     "ODBC;database=Orders;uid=SomeUser;pwd=;dsn=OrderEntry;"
 .ReturnsRecords = False
 .SQL = "INSERT tblCustomers values ('" & strFirst & _
 "', '" & strLast & "')"
     .Execute dbSQLPassThrough
 End With
 NewCustomer = True

NewCustomer_Exit:
 Exit Function

NewCustomer_Error:
 NewCustomer = False
 Resume NewCustomer_Exit
Exit Function
```

Using Correct Syntax in Passthrough Queries

In the move from Access-only to Access and SQL Server, the differences between Access SQL and Transact-SQL become much more important, especially when dealing with passthrough queries (in which Jet does not protect you from sending a query with the wrong syntax to the server). For example, the following Access/Jet query will return all of the customer records from tblCustomers that begin with the letters "Sm":

```
SELECT * FROM tblCustomers WHERE LastName Like 'Sm*'
```

This works because Jet uses the asterisk for a wildcard character. SQL Server, on the other hand, uses the percent (%) symbol for a wildcard. In a regular Select query this would not matter because Jet automatically maps these differences when the query is compiled. However, if you wanted to do the same thing with a passthrough query you would have to change the statement to

```
SELECT * FROM tblCustomers WHERE LastName Like 'Sm%'
```

as Jet does not compile a passthrough query. As the name implies, Jet *passes* whatever SQL you code in the query straight *through* to the server without modification.

Using Stored Procedures

A *stored procedure* is a compiled set of Transact-SQL statements in the SQL Server database that performs some function. It extends the capabilities of a SQL Server query by allowing you to use variables, expressions, and conditional flow logic that would not otherwise be available. Stored procedures are often used to handle maintenance, administrative, and other kinds of tasks on the server.

A simple example of a stored procedure is seen below:

```
CREATE PROCEDURE test_info @last_name varchar(30) = null as
 IF @last_name = null
 print "You must supply a last name!"
 ELSE
 SELECT test_name, test_score
 FROM tests, customers
 WHERE last_name LIKE @last_name
OUTPUT:
```

This procedure takes a last name as a parameter and then returns a list of the tests this person took and the scores for each test. To run it, execute a passthrough query such as this:

```
test_info "Smith"
```

If you have the ReturnRecords property set to True (either through the user interface or in code), the recordset created will contain the list of tests.

As another example, you may have a stored procedure called archive_records that archives data from a previous month. Assuming that archive_records has no parameters (as it performs a set task and already knows to run from the last month), to run it you would just need a passthrough query that simply sends the name of the function, as in

```
archive_records
```

If you save this procedure as a query named qsptArchive in your Access client database, then you can execute qsptArchive and it will run the procedure. If the stored procedure returns rows, you can create a recordset with it just as you would with any other passthrough query. You can even send parameters (such as data to enter into a specific table or information on what records to archive) to the procedure.

For the most part, your stored procedures will be much more complex than this; sometimes the procedures themselves will be enormous. As mentioned, you can create them from Access via passthrough queries (using CREATE PROCEDURE) and delete them if needed by using DROP PROCEDURE.

Which Method Is Best?

Is it better to use linked tables or passthrough queries? Although the answer to this question seems vital, unfortunately it is always, "It depends." In most cases you will use a combination of these techniques, using mainly linked tables and passthrough queries to get most work done. This gives you the ability to do much of the server administration via the client, as well as the ability to control access to your tables (you can design your application so that it can only be accessed through stored procedures called from passthrough queries). The key is to carefully weigh each method and sometimes do benchmarking of various methods to determine which one is best. (Turn to the Performance Issues section of Chapter 5 for more information on running performance tests.)

Optimizing Queries for the Jet Engine

Any time you create a query that uses a SQL Server table, you will want to look out for many things that can drastically affect performance and functionality, such as:

- Deciding when to use heterogenous (versus homogenous) joins
- Making use of user-defined or Access-specific functions
- Determining whether the recordset is updateable
- Using transactions properly
- Using the Find methods
- Caching remote data

We discuss each of these items in the following sections.

Heterogeneous (versus Homogeneous) Joins

The Jet Engine's ability to mix different data sources, connecting different database formats in heterogeneous joins (for example, joining an

Access table with one linked from SQL Server) is a powerful feature. However, a query using a heterogeneous join will always run slower (sometimes *much* slower) than the same query performing a join across homogeneous tables. For the most part, a heterogeneous join forces at least part (and sometimes all) of a query to be run on the client rather than on the server.

Performing a join on the client may mean that all of the rows from each of the tables must be retrieved over the network to correctly solve the query. If you do need to create a query that joins local data with remote, it is important to plan the query to make sure that the majority of processing is done on the server. This can be very difficult, as it's hard to predict how the Access Jet Engine may attempt to optimize your query.

Although we have recommended in earlier chapters that you consider moving certain static or infrequently-updated tables to the client to improve performance, this may not be a good idea if many of your uses of the local table involve a heterogeneous join with a table on the server. You may want to keep a local copy to enhance the performance of single-row lookups, but use the remote copy when you need to run a query that involves a join.

Using User-Defined and Access-Specific Functions

Another of the strengths of the Jet Engine that can at times be a weakness is its support for Access' built-in and user-defined functions. In any Jet-compiled query you run, you can call any function in the current database or one of the currently loaded library databases. You can also call any of the rich set of functions that are built into Access.

The problem is that SQL Server does not support most of these built-in functions (or any of the user-defined ones), so that including them in the query forces part of it (and sometimes all of it) to run locally. If possible, you should remove built-in and user-defined functions from the query entirely.

Sometimes you must include a user-defined function in the query; in those cases Jet will try to send as much of the query to the server as it can. For example, if you have a user-defined Access VBA function called IsApproved(), that determines whether the person is approved for a certain benefit, and you use it in the following query:

```
SELECT FirstName, LastName, DOB, HireDate
FROM Employees
WHERE LastName Like "A*"
 AND DOB > #1/1/70#
 AND HireDate < #1/1/90#
 AND IsApproved(EmployeeID)
```

then Access cannot send the IsApproved() function to the server because it is a user-defined VBA function in the database. It can only be run on the client, by Access. It can, however, send a query such as:

```
SELECT FirstName, LastName, DOB, HireDate
FROM Employees
WHERE LastName Like "A*"
 AND DOB > #1/1/70#
 AND HireDate < #1/1/90#
```

and then run the IsApproved (EmployeeID) locally on all the records that this query returns. You can take advantage of this by looking at the functions themselves and seeing if you can filter the data with additional WHERE clause restrictions, minimizing the number of rows that need to be returned to solve the query.

There are other times (such as with the IsApproved function example discussed above) that you can duplicate the functionality of a user-defined function that *will* run on the server by creating the same logic in a stored procedure. When this is possible, it is usually the best solution in terms of performance, because the function will run much more quickly on the server. This type of optimization would mainly depend on what you need from the function (as Access VBA supports a much larger functionality than SQL Server's stored procedures do).

In a related way, Jet SQL clauses such as TOP N and TOP N PERCENT are not supported by SQL Server (or, for that matter, by any other server that supports SQL), so it is best to avoid using them as much as you can. As you might guess, SQL Server also does not support other Access extensions to the SQL language such as the DISTINCTROW keyword and Crosstab queries.

Is the Recordset Updateable?

Whenever you link to a remote table, Jet attempts to create a *dynaset*-type recordset (a recordset that lets you update the data in it, as opposed to a *snapshot* recordset that is read-only). In order to do this, it needs (as was mentioned earlier in this chapter in the discussion of SQL views) a unique index so that it has a way of identifying each record. Jet looks for indexes using the SQLStatistics ODBC operator, which will look for clustered indexes, hashed indexes, and other indexes, searching each group alphabetically until it finds a unique one. If it cannot find one (as would be the case with a SQL View for which you do not create an index specification, or a table that simply has no unique indexes), then a snapshot is opened and data cannot be updated.

Using Transactions Properly

You should use transactions any time you need several operations to be processed as a single unit. The classic example is a banking application, in which, when transferring funds between accounts, the withdrawal from one account must succeed if and only if the deposit to the other account for the same amount is successful. Database systems use something called a *transaction* to define a group of updates that must either all succeed or none succeed. This type of model, the *transaction model*, is vital in many different types of applications, so strong support for transactions is often one of the most important features that a user

Index Specifications versus Indexes

The proper use of indexes can be crucial to the performance of your application. As you can see from the explanation of how Jet tries to create a dynaset, there is not a strict mapping of index types between Access and SQL Server, and a little bit of "translation" must be done. One option you have, however, is to create an index specification, as you do for views. Essentially, you are putting an index on the linked TableDef rather than on the server.

However, you must make sure that you are indexing the field you want to use. When linking to views, you must use Jet (rather than a passthrough query) to make use of the index specification, because no index has been created on the server. It is easy to miss that point and, thinking that the field has been indexed, wonder why a search on a given field takes such a long time!

is looking for, whether in Access or SQL Server. As Jet needs to store the data in memory in order to be able to roll back a transaction, the use of transactions can also help performance as well.

As a rule, each SQL statement that Jet sends to the server has an implicit transaction wrapped around it. The only time this is not true is when you either do an explicit transaction yourself (in DAO) or when you use an action query (such as UPDATE or APPEND). In this case the entire statement that you give to Jet is put into a single transaction, as Jet may split the statement up into several different statements for the server.

Although it is technically possible to use a passthrough query to utilize SQL Server's native transaction commands (such as BEGIN TRAN), you should avoid this and instead employ Jet's BeginTrans, CommitTrans, and Rollback methods. The reason for this is that Jet tries to keep track internally of the current transactions and it can't do so if you start or end transactions that it does not know about.

There are a couple of limitations on the use of transactions with SQL Server:

- SQL Server does not support nested transactions, so Jet will ignore any nested transactions in your code.
- Many types of passthrough queries are not allowed to appear within a transaction, including data definition, permission, or backup-related SQL statements.

Using the Find Methods

One of the biggest headaches in the switch from an Access-only to an Access/SQL Server application is the conversion of the "Seek" method of table-type recordsets. As the tables can only be opened as dynasets or snapshots, Seek is unavailable and the only easy replacements (the Find methods) are significantly slower. In an Access-only solution, you can get around this by using OpenDatabase to open up the DATA.MDB directly, so that Seek works as it does in a local table. This will not, however, work with a SQL Server database, because ODBC sources do not support the Seek method.

The performance of the Find methods (such as FindFirst and FindNext) are usually only acceptable under the following circumstances:

- **For Dynasets:** When the search field is a single field that is indexed on the server, you are either using a Like expression or testing for equality, and the recordset is reasonably small (fewer than 800 records).
- **For Snapshots:** When the number of records in the snapshot is small (fewer than 500 records) and there is sufficient room in memory for data buffering.

If these conditions don't apply, you should usually avoid Find and instead consider other search methods (such as stored procedures that take parameters or passthrough queries that return a single row) to execute on the server. Otherwise, you might find yourself doing table scans of large tables to find a single record.

Caching Remote Data

Jet provides several properties or recordset objects (CacheSize and CacheStart) and a method (FillCache) which you can use to significantly improve the speed of dynaset-type recordset operations. To use them, set the CacheSize (a long integer between 5 and 1200) to specify the number of rows you wish to cache, and then set the CacheStart (a string) to the bookmark value of the first record to cache. All you need to do then is apply the FillCache method and the cache will be filled with data from the server. To recover cache space, set the value of CacheSize to zero.

When using the recordset cache, keep the value of CacheStart synchronized as you move through the recordset so that it tries to fill the cache with the data you will need rather than the data you just saw.

The Dynamic Nature of Jet Query Compilation

When optimizing your application so that the Jet Engine will perform a query with properly distributed processing, keep in mind that the Jet Engine compiles all queries (except passthrough queries) in the following manner:

- **For SQL Statements:** The query is compiled each time it is executed. Jet keeps none of the compiled query information after it is executed.

- **For Saved Queries:** The query is compiled the first time it is run. It must be re-compiled any time you save the query and also after you compact the database.

Because Jet makes the query plan according to the statistics it has on the tables that make up the query, it is possible that an optimized query that it runs might (as more data is added to the database) be compiled according to a different plan if the statistics on the database change. Database statistics from ODBC sources are also not usually as accurate as the ones that Jet keeps for its own local .MDB databases. This is, in fact, another very strong argument for using passthrough queries, which will never run into the problem of how Jet saves a compiled plan (as Jet doesn't compile or save them!). Although the server must compile a passthrough query each time you execute it, the overhead is tiny compared to the potential gain from always running with the latest and best execution plan.

Sometimes Less Is More

When using Access alone, dynasets are usually faster because only the key values need to be sent over the wire (as opposed to snapshots, where all the data would have to be sent). When you are using SQL Server, however, there are times that a snapshot will give you better performance. The reason for this is that when a recordset is updateable, there is a lot of information that Jet has to keep track of in order to handle the updating, and that extra information can lead to a performance decline across a network. It is usually worth setting the Allow-Updating property to No Tables (causing Jet to create a snapshot for the form's RecordSource) if the following are true:

- You don't need the recordset to be updateable
- The recordset contains fewer than 500 records

Otherwise, it is often better to use a dynaset than a snapshot, especially if the table contains OLE object or memo fields (which are only retrieved if they need to be displayed on screen). The best rule is to try both methods out.

A form that has multiple subforms can also hurt performance. Although the interface is convenient, a separate query must be sent to the server for each RecordSource. This can significantly slow down queries (similar to the way using combo boxes with a remote data source can, as discussed in Chapter 3). Because a multi-table query will usually be updateable anyway, it is often much faster to combine the form and subform queries into a single query.

Adding Timestamps

One thing you can do to speed up the update and deletion of records is to add a timestamp field to the remote table. This field will change any time the record is updated, and is entirely maintained by the server. When a timestamp exists, the Jet Engine will check to see if the timestamp has changed, so as to determine whether it needs to cancel the update or deletion.

If you do not include a timestamp field, then Access must check each of the old fields to see if there have been any changes made. In tables with many fields this can cause extremely poor performance, especially in batch updates or deletions.

Handling SQL Server Errors in Access 95

Any time your code or some other problem causes an error on the server, Access 95 will detect both its own local error (one of the ODBC errors that range from 3146 to 3299) and an error from the server. You can find all errors that occur stored in the Errors collection of the

DBEngine object. To scroll through them and display each one, you can use a procedure such as the one shown here:

```
Public Function EnumerateErrors()
 Dim errValue As Error
 Dim lngCounter As Long

 Select Case Err
  Case 3146 To 3299
   lngCounter = 0
   For Each errValue In DBEngine.Errors
    MsgBox "Server Error " & _
    lngCounter & " Number: " & errValue.Number & _
    " Description: " & errValue.Description
    lngCounter = lngCounter + 1
   Next errValue
  Case Else
   'Not an ODBC error. Add your own code in here
   'for error trapping or just do nothing and let
   'the calling function handle the error.
  End Select
End Function
```

You can call such a function globally from the various error handlers in your code so that any time an error occurs on the server all of the messages that came back can be displayed. In addition, you can also add other global error handling code to the Case Else section of this procedure to make it a more generic error handler.

Mapping Datatypes from SQL Server to Access

The datatypes that are used by SQL Server and Access are not identical. Therefore, any time you use SQL Server data in an Access client, the Jet engine must "translate" between the datatypes. Unless a linked table is used, this information must be obtained every time a query is run. In that case, this information is cached, but you need to relink the table if you change any of the datatypes or sizes (unless you want Jet to assume the old ones are still valid).

The conversion types between SQL Server and Jet are listed in Table 4.1, and the conversions from Jet to SQL Server are in Table 4.2. When more than one possible type is listed on the "convert to" side, they are listed in the order that is used to try to find an appropriate type.

As you can see, the mappings are not identical, which can lead to some problems if you don't choose your data types with care. Floating-point numbers present a common area to run into problems, because SQL Server and Jet store these values somewhat differently. If you use a floating-point value in a table's Primary Key, then it is possible that Jet will think a record has been deleted when it looks for a specific record because the index values may not match exactly. In these cases it is

TABLE 4.1: Conversion from SQL Server datatypes to Jet datatypes

SQL Server	Access/Jet SQL
bit	Yes/No
tinyint smallint	Number (Integer)
int	Number (Long Integer)
real	Number (Single)
float	Number (Double)
datetime smalldatetime timestamp	DateTime Text
char(n) varchar(n)	Text if less than or equal to 255 characters, Memo if it is more than 255 characters
binary varbinary	Binary if size is less than or equal to 255, OLE object if it is more than 255
decimal numeric	Integer, Long Integer, or Double (depending on lprecision and wScale values)
money smallmoney	Currency

TABLE 4.2: Conversion from Jet datatypes to SQL Server datatypes

Access/Jet SQL	SQL Server
Yes/No	bit Byte smallint
Number (Integer)	smallint int
Number (Long Integer)	int
Currency	decimal (with wScale of 4 and lPrecision of 19)
Number (Single)	real float
Number (Double)	float
DateTime	timestamp
Text (Field Size)	varchar(n)
Binary (Field Size)	varbinary(n)
OLE Object	varbinary(n)

important to specify some other unique index that Access can use (one that will remain constant).

To determine the appropriate datatype, Jet calls the SQLColumns ODBC function (see Chapter 5 for more information on the ODBC API), which returns three values that Jet uses to determine what datatype it should use:

- **fSQLType:** the ODBC SQL type
- **lPrecision:** the maximum size of the field
- **wSize:** the number of digits to the right of the decimal place

Because you do not always have a choice as to the structure of the SQL Server table (you may be linking to someone else's data, for example), it is important to keep the procedure that Jet uses to determine datatype in mind to make sure you do not cause any data anomalies (such as truncation) during the conversion.

Summary

The change from making use of data through queries in Access alone to client/server requires you to rethink your data access strategies. Although most of the querying methods that you used for Access will still work, many of the commonly used methods for retrieving and changing data can lead to severe performance problems in the client/server environment. This chapter looked at many of the issues involved and optimizations that you can use to make these operations faster for your application.

Although passthrough queries do allow you to bypass Jet for enhanced performance and access to "native" features on the server, you give up the benefits data mapping and "transparent" data management you find in native Access queries. Also, using passthrough queries doesn't give you access to some of the rich features of the ODBC API, from which Access DAO and SQL try to shield you. Chapter 5 will discuss how to use the ODBC API directly to work with the server, as well as continuing the discussion on optimizing your application, comparing use of the ODBC API with other methods.

CHAPTER

FIVE

Using the ODBC API

- Understanding ODBC

- Using ODBC

- A set of ODBC wrapper functions

- Remote Data Objects

- Testing performance

In the first four chapters, we've shown you how to manipulate data stored on SQL Server using the Jet Engine built into Access. Now we're going to drill down to another level and look at using the Open Database Connectivity Applications Programming Interface—usually abbreviated simply as ODBC API—to retrieve and update data. By writing code in Access that is executed directly by the ODBC API, you can skip the Jet Engine entirely, and in some circumstances gain increased processing speed. As we'll demonstrate, though, this speed comes at the cost of a substantial increase in programming complexity.

What is ODBC?

Open Database Connectivity (ODBC) is a common language definition and a set of protocols that allow a client such as Access to interactively determine a server's capabilities and adapt the processing to work within the functions supported by the server. ODBC sits between the application and the data and handles the communications between the two. In normal Access-to-SQL-Server querying using linked tables, you never see this ODBC layer, but it's still there. The Jet Engine transparently converts your queries to the ODBC format and uses this standard for communicating with SQL Server. All of the examples in the previous chapters have used ODBC in this transparent manner, with the Jet Engine managing all the details.

In order to take advantage of ODBC, you need a network that allows communications between the client machine and the machine that holds the database, and the appropriate ODBC Driver Manager and drivers that can work with both the application database and the back-end database. If you can connect to SQL Server at all from Access, you've already got this part worked out. In theory, at least, you should be able to switch from one server to another, even another server of a different type, without having to rewrite any part of your client application. In practice, though, differing levels of ODBC conformance can make this difficult.

ODBC defines a core standard SQL grammar and set of function calls, with two levels of optional extensions. ODBC also includes mechanisms for calling server-specific features that are not included in the ODBC standard. In general, this allows application developers to decide on the level of functionality they want to use when accessing a database server. The developer can choose between using the least common denominator of functionality provided by ODBC or exploiting the full capabilities of the server.

With core ODBC functionality, the developer can establish a connection with a data source through a standard logon interface, execute SQL statements, and retrieve data and error messages should something go wrong on the other end.

With extended ODBC functionality, the developer can use additional parts of the standard SQL grammar and ODBC-defined functions to exploit advanced capabilities of a particular database management system (DBMS). ODBC extensions also include such additional features as asynchronous query execution, unusual datatypes (date, time, timestamp, and binary), scrollable cursors, SQL grammar for scalar functions, outer joins, and procedures, as well as the use of server-specific SQL grammar.

Fortunately, the latest ODBC drivers for SQL Server support most of the optional extensions to the ODBC core functionality. In this chapter, we'll take advantage of many of these extensions. If you are trying to work with a server other than SQL Server, keep in mind that some of the code presented here may simply not work, depending on your ODBC driver. If you're unsure of the capabilities of your particular ODBC driver, you can use the SQLGetInfo, SQLGetFunctions, and SQLGetStmtOption API calls to retrieve this information. Note, though, that SQLGetInfo is a Level 1 Extension to the ODBC API. Access itself is incapable of using ODBC drivers that do not conform to ODBC Level 1; if you have such a driver, you'll have to upgrade before proceeding. In other words, if a call to SQLGetInfo fails to return any information, then you cannot use this driver from Access.

NOTE The sample database CH5ODBC.MDB includes a function, ODBCGetInfo, which demonstrates the use of the SQLGetInfo API call to retrieve information on a particular ODBC driver, including the ODBC level that it supports.

One of the design goals of ODBC is to hide the complexity of the underlying communications necessary for an application to retrieve data from a data source such as SQL Server. ODBC uses an abstraction that maps the data source name to a specific server so that the mechanics of drivers, server addresses, networks, and gateways are hidden from the user. Of course, as a developer, you need to know all the pieces of plumbing that go into making a connection so that your users can be protected from them. Table 5.1 lists the major ODBC components.

When writing ODBC API code, you'll be communicating directly with either the Driver Manager or the driver. In general, the Driver Manager handles connecting and disconnecting chores, while the driver is concerned with the actual data retrieved from the server. You don't need to be concerned with directing your commands to the correct component. The ODBC libraries will automatically choose the driver or the Driver Manager as necessary.

TABLE 5.1: Major ODBC Components

Component	Description
Application	Uses ODBC to connect to a data source, send and receive data, and disconnect. The application might use the SQLConnect function to pass the connection handle, a data source name, user ID, and password to the Driver Manager.
Driver Manager	Communicates between the application and the data source by providing information to the application and loading drivers dynamically as they are needed. ODBC allows an application to talk to many types of data sources through DBMS-specific drivers by using the Driver Manager to handle the communications. The Driver Manager and the drivers are implemented as dynamic-link libraries (DLLs), which means that you can use ODBC either through the UI as attached tables (in Access) or through code. The Driver Manager loads the correct library and then connects to the server through the driver, which actually processes the SQLConnect function call.
Driver	Processes ODBC function calls, manages all exchanges between an application and a specific DBMS, and translates SQL syntax for the target data source. Drivers are generally supplied by the vendor, and it is advisable to obtain the latest one since there are usually frequent updates and bug fixes. The driver handles all error codes by mapping them to standard ODBC error codes. The driver also handles catalog functions, which provide information about the objects in the database, such as tables, columns, indexes, etc.
Server	Stores and retrieves data in response to requests from the ODBC driver. The server returns data or error codes which are ultimately passed back to the original calling application.

ODBC Grammar

The designers of ODBC faced a problem when deciding what dialect of SQL to support. With hundreds of different SQL products on the market, there are hundreds of variations of SQL. Rather than pick any one of these as being the one to support, the ODBC designers chose to come up with yet another SQL grammar, "ODBC SQL," and a component design to allow products to translate their own SQL to and from this universal SQL dialect.

The ODBC standard defines three levels of grammar: minimum, core, and extended. In a perfect world, we'd be able to say that any ODBC driver supported one of these three variants of ODBC SQL. Unfortunately, drivers tend to pick and choose, with most supporting some but not all of the core and extended grammars. In addition, ODBC includes a mechanism for a driver to define its own extensions beyond extended ODBC SQL.

To determine exactly which SQL statements you can send to any particular database via ODBC, you have to check two sources. The formal definitions of the minimum, core, and extended ODBC grammars are contained in Appendix D of the ODBC Software Development Kit (available on the Microsoft Developer's Network CD-ROM). The help file that ships with your particular driver will tell you which of these three levels of ODBC it supports, together with notes about added or deleted functions.

The Microsoft SQL Server ODBC driver that ships with SQL 6.0 supports the entire core and extended ODBC grammar with just a few exceptions, most of which only apply when you are connecting to a 4.21 SQL Server. Table 5.2 lists the major SQL statements that are supported via ODBC to SQL Server. Fortunately, the ODBC syntax for SQL statements is almost always identical to the syntax used by SQL Server itself.

TIP

If you're unsure of the correct ODBC SQL for a particular query, there's an easy way to generate it. Enable the SQLTraceMode Registry setting (discussed later in this chapter) and run the query in Access on a linked SQL Server table. The ODBC version of the SQL will be saved in your trace file.

TABLE 5.2: Statements Supported in Extended ODBC Grammar

SQL Statement
ALTER TABLE
CREATE INDEX
CREATE TABLE
CREATE VIEW
DELETE
DROP INDEX
DROP TABLE
DROP VIEW
GRANT
INSERT INTO
REVOKE
SELECT
UPDATE

ODBC Access versus Jet

To understand ODBC connectivity, it helps to visualize the components used in the various different ways that you can retrieve data from your server. Figure 5.1 shows some of the ways that you can retrieve data from SQL Server using Access.

Queries against linked tables use ODBC implicitly to retrieve data. When you write an Access query to retrieve data from a linked ODBC table, the Jet Engine translates your Access SQL into a universal ODBC SQL dialect and sends this to the Driver Manager. The ODBC Manager then handles the connection chores and passes the universal SQL to the appropriate driver. The ODBC driver then translates this universal SQL to the correct SQL dialect understood by the server so

FIGURE 5.1:

Different methods for
retrieving SQL Server data

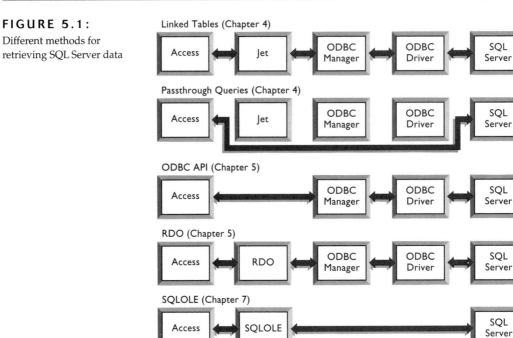

that the server can process it. Results follow the same pathway in reverse. This cuts down on network traffic compared to using linked
Access tables, since you only have the outgoing SQL statement and
the incoming final results set to contend with. We've reviewed this
sort of attached table ODBC in previous chapters.

Chapter 4 also covered SQL pass-through queries. In these queries,
you can think of the SQL statement as going directly from your Access
application to the server for execution. It's passed along by all of the
normal ODBC components, but none of them actually manipulate
the SQL in any way.

Writing to the ODBC API, as we'll do in this chapter, allows you to skip
the Jet Engine part of the equation entirely. Instead, we'll send our connection information and queries directly to the Driver Manager, which

will handle the rest of the details. As you might guess from looking at Figure 5.1, though, your code will have to supply all the functionality normally taken care of by the Jet Engine.

Finally, we'll also look at Remote Data Objects (RDO) in this chapter. RDO, introduced with the Enterprise Edition of Visual Basic 4.0, treats ODBC queries as OLE objects. Querying becomes a matter of specifying properties of these objects and using their methods to return data. In turn, RDO converts everything into ODBC API calls, just as Jet does. RDO is a faster solution than Jet in many situations. However, RDO also requires you to write more code than Jet does to accomplish the same tasks.

Mechanics of Query Execution

Let's consider the differences in Jet query execution using each of the ODBC methods. Jet can handle a query for an ODBC connection as a regular Jet-optimized Access query, an SQL pass-through (SPT) query, or as a query performed by RDO. With a regular Access query, Jet interprets and optimizes the query locally in order to determine the optimal path of execution. It may choose to send the entire query to the server as a unit, or break it up into several queries for greater efficiency. Jet may even choose to do only part of the query on the server and finish creating the result set by executing further operations on the client.

For SPT queries, Jet becomes more of a bystander. Jet doesn't check the syntax of an SPT query at all. Instead, it merely looks at the query's Connect property to properly address the message sent to the Driver Manager. The overhead to doing this is very small compared to regular query optimization.

With RDO, Jet is bypassed entirely. There is no Jet overhead at all since Access considers it to be merely another OLE object with its own methods and properties. RDO queries are executed by setting an RDO property to the appropriate back-end SQL and using methods to retrieve rows of the results. Any overhead involved is not through Jet, but through the OLE libraries themselves.

SQL passthrough and RDO queries generally work best when the server has to do a large amount of processing, or when Access is incapable of expressing the query in native SQL. Data Definition Language (DDL) operations, administrative actions on the server, and execution of non-Access SQL syntax are well-suited to these methods since there is no Access equivalent.

For the absolute least amount of overhead, you'll need to use the ODBC API directly. This bypasses all but the essential connectivity and translation layers contained in the driver and the Driver Manager. As we'll discuss in this chapter, though, this requires extensive programming on your part. You'll need to carefully focus your development efforts so that you only spend time optimizing those parts of your application that will really repay the effort. In many cases you'll find that executing queries directly on linked tables will provide more than adequate performance.

When and Why to Use ODBC Instead of Jet

Given all these different methods of retrieving data from the server, how do you choose the most appropriate one for your particular application? In general, there's a tradeoff between performance and maintenance here: Although using the ODBC API is often faster than Jet, it also requires doing a lot more programming to execute even a simple query. Our own preference is to start most applications by assuming that the Jet Engine with attached tables will be fast enough, and then migrate to passthrough queries, the ODBC API, or Remote Data Objects in areas where this assumption is untrue.

To find these areas, you'll need to actually time the operation of queries in your application. The section "Timing Queries" later in this chapter discusses how to do this. When you've identified a particular query that seems to be taking too long to execute, you can use Table 5.3 as a guide to revising it.

TABLE 5.3: Query Optimization Strategies

If...	Try This
...the query is slow because Jet is picking a less-than-optimal execution strategy	convert to SQL pass-through query using more efficient server-side SQL.
...the query is slow because of Jet overhead, and you have Visual Basic 4.0, Enterprise Edition, installed	convert the query to use Remote Data Objects.
...the query is slow because of Jet overhead, and you have no additional software	convert the query to use the ODBC API directly.

Performance Issues

There's no doubt that ODBC is faster than Jet at retrieving information. After all, that's all ODBC does. If you use Jet to fetch information from attached tables, you're still using ODBC as well, plus you have whatever overhead the Jet Engine adds to the picture.

However, don't conclude from this that you'll always need to switch to the ODBC API for acceptable performance. ODBC has the greatest advantage when you can place most of the processing on the server. For example, if you're looking for a few records in a large table, you'll find ODBC has a substantial speed advantage. If you're preparing a report on all your customers, with several different sort orders, you might discover that the data caching of the Jet Engine is more efficient than anything you can easily program yourself. In addition, the Jet Engine contains very sophisticated programming to optimize its own use of ODBC. By being smart about breaking a single query up into multiple steps, all executed on the server, Jet can often more than make up for its own speed overhead when compared to sending the original query direct to the ODBC API.

Maintenance Issues

You'll see in this chapter that ODBC API code is quite complex. This translates into more difficult code maintenance. Any time you step away from using Jet-provided recordsets into manipulating server cursors directly, you're adding another bit of code that will need to be maintained and checked for errors. There's a tradeoff here between the speed of your application and the time that it takes you to complete it.

As the operating system changes, you're also more likely to have to change ODBC API calls than code written using the native Jet objects and methods. Each new release of ODBC (the current release is version 2.10) includes new functions and sometimes modifications to existing functions. Although new releases of ODBC can generally continue to use the syntax of previous versions, there have been some major revisions along the way. For example, the 32-bit ODBC calls used in this chapter are in a different library than the 16-bit ones Access 2.0 could call. Existing Access 2.0 applications that use ODBC require major rewrites when being ported to Access 95.

Understanding the ODBC API Examples

The CH5ODBC.MDB database contains functions for using the ODBC API direct from Access 95. This database includes:

- ODBC API Declare statements
- Low-level ODBC utility functions
- High-level ODBC sample functions

All of the ODBC Declares and constants are contained in the single module basODBCDeclares. This makes it easy for you to import this module to your own database and use any of the ODBC functions that we've used in this chapter. You may wish to edit this module to remove declarations you're not using, since it is quite lengthy.

NOTE There are many ODBC API functions that we do not use in this chapter. The full documentation of the ODBC API is contained in the ODBC Software Development Kit, which is available as part of the Microsoft Developer's Network Level 2 CD-ROM series. If you intend to do substantial ODBC programming, you need this reference. If you own Visual Basic 4.0, Enterprise Edition, you'll also find the ODBC32.TXT file that ships with the sample databases a useful reference, since it includes Visual Basic declarations for the entire API.

General ODBC Programming

In general, ODBC API programming involves a fixed series of actions:

1. Initialize the necessary data structures

2. Send SQL statements to the server for execution

3. Retrieve results from the server

4. Destroy the data structures

The data structures which ODBC uses are an environment, a connection, and a statement. The environment contains high-level information of interest to ODBC itself, and you'll seldom, if ever, need to manipulate it after creating it. The connection contains information on the particular server—you need to somehow associate this to a Data Source Name (DSN). The statement relates to a particular SQL statement sent to the connection.

We'll see below how to create and use each of these data structures. Each data structure can be passed back and forth by means of a *handle*—a 32-bit address that can be stored in an Access long integer. We'll use module-level variables for all handles so that they remain in scope between calls to the various functions that we declare. Figure 5.2 provides an overview of the specific ODBC calls we'll be using in these examples.

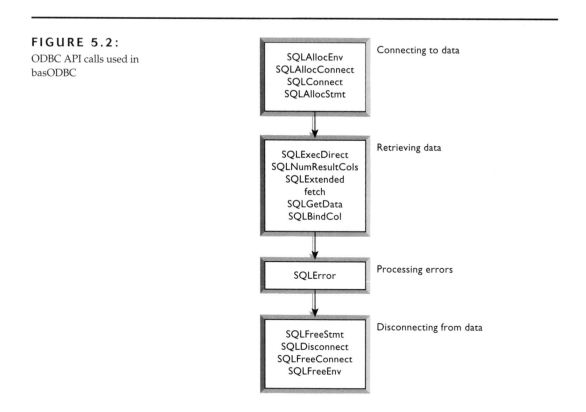

FIGURE 5.2:
ODBC API calls used in basODBC

Connecting to data

SQLAllocEnv
SQLAllocConnect
SQLConnect
SQLAllocStmt

Retrieving data

SQLExecDirect
SQLNumResultCols
SQLExtended
fetch
SQLGetData
SQLBindCol

Processing errors

SQLError

Disconnecting from data

SQLFreeStmt
SQLDisconnect
SQLFreeConnect
SQLFreeEnv

Creating the Environment

To create an ODBC environment, your code needs to call SQLAllocEnv, which we have aliased as oSQLAllocEnv. Since our examples are written to use only a single server, our utility functions create the environment at the same time that they make the connection to a particular server. If you have an application that frequently connects to and disconnects from various servers, you'll want to create the environment once in a function of its own, and have it available for multiple connections, one after the other.

> **NOTE** **Aliasing** is the process of assigning a new name to an API call in your Access code. It's generally a good idea to use an aliased name. Although Access 95 lets you have the same public procedure name in multiple modules, you will have to use the full **modulename.procedurename** syntax every time you wish to call the function. In our ODBC examples, we've aliased all the ODBC API calls by putting the letter "o" on them as a prefix.

SQLAllocEnv takes only a single argument, hEnv. The function uses this to return the environment handle which is used in subsequent calls within that environment.

Making the Connection

The ODBCConnect function is an Access function that connects your application to a specific SQL Server via the ODBC API. It takes three arguments, as shown in Table 5.4.

TABLE 5.4: Arguments to ODBCConnect()

Argument	Meaning
strServer	Data Source Name to which to connect. This must be set up with ODBC Administrator before running the function.
strUID	User ID to use when logging on to the server. Leave empty to use integrated security.
strPassword	Password with which to log on. Leave empty to use integrated security.

```vb
Function ODBCConnect(strServer As String, _
    strUID As String, strPassword As String) _
    As Boolean
' Take a hard-coded ODBC data source, connect
' to it, and open a statement. Returns True on
' success, False on any error
    Dim intRet As Integer
    Dim strConnIn As String
    Dim strConnOut As String * 256
    Dim intConnOut As Integer

    On Error GoTo ODBCConnectErr
    ODBCConnect = True
    ' Allocate the environment
    intRet = oSQLAllocEnv(mlngHenv)
    If intRet <> SQL_SUCCESS Then
        Call ODBCErrorInfo(mlngHenv, _
            SQL_NULL_HDBC, SQL_NULL_HSTMT)
    End If
    ' Allocate the connection
    intRet = oSQLAllocConnect(ByVal _
        mlngHenv, mlngHdbc)
    If intRet <> SQL_SUCCESS Then
        Call ODBCErrorInfo(mlngHenv, _
            mlngHdbc, SQL_NULL_HSTMT)
    End If
    ' Connect to the server
    intRet = oSQLConnect(ByVal mlngHdbc, _
        strServer, Len(strServer), strUID, _
        Len(strUID), strPassword, Len(strPassword))
    strConnIn = ""
    If intRet <> SQL_SUCCESS Then
        Call ODBCErrorInfo(mlngHenv, _
            mlngHdbc, SQL_NULL_HSTMT)
    End If
    ' Allocate the statement
    intRet = oSQLAllocStmt(ByVal mlngHdbc, _
        mlngHstmt)
    If intRet <> SQL_SUCCESS Then
        Call ODBCErrorInfo(mlngHenv, _
            mlngHdbc, mlngHstmt)
    End If
ODBCConnectExit:
    Exit Function
```

```
ODBCConnectErr:
    MsgBox Err.Number & ": " & Err.Description, _
        vbCritical, "ODBCConnect()"
    ODBCConnect = False
    Resume ODBCConnectExit
End Function
```

ODBCConnect first uses SQLAllocEnv to set aside storage for an environment, and then SQLAllocConnect to set aside storage for a connection. SQLAllocConnect requires two arguments. The first argument is the environment handle from the call to SQLAllocEnv. The second is the connection handle, which the function will return after successfully setting aside storage space for the connection.

The call to SQLConnect does the actual work of connecting from our program to an individual SQL Server (or other ODBC data source). This function takes a number of arguments, as shown in Table 5.5. Finally, we call SQLAllocStmt to set aside storage for a statement. This initializes the statement handle mlngHstmt, which can then be used to send SQL straight to the server. SQLAllocStmt takes two arguments: the connection handle to contain the statement, and the statement handle to be returned.

TABLE 5.5: Arguments to SQLConnect

Argument	Meaning
hdbc	Connection handle to use in making this connection.
szDSN	Data Source Name (DSN) to which to connect.
cbDSN	Length of szDSN.
szUID	User ID to log on to the server.
cbUID	Length of szUID.
szAuthStr	Password to log on to the server.
cbAuthStr	Length of cbAuthStr.

As an alternative to using SQLConnect with the DSN of a server, you can use SQLConnectWithPrompt. This allows you to supply incomplete DSN information as part of the connect call. If the information is incomplete, the user is prompted via the standard ODBC dialog boxes to supply the missing information. In the sample database, the ODBCConnectWithPrompt function uses this API call to allow the user to select a data source at runtime.

```
strConnIn = ""
intRet = oSQLDriverConnect(ByVal mlngHdbc, _
    hWndAccessApp, strConnIn, 0, strConnOut, _
    255, intConnOut, SQL_DRIVER_PROMPT)
```

Table 5.6 shows the arguments to SQLDriverConnect.

TABLE 5.6: Arguments to SQLDriverConnect

Argument	Meaning
hdbc	Connection handle to use in making this connection.
hwnd	Window handle to anchor any required dialog boxes.
szConnStrIn	A (possibly incomplete) ODBC Connect string.
cbConnStrIn	Length of szConnStrIn.
szConnStrOut	Storage for the actual connect string. If the function is successful, this will be filled in by the driver.
cbConnStrOutMax	Available length of szConnStrOut.
pcbConnStrOut	Actual length used in szConnStrOut.
fDriverCompletion	Flag that controls how the user will be prompted for more information if necessary. Use SQL_DRIVER_PROMPT to prompt the user for all necessary information.

Handling Errors

The functions in ODBCDemo include standard Access error-trapping for errors that occur on the Access side of the connection. However, trapping and reporting on error messages from ODBC itself requires extra effort. Every ODBC call returns an integer indicating the success or failure of the call. Possible values for this return value are shown in Table 5.7.

TABLE 5.7: ODBC API Return Values

Constant	Meaning
SQL_INVALID_HANDLE	One or more of the handles (environment, connection, or statement) supplied to the call was invalid.
SQL_ERROR	An error occurred within the ODBC layer.
SQL_SUCCESS	The call succeeded.
SQL_SUCCESS_WITH_INFO	The call succeeded, but further information is available via SQLError.
SQL_STILL_EXECUTING	An asynchronous call is still processing on the server.
SQL_NEED_DATA	The server is waiting for further information.
SQL_NO_DATA_FOUND	A call to SQLError found no further data.

Any ODBC call can post an error or multiple errors. The technique we use in ODBCDemo is to check the return value after each call. If it's not SQL_SUCCESS, we call the ODBCErrorInfo function to tell us about all of the errors and warnings that occurred during the call.

```
Sub ODBCErrorInfo(lngHenv As Long, _
    lngHdbc As Long, _
    lngHstmt As Long)

    Dim strSQLState As String * 5
    Dim strErrorMessage _
        As String * SQL_MAX_MESSAGE_LENGTH
    Dim lngNativeError As Long
    Dim intRet As Integer
    Dim intErrorLength As Integer
    intRet = SQL_SUCCESS
    Do Until intRet = SQL_NO_DATA_FOUND
    Debug.Print intRet
        intRet = oSQLError(lngHenv, _
            lngHdbc, lngHstmt, strSQLState, _
            lngNativeError, strErrorMessage, _
            SQL_MAX_MESSAGE_LENGTH - 1, _
            intErrorLength)
        #If FDEBUG Then
            If intErrorLength <= 255 Then
                MsgBox Left$(strErrorMessage, _
                    intErrorLength)
```

```
            Else
                MsgBox strErrorMessage
            End If
        #Else
            If intErrorLength <= 255 Then
                Debug.Print Left$(strErrorMessage, _
                    intErrorLength)
            Else
                Debug.Print strErrorMessage, _
                    intErrorLength
            End If
        #End If
    Loop
End Sub
```

ODBCErrorInfo is able to report on errors generated on any of the ODBC handles, so it takes all of the current handles as arguments. In turn, it calls the SQLError API function to return information from the ODBC layer. Table 5.8 describes the arguments to this call. This procedure also uses the FDEBUG conditional compilation constant to decide whether to post the messages to the user interface or just to the Debug Window. You can set this constant by using Tools ➤ Options ➤ Module.

TABLE 5.8: Arguments to SQLError

Argument	Meaning
henv	Current environment handle. Use the constant SQL_NULL_HENV if there is no environment handle.
hdbc	Current connection handle. Use the constant SQL_NULL_HDBC if there is no connection handle.
hstmt	Current statement handle. Use the constant SQL_NULL_HSTMT if there is no statement handle.
szSQLState	Current state of the SQL connection. String value supplied by the server.
pfNativeError	Native error code supplied by the server.
szErrorMsg	Native error message supplied by the server.
cbErrorMsgMax	Length of the szErrorMsg buffer.
pcbErrorMsg	Actual length used in the szErrorMsg buffer.

The SQL Server ODBC driver returns SQL_ERROR any time it encounters a severity 11 or higher error on the server. Errors of severity 10 or less return SQL_SUCCESS_WITH_INFO instead. During the process of connecting to a server, for example, several low-severity messages are returned. If you connect to the pubs database with FDEBUG set to a non-zero value, you'll get a message box for each of these messages:

```
Changed database context to 'master'.
Changed language setting to 'us_english'.
Changed database context to 'pubs'.
```

Sending a Query

The end result of calling either ODBCConnect or ODBCConnectWith-Prompt (assuming that there are no errors in connecting to the server) is to allocate a *statement handle* at the module level, mlngHstmt. This serves as a pipeline you can use to execute queries on the server. The simplest way to do this is to use the SQLExecDirect call, followed by the SQLFetch call. SQLExecDirect sends a query to the server and returns the results to a statement handle. SQLFetch fetches the next row of results queued up to a statement handle. Table 5.9 shows the arguments to SQLExecDirect and Table 5.10 shows the argument to SQLFetch.

TABLE 5.9: Arguments to SQLExecDirect

Argument	Meaning
hstmt	Statement handle to use for this query. This determines which server will handle the query. You must already have used SQLConnect or SQLDriverConnect to provide a valid connection to the server.
szSQLStr	SQL String to execute on the server. You must supply this in standard ODBC SQL.
CbSQLStr	Length of szSQLStr.

TABLE 5.10: Argument to SQLFetch

Argument	Meaning
hstmt	Statement handle from which to fetch data. You must already have used SQLExecDirect to make results available on this handle.

In the sample database, we have wrapped an example of doing this in the ODBCDebugFetch function, which prints the results of a SQL statement out to the Debug Window.

```
Function ODBCDebugFetch(strSQL As String) _
    As Boolean
' Execute a SQL statement over an existing
' statement handle and print the results '
' to the Debug window. Returns True on
' success and False on any error
    Dim intRet As Integer
    Dim intCols As Integer
    Dim i As Integer
    Dim strRet As String * 1024
    Dim lngLength As Long

    ODBCDebugFetch = True

    intRet = oSQLExecDirect(ByVal mlngHstmt, _
        strSQL, Len(strSQL))
    If intRet <> SQL_SUCCESS Then
        Call ODBCErrorInfo(mlngHenv, _
            mlngHdbc, mlngHstmt)
    End If
    If intRet <> SQL_SUCCESS And _
        intRet <> SQL_SUCCESS_WITH_INFO Then
        ODBCDebugFetch = False
        GoTo ODBCDebugFetchExit
    End If
    ' Find the number of columns in the result
    intRet = oSQLNumResultCols(ByVal mlngHstmt, _
        intCols)
    If intRet <> SQL_SUCCESS Then
        Call ODBCErrorInfo(mlngHenv, mlngHdbc, _
            mlngHstmt)
    End If
```

```
        intRet = oSQLFetch(ByVal mlngHstmt)
        Do While intRet <> SQL_NO_DATA_FOUND
            For i = 1 To intCols
                intRet = oSQLGetData(ByVal mlngHstmt, _
                    i, SQL_C_CHAR, ByVal strRet, _
                    1024, lngLength)
                If intRet <> SQL_SUCCESS Then
                    Call ODBCErrorInfo(mlngHenv, _
                        mlngHdbc, mlngHstmt)
                End If
                If lngLength = -1 Then
                    Debug.Print Space(i) & "#NULL#"
                Else
                    Debug.Print Space(i) & Left$(strRet, _
                    lngLength)
                End If
            Next i
            intRet = oSQLFetch(ByVal mlngHstmt)
        Loop
ODBCDebugFetchExit:
    Exit Function
ODBCDebugFetchErr:
    MsgBox Err.Number & ": " & Err.Description, _
        vbCritical, "ODBCDebugFetch()"
    ODBCDebugFetch = False
    Resume ODBCDebugFetchExit
End Function
```

SQLExecDirect sends the SQL statement directly to the server for execution. Assuming it succeeds, the statement handle mlngHstmt now points to a data structure that can be used to retrieve results. We next use the SQLNumResultsCols API call to determine how many columns are in the result.

Looping through the entire set of results is done by calling SQLFetch repeatedly. Each call to SQLFetch loads another record into the statement handle, until finally SQL_NO_DATA_FOUND is returned. The inner loop uses the SQLGetData call to get the data out of each column of the result set in turn and then dump it to the debug window. SQLGetData provides a general-purpose way to retrieve a column from the most recently fetched row of data. It takes the arguments shown in Table 5.11.

TABLE 5.11: Arguments to SQLGetData

Argument	Meaning
hstmt	Statement handle from which to get data. You should already have used SQLFetch to make data ready on this statement handle.
icol	Column number of the data to retrieve. Columns are numbered starting at 1.
fcType	C Data type to use when fetching the data. The easiest thing to do from Access is to always use SQL_C_CHAR and depend on Access to convert from the returned string to the data type you want to use.
rgbValue	Storage for the data. If you're using SQL_C_CHAR for the type, this should be a string variable passed by value.
cbValueMax	Length of the storage buffer.
pcbValue	Length of the data actually returned.

After you've called SQLGetData, the first pcbValue bytes of the rgbValue buffer will contain the data returned by ODBC.

Binding Columns

As an alternative to using SQLGetData, you can bind columns to an ODBC statement. Just as binding a control on an Access form connects that control to a field in the underlying data source, binding in ODBC connects a variable in your code to a field in the ODBC statement. In the ODBC sample database, basODBC contains the BindDemo sub to demonstrate data binding. To simplify data management, we've defined a user-defined type on the module's Declarations page:

```
' Type used to hold information from the Dieter table
Private Type Dieter
    intDieterID As Integer
    lngDieterIDLen As Long
    chrDieterName(50) As Byte
    lngDieterNameLen As Long
End Type
```

This type matches a single row in tblDieters in the Food database. For each field, we've provided storage for the returned data and storage for the length of the returned data.

If you're unsure what data type to use in Access Basic to represent a particular SQL Server field, it's easy to find out. Just link the table directly to your Access database and open it in design view. You won't be able to change anything, but you'll be able to quickly determine how Access sees the data type for each field.

BindDemo declares a particular variable of this type:

```
Dim typDieter As Dieter
```

After making a connection to the database and setting some options for the statement, here's the code that BindDemo uses to retrieve records from the table:

```
intRet = oSQLExecDirect(ByVal mlngHstmt, strSQL, _
      Len(strSQL))
   If intRet <> SQL_SUCCESS Then
       Call ODBCErrorInfo(mlngHenv, mlngHdbc, _
          mlngHstmt)
   End If
   intRet = oSQLBindCol(mlngHstmt, 1, SQL_C_USHORT, _
       typDieter.intDieterID, _
       Len(typDieter.intDieterID), _
       typDieter.lngDieterIDLen)
   If intRet <> SQL_SUCCESS Then
       Call ODBCErrorInfo(mlngHenv, mlngHdbc, _
          mlngHstmt)
   End If
   intRet = oSQLBindCol(mlngHstmt, 2, SQL_C_CHAR, _
       typDieter.chrDieterName(0), 50, _
       typDieter.lngDieterNameLen)
   If intRet <> SQL_SUCCESS Then
       Call ODBCErrorInfo(mlngHenv, mlngHdbc, _
          mlngHstmt)
   End If
```

```
intRet = oSQLFetch(ByVal mlngHstmt)
Do While intRet <> SQL_NO_DATA_FOUND
    strDieter = StrConv(LeftB(typDieter.chrDieterName, _
        typDieter.lngDieterNameLen), vbUnicode)
    Debug.Print typDieter.intDieterID, _
        typDieter.lngDieterNameLen, strDieter
    intRet = oSQLFetch(ByVal mlngHstmt)
Loop
```

As before, the SQLExecDirect call actually executes the query and sets up the result set. But now, before moving through the rows with SQLFetch, we call the SQLBindCol function. This function takes the arguments shown in Table 5.12.

TABLE 5.12: Arguments to SQLBindCol

Argument	Meaning
hstmt	Statement handle to use.
icol	Column number to bind, starting at 1.
fcType	C data type of the column.
rgbValue	Storage for the data returned from the column.
cbValueMax	Length of the rgbValue buffer.
pcbValue	Number of bytes actually returned by the most recent SQLFetch call.

Once the column has been bound to a particular variable, each call to SQLFetch sets the variable to hold the data from the current row of the query results. You can read this value freely without needing to make a call to SQLGetData.

One additional thing you need to watch out for in this case, though, is Unicode. Strings are returned as arrays of bytes rather than as Access strings. You will need to use LeftB and StrConv, as shown in the sample, to actually convert these strings to something that your Access code can use.

Dropping the Connection

When you are done with an ODBC connection, you should drop it. This will preserve resources on your local machine, as well as keep your server from being bogged down by excess connections. There are calls to deallocate each of the data structures in turn, which we've wrapped in a single function:

```
Function ODBCDisconnect() As Boolean
' Disconnect from the module-level data source
    Dim intRet As Integer
    On Error GoTo ODBCDisconnectErr
    ODBCDisconnect = True
    ' Close the query and drop the statement
    intRet = oSQLFreeStmt(ByVal mlngHstmt, _
        SQL_DROP)
    If intRet <> SQL_SUCCESS Then
        Call ODBCErrorInfo(mlngHenv, _
            mlngHdbc, mlngHstmt)
    End If
    ' Close the connection
    intRet = oSQLDisconnect(ByVal mlngHdbc)
    If intRet <> SQL_SUCCESS Then
        Call ODBCErrorInfo(mlngHenv, mlngHdbc, _
            SQL_NULL_HSTMT)
    End If
    ' Free the connection memory
    intRet = oSQLFreeConnect(ByVal mlngHdbc)
    If intRet <> SQL_SUCCESS Then
        Call ODBCErrorInfo(mlngHenv, mlngHdbc, _
            SQL_NULL_HSTMT)
    End If
    ' Close the environment and free its memory
    intRet = oSQLFreeEnv(ByVal mlngHenv)
     If intRet <> SQL_SUCCESS Then
        Call ODBCErrorInfo(mlngHenv, _
            SQL_NULL_HDBC, SQL_NULL_HSTMT)
    End If
ODBCDisconnectExit:
    Exit Function
```

```
ODBCDisconnectErr:
    MsgBox Err.Number & ": " & Err.Description, vbCritical,
"ODBCDisconnect()"
    ODBCDisconnect = False
    Resume ODBCDisconnectExit
End Function
```

There are four steps to shutting down the ODBC connection entirely:

1. Use SQLFreeStmt to stop any query processing and discard the statement handle.

2. Use SQLDisconnect to break the connection with the server.

3. Use SQLFreeConnect to free the memory used by the connection handle.

4. Use SQLFreeEnv to free the memory used by the environment handle.

A Set of Access Wrappers for ODBC

Once you understand the basic principles of ODBC, it's not too hard to write a set of *wrapper functions* to make ODBC resemble Access recordsets. The basWrappers module in CH5ODBC.MDB includes the following functions:

rODBCConnect	Connect to a data source
rODBCOpenRecordset	Open a recordset (a SQL cursor) given a particular SQL statement
rODBCMoveFirst	Move to the first row of the recordset
rODBCMoveLast	Move to the last row of the recordset

rODBCMovePrevious	Move to the previous row of the recordset
rODBCMoveNext	Move to the next row of the recordset
rODBCGetField	Retrieve data from the recordset
rODBCCloseRecordset	Close the recordset and the connection
rODBCDelete	Delete a record
rODBCUpdate	Update a record

Rather than review every line of code in detail, we'll discuss the interesting points of these functions here. You'll find the full implementation in the basWrappers module in the ODBC sample database. We've also included a second version on the companion CD as MULTIW.TXT. This version uses arrays of structures to allow you to have more than one open ODBC recordset at the same time. You'll find that this approach involves a performance tradeoff, since Access is doing considerable extra work in finding the correct data structure to work with at any given time.

rODBCConnect

The rODBCConnect function allocates the environment and connection handles used by the other rODBC functions. It does not allocate a statement handle, however. We reserve that for the next step. This way, if it becomes possible to use multiple statements on a single connection in a future version of SQL Server, we won't have to rewrite this part of the code.

rODBCOpenRecordset

rODBCOpenRecordset is written to be as close to the DAO.OpenRecordset method as possible. It takes as arguments a SQL string and a recordset type, which can be either dbOpenDynaset or dbOpenSnapshot. (ODBC tables, of course, cannot generate a table-type recordset.) rODBCOpenRecordset does a large amount of setup processing while preparing the recordset:

- Allocates the statement handle
- Initializes various values in the structure used to keep track of the recordset
- Sets the rowset size for the statement
- Sets the cursor type for the statement
- Sets the concurrency type for the statement
- Sets the cursor name for the statement
- Sets the maximum rows for the statement
- Uses SQLExecDirect to actually execute the query
- Retrieves information about column names and widths for this query

Most of this setup is concerned with getting the best possible options for recordset processing. Rather than use the SQLFetch call to retrieve data, the rODBC functions use SQLExtendedFetch, which can bring back multiple rows of server data in a single operation. This helps keep the overhead down to a minimum. The cursor type and concurrency type control the way in which the recordset is handled. Our function chooses a keyset-driven cursor and optimistic record locking, just as Access itself does. We also assign a name to the cursor. This will be used later in Update and Delete operations.

rODBCMove Functions

All of the recordset movement functions ultimately call the helper function rODBCMoveLowLevel. This function uses the SQLExtended-Fetch call to retrieve a set of rows. There's a great deal of additional code in functions such as rODBCMoveNext, since we need to keep careful track of whether we've already fetched a particular row from the server.

rODBCGetField

rODBCGetField is our analog to retrieving the value of a field in DAO. Unfortunately, there is no Fields collection with an ODBC recordset, so we have to actually look at column names to determine which field to return. This is a general, but not particularly efficient, solution. If you decide to use these functions in your own application, you may want to write specific fetching functions for each field you need to deal with. These will be less portable but far more efficient than searching for each field every single time you want to read data from it.

rODBCDelete

rODBCDelete is a function to delete an entire row from the result set. It takes advantage of SQL Server's ability to handle a *positioned delete*. A positioned delete is an SQL statement of the form:

```
DELETE FROM TableName
WHERE CURRENT OF CursorName
```

Positioned deletes depend on named cursors, so our rODBCOpen-Recordset function assigned a name to the statement handle before executing the query.

rODBCUpdate

A positioned update is an SQL statement which can update a row on the server. It has the general form:

```
UPDATE TableName
SET Field1 = Expression1
{,Field2 = Expression2 ...}
WHERE CURRENT OF CursorName
```

By taking advantage of positioned updates and deletes, our functions can offer general-purpose modification of data on the server without needing any special knowledge of the table structure there.

> **NOTE** Positioned updates and deletes are included in the Extended ODBC grammar. You can use these functions with any driver that supports the full extended grammar.

rODBCCloseRecordset

rODBCCloseRecordset frees up all the handles associated with the ODBC connection to give memory and resources back to other operations. In the MULTIW.TXT implementation, we keep the connection and environment open for execution of another SQL Statement.

Using the rODBC Functions

The ODBC sample database includes a function that demonstrates the use of these functions. As you can see, you don't need any understanding of the underlying ODBC calls to use them in an application.

```
Function wraptest()
    Dim intRet As Integer
    Dim rstX As ORecordset
    Dim strName As String
```

```
        Debug.Print "---Starting Test---"
        rstX = rODBCConnect("Food", "sa", "")
        Debug.Print "ODBCConnect: " & intRet
        intRet = rODBCOpenRecordset(rstX, _
            "SELECT * FROM Food.dbo.tblDieters FOR UPDATE", _
            dbOpenDynaset)
        Do Until rODBCEOF(rstX)
            intRet = rODBCMoveNext(rstX)
            strName = rODBCGetField(rstX, "DieterName")
            Debug.Print strName
            If strName = "Stan Pardo" Then
                intRet = rODBCUpdate(rstX, _
                    "Food.dbo.tblDieters", _
                    "DieterID", "27")
            End If
        Loop
        intRet = rODBCCloseRecordset(rstX)
        Debug.Print "ODBCCloseRecordset: " & intRet
        Debug.Print "---Test Over---"
End Function
```

Three Ways to Update Data

Positioned updates and deletes provide a general purpose way to modify data via ODBC. They do require you to be using SQLExtendedFetch to retrieve your data, however. If you're using SQLFetch, you'll need to find another alternative.

There are two other ways to update data via ODBC. One is to issue a single-row UPDATE statement, either by opening a second statement handle or closing the first one and reusing it. In the general case, you must know the value of a unique index to write this update. If you like, you can call the SQLPrimaryKeys function to determine the primary key of a table, and use this information in constructing the SQL statement to send to SQLExecDirect.

The other way to perform an update via ODBC is through the SQLSetPos function. If you issue this call with a parameter of SQL_UPDATE, it will take the values you have stored locally and send them back to the server via an ODBC-constructed stored procedure. Unfortunately, there's no way to do this in the general case in Visual Basic for Applications. To do an update this way, you must make use of ODBC Binding, the process of assigning retrieved data to local variables. This requires a foreknowledge of your recordset's structure to create an appropriate user-defined Type structure within Access.

In general, if you want to do updates, we recommend not trying to write direct ODBC API calls yourself. Either retreat to using regular recordsets within Access, use the ODBC recordset wrappers with positioned updates and deletes, or use the Visual Basic Remote Data Objects discussed below. Any of these alternatives will allow updating your data without the necessity of writing large amounts of code.

Installing ODBC Data Sources Automatically

One last piece of the puzzle you'll need to consider is installing ODBC data sources. There are two ways to do this: from the user interface with ODBC Administrator, and directly from your code using the RegisterDatabase method of the DBEngine object. We'll discuss both of these in turn.

Using ODBC Administrator

The ODBC Administrator Control Panel applet provides a handy method for setting up a connection to a remote database. ODBC Administrator makes entries to your Registry, but the user interface hides this level from you unless you go looking for it.

To start the ODBC Administrator, access the Windows Control Panel and double-click the 32-bit ODBC icon (you may also have a separate icon for 16-bit data sources, but Access 95 can only use 32-bit drivers). You'll see a dialog box similar to that in Figure 5.3, though perhaps with different installed data sources.

FIGURE 5.3:
ODBC Administrator showing installed data sources

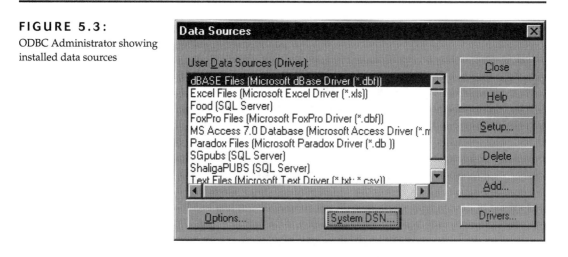

To add a new data source using the ODBC Administrator, follow these steps:

1. Run ODBC Administrator.

2. Click the Add button.

3. Select "SQL Server" from the list of available drivers and click the OK button.

4. Fill in the details about your server and click OK.

Figure 5.4 shows the data source we've been using in our examples in the ODBC Administrator.

Using RegisterDatabase

The major problem with using ODBC Administrator to set up your data sources on a network is that someone has to run through these user interface steps on every single machine. Fortunately, there's a programming alternative. The Jet DBEngine object has a RegisterDatabase method that can be used to add a data source to the Registry, making it available to applications.

FIGURE 5.4:

Setting up a data source using ODBC Administrator

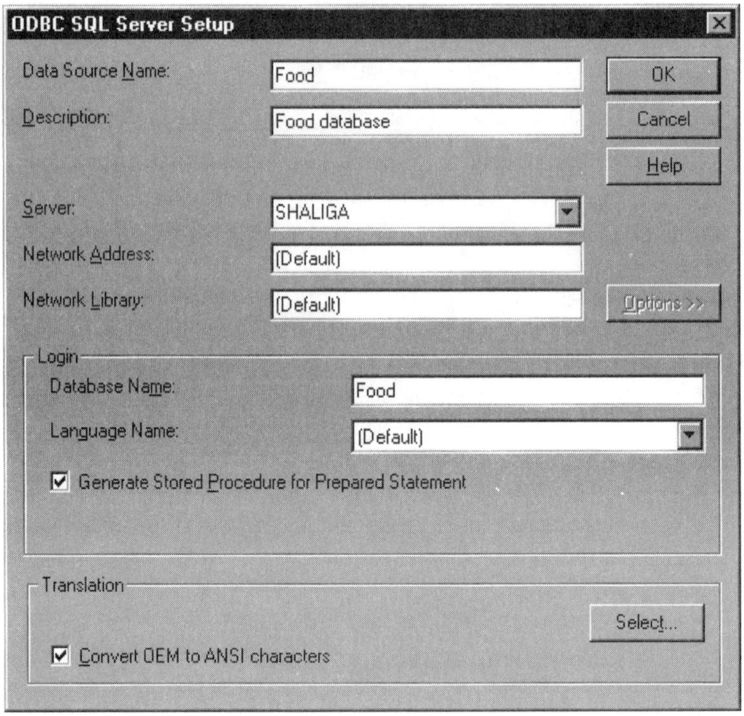

In the sample database, basODBC contains a function showing how to register a database. To use this in your own applications, you'll need to build up a string containing the necessary information for your server. Once you've used Workgroup Administrator on one computer, you can check the Registry to see the necessary strings. Figure 5.5 shows the applicable part of the Registry.

```
Function ODBCRegisterDatabaseDemo() As Boolean
    Dim strKeys As String
    ' Build string containing all the Registry info
    strKeys = "Database=Food" & Chr$(13) & _
        "Description=USDA Database" & Chr$(13) & _
        "Driver=c:\windows\system\sqlsrv32.dll" _
        & Chr$(13) & _
        "LastUser=sa" & Chr$(13) & _
        "OEMTOANSI=Yes" & Chr$(13) & _
```

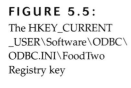

FIGURE 5.5:

The HKEY_CURRENT
_USER\Software\ODBC\
ODBC.INI\FoodTwo
Registry key

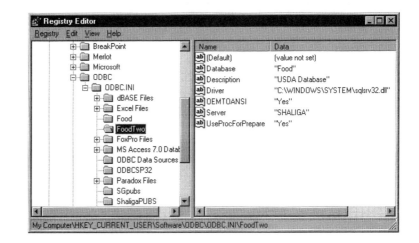

```
        "Server=SHALIGA" & Chr$(13) & _
        "UseProcForPrepare=Yes"
    ' Register the database
    On Error Resume Next
    DBEngine.RegisterDatabase "FoodTwo", _
        "SQL Server", True, strKeys
    ODBCRegisterDatabaseDemo = (Err = 0)
End Function
```

The RegisterDatabase method takes four arguments, as shown in Table 5.13. If you choose to register an already registered database, no error occurs, so you can just put a registration function in your AutoExec and not worry about it after that.

TABLE 5.13: Arguments to RegisterDatabase

Argument	Meaning
dbName	Name to use for this ODBC data source.
driver	Name of the ODBC driver to use. For SQL Server, this should be "SQL Server."
silent	True to suppress all the ODBC Administrator dialog boxes, false to show them.
attributes	Carriage-return-delimited string of registry entries to make.

Using Remote Data Objects

If you own Visual Basic 4.0, Enterprise Edition, you have another alternative to using either linked tables via Jet or direct calls to the ODBC API. This alternative is Remote Data Objects (RDO). You can think of RDO as a kind of "mini-Jet" when dealing with ODBC databases. RDO supports its own hierarchy of objects, methods, and properties for access to data. Unlike Jet, it has no native file format of its own. Instead, RDO can only be used with ODBC data sources. For these data sources, though, it can be very fast, with speed that sometimes rivals that of direct API calls. Because programming RDO is much easier than programming to the ODBC API, it deserves a closer look.

Licensing Issues

Before using RDO in your Access applications, you need to understand the licensing issues involved. Unfortunately, RDO was developed within the Visual Basic product team, and the license terms are not favorable for Access programmers.

RDO is implemented as an OLE Automation in-process server—that is, it runs in the memory space of whatever application is acting as its host. RDO can run within any VBA host, including Visual Basic 4.0, Excel 95, Project 95, and Access 95. However, VBA can be in two different states. The first is design/debug mode; the second is executable mode. In Access, Excel, and Project, VBA is always in design/debug mode. If you use Visual Basic's Setup Wizard to create a standalone VB program, then that program runs in executable mode.

If RDO is used in a design/debug mode host, then it checks the Registry for a special licensing key that's placed there when VB4, Enterprise Edition, is installed on the machine. If that Registry key isn't present, RDO will refuse to create its objects, even if the server is installed on the machine. If you install a VB4 application that uses RDO on a computer that does not have VB4, Enterprise Edition, RDO will be added to the list of things to which you can set a reference in your VBA code. However, if you try to use this reference from within Access, your RDO programs will fail with a "Can't Create Object" message.

If RDO is used in an executable mode application (a compiled Visual Basic program), then the executable itself contains the licensing key.

The bottom line is that RDO will only work in Access applications if Visual Basic 4.0, Enterprise Edition, is installed on the machine where you're trying to run the program. Since this amounts to a nearly $1,000 per seat licensing fee, we hope Microsoft examines this policy for possible future modification. Meanwhile, we'll discuss the use of RDO for those who have the necessary software installed.

What Are Remote Data Objects?

Remote Data Objects function very much like Jet objects in that they are a hierarchy of collections and objects with methods and properties. RDO is implemented over the ODBC API and Driver Manager to establish connections, create recordsets (which, in a strange bout of inconsistency, are called result sets in RDO) and cursors, and execute procedures, all without using Jet. You can configure RDO to permit either synchronous or asynchronous operation.

Using RDO

We'll start with a review of the major objects in the RDO hierarchy. The full hierarchy is shown in Figure 5.6. In our examples, we'll only use a few of these objects. If you get deeply involved with RDO (perhaps through Visual Basic), you'll want to investigate the rest of the RDO objects.

FIGURE 5.6:

RDO Object Hierarchy

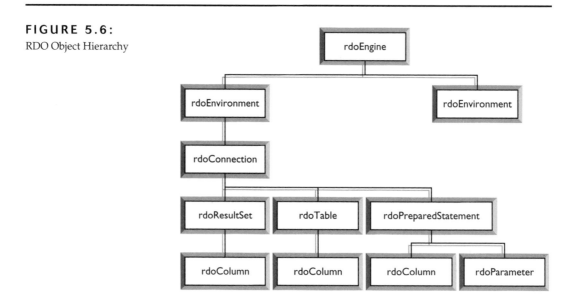

rdoEngine

rdoEngine is the top-level object in the RDO hierarchy (similar to the DBEngine object in Jet) and contains all of the other RDO objects. It represents the database engine or other ODBC data source. Its child collection is rdoEnvironments, which is used to collect information about open rdoEnvironment objects (which represent ODBC environment handles). The rdoEngine has several properties, including rdoDefaultCursorDriver (used to determine whether cursors are created locally or on the server), rdoDefaultLoginTimeout, rdoDefaultPassword, rdoDefaultUser, and rdoVersion. Its methods are rdoCreateEnvironment (which starts a session so you can refer to the rdoEnvironment object in your code) and rdoRegisterDataSource (which registers connection information for an ODBC data source).

rdoEnvironment

An rdoEnvironment object is created using Name, Password, and UserName properties. Behind the scenes, this object maps to the Environment level of the ODBC API. Within a single rdoEnvironment, you can have multiple connections and open multiple databases. The OpenConnection method opens an existing connection in that rdoEnvironment. BeginTrans, CommitTrans, and RollbackTrans methods can be used to manage transaction processing, and you can have several rdoEnvironment objects conducting multiple transactions. The Close method terminates an environment and its connection.

rdoConnection

The rdoConnection object maps to the Connection level of the ODBC API. Using a connection, you can open one or more result sets. Typically, your identity on a server is established using the properties of the rdoConnection object.

rdoResultset

The rdoResultset is roughly analogous to the recordset in Access, although without many of its features. You might think of an rdoResultset as something of a lightweight recordset. Although a single SQL statement can return many result sets (if, for example, it calls a stored procedure on the server), you can only have one of these open at a time, which is zero or more rows of data returned by an SQL query. rdoResultset objects are created using the OpenResultset method of the rdoPreparedStatement, rdoTable, or rdoConnection object. (Visual Basic includes a Remote Data Control, but this can't be used in Access since it depends on row-binding of data.) The Type argument of the OpenResultset method allows you to specify the type of cursor that is created to access the data. The methods and properties of the rdoResultset object allow you to manipulate data and navigate the rows of a result set, which we will discuss more fully when investigating our sample application below. Tables 5.14 and 5.15 show these methods and properties. As you can see, it's a less rich set than you'll find in Jet recordsets.

TABLE 5.14: Properties of rdoResultset Objects

Property	Explanation
AbsolutePosition	Position of the current row in the rdoResultset as an integer.
BOF	True when at the beginning of the rdoResultset.
Bookmark	Bookmark for the current row.
Bookmarkable	True if this rdoResultset supports bookmarks.
EOF	True when at the end of the rdoResultset.
hStmt	ODBC hStmt this rdoResultset is open on.
LastModified	Bookmark of the most recently modified row.
LockEdits	True for pessimistic locking, false for optimistic locking.
Name	Name of the rdoResultset.
PercentPosition	Position of the current row, from 0 to 100%.
Restartable	True if this rdoResultset supports the Requery method.
RowCount	Number of rows that have been retrieved.
StillExecuting	True in an asynchronous rdoResultset that has not yet finished returning rows.
Transactions	True if this rdoResultset supports transactions.
Updatable	True if this rdoResultset can be edited.

rdoColumn

A column of data (with a consistent data type and common properties) is represented by an rdoColumn object. The rdoColumn object is used to map a base table's column structure to a database table (but not to alter its structure). In our example we'll take advantage of

TABLE 5.15: Methods of rdoResultset Objects

Method	Explanation
AddNew	Prepare a new row for adding a record.
CancelUpdate	Discard an unsaved new row.
Close	Close the rdoResultset.
Delete	Delete the current row.
Edit	Prepare the current row for editing.
GetRows	Get multiple rows of data into an array.
MoreResults	Retrieve a second rdoResultset from the same statement.
Move	Move to an arbitrary record.
MoveFirst	Move to the first record.
MoveLast	Move to the last record.
MoveNext	Move to the next record.
MovePrevious	Move to the previous record.
Requery	Re-execute the query on which the rdoResultset is based.
Update	Save a new or edited row.

the fact that rdoColumn objects have names to retrieve the data from the current row.

Programming RDO in Access Forms

Our sample Access database, rdoForms, consists of a single form which is used to fetch and display data from the Food database in SQL Server. To make connections as seamless as possible, we have used Access properties such as the Tag property to store useful information so that it can be retrieved quickly. You can adapt the methods shown here to retrieve data from any SQL Server via RDO. We've kept the functions involved as generic as possible.

In the Declarations section of the form module, we declare an rdoResultset variable in order to hold the data that we want to display in the controls on our form, since the form of necessity has to be unbound. Keeping this rdoResultset at the module level makes sure that it stays in scope as long as the form is open.

```
Option Compare Database
Option Explicit

Dim rstRDF As rdo.rdoResultset
```

In the Load event of the form, we call the global procedure rdfInitialize() to initialize the shared variables for the RDO connection and open the connection to the data source. Here's the essential part of this global procedure:

```
If grdfEnv Is Nothing Then
        rdoEngine.rdoDefaultCursorDriver = rdUseOdbc
    Set grdfEnv = rdoEngine.rdoCreateEnvironment _
        ("", "", "")
    Set grdfConn = grdfEnv.OpenConnection _
        (rServerDSN, rdDriverNoPrompt, False, _
        rServerUser)
    grdfConn.QueryTimeout = 0
    End If
```

Then we open the rdoResultset using an SQL string retrieved from the form's Tag property ("SELECT * FROM tblFoods ORDER BY FoodID" in our sample database). By moving to the last record and storing the AbsolutePosition property in a variable, we can store the record count so that our navigation buttons function properly.

```
    Set rstRDF = grdfConn.OpenResultset _
            (Me.Tag, rdOpenDynamic, rdConcurRowver)
    ' Get the number of records
    rstRDF.MoveLast
    lngRecordcount = rstRDF.AbsolutePosition
    rstRDF.MoveFirst
    ' And populate the first record on to the form
    booRet = rdfGetRecord(Me, rstRDF)
```

The first record is populated by calling the rdfGetRecord function and passing it the form and the rdoResultset variable. Each text box control on the form stores the column name in the Tag property. The rdfGetRecord function will store the value in the Default Value property. We are using Default Value to store the retrieved value so that we can use it later to perform a rollback if the user chooses not to save a record while editing. This is safe, since a Default Value can't actually be used for anything on an unbound form.

```
Function rdfGetRecord(frm As Form, rst As rdo.rdoResultset)
' Get the current record from the Resultset and place
' fields on to the form in matching controls
    On Error GoTo rdfGetRecordErr
    Dim errX As Error
    Dim ctl As Control
    rdfGetRecord = True

    ' Walk through the controls on the form, looking for
    ' text boxes whose Tag property is not empty. We store
    ' the column name in the Tag and the value in the
    ' Default Value
    For Each ctl In frm.Controls
        If ctl.ControlType = acTextBox Then
            If Len(ctl.Tag & "") > 0 Then
                ctl = rst.rdoColumns(ctl.Tag).Value
                If Not _
IsNull(rst.rdoColumns(ctl.Tag).Value) Then
                    ctl.DefaultValue = _
 CStr(rst.rdoColumns(ctl.Tag).Value)
                End If
            End If
        End If
    Next ctl

rdfGetRecordExit:
    Exit Function

rdfGetRecordErr:
    If DBEngine.Errors.Count > 0 Then
        If Err.Number = DBEngine.Errors(0).Number And _
            DBEngine.Errors.Count > 1 Then
            For Each errX In DBEngine.Errors
                MsgBox "Error " & errX.Number & " raised by "
```

—

```
                    & errX.Source & ": " & errX.Description, _
                        vbCritical, "rdfGetRecord()"
                Next errX
            End If
        Else
            MsgBox "Error " & Err.Number & " raised by " _
                & Err.Source & ": " & Err.Description, _
                vbCritical, "rdfGetRecord()"
        End If
        rdfGetRecord = False
        Resume rdfGetRecordExit
End Function
```

The major difference between using RDO and attached tables is that you have to perform all form operations in code since nothing is built-in. We have built navigation buttons for our form that perform navigation by moving from record to record or to the beginning or the end of the rdoResultset. If the user is positioned at the beginning of the rdoResultset, the Move First and Move Previous buttons are disabled; if the user is positioned at the end of the rdoResultset, the Move Next and Move Last buttons are disabled. We achieve this by checking the AbsolutePosition property of each record. If you are on the first record, the AbsolutePosition property will be 1 (contrary to online help) and if you are on the last record, the AbsolutePosition property will match lngRecordCount, which we initialized when we fetched the data. The code for the navigation buttons advances to the specified record in the rdoResultset (rdfGetRecord), then runs the EnableButtons subprocedure to figure out where in the rdoResultset the record is located by checking the AbsolutePosition property:

```
Private Sub EnableButtons(strControl As String)
' check AbsolutePosition property against recordcount
' to enable buttons
    Select Case rstRDF.AbsolutePosition
        ' EOF
        Case lngRecordcount
            DoAllButtons "AtLast", "cmdPrevious"
        ' BOF
        Case 1
            DoAllButtons "AtFirst", "cmdNext"
```

```
        Case Else
            DoAllButtons "DisplayAll", strControl
    End Select
End Sub
```

One interesting thing to note about RDO properties is that the AbsolutePosition property seems to be the only way to reliably check where you are. The PercentPosition, which initially looked promising, turned out to always return "50%" on SQL Server Resultsets, even when on the last record.

The other command buttons on our form allow us to edit, delete, and add new records. We call our button activation code to enable the appropriate buttons for each state the user might be in. For example, when a value changes in a field, we call our DoAllButtons subprocedure from the OnChange property, which will enable the Save and Cancel buttons while disabling other inappropriate buttons. This gives the user explicit save and rollback functionality.

```
    If Me!cmdAddNew.Enabled Then DoAllButtons _
"Edit", "txtFoodName"
```

When you press the Save button, the value of the tag property of the AddNew button is checked (this is set to "True" if the button is clicked). If the tag property is empty, then the controls on the form are updated; otherwise a new record is added by calling the AddNew-Record procedure:

```
' add new record and refresh Resultset
    Dim errX As Error
    Dim varBookmark As Variant
    Dim booRet As Boolean
 On Error GoTo AddNewRecordErr
    rstRDF.AddNew
    rstRDF.rdoColumns(Me!txtFoodID.Tag).Value = Me!txtFoodID
    rstRDF.rdoColumns(Me!txtFoodName.Tag).Value = Me!txtFoodName
    rstRDF.rdoColumns(Me!txtServingCalories.Tag).Value =
Me!txtServingCalories
    rstRDF.rdoColumns(Me!txtServingDesc.Tag).Value =_
Me!txtServingDesc
    rstRDF.rdoColumns(Me!txtServingSize.Tag).Value =_
Me!txtServingSize
```

```
    rstRDF.UPDATE
    ' requery the Resultset so the new record shows up
    rstRDF.Requery
    rstRDF.MoveLast
    lngRecordcount = rstRDF.AbsolutePosition
    rstRDF.MoveFirst
    booRet = rdfGetRecord(Me, rstRDF)
    If booRet Then EnableButtons "cmdFirst"

AddNewRecordExit:
Debug.Print rstRDF.AbsolutePosition, lngRecordcount; "after
add new"
    Exit Sub

AddNewRecordErr:
    If DBEngine.Errors.Count > 0 Then
        If Err.Number = DBEngine.Errors(0).Number And _
            DBEngine.Errors.Count > 1 Then
            For Each errX In DBEngine.Errors
                MsgBox "Error " & errX.Number & " raised by " _
                    & errX.Source & ": " & errX.Description, _
                    vbCritical, "AddNewRecord()"
            Next errX
        Else
            MsgBox "Error " & Err.Number & " raised by " _
                & Err.Source & ": " & Err.Description, _
                vbCritical, "AddNewRecord()"
        End If
    Else
        MsgBox "Error " & Err.Number & " raised by " _
            & Err.Source & ": " & Err.Description, _
            vbCritical, "AddNewRecord()"
    End If
    RollbackRecord
    Resume AddNewRecordExit
End Sub
```

The RollbackRecord procedure restores the original values in the controls that were initially stored in the Default Value property of each control. This should leave the original position in the rdoResultset and the restored values in each text box. We then check to see where we are in the rdoResultset to enable or disable the appropriate buttons:

```
Dim ctl As Control
    For Each ctl In Me.Controls
        If ctl.ControlType = acTextBox Then
            If CStr(ctl.DefaultValue) <> CStr(ctl.Value) Then
                ctl.Value = ctl.DefaultValue
            End If
        End If
    Next ctl
    If rstRDF.AbsolutePosition = 1 Then
        DoAllButtons "AtFirst", "txtFoodID"
    ElseIf lngRecordcount = rstRDF.AbsolutePosition Then
        DoAllButtons "AtLast", "txtFoodID"
    Else
        DoAllButtons "Edit", "txtFoodID"
    End If
End Sub
```

Using RDO to Fetch Data for Access Reports

In most cases, RDO is not an especially good choice for reporting. The problem is that rdoResultsets end up in memory, and reports really want to be bound objects. There's no good way to transfer the rows of an rdoResultset in memory to the controls in the detail section of a report. If you're using RDO and need to produce a report on some subset of the server data, you may wish to investigate creating a local temporary table, moving the records to that table from the rdoResultset (using a Jet recordset to transfer them) and then basing the report on this temporary table.

Performance Issues

At this point, you have seen all the major ways to get data from SQL Server to Access:

- Attached tables and ODBC
- Direct ODBC API calls
- RDO

As you've seen, writing code to call the ODBC API directly can be substantially more work than using regular Access queries and bound forms. Is it worth the effort? There's no hard and fast answer to that question. Think about some of the variables involved in any client/server installation:

- The number of users on the system
- The network server used to handle logins
- The size of the database
- The number of simultaneous transactions
- The physical layout of the network

The only thing one can say with certainty is that every application is different. This is why monitoring and timing client/server applications is so important.

We use *monitoring* and *timing* to mean two very different activities. *Monitoring* is the act of recording some information on a process while it's going on, with the goal of analyzing it later. *Timing* is the act of recording the time the process takes to compare it with alternatives. Monitoring can tell you what's going on with a particular query strategy; timing can tell you whether it is better than another particular strategy.

Monitoring ODBC

There are a number of Microsoft tools available to monitor an ODBC connection. (Remember, even if you aren't using the ODBC API directly, any connection between Access and SQL Server is an ODBC connection.) Access is capable of producing trace files that show its activities when dealing with an ODBC data source. There are also various utilities for monitoring the ODBC connection in real time. Let's look at each of these in turn.

Access Registry Settings

To have Access automatically generate ODBC trace files, you'll need to modify your Windows Registry. The Registry is a database of configuration information maintained by Windows itself. Almost everything about the way your copy of Windows is set up—your default colors, the OLE Servers you have installed, even the documents you have most recently used—is stored in the Registry.

You can't read the Registry directly. However, Windows NT and Windows 95 ship with a special utility called the Registry Editor, REGEDT32.EXE. By default, there is no icon for this application in any version of Windows. You'll have to use Program Manager or Explorer to create your own. You'll find the tool in the Windows system directory.

Depending on your operating system, the Registry Editor will look like something like Figure 5.7. (The Windows NT version of the Registry Editor is somewhat less flashy than the Windows 95 version.) The Registry stores all of its information in a hierarchical view. The levels of the hierarchy are called *keys*. The top level consists of six to eight root keys. All of the information which controls Access and Jet is somewhere under the HKEY_LOCAL_MACHINE root key.

To set up ODBC tracing, you'll need to make some changes under the key \HKEY_LOCAL_MACHINE\SOFTWARE\Microsoft\Jet\3.0\Engines.

FIGURE 5.7:

Registry Editor showing ODBC tracing keys

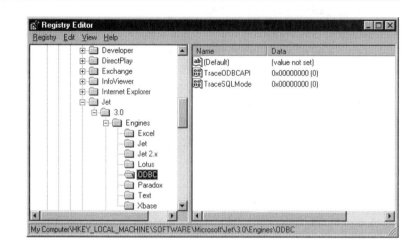

First, you need to add a new key under this key named ODBC. To do this, you can select Edit ➤ Add Key from the menu. Once you have created this key, you can create values directly in it with Edit ➤ Add Value. The two values that enable ODBC tracing are shown in Table 5.16.

NOTE   Settings made under this key will affect all software, including Access 95, Excel 95, and Visual Basic 4.0, that use the Jet 3.0 Engine. If you want to make settings that only affect Access, use the key \HKEY_LOCAL_ MACHINE\SOFTWARE\Microsoft\ Access\7.0\Jet\3.0\Engines instead.

To turn on either of these tracing modes, set the value of the appropriate key to 1. These options will take effect as soon as you restart Access.

You'll find that the trace files turn up in whatever your current default directory is under Windows 95. You can check the current directory from within Access with the CurDir function, and set it with the ChDir and ChDrive functions.

TABLE 5.16: Registry Settings for ODBC Tracing

Key	Purpose	File Name
TraceSQLMode	Trace all SQL Statements sent to the ODBC driver.	SQLOUT.TXT
TraceODBCAPI	Trace all ODBC calls made to the driver.	ODBCAPI.TXT

To see how these trace files work, look at the query in Figure 5.8. This query joins six tables from our Food sample database to produce a query that takes some time to run (long enough that sample timings can be meaningful). We'll be using this query for all of our tracing examples.

FIGURE 5.8:

The sample query for tracing

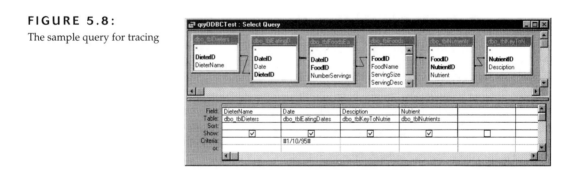

The simpler of the trace files is the SQLOUT.TXT. This file records all of the ODBC SQL calls made by Jet and sent to the Driver Manager for transmission to the driver and, ultimately, the database. When you run this query, here's the resulting SQLOUT.TXT:

```
SQLExecDirect: SELECT "dbo"."tblEating-
Dates"."DateID","dbo"."tblEatingDates"."DieterID" FROM
"dbo"."tblEatingDates"

SQLExecDirect: SELECT "DateID","Date","DieterID"  FROM
"dbo"."tblEatingDates"
```

```
SQLExecDirect: SELECT
"dbo"."tblDieters"."DieterID","dbo"."tblEating-
Dates"."DateID","dbo"."tblEatingDates"."DieterID","dbo"."tblFoo
ds"."FoodID","dbo"."tblFoodsEaten"."DateID","dbo"."tblFood-
sEaten"."FoodID","dbo"."tblKeyToNutrientIDs"."NutrientID","dbo"
."tblNutrients"."FoodID","dbo"."tblNutrients"."NutrientID"
FROM "dbo"."tblEatingDates","dbo"."tblFood-
sEaten","dbo"."tblFoods","dbo"."tblNutrients","dbo"."tblKeyToNu
trientIDs","dbo"."tblDieters" WHERE ((((((("dbo"."tblEating-
Dates"."Date" = {d '1995-01-10'} ) AND
("dbo"."tblEatingDates"."DateID" = "dbo"."tblFood-
sEaten"."DateID" ) ) AND ("dbo"."tblFoods"."FoodID" =
"dbo"."tblFoodsEaten"."FoodID" ) ) AND
("dbo"."tblFoods"."FoodID" = "dbo"."tblNutrients"."FoodID" )
) AND ("dbo"."tblKeyToNutrientIDs"."NutrientID" =
"dbo"."tblNutrients"."NutrientID" ) ) AND
("dbo"."tblDieters"."DieterID" = "dbo"."tblEating-
Dates"."DieterID" ) )

SQLPrepare: SELECT "DieterID","DieterName"  FROM
"dbo"."tblDieters"  WHERE "DieterID" = ? OR "DieterID" = ? OR
"DieterID" = ? OR "DieterID" = ? OR "DieterID" = ? OR
"DieterID" = ? OR "DieterID" = ? OR "DieterID" = ? OR
"DieterID" = ? OR "DieterID" = ?

SQLExecute: (MULTI-ROW FETCH)

SQLPrepare: SELECT "DateID","Date","DieterID"  FROM
"dbo"."tblEatingDates"  WHERE "DateID" = ? AND "DieterID" = ?
OR "DateID" = ? AND "DieterID" = ? OR "DateID" = ? AND
"DieterID" = ? OR "DateID" = ? AND "DieterID" = ? OR "DateID"
= ? AND "DieterID" = ? OR "DateID" = ? AND "DieterID" = ? OR
"DateID" = ? AND "DieterID" = ? OR "DateID" = ? AND
"DieterID" = ? OR "DateID" = ? AND "DieterID" = ? OR "DateID"
= ? AND "DieterID" = ?

SQLExecute: (MULTI-ROW FETCH)

SQLPrepare: SELECT "NutrientID","Desciption"  FROM
"dbo"."tblKeyToNutrientIDs"  WHERE "NutrientID" = ? OR "Nutri-
entID" = ? OR "NutrientID" = ? OR "NutrientID" = ? OR
"NutrientID" = ? OR "NutrientID" = ? OR "NutrientID" = ? OR
"NutrientID" = ? OR "NutrientID" = ? OR "NutrientID" = ?

SQLExecute: (MULTI-ROW FETCH)
```

```
SQLPrepare: SELECT "FoodID","NutrientID","Nutrient"  FROM
"dbo"."tblNutrients"  WHERE "FoodID" = ? AND "NutrientID" = ?
OR "FoodID" = ? AND "NutrientID" = ? OR "FoodID" = ? AND "Nu-
trientID" = ? OR "FoodID" = ? AND "NutrientID" = ? OR
"FoodID" = ? AND "NutrientID" = ? OR "FoodID" = ? AND "Nutri-
entID" = ? OR "FoodID" = ? AND "NutrientID" = ? OR "FoodID" =
? AND "NutrientID" = ? OR "FoodID" = ? AND "NutrientID" = ?
OR "FoodID" = ? AND "NutrientID" = ?

SQLExecute: (MULTI-ROW FETCH)
SQLExecute: (MULTI-ROW FETCH)
SQLExecute: (MULTI-ROW FETCH)
SQLExecute: (MULTI-ROW FETCH)
SQLExecute: (MULTI-ROW FETCH)
SQLExecute: (MULTI-ROW FETCH)
SQLExecute: (MULTI-ROW FETCH)
SQLExecute: (MULTI-ROW FETCH)
SQLExecute: (MULTI-ROW FETCH)
SQLExecute: (MULTI-ROW FETCH)
SQLExecute: (MULTI-ROW FETCH)
SQLExecute: (MULTI-ROW FETCH)
SQLExecute: (MULTI-ROW FETCH)
SQLExecute: (MULTI-ROW FETCH)
SQLExecute: (MULTI-ROW FETCH)
SQLExecute: (MULTI-ROW FETCH)
SQLExecute: (MULTI-ROW FETCH)
SQLExecute: (MULTI-ROW FETCH)
SQLExecute: (MULTI-ROW FETCH)
SQLExecute: (MULTI-ROW FETCH)
SQLExecute: (MULTI-ROW FETCH)
SQLExecute: (MULTI-ROW FETCH)
SQLExecute: (MULTI-ROW FETCH)
SQLExecute: (MULTI-ROW FETCH)
SQLExecute: (MULTI-ROW FETCH)
```

The SQLOUT.TXT file is mainly of interest when you're suspicious that Jet is not doing a good job of breaking the query up to send to the server. Here you're in pretty good shape. The Jet Engine has chosen to fetch all the rows from one of the smaller tables, and then it has used prepared statements on the server to resolve the query.

The ODBCAPI.TXT file is considerably more detailed. It records the actual API calls made between Jet and the ODBC layer. Here's a small portion of the ODBCAPI.TXT file for this query:

```
SQLAllocStmt(hdbc004321DC, phstmt00432E7C);
SQLGetStmtOption(hstmt00432E7C, 0, pvParam);
SQLSetStmtOption(hstmt00432E7C, 0, 0000003C);
SQLGetStmtOption(hstmt00432E7C, 3, pvParam);
SQLSetStmtOption(hstmt00432E7C, 3, 7FFFFFFE);
SQLStatistics(hstmt00432E7C, "(null)", -3, "dbo.tblEating-
Dates", 3, "tblEatingDates", -3, 1, 0);
SQLNumResultCols(hstmt00432E7C, pccol);
SQLFetch(hstmt00432E7C);
SQLGetData(hstmt00432E7C, 2, 99, rgbValue, 63, pcbValue);
SQLGetData(hstmt00432E7C, 3, 99, rgbValue, 63, pcbValue);
SQLGetData(hstmt00432E7C, 4, 99, rgbValue, 2, pcbValue);
SQLGetData(hstmt00432E7C, 5, 99, rgbValue, 254, pcbValue);
SQLGetData(hstmt00432E7C, 6, 99, rgbValue, 254, pcbValue);
SQLGetData(hstmt00432E7C, 7, 99, rgbValue, 2, pcbValue);
SQLGetData(hstmt00432E7C, 11, 99, rgbValue, 4, pcbValue);
SQLGetData(hstmt00432E7C, 12, 99, rgbValue, 4, pcbValue);
SQLFetch(hstmt00432E7C);
```

As you can see, the ODBCAPI.TXT file presumes substantial understanding of the API, since it shows you the individual calls and their parameters. To decipher this, you'll need a copy of the ODBC Software Development Kit, which may be found on the Microsoft Developer's Library CD-ROM. These ODBCAPI.TXT trace files are mainly of interest when you're working with a driver vendor trying to track down some sort of conformance problem.

WARNING If you enable either of these tracing flags, be absolutely sure to go back into the registry and disable them (by setting the values of the appropriate keys back to zero) when you're done. Trace files can build up on your drive at an alarming rate. For example, the ODBCAPI.TXT file for just running this one query takes up over a megabyte of disk space.

ODBC Spy

The ODBC Software Development Kit (SDK) contains a utility called ODBC Spy. This utility provides a real-time equivalent of the TraceSQlMode Registry setting. Figure 5.9 shows a part of our test query as it appears in ODBC Spy.

FIGURE 5.9:

Query tracing with ODBC Spy

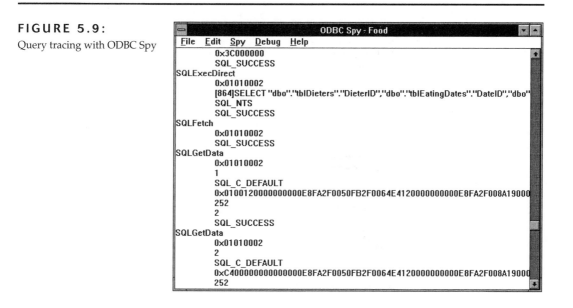

To install ODBC Spy, you'll need to obtain the Microsoft Development Platform (also known as the Microsoft Developer's Network, Level 2). The ODBC SDK is just one of the many development kits and operating system utilities contained on this series of CD-ROMs. When you run the ODBC SDK Setup, one of the utilities installed is ODBC Spy. If you're installing to Windows NT, both 16- and 32-bit versions of ODBC Spy are provided. If you install to Windows 95, only the 16-bit version is installed. To trace ODBC calls from Access 95, you must use the 32-bit ODBC Spy, and it must be installed on the same machine as Access 95 itself.

NOTE   If you have both Windows NT and Windows 95 available, you can copy the contents of the odbcsdk\bin32 directory from a Windows NT installation of the ODBC SDK to your Windows 95 machine. This directory contains ODBCSP32.EXE, which is the 32-bit version of ODBC Spy, and it will run on Windows 95. However, as recently as October 1995 (the most recent version we were able to test for this book), the 32-bit version of ODBC Spy seems to be somewhat unstable on Windows 95, producing random "illegal operation" faults. Presumably, the next release of the ODBC SDK will contain a native Windows 95 version of this utility.

To start tracing ODBC calls with ODBC Spy, choose Spy ➤ Capture from the menus. This allows you to choose a data source and decide whether you want to trace to the screen, a disk file (to which you can assign a name), or both. Figure 5.10 shows ODBC Spy being configured to spy on our Food database.

FIGURE 5.10:

Configuring ODBC Spy

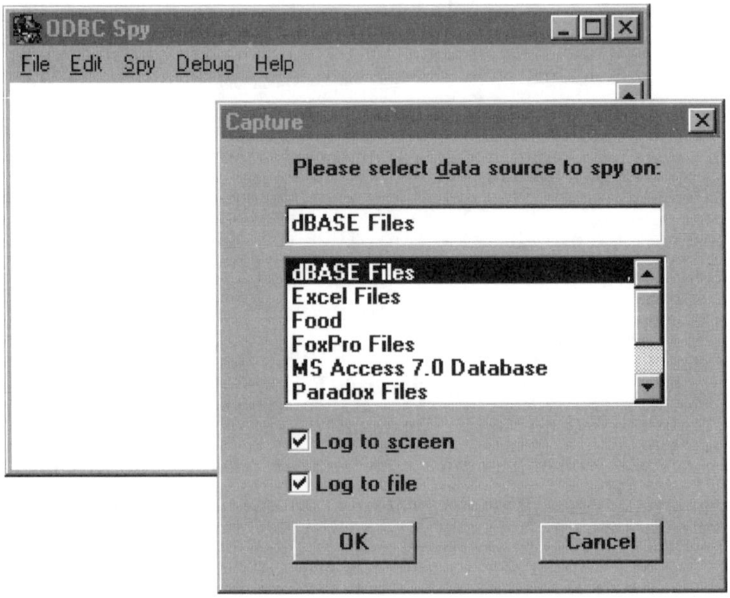

Once you've activated the capture in this way, simply proceed to use your Access database just as you otherwise would. Every bit of ODBC SQL sent from Jet to the Driver Manager will appear on screen, and, if you've specified a disk file, be saved to disk as well. In fact, ODBC Spy will even capture some calls that you won't see in the SQLOUT.TXT file. This utility inserts itself between the Driver Manager and the driver, so it will show you calls that originated in the Driver Manager in addition to those that originated in your application.

ODBC Spy also has the ability to play back calls if you've recorded them to a disk file. This is very useful if some call is failing and you don't quite understand why. You can load a log file, set a breakpoint just before the failing line, and then single step through it.

WARNING ODBC Spy works by actually modifying your ODBC.INI file to redirect calls to it on the way to the driver. You'll want to save a backup of this file before using ODBC Spy; otherwise, a system crash could leave this .INI file permanently damaged.

SQLEYE

If you would like to see what's going on at the last step of the ODBC calling chain, between the driver and SQL Server itself, you can use the SQLEYE utility. This is a freeware utility available from Microsoft. You can get it from the MSSQL forum on CompuServe, or from the TechNet CD-ROM subscription. For use with SQL Server 6.0, you'll need to get SQLEYE 2.0, which also includes a version for SQL Server 4.21. You can also use the earlier SQLEYE 1.0 with SQL Server 4.21.

SQLEYE provides real-time monitoring of the communications between your driver and the SQL Server, in both directions. Figure 5.11 shows a fairly typical moment in the progress of an Access query. Here Access has opened two connections to the server, one for the key set and one for the actual data.

FIGURE 5.11:

Monitoring a SQL connection
with SQLEYE

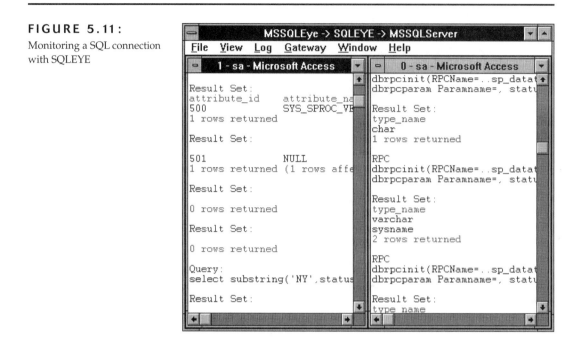

SQLEYE can show you all of the communications in both directions,
including:

- Queries being sent to the SQL Server
- Results returned
- Row counts
- Messages
- Errors
- Attentions

SQLEYE runs on the server, and will track all of the connections to the
server at the same time. This makes it an ideal tool for the network administrator who wants to keep an eye on network traffic, as well as the

programmer trying to debug a specific problem. Installing SQLEYE requires modifying the Registry, so it's not for the faint of heart, but there are full instructions supplied with the program.

Timing Queries

Monitoring is fine when you're trying to track down a logic error in your application, or when you need to diagnose a driver conformance problem. But all the monitoring in the world won't show you where the bottlenecks in your application are. For that, you need to dig in and actually time your queries, and decide which ones need to be rewritten.

Unfortunately, timing is really the only way to do this. There's no rule of thumb that works for all queries at all times. Many factors go into determining the relative speed of different ways of retrieving data. These include:

- Complexity of the query
- Speed of the client machine
- Amount of memory on the client
- Amount of memory on the server
- Size of the server database
- Actual network topology
- Number of network users

If you want to do serious performance tuning, you'll need to test in an environment that resembles your production environment as closely as possible.

Windows Timing Functions

Since there's a clock in your computer, it's not surprising that Windows itself has an API call for timing. Actually, it has at least three different

API calls, all of which are illustrated in the basTimer module in CH5ODBC.MDB:

- GetTickCount
- timeGetTime
- QueryPerformanceCounter

GetTickCount is the original Windows timing function introduced with Windows 2.0. It returns the number of milliseconds since Windows was started on the machine. (One trivia note: Since GetTick-Count returns a long integer, after 49.7 days it wraps around and starts counting up from zero. This assumes that any Windows machine could ever be kept running for 49.7 days without a reboot.) Or rather, that's what the documentation claims. Actually, although the value returned by GetTickCount is a number of milliseconds, it's only updated once every 18.5 milliseconds. So although the number claims to be accurate to a single millisecond, it's only precise to 18.5 milliseconds.

The timeGetTime function was introduced with the multimedia extensions to Windows 3.0, and it still resides in the main Windows multimedia library (now WINMM.DLL rather than the original MMSYSTEM.DLL). To handle tasks such as playing sound files and precisely updating graphics, Windows needed a timer with more precision. The hardware was there; it was merely a matter of providing a software interface.

Even more precision was required when developing the Performance Monitor interface in Windows NT. Since Windows NT is cross-platform, the QueryPerformanceFrequency and QueryPerformanceCounter functions were introduced to provide a way to utilize the maximum precision of the hardware, whatever that might be. QueryPerformanceFrequency returns the number of beats per second that this counter measures, and QueryPerformanceCounter returns the actual number of counts. On one Intel Pentium system we tested, this gives a precision to roughly 800 nanoseconds.

In our timing measurements, we've taken the middle road and used the timeGetTime API call. There are two reasons for using this instead of QueryPerformanceCounter. First, there is no guarantee that any particular 32-bit system actually supports this call. Second, the counts and frequencies from the QueryPerformance calls are returned as 64-bit integers, which Access has no native capability to deal with. If you want to use these calls, you'll have to work out your own 64-bit math routines to manipulate them. The sample database includes the procedure TestPerformanceCounter to show you the frequency of the counter in your own hardware.

Setting up a Reliable Testbed

There are many factors you need to consider when running timing tests. It's simply not enough to compare the time it takes to run a query two separate ways. The same query won't take the same amount of time twice in a row. To do reasonable comparisons, you'll want to:

- Run the query multiple times, since Access, Windows, and the server may all cache data.
- Use a realistic amount of data on the server side. You want to be sure the server is using the same execution plan that it will use in practice.
- Test during a normal network load. It may be tempting to delay your testing to off hours so as not to inconvenience users, but you must confirm it with the usual number of people logged in to the system.

You'll also need to give some consideration to deciding exactly what you want to test. Is it the time it takes to retrieve the first record in a set? The time it takes to retrieve all records from a SELECT statement? The time it takes to process an UPDATE or DELETE? The only way to decide what's important is to look at your application and locate the places where your users feel processing is too slow. Concentrate your resources on the trouble spots first. You also need to consider the pattern of access. An application where users frequently retrieve the same set of data multiple times will differ in performance from one where querying tends to be more evenly distributed across the data. Your goal when doing timings should be to invent a set of tests that reflect the actual usage patterns of your application as accurately as possible.

You also need to consider whether you're comparing identical queries with two different execution methods or something else might be interfering. For example, by default the SQL Server ODBC driver will create temporary stored procedures for prepared queries, and Access itself will send prepared queries. If you test this against just passing the query through ODBC, you'll find that Access shows up as being much faster than ODBC. But if you rewrite your ODBC call to use stored procedures so it's on an even footing with Access, you'll see that it becomes faster once again.

Sample Timings

As an example of timing, we tested a single query using the three methods explored in this chapter: directly against linked tables, through the ODBC API, and using RDO. The timings were done on a Pentium 90 with 32 MB of RAM, and no applications besides Access 95 were running on Windows 95. The server was a 486-DX266 with 32 MB of RAM, running Windows NT Server 3.51. The network was a very lightly loaded 10BaseT network with 6 machines connected to it.

The query we tested was run five times with each method. Figure 5.12 shows this query in design view, though we actually used SQL statements in code to compare timings.

In this particular situation, we received the results shown in Figure 5.13, which was taken from the Debug Window in Access. We found RDO mildly superior to using attached tables, and the ODBC API markedly faster than either of the other alternatives. As you'll see

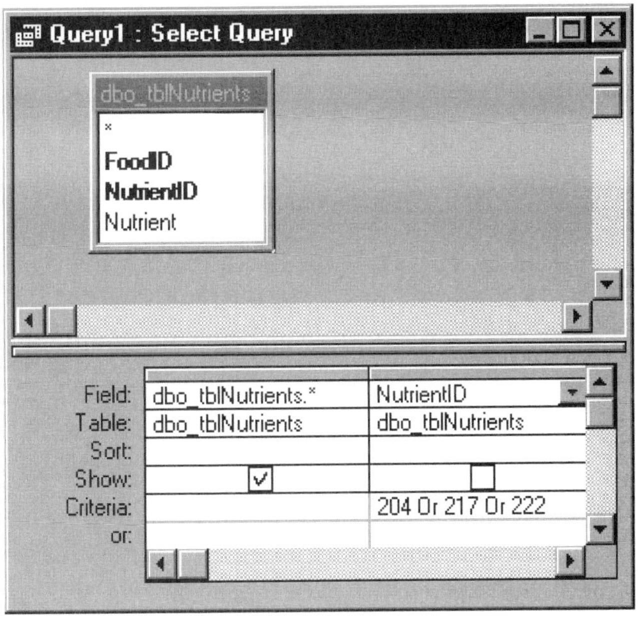

FIGURE 5.12:

Sample query used in timing tests

in the code, what we measured was the time it took to open and close the identical dynaset using all three methods. Depending on your application, of course, you may want to construct a more realistic test than this, perhaps one which uses a mix of queries to simulate people working with different data over the course of a day.

NOTE   In general, it seems that the Jet Engine keeps up well with the other methods of querying when you're executing SELECT statements. UPDATE, APPEND, and DELETE statements (the equivalent of Access action queries) are much better candidates for optimization by moving to passthrough or RDO. It's not unusual to see a 100-to-1 speedup when executing a DELETE via passthrough.

FIGURE 5.13:

Timings for the sample query.

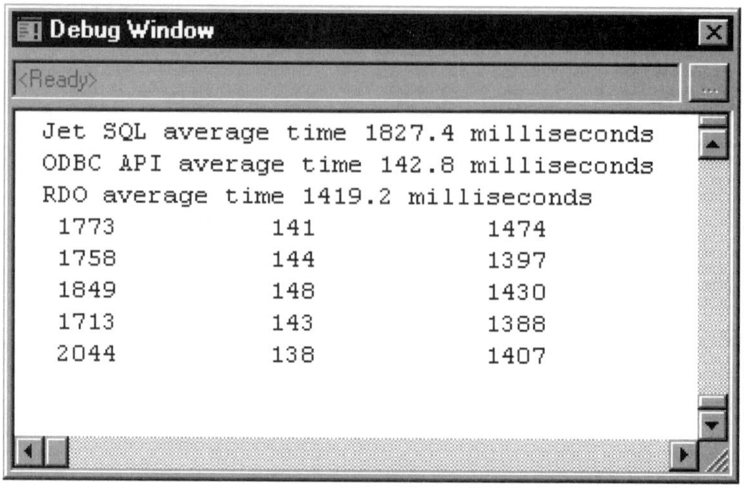

```
Debug Window

<Ready>

Jet SQL average time 1827.4 milliseconds
ODBC API average time 142.8 milliseconds
RDO average time 1419.2 milliseconds
    1773            141            1474
    1758            144            1397
    1849            148            1430
    1713            143            1388
    2044            138            1407
```

These timings were generated by the CompareTimes sub in basTimer. Let's take a look at this procedure. It starts by doing the necessary work to set up both an ODBC connection and an RDO connection. For ODBC, we'll use the "recordset" wrappers previously discussed. For RDO, we'll simply write the code directly in this function. In a real application we'd likely open a connection and then use it a number of times; therefore we've chosen to do this outside of the timing loop. This heading section is also where we specify the number of times we want to run each test, and include the SQL statements to test. Note that two SQL statements are needed—the Jet Engine version and the equivalent SQL Server statement. This is one more place where ANSI SQL compliance in all Microsoft products would help immensely.

All code relating to RDO is between #If...#End If pairs. This way, if you don't have RDO installed on your machine, you only have to change a single compilation constant in the module's Declarations section.

```
Sub CompareTimes()
' Compare times for a query run in multiple ways
    Const intRuns = 5
```

```
Dim rst As Recordset
Dim lngCount(3, intRuns) As Long
Dim lngTotalCount As Long
Dim i As Integer
Dim strJetSQL As String
Dim strSQL As String
Dim intRet As Integer
Dim rdoEnv As RDO.rdoEnvironment
Dim rdoConn As RDO.rdoConnection
Dim rdoResults As RDO.rdoResultset

' SQL Statement to use with Jet
strJetSQL = "SELECT * FROM dbo_tblNutrients WHERE " & _
    "((NutrientID = 204) OR (NutrientID = 217) " & _
    "OR (NutrientID = 222));"
' Equivalent ODBC SQL Statement
strSQL = "SELECT * FROM Food.dbo.tblNutrients WHERE " & _
    "((NutrientID = 204) OR (NutrientID = 217) OR " & _
    "(NutrientID = 222))"

' Set up test parameters and connections
' Jet
CurrentDb.QueryTimeout = 0
' ODPC API
intRet = rODBCConnect("Food", "sa", "")
'RDO
#If RDOInstalled Then
    rdoEngine.rdoDefaultCursorDriver = rdUseOdbc
    Set rdoEnv = rdoEngine.rdoCreateEnvironment _
        ("", "", "")
    Set rdoConn = rdoEnv.OpenConnection _
        ("Food", rdDriverNoPrompt, False, _
        "UID=sa;DATABASE=Food")
    rdoConn.QueryTimeout = 0
#End If
```

Testing the Jet Engine with linked tables is relatively simple. We've already linked the tables directly through the Database Explorer, so all the timing function needs to do is open a dynaset on the records. Notice that we take times before and after using oTimeGetTime and store the difference in an array.

```
For i = 1 To 5
    ' Test Jet
    Debug.Print "Jet SQL Run #" & i
    lngCount(1, i) = oTimeGetTime()
    Set rst = CurrentDb.OpenRecordset(strJetSQL, dbOpen_
Dynaset)
    rst.Close
    lngCount(1, i) = oTimeGetTime() - lngCount(1, i)
```

For ODBC, we do the same operations, only here we use our wrapper functions. Since we're trying to compare as evenly as possible, we need to make sure to pass the same flags, in this case opening an ODBC dynaset.

```
' Test direct ODBC API
Debug.Print "ODBC API Run #" & i
lngCount(2, i) = oTimeGetTime()
intRet = rODBCOpenRecordset(strSQL, dbOpenDynaset)
intRet = rODBCCloseRecordset()
lngCount(2, i) = oTimeGetTime() - lngCount(2, i)
```

To test RDO, we do the same thing a third time, making allowances for the differing syntax enforced by RDO (rdoResultset instead of recordset, rdOpenDynamic instead of dbOpenDynaset, and so on).

```
#If RDOInstalled Then
    ' Test RDO
    Debug.Print "RDO Run #" & i
    lngCount(3, i) = oTimeGetTime()
    Set rdoResults = rdoConn.OpenResultset _
        (strSQL, rdOpenDynamic, rdConcurRowver)
    rdoResults.Close
    lngCount(3, i) = oTimeGetTime() - lngCount(3, i)
#End If
Next i
```

The function ends by closing down the connections and then calculates the relative times taken by each method of running the query.

```
' Cleanup
#If RDOInstalled Then
    rdoConn.Close
    rdoEnv.Close
#End If
intRet = rODBCDisconnect()
```

```
' And tote up the results
lngTotalCount = 0
For i = 1 To intRuns
    lngTotalCount = lngTotalCount + lngCount(1, i)
Next i
Debug.Print "Jet SQL average time " & _
    lngTotalCount / intRuns & " milliseconds"
lngTotalCount = 0
For i = 1 To intRuns
    lngTotalCount = lngTotalCount + lngCount(2, i)
Next i
Debug.Print "ODBC API average time " & _
    lngTotalCount / intRuns & " milliseconds"
#If RDOInstalled Then
    lngTotalCount = 0
    For i = 1 To intRuns
        lngTotalCount = lngTotalCount + lngCount(3, i)
    Next i
    Debug.Print "RDO average time " & _
        lngTotalCount / intRuns & " milliseconds"
#End If
For i = 1 To intRuns
    Debug.Print lngCount(1, i), _
        lngCount(2, i), lngCount(3, i)
Next i
End Sub
```

We can't emphasize enough that you should not conclude anything about speed from this single test! We could run other examples that would show Jet faster than ODBC, or RDO slower than Jet. You need to think long and hard about what your testbed situation should look like to most accurately reflect the way that your application is used in practice. And remember, there are other tradeoffs besides speed. You also need to consider ease of coding and ease of maintenance when planning the query strategy for your application.

Summary

In this chapter, we've drilled down into the real heart of the Access-SQL Server connection: Open Database Connectivity. All of the methods we've looked at for retrieving data, including linked tables, passthrough queries, API calls, and Remote Data Objects, use this same pipeline to get their results. For the most part, once you're hooked up to a data source, you can ignore these low-level details entirely. However, you may find from time to time that your application has performance problems that can only be solved by working at a very low level. If this is the case, the code described in this chapter should provide a solid base for increasing your understanding of how ODBC functions.

CHAPTER

SIX

The Access Upsizing Tools

- What is upsizing?

- Using the Upsizing Wizard

- Using the SQL Browser

- Optimizing upsized applications

Y ou'll find many references to "upsizing" and "downsizing" in the computer world these days. As traditional mainframe-based organizations introduce desktop PCs into their operations, they often undertake a downsizing process to bring data to the individual desktops. Conversely, small businesses that grow large enough to require a database server find themselves needing to upsize databases developed for individual users into client/server applications. To help this second population of users, Microsoft has developed a set of Upsizing Tools for Access. These tools can help you take an existing Access application and move its data to SQL Server.

The Upsizing Tools package consists of the Upsizing Wizard and the SQL-Server Browser. The Upsizing Wizard makes upsizing an Access database to SQL Server practically pain-free. It takes your tables and creates equivalent (or nearly equivalent) tables in SQL Server. These tables are created with fields, indexes, and defaults that match those in the original Access database as closely as possible. The Upsizing Wizard also translates validation rules and relations by creating triggers in the SQL Server database. If necessary, the Upsizing Wizard will build queries that hide differences in field and table names on Access and SQL Server from the rest of your application. If you choose, you can have the newly created SQL Server tables linked directly to your Access database. The original tables will be saved as local tables.

Versions of Upsizing Tools

Microsoft originally released the Upsizing Tools for Access as a commercial product. This Upsizing Tools 1.0 release runs in Access 2.0. The new Upsizing Tools 2.0 runs in Access 95 and comes in two versions, one each for SQL Server 4.21 and SQL Server 6.0. Upsizing Tools 2.0 is free, available for download from the Microsoft Network and on the Microsoft Developer's Network CD-ROM.

Upsizing Tools 1.0

Upsizing Tools 1.0 works only with Access 2.0 databases and Microsoft SQL Server 4.21. It installs like any other Access 2.0 add-in and creates two entries on the File ➤ Add-Ins menu, one for the Upsizing Wizard and one for the SQL-Server Browser.

Upsizing Tools 2.0

Upsizing Tools 2.0 works only with Access 95. This new release exists in two different versions. The first is a direct port of the existing version, which supports upsizing Access 95 databases to either SQL Server 4.21 or SQL Server 6.0. This version acts very much like Upsizing Tools 1.0 in building triggers—in other words, it does not take advantage of new SQL Server 6.0 functionality. The second version supports upsizing Access 95 databases to SQL Server 6.0 only. This version takes advantage of new SQL Server 6.0 functionality including the Identity datatype to replace Access AutoNumber fields and SQL Server's Declarative Referential Integrity (DRI) support.

NOTE The conversion from Access 95 referential integrity to SQL Server 6.0 DRI is not perfect. SQL Server 6.0 does not support cascading updates or cascading deletes. If you upsize an Access database that makes use of these features, Upsizing Tools will offer you the option of either using SQL Server DRI and losing cascades, or using triggers and preserving cascades.

Upsizing from Access 2.0 to SQL Server 6.0

You cannot upsize directly from an Access 2.0 database to SQL Server 6.0 with either version of Upsizing Tools. If you need to upsize from Access 2.0 to SQL Server 6.0, you have two options. The first option is to convert your Access 2.0 application to Access 95 and run the Upsizing Wizard 2.0. The other option is to use the Access 2.0 Upsizing Wizard to upsize to SQL Server 4.21, and then use the Transfer Manager to convert your SQL database to SQL Server 6.0. Either option requires some additional manual work to finish the process.

If you convert and then upsize, the end result will be an Access 95 version of your database with linked SQL Server 6.0 tables. To finish the process in this case, you need to return to your original Access 2.0 database and make these changes:

- Rename the existing Access tables with the "_local" suffix.

- Link the new SQL Server tables to the Access 2.0 database.

- For cases where the Upsizing Wizard created an alias query, because either a table name or a field name needed to be changed in SQL Server, recreate the same queries in the Access 2.0 database. (You should be able to just cut and paste the SQL statement from the Access 95 alias query.)

If you upsize and then transfer, you need to do some manual work before running Transfer Manager. In particular, you must check all of the triggers created by the Upsizing Wizard. Upsizing Wizard 1.0 will create triggers that include double quotes embedded in single-quoted strings. This syntax is illegal on SQL Server 6.0. You can use a tool such as SQL Object Manager from SQL Server 4.21 to review and edit all of the triggers. After you do this, you should have no trouble using Transfer Manager to move the SQL Server 4.21 database to SQL Server 6.0. You'll then need to change the ODBC data source being used by the Access database to point to the 6.0 version of the data.

Why Upsize?

The major reasons for upsizing are the same reasons for moving to client/server computing in the first place. The end result of upsizing an existing Access application should be identical to originally creating the application as client/server. Upsizing can make this process easier by taking tables that you've already designed and moving them to the server.

In general, it makes sense to upsize an Access database when you feel you've reached the limits of Access and need some of the additional capabilities that SQL Server provides. Many people choose to upsize to address performance issues, but there are many other good reasons to move your data from Access to SQL Server.

Performance

Probably the most popular reason to upsize an Access database is the perception that "client/server is faster." This is an assumption many people seem to make because it costs so much more to set up a client/server database than a file/server database. Unfortunately this assumption is not necessarily true. There are many good reasons to move your data from Access to a server database, but you shouldn't count on additional speed without testing and retuning your application. Upsizing will quickly move your data from the client to the server, but you must be prepared to apply the new query techniques and other optimizations discussed in the first several chapters of this book after the upsizing process is finished.

Better Reasons

Better reasons to upsize an Access database to SQL Server revolve around the relative capabilities of the two products. SQL Server has many features that just aren't offered in Access. As your data becomes more critical, and you need better management tools to keep track of it and protect it from accidental damage, storing your data in SQL Server becomes more and more attractive. Table 6.1 sums up some of the important areas where SQL Server has an advantage over Access.

TABLE 6.1: Comparing SQL Server to Access

Feature	Access	SQL Server
Management of distributed data	If your data is stored on multiple computers, you must manage each individual database separately.	Can manage multiple databases on different servers from a single computer using tools such as SQL Enterprise Manager.
Scalability	Only uses a single CPU, even in multi-processor machines.	Will use multiple CPUs for increased performance.
Maximum database size	1 gigabyte.	1 terabyte (1,000 gigabytes).
Querying via Mail	Not available.	Supports queries via Microsoft Mail.
Transaction logging	Not available.	All transactions are logged by default.
Deadlock and livelock resolution	Not available.	Automatic.
Dynamic backup	Database must be closed before being backed up.	Database can be backed up even when it is in active use.
Automatic Recovery	Not available.	Automatic.
Device mirroring	Not available.	Can be installed for any device.
Integrated security	Uses its own security system.	Can be set up to use operating system security.

So It Exports Tables—What Else Does It Do?

If you think that the upsizing process only includes exporting Access tables to SQL Server and linking to the exported tables, you might wonder why a product like the Upsizing Wizard is even necessary. Although the upsizing process is the basis of its operation, the Upsizing Wizard performs a number of other functions. First, it makes any changes necessary to make table and field names legal on SQL Server. In an Access table, you can name a field with a space in the name, or give a field the same name as a SQL Server keyword such as "count." The Upsizing Wizard will translate these to legal names on the server tables, and then build queries to map the server tables back to the original Access names. For example, an Access field named "Customer ID" will be upsized to a SQL Server field named "Customer_ID." The Upsizing Wizard will then build a query named "Customers" to replace the original "Customers" table. In this query, it will include a calculated field using the expression "Customer ID: Customer_ID" to map the new field name back to the old one.

In addition to exporting your Access tables, the Upsizing Wizard will also duplicate the data structure and rules by converting Access indexes and default values to indexes and defaults on the server. It will translate relationships into equivalent triggers. None of these actions occur by default if you just use the Access menus to export tables to a SQL Server database. The Upsizing Wizard can save you a great deal of tedious work by automating these processes.

When it's all finished exporting your tables, the Upsizing Wizard will link the finished SQL tables back to your original Access database.

The Upsizing Process

When you install Upsizing Tools 2.0, two options will appear on your Tools ➤ Add-ins menu:

- SQL-Server Browser
- Upsize to SQLServer

The SQL-Server Browser allows you to connect to an existing SQL Server data source. It provides a user interface for the database you select that looks a lot like the Access user interface. Instead of tabs for Tables, Queries, Forms, Reports, Macros, and Modules, it has tabs for Table, View, Default, Rule, and Proc. SQL-Server Browser is discussed in more detail later in this chapter.

To start the upsizing process, you must load the existing database that you want to upsize, and then choose Tools ➤ Add-ins ➤ Upsize to SQLServer.

Creating a New Database

When you select Upsize to SQLServer, Access loads the Upsizing Wizard. The first page of the wizard asks you if you want to create a new database or upsize to an existing one, as shown in Figure 6.1. Generally speaking, if you are upsizing for the first time you will want to create a new database out of your Access database. If you select Create New Database you will then be asked to log on to the master database. If you are adding tables to an existing database, select the Use Existing Database option. When you click the Next button, you will be prompted to select a data source from the list of available ODBC data sources and log on to the server. You will need to supply a valid ID and password for this server database to continue.

FIGURE 6.1:

The first page of the Upsizing Wizard

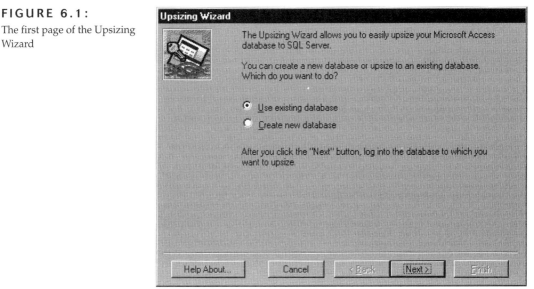

FIGURE 6.1:

The first page of the Upsizing Wizard

Choosing a Device

The next screen of the Upsizing Wizard, shown in Figure 6.2, asks you if you want to place your upsized database on an existing SQL Server device or create a new SQL Server device. You will most likely want to create a new device, especially if you are creating a new database. Of course, if you do not have room on an existing device you must create a new device. If you do not specify a device, the wizard will use the default device. Make sure that you create a sufficiently large device, as the device's size can't be easily modified once it's created. You will usually want to create a device with at least twice as much room as the Access database you are upsizing, and then add on another 2MB for good measure as it will also need to accommodate the log file. If you have multiple hard drives available on your SQL Server, you should create a second new device to hold the log file and place it on a drive other than the drive containing the main device.

FIGURE 6.2:

Creating a device

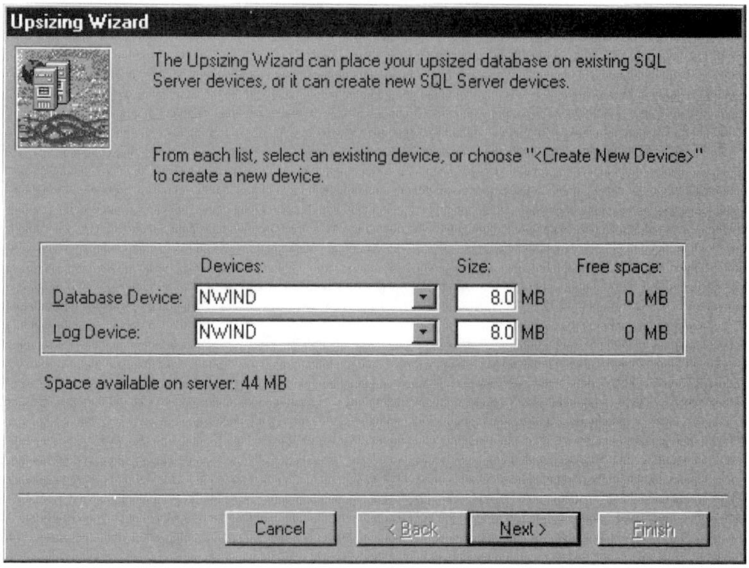

Naming the Database

The next screen of the Upsizing Wizard, as shown in Figure 6.3, asks you what you would like to name your new SQL Server database and how much space you would like to reserve for it. Database names are subject to the usual SQL Server rules for identifiers. That is, they can be up to 30 characters long and include letters, numbers, and the symbols #, $, and _. Spaces are prohibited. The size allowed must be at least 2MB, but can be up to the maximum available on the selected device. You will also need to fill in information about your required log size. Any log device you select must have at least 1MB of free space. If you do not have enough space for the database and the log file, you will run into errors during the upsizing process, and the wizard will not be able to finish its work.

FIGURE 6.3:

Naming the new database

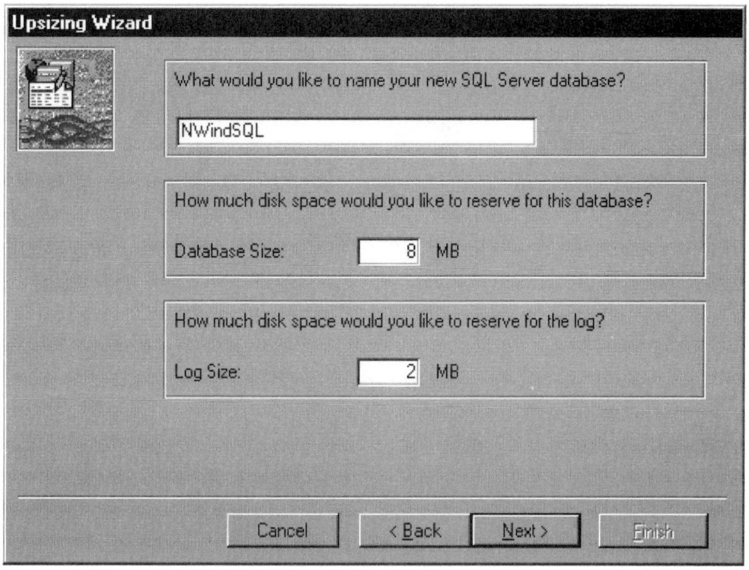

Selecting the Tables

The next screen asks you which tables you want to export to SQL Server. This is a useful option as you may want to keep some tables local, especially ones which are not updated frequently. For example, a lookup table whose values are fairly static, like a list of state abbreviations, is a good candidate for a local table. Figure 6.4 shows the table selection screen of the Upsizing Wizard.

Upsizing Attributes Options

The next screen lists table attributes you may want to upsize. Table 6.2 shows the choices you can make here and their consequences.

On this screen, shown in Figure 6.5, you can also select whether to link the newly created SQL Server tables to your Access database. If you

FIGURE 6.4:

Selecting tables to upsize

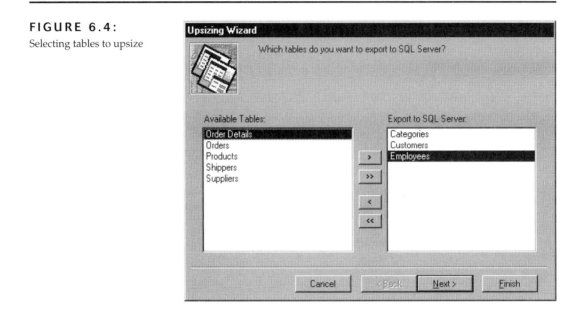

TABLE 6.2: Table Attributes You Can Upsize

Option	Effect
Indexes	Creates a SQL Server index on each field that was indexed in the original Access table.
Validation rules	Translates Access table validation rules to their equivalent stored procedures on SQL Server.
Defaults	Converts Access default values to insert triggers.
Table relationships	Maintains existing Access relationships and enforces referential integrity by creating insert, update, and delete triggers.
Add timestamp fields	Provides a unique key for any table containing Memo or OLE objects. This optimizes locating and updating records and ensures that changes to a record aren't improperly overwritten.
Structure only, no data	Creates an empty shell with the same structure as the Access database but leaves the data behind in the Access database.

FIGURE 6.5:

Upsizing table attributes

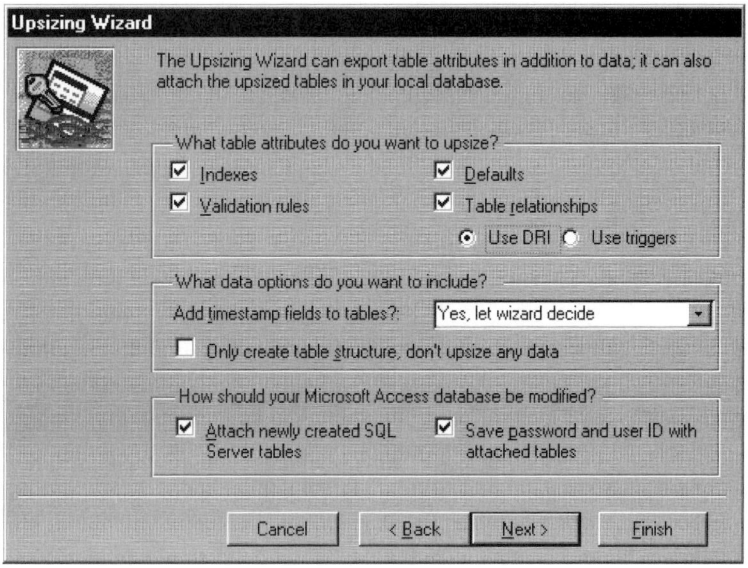

choose to link, the Wizard will link the SQL Server tables to your database and rename the original tables with the suffix "_local." For example, if you upsize the sample Northwinds database that ships with Access, the Orders table will be renamed Orders_local and the corresponding SQL Server table will be named Orders so that any objects referencing the Orders table will now point to the linked table instead of the original version.

SQL Server does not allow spaces in object identifiers, so if a table or field name includes spaces, these objects will be renamed, and the Upsizing Wizard will create a suffix "_remote" for the SQL Server table. Aliasing queries will then be created to reference the table. For example, if the Orders table had a field name with spaces in it, the aliasing query would be named Orders, the actual SQL Server table would be named Orders_remote, and the original local table would be renamed Orders_local. In this case, queries, forms, and reports based on the original Orders table will still work, since Access tables and queries are interchangeable as recordsources.

You can also specify whether or not to save your password and login ID with linked tables. You must enter your password and login ID when opening a linked table; this gives you the option of storing the user ID and password locally. This option can be a bit of a security risk—if you are logged on as the administrator when you upsize and select this option, subsequent users of the Access database will be using it under your permissions.

Creating an Upsizing Report

The last screen of the wizard, shown in Figure 6.6, gives you the option to create an upsizing report. Creating one is generally a good idea in case you need to document the process. If you close this report without saving or exporting it, the report is not saved in your local database; be sure to print the report before closing it.

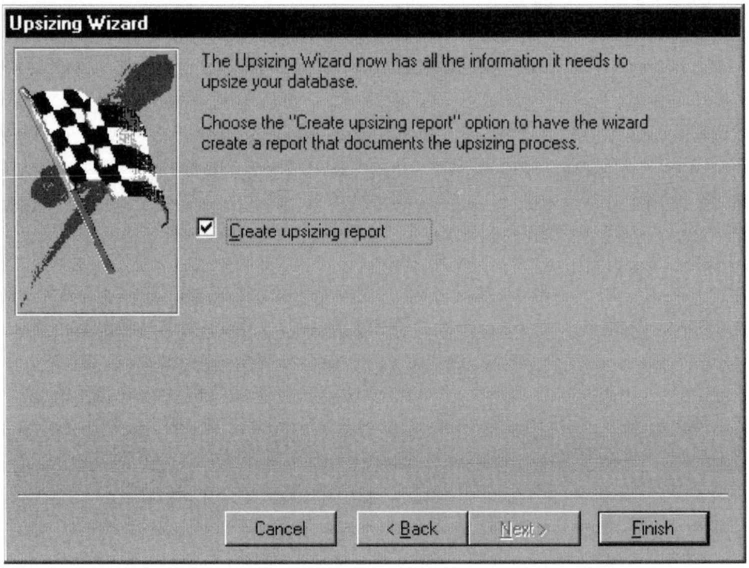

FIGURE 6.6:

The closing screen of the wizard

TIP

You can use the Office Links button on the Report toolbar and choose Publish It with MS Word to create an RTF file. You can then save it for later reference. This will take some time to run, depending on the size and complexity of your database. If you forget to do this, you can always open the Upsizing Wizard and print the report again since the information is stored in local tables in the wizard. Or you can simply link to the tables in the Wizard that store this information—the five tables whose names start with "UT_tblReport"—and browse the information that they contain at your leisure.

When you click Finish, the Upsizing Wizard warns that the upsizing process may be lengthy, but it will provide screens to keep you updated as to what it's doing along the way.

What the Wizard Does

As you'll see when you run the Upsizing Wizard, it does a great deal of work with your database. We'll explore the details of its operation in six areas:

- Indexes and validations
- Defaults
- Referential integrity
- Validation rules
- Datatypes
- Timestamps

Exporting Indexes and Validations

Since Access indexes are similar to SQL Server indexes, they convert well. Unique and non-unique indexes are the same in both products. The Upsizing Wizard converts an Access primary index into a SQL Server clustered, unique index named "AAAAA_PrimaryKey". This ensures that this index is chosen as the primary key when the table is linked back to Access. Access decides which index to use for a primary key by choosing the first one in alphabetical order. This comparison is case-sensitive, so be aware that an index named "ZABAR" will be chosen ahead of an index prefaced with "aaa," even though "a" precedes "Z" in the alphabet.

WARNING When upsizing tables, you must beware of floating point values (either single or double) used as primary keys. Floating point primary keys will not function properly when these tables are linked back to Access. When Access goes to read data from a table, it first reads the primary key and then uses that key to request other fields from the table. SQL Server can store floating point values with more precision than Access—when the stored key is sent back to the server there might not be a match, and Access will be unable to find the data.

Access exports table and field validation rules by creating custom UPDATE and INSERT triggers on the SQL Server table. It might seem that SQL Server Rules would be a more natural translation, but the designers of the Upsizing Wizard opted to use triggers instead so that they could return custom error messages when the user attempts to violate the validation rule. SQL Server Rules have no provision for an error message that could be mapped back to the Access Validation Text property so that custom error messages can be displayed. Any Table or

Field validation rules are converted to Transact-SQL fragments. These fragments are then combined with any other fragments created later by the wizard to create the final UPDATE and INSERT triggers.

Exporting Defaults

Default expressions map more or less one-to-one from Access to SQL Server, with a few differences. In Access, defaults are associated with a particular field in a specific table. In SQL Server, they are independent and can be bound to any number of different fields. Any converted counter fields automatically have a zero default expression bound to them. Fields with a default of zero are bound to UW_ZeroDefault. Yes/No fields will have "no" default bound to them if you have not specified a default in Access.

Dealing with Referential Integrity

How relationships between tables are upsized depends on which version of the Upsizing Tools you are using. If you're using version 1.0 or the ported version 2.0, table relationships are converted to triggers. If you're using the rewritten version 2.0, table relationships are translated into PRIMARY KEY, FOREIGN KEY, and UNIQUE constraints on the tables. However, if you use the 2.0 Upsizing Tools and choose to preserve cascades when upsizing, the relationships are translated to triggers.

Relationships As Triggers

With the older version of the Upsizing Wizard, table relationships established in Access will be converted to Transact-SQL code in triggers. One relationship in Access maps to four SQL Server triggers: two for the parent table and two for the child table. If two tables are related in Access and only one is upsized, no triggers will be created in SQL Server.

Like Access relationships, SQL Server triggers cannot cross database boundaries.

The type of trigger created in SQL Server depends on the options selected in Access for enforcing referential integrity. If you selected to enforce referential integrity and cascade updates, then the trigger will also cascade updates to the child table and prevent deletions to the parent table where child records exist. The trigger on the child table will prevent users from making changes to the foreign key that would orphan the record or prevent them from adding a record that had no matching key in the parent table. The following code shows the trigger created to prevent deletion of category items if records exist in the Products table:

```
CREATE TRIGGER Categories_DTrig ON Categories FOR DELETE AS
/*
 * PREVENT DELETES IF DEPENDENT RECORDS IN 'Products'
 */
IF (SELECT COUNT(*) FROM deleted, Products WHERE
(deleted.CategoryID =
Products.CategoryID)) > O
    BEGIN
        RAISERROR 44445 'Cannot delete or change record. ⏎
Since related records exist in table ''Products'', ⏎
referential integrity rules would be violated.'
        ROLLBACK TRANSACTION
    END
```

NOTE   Upsizing Tools 1.0 used double quotes in triggers, whereas Upsizing Tools 2.0 uses a pair of single quotes. Double quotes nested inside single quotes are illegal in SQL Server 6.0.

Relationships As Constraints

When you use the newer revision of the 2.0 Upsizing Wizard, relationships are handled by the wizard when it creates the table. After exporting the tables from Access, the wizard uses an ALTER TABLE Transact-SQL Statement with the PRIMARY KEY clause on each table that has a primary key, and a similar statement with the FOREIGN KEY clause on each table that contains a foreign key.

NOTE Because SQL Server's Declarative Referential Integrity (DRI) does not support cascaded updates or deletes, it's impossible to map some Access relationships directly to SQL Server when using the newer version of the Upsizing Wizard. You may wish to use the older method of converting relationships to triggers when you are upsizing a database that makes heavy use of these cascade features.

Validation Rules

Triggers are also created for field-level validation and referential integrity rules. The following example shows the trigger created that does not allow a null value in the CompanyName field of the Customers table:

```
CREATE TRIGGER Customers_UTrig ON Customers FOR UPDATE AS
/*
 * PREVENT NULL VALUES IN 'CompanyName'
 */
IF (SELECT Count(*) FROM inserted WHERE CompanyName IS NULL) > 0
    BEGIN
        RAISERROR 44444 'Field ''CompanyName'' cannot contain
a null value.'
        ROLLBACK TRANSACTION
    END
```

The Upsizing Wizard is able to convert most, but not all, Access validation rules to equivalent checks on the SQL Server. If it's unable to convert a particular rule, an entry will appear on the upsizing report to indicate this.

Dealing with Datatypes

Most fields are converted to their SQL Server equivalent, with the possible exception of Counter fields, which are an unsupported datatype in SQL Server 4.21. The older version of the Upsizing Wizard creates a trigger to emulate the counter. This code fragment shows the part of the INSERT trigger for the CategoryID field in the Categories table:

```
/*
 * COUNTER-EMULATION CODE FOR FIELD 'CategoryID'
 */
SELECT @maxc = (SELECT Max(CategoryID) FROM Categories)
SELECT @newc = (SELECT CategoryID FROM inserted)
IF @newc = 0 OR @maxc <> @newc SELECT @maxc = @maxc + 1
UPDATE Categories SET CategoryID = @maxc WHERE CategoryID = @newc
```

In the newer version of the Upsizing Wizard, Access counter fields are converted to SQL Server Identity columns.

WARNING   Tables containing GUID fields cannot be successfully upsized. GUIDs are generated by code within the Jet Engine that uses a special function built into Jet. SQL Server does not offer an equivalent function.

Adding Timestamps

The Upsizing Wizard creates a timestamp field in each upsized table in which there are fields with Memo, OLE, or floating point datatypes. This is done to increase performance on updates. A timestamp is a special datatype on SQL Server which is automatically updated by the system whenever a record in a table is edited. Before it will save changes to a record, Access always checks to make sure it hasn't been edited by another user. If the table contains a timestamp column, Access only needs to check the value of the timestamp to determine whether data in the field has been changed before updating it. Without a timestamp, Access would have to read the data in every field, which could conceivably be a costly operation in terms of time and network resources. If Access has to read floating point data, a value can erroneously appear to have been changed when it hasn't. Unless you have a very good reason, you should allow the Upsizing Wizard to create timestamps where it thinks they are necessary.

NOTE
A timestamp is a binary (8) datatype that is automatically updated every time a row containing a timestamp column is inserted or updated. You are only allowed one timestamp column per table. Timestamp datatypes store a counter value always guaranteed to be unique within a database, not the system date/time. You can automatically create a timestamp in a database merely by naming it "timestamp" and not specifying a datatype, which is what the Upsizing Wizard does. You can also name another column "timestamp" and assign another datatype to it, but as it can't be browsed with the DB-Library Browse functions, it can only serve as a source of confusion.

Sending Data versus Sending Structure

The Upsizing Wizard gives you the option of either transferring data to SQL Server or just building the server tables but not putting any data into them. If you send the data, your tables will be upsized and all of the data exported as well. However, if you have developed a prototype in Access using sample data, you may want to just upsize the structure and worry about getting data into the SQL Server tables after the fact.

A Typical Upsizing Wizard Report

The report generated by the Upsizing Wizard contains valuable information about the progress of your upsizing. Any errors found will be logged here, as well as the entire structure of your SQL Server database. Figure 6.7 shows typical output on an upsizing report with error messages showing where triggers were not created on the Categories table due to lack of space on the transaction log.

> **NOTE**
>
> If you run into problems or errors upsizing, you will often need to fix them on the SQL Server end. After you have fixed the cause of the errors, you will need to resume upsizing. Depending on how much of the upsizing was actually completed successfully, you may want to start completely over again. You will need to delete any attached tables from the Access database and rename any local tables named with the _local suffix back to their original Access names. If you don't rename the tables, they won't show up on the list of available tables in the wizard.

Figure 6.8 shows the Table section of the report and the parts of the Categories table that were modified. As you can see, a timestamp column was added. The column on the left represents the Access properties and the column on the right represents their SQL Server translations.

Figure 6.9 shows the output of an Insert trigger created for the Categories table which is clearly labeled as being for counter-emulation code. The original Access table had a counter as the primary key, so this trigger translates the autoincrementing behavior of the counter to its SQL Server equivalent.

Upsizing Wizard Report

Database and Log:

Microsoft Access Database:	D:\Pubs\upsize\Northwind.mdb
SQL Server Database:	NorthwindSQL
Database Size:	2
Log Size:	1

Devices:

	Database Device	Log Device
		Northwind
Logical Name:	Northwind	
Physical Name:	Northwi	
Size:	1536	1536

Errors

Table: Categories

Insert trigger was not created.   FatalError

Table: Categories

	Microsoft Access	SQL Server
Table Name:	Categories_local	Categories
Attached Table Name:	Categories	
Validation Rule:Aliasing Query:		*Timestamp field added to SQL Server table.*

Fields	Microsoft Access	SQL Server
Field name:	CategoryID	CategoryID
Data Type:	Number (Long)	int
Default:	(none)	0 (Name: UW_ZeroDefault)
Validation Rule:		
Field name:	CategoryName	CategoryName
Data Type:	Text(15)	varchar(15)
Default:Validation Rule:		
Field name:	Description	Description
Data Type:	Memo	text
Default:Validation Rule:		
Field name:	Picture	Picture

In addition to counters, indexes are also created and documented. Figure 6.10 shows the indexes created on the first few tables when upsizing the sample Northwinds database.

FIGURE 6.9:

Triggers

```
Triggers

Insert Trigger:      Categories_ITrig, not exported

CREATE TRIGGER Categories_ITrig ON Categories FOR INSERT AS
DECLARE @maxc int, @newc int    /* FOR COUNTER-EMULATION CODE */

/*
 * PREVENT NULL VALUES IN 'CategoryName'
 */
IF (SELECT Count(*) FROM inserted WHERE CategoryName IS NULL) > 0
    BEGIN
        RAISERROR 44444 'Field ''CategoryName'' cannot contain a null value.'
        ROLLBACK TRANSACTION
    END
/*
 * COUNTER-EMULATION CODE FOR FIELD 'CategoryID'
 */
SELECT @maxc = (SELECT Max(CategoryID) FROM Categories)
SELECT @newc = (SELECT CategoryID FROM inserted)
IF @newc = 0 OR @maxc <> @newc SELECT @maxc = @maxc + 1
UPDATE Categories SET CategoryID = @maxc WHERE CategoryID = @newc
```

FIGURE 6.10:

Indexes

Indexes	Microsoft Access	SQL Server
Name:	CategoriesProducts	CategoriesProducts
Fields:	CategoryID	CategoryID
Type:	DuplicatesOK	*DuplicatesOK*
Name:	CategoryID	CategoryID
Fields:	CategoryID	CategoryID
Type:	DuplicatesOK	DuplicatesOK
Name:	PrimaryKey	aaaaa_PrimaryKey
Fields:	ProductID	ProductID
Type:	Unique, Primary	Unique, Clustered
Name:	ProductName	ProductName
Fields:	ProductName	ProductName
Type:	DuplicatesOK	DuplicatesOK
Name:	SupplierID	SupplierID
Fields:	SupplierID	SupplierID
Type:	DuplicatesOK	DuplicatesOK

Finally, Figure 6.11 shows the documenting of the relationships in the Categories and Customers tables. As you can see, the Upsizing Wizard documents the triggers required to manage each of the referential integrity constraints. You can refer back to the Triggers section of the report if you need to see the actual text of the triggers.

FIGURE 6.11:

Relationships

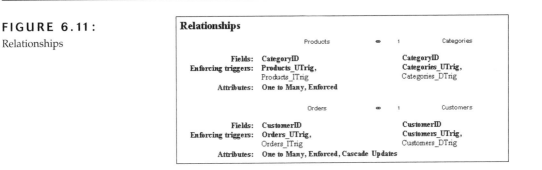

The SQL Browser

The SQL Browser looks a lot like the Access Database Explorer window, with tabs for Table, View, Default, Rule, and Proc. You can use it to perform many useful functions on the server. If you're used to the Access user interface, you may find SQL Browser much more convenient than using the SQL Server Enterprise Manager, Administrator, or Object Manager tools.

You can use the Browser to create, edit, and view SQL Server objects. You can also use it to link objects and connect to data. In addition, it comes with an ad-hoc query editor which lets you type in SQL statements to be immediately executed.

When you install the Upsizing Wizard, the Browser comes with it and appears as another item in the Add-ins menu. You can use it to open, modify, create, or link tables and views, although you can only open one table at a time. You can also modify or create validation rules and triggers or run stored procedures.

When you select the Browser from the Add-ins menu, you will be prompted to log in and select a database. Figure 6.12 shows the Browser with our recently upsized database.

FIGURE 6.12:

The SQL-Server Browser

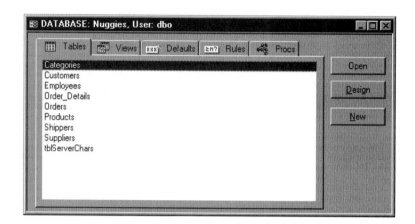

You can open tables through the Browser to view their data, although you cannot update data. You can modify table definitions up to a point, but you cannot delete any fields. (This is because SQL Server doesn't allow deleting fields from tables after they have been created. The SQL Browser doesn't add any new capabilities to the server, just a new user interface for existing capabilities.) You can also create new tables in the Browser by clicking the New button from the main window. Fields and properties are also editable. Figure 6.13 shows the Categories table open in design view. If you want to delete a table, you can use the Drop option from the Edit menu. You can also link tables directly from the Browser by choosing Link from the File menu.

You can edit views from the Browser by clicking on the View tab and then clicking Design. This allows you to change the Transact-SQL definition of the view and save your changes to the server. You can also use the Open button to see the data returned by the view.

You can edit SQL Server defaults, rules, and procedures by selecting the appropriate tab and then clicking Design. In each case, you can edit the SQL statement that defines these objects. Stored procedures can

FIGURE 6.13:

The categories table in design view

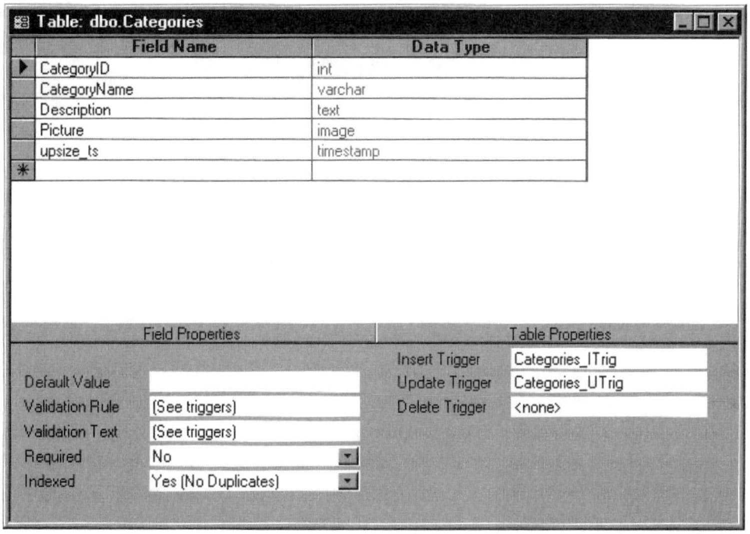

also be executed directly from the SQL Browser. If they return any rows, the Browser will display a datasheet with the results.

You can create or modify stored procedures using the Browser by clicking the Proc button and typing SQL code directly into the editing window. There is a Parameters button for specifying parameters for stored procedures. You can also run an existing stored procedure or link it to the existing Access database. This will create a passthrough query which contains the connection information and name of the stored procedure. Figure 6.14 shows the result of executing a stored procedure in the Pubs sample database.

The Ad Hoc SQL tool lets you execute SQL commands directly on the server. To open the Ad Hoc query window, select Ad-Hoc SQL from the View menu. This will let you execute any Transact-SQL commands you like. The SQL Browser will build a datasheet with the results (if any) returned from the SQL Server. Figure 6.15 shows an example datasheet from this part of the Browser.

FIGURE 6.14:

Running a stored procedure
from the SQL Browser

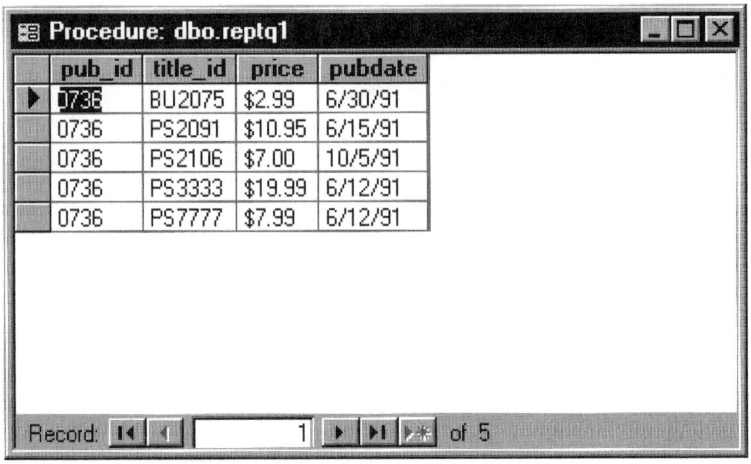

	pub_id	title_id	price	pubdate
▶	0736	BU2075	$2.99	6/30/91
	0736	PS2091	$10.95	6/15/91
	0736	PS2106	$7.00	10/5/91
	0736	PS3333	$19.99	6/12/91
	0736	PS7777	$7.99	6/12/91

FIGURE 6.15:

Executing an SQL statement
with the SQL Browser's
Ad-Hoc SQL tool

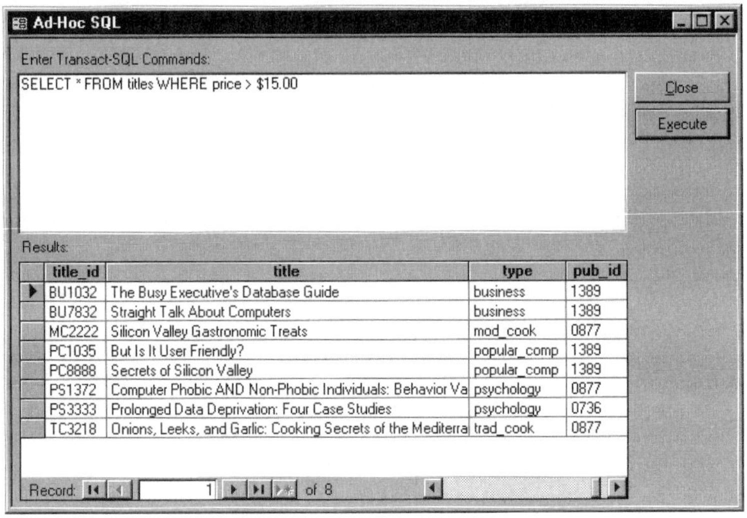

Enter Transact-SQL Commands:

SELECT * FROM titles WHERE price > $15.00

Results:

title_id	title	type	pub_id
▶ BU1032	The Busy Executive's Database Guide	business	1389
BU7832	Straight Talk About Computers	business	1389
MC2222	Silicon Valley Gastronomic Treats	mod_cook	0877
PC1035	But Is It User Friendly?	popular_comp	1389
PC8888	Secrets of Silicon Valley	popular_comp	1389
PS1372	Computer Phobic AND Non-Phobic Individuals: Behavior Va	psychology	0877
PS3333	Prolonged Data Deprivation: Four Case Studies	psychology	0736
TC3218	Onions, Leeks, and Garlic: Cooking Secrets of the Mediterra	trad_cook	0877

You can also create and modify views using the Browser, but as views involving multiple tables are read-only in Access they may be of limited use. You also need to make sure that you have permission to edit views created by other users. (Further details on SQL Server permissions are explained in Chapter 9.)

A view can be linked to your Access database in much the same way that a table is, and will show up in the Tables tab on the Database Explorer. Figure 6.16 demonstrates editing a view from the Pubs sample database.

FIGURE 6.16:

Designing a view

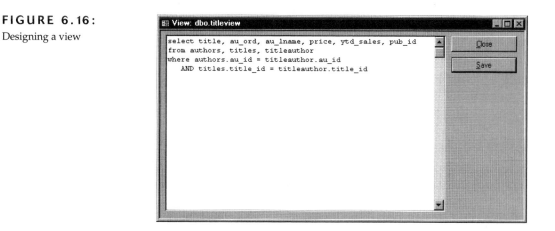

Common Upsizing Problems

Like any other tool, the Upsizing Wizard isn't perfect. You may run into trouble dealing with multiple databases, as well as with parts of Access that can't be completely converted to SQL Server. We'll review some of these common problems here and tell you how to work around them. You should also review the suggestions for writing more efficient queries in Chapters 3 and 4 and apply them to your newly upsized application.

How to Handle Split Databases

Many people are confused when they attempt the upsizing process on a database split into a front-end database of forms and reports and a back-end database containing shared tables. Since upsizing only works on tables and not on other objects, you only need to upsize the back-end database. The front-end database may remain largely unchanged.

Once you have upsized the back-end, you need to modify the front-end to use the new SQL Server tables instead of the old local tables. First, delete the linked local tables from the front-end database. You can then simply import the back-end database into the front-end database. This will bring in all of the necessary links and aliasing queries to make the front-end work with the new SQL Server back-end.

Limits on Names

Although the Upsizing Wizard will take care of most naming problems by writing aliasing queries, you still need to watch out for case sensitivity on names. SQL Server treats all field names as case-sensitive. You need to be aware of this any place that you refer to a field name directly in VBA code within Access.

Limits on Defaults

Some default values are not properly handled by the Upsizing Wizard. Date$ and Now$, although legal in Access, are not properly translated to SQL Server defaults. The Date() and Now() functions, on the other hand, upsize well. The Upsizing Wizard also has problems handling a default explicitly set to Null. You can eliminate this problem simply by eliminating the default, as it doesn't do anything in Access.

Drivers for Upsizing

There are two driver issues to be aware of when running the Upsizing Tools. First, you must have a default printer installed if you're running the Upsizing Wizard under Windows NT. Otherwise, the process will fail entirely when it goes to construct the upsizing report. Second, you should always use the most recent ODBC drivers for SQL Server that you can find. The ODBC drivers shipped with SQL Server 6.0 will speed up Upsizing Tools 1.0 immensely.

Next Steps: Optimizing Upsized Applications

Now that you've upsized your database, what do you do to make it perform? It isn't enough just to port the application over to SQL Server to see performance benefits. There are some general rules: fetch only needed data, store some data locally, don't use scrollable or updateable cursors unless you need them, and move as much functionality to the server as is feasible. We'll cover these points in more detail next.

Optimizing Problem Tables and Queries

As with any other client/server application, the best thing you can do to improve performance of an upsized application is to retrieve only the data you need from SQL Server. Access encourages a design strategy of binding entire tables or queries to forms and reports. This strategy is disastrous when these tables and queries are replaced by SQL Server tables or views. As all data has to travel across a network after you upsize, such a straight swap of tables might actually slow the application down.

We discussed optimizing SQL Server queries extensively in the first chapters of this book. In general, you'll need to add a sufficiently restrictive WHERE clause to each query to be sure that it returns only a limited subset of the data from the server.

You also need to beware of the particular problems we discussed earlier involving floating point primary keys on linked SQL Server tables. In general, you'll find that an SQL Server table with a primary key that is a floating point or date type just won't work well with an Access application. In such cases, if you can't find another natural key to use in the table, you'll have to add an Access counter field before upsizing.

Converting Queries to Updateable Views

Views are similar to Access select queries, although unlike Access queries, they don't allow you to update data if they involve multiple tables. If you want to use Access forms for adding and editing data, you can link them directly to an SQL Server table, although you'll get better performance by using a query based on the SQL Server table to limit the records returned. This strategy of basing a local query on server tables will work even if there are multiple tables involved. However, if your form is based on multiple tables, you will probably want to use an updateable view.

Views created in SQL Server are read-only when retrieved by Access. So, if you base a form on one of these read-only views, you will not be able to edit data. You need to create a unique index on the view to be able to edit the data using a form. This is a trick that depends on Jet's ability to maintain the index locally even though the view itself is constructed on a remote server. To add an index to a view, you run a CREATE INDEX query within Access. For example, we might index a view named TitleAuthor on the TitleName field by running this query within Access after linking the view:

```
CREATE UNIQUE INDEX TitleNameIndex ON TitleAuthor (TitleName ASC)
```

Once you've created such an index on a SQL Server view, Access will treat it as updateable.

Adding Timestamps

Timestamps are automatically added by the Upsizing Wizard to any floating point, memo, or OLE fields to speed up execution. The time-stamp prevents Access from having to actually inspect the data inside of these fields to find out whether or not it has been changed.

You can also use timestamp fields to improve performance on tables that have many fields. To create a timestamp on a remote table, use the ALTER TABLE command. You will then need to relink the remote table so that Access will see the new timestamp field.

Optimizing Problem Forms

Changing tables and queries allows you to tackle some performance problems at the source. But you'll also need to modify the forms in your Access application to work more efficiently with the remote data. Generally, this means changing the recordsource of the forms to retrieve fewer records at any given time.

Modifying Recordsources

Access forms, when used exclusively with Access, are often con-structed to have as their recordsource an entire table or joins of multi-ple tables with no restrictions on the number of rows returned. While this is reasonably efficient when dealing with local tables, it just doesn't work in the client/server world. Since bound forms in Access are most often used for editing data, it makes no sense at all to return several hundred (or several thousand) rows from the server when the user can only manipulate one record at a time. In addition, a dynaset containing fewer than 100 records requires only a single connection, whereas dynasets over 100 records require two connections: one to fetch key values and another to fetch data to display on the form. Speed and performance will dramatically increase if only the record being edited is actually returned from the server.

Other resource hogs are bound combo boxes and list boxes, since they each require that a separate query be sent to the server, thereby increasing the number of connections and the amount of data that needs to be fetched. You should consider keeping any table that's used as a row source local to your Access application instead of upsizing it. If you do this, of course, you must provide some mechanism to allow these local tables to be updated. Often downloading the newest versions of these lookup tables at AutoExec time makes sense.

If you are used to displaying OLE and Memo fields on your forms, you might want to reconsider so that these fields are not actually retrieved from the server until they are displayed on the screen. It is easy enough to set the Visible property for these controls to False and provide a button the user can press if they want to view or edit the contents. Only at that point will the data actually be fetched from the server.

If you have many fields to display on the form and some of the fields are used more often than others, you may want to consider breaking the form into multiple forms. Provide a button to open the second form should the user request the data from the less-used fields. Again, this approach serves to leave the data on the server until it is required.

Using Passthrough Queries and Stored Procedures

A pass-through query in Access is an SQL statement which, once identified as a pass-through query by selecting that option in the Query window, is not compiled by Access. Instead it is passed directly to the server for execution. This causes all processing to occur on the server instead of locally, so network traffic is reduced. For update, delete, and append queries you are likely to get better performance from pass-through queries than from the Access equivalent queries based on attached remote tables. Pass-through queries also allow you to use SQL-specific functionality that is not found in Access, such as stored procedures and server-based intrinsic functions as well as Data Definition Language, administrative, and security functions.

The following are some disadvantages of passthrough queries:

- They always return a non-updateable snapshot.
- They can't be built with the query editor in Access. You must be familiar with the correct SQL grammar.
- User-defined functions are not supported, nor are parameter queries.
- If an action query is unable to execute completely, it will not update partial rows as Access does.

A stored procedure is created, named, and saved on the server. You can use stored procedures if you only need to retrieve data and don't need to update it, as the results are read-only. You call the stored procedure on the server by using a passthrough query.

Although the data returned by passthrough queries and stored procedures can't be directly edited, you can issue single-row UPDATE queries to the same table via pass-through to work around this problem. This makes them viable solutions for data-editing forms that are simply too slow when based directly on attached tables. You should certainly consider using this technique when you have a form that's only used for data display. The more query processing you can push on to the server, the less network traffic you'll have to deal with and the faster these forms will be.

Optimizing Problem Reports

Reports may also benefit from post-upsizing changes. In addition to using more restrictive queries to limit the report to only those rows you really need to see, you may want to consider using local shadow tables when you need to produce a series of reports based on the same data.

Local Shadow Tables

Many applications have reporting needs which require using the same data several times in a row. For example, you may have an accounting report which prints annual data, then quarterly data, then detail data using three subreports based on the same table. If this report is based directly on tables on the server, it will retrieve each record three times whenever you print it.

When you have this situation, you should change your processing so that the rows are first moved to a local shadow table using an append query. Then you can base the reports on this local table. Making this change means that the data will only be retrieved across the network once and used locally after that. Of course, you need to be sure to update the local shadow tables every time you want to run the report.

Optimizing Problem Code

If you've been planning on a move to client/server, VBA code in Access often does not require any changes. However, you must beware of expressions that are unsupported on your server and table-specific methods in your code.

Unsupported Expressions

User-defined functions and some Access functions are not supported by SQL Server. If you use these expressions in constructing query fields, you may cause your application to slow down or possibly not work at all. Things to watch out for in queries include:

- User-defined functions
- Iif

- Switch

- Choose

- Parameter queries

Unfortunately it's not possible to provide an overall "cookbook" method of fixing these problems. You'll need to rethink the logic of your application to determine whether you can eliminate these functions from expressions. If not, you'll find that much more processing is done locally, as Access will likely retrieve entire tables from the server in the process of evaluating these expressions.

Removing Table-Specific Methods

Finally, since you cannot base a table-type recordset on a server table, you must rewrite any code which uses functionality that is specific to this type of recordset. For the most part, this means eliminating the Seek method from your code. You have two alternatives for doing this in most cases. The first is to change the table-type recordset to a dynaset-type recordset and use the Find method. The second is to change the recordsource of the recordset to use a WHERE clause to only retrieve the records of interest when the recordset is created. When it makes sense, the second alternative is usually faster, since it serves to move the processing from the client to the server and eliminates network traffic.

Summary

For developers moving from Access to client/server using SQL Server, the Access Upsizing Tools can represent a significant time savings. In this chapter, we reviewed the operation of these tools, as well as some steps that need to be taken to optimize an upsized application. As long as you treat the Upsizing Wizard as a tool rather than as a magic cure for all the problems of your Access application, you will find it useful.

CHAPTER

SEVEN

Managing SQL Server with DMO

- What is SQL-DMO?

- Programming with SQL-DMO

- SQL-DMO objects

- The SQL Explorer Application

SQL Distributed Management Objects (or SQL-DMO) allow a developer to use either 32-bit Visual Basic or 32-bit C++ as an OLE Automation controller with SQL Server. Since Visual Basic is also implemented in products including Access, Excel, and Project, this means you can write programs that use SQL-DMO objects that directly interact with SQL Server objects. We will cover only programming with Visual Basic since C++ programming is beyond the scope of this book.

What Are Distributed Management Objects?

Distributed Management Objects are 32-bit, OLE Automation-compatible objects which can only be used on Windows 95 and Windows NT operating systems. The object model includes objects, methods, properties, and collections for the purpose of writing code in either 32-bit Visual Basic (any dialect—for example, those included in Access 95, Excel 95, or Visual Basic 4.0) or C++ to administer multiple SQL Servers distributed across a network.

It's important to understand that these are *management* objects, not data objects. Although there is a method for retrieving data from SQL Server using these objects (the ExecuteWithResults method of the SQLServer or Database object), their primary use is in managing SQL Servers and the objects they contain. You can think of them as being a tool for manipulating what you could change in design view if your application were written in Access. However, SQL-DMO has an additional set of methods which allow you to actually control the servers themselves. For example, you can start, stop, or begin a backup on a server using the appropriate methods of these objects.

If you are familiar with Data Access Objects (DAO) in Access and Excel, you can easily grasp that DMO is the hierarchical framework of objects in SQL Server that is used for its programming interface via OLE Automation. Access DAO, for example, has a single object, DBEngine, at the top of the hierarchy (the parent of all other objects), with Workspaces, Groups, Users, Databases, etc. as child objects. SQL-DMO works in much the same way, as a hierarchy of objects, with Application as the parent object and SQLServer, Executive, IntegratedSecurity, Database, etc. as child objects of Application. Referring to the child objects necessitates referencing them through the hierarchy. There are many parallels between the two hierarchies. For example, in Access you might retrieve properties of a particular field by referring to

```
DBEngine.Workspaces(0).Databases(0) _
    .Tables("Customers").Fields("CustomerName")
```

With SQL-DMO, you might look for similar information under

```
SQLServer("Server1").Databases(0) _
    .Tables("Customers").Columns("CustomerName")
```

If you're already familiar with the notation used by VBA for objects, collections, methods, and properties, you'll be right at home with SQL-DMO.

Each object and collection has its own methods and properties, with a few properties common to all (for example, every object has a property named Type that describes itself, and all Collections have a Count property). Referencing these objects in code follows the same general syntax rules as working with any OLE objects in Visual Basic. If you are already comfortable with DAO and OLE in Visual Basic, you need only learn the SQL-DMO hierarchy and its properties and methods to directly manipulate objects in SQL Server and manage the server itself.

Installing SQL-DMO

You can install the SQL-DMO library on any machine running Windows NT 3.51 (or higher) or Windows 95. The install procedure differs slightly depending on whether you are installing to the same computer with the server, to a different Windows NT computer, or to a Windows 95 computer.

Installing on the SQL Server

SQL-DMO is automatically included when you choose "Install SQL Server and Utilities" during SQL 6.0 installation. By default, it only works with SQL 6.0 servers. However, it also includes a script which you can run on a SQL 4.21 server, adding it to the list of servers that SQL-DMO can manage. To install SQL-DMO on an existing 4.21 server, use the following steps:

1. Copy the SQLOLE42.SQL script from a version 6.0 SQL server to your old SQL Server. (You'll find this script in the install subdirectory.)

2. On the SQL 4.21 machine, run ISQL/W.

3. Connect to the server.

4. Use the Open button on the toolbar to load the SQLOLE42.SQL script.

5. Use the Execute button to run the script. (Note: As a side effect, this script will also dump the server's transaction log.) This will

install the tables needed for the SQL-DMO to connect to this
server. The last few lines of output should be:

```
Successful installation.
Microsoft SQLOLE Scripts Version
------------------------_---------
393216                      0x00060000
```

Installing on Another Windows NT Machine

To get the SQL-DMO objects installed on a Windows NT machine that
does not also serve as the host for the SQL Server install, run SQL Server
setup and choose "Install Utilities Only" when you're prompted for
the type of installation.

Installing on Windows 95

You can also install SQL-DMO on a Windows 95 machine, which allows
you to manage your SQL Servers from this platform as well. To do this,
just run the SETUP.EXE program from the i386 subdirectory of the SQL
Server installation CD and choose Install Client Utilities, as shown in
Figure 7.1.

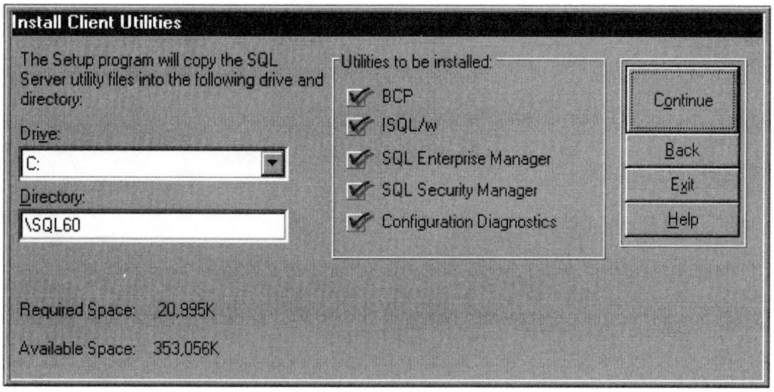

FIGURE 7.1:

Installing SQL-DMO on
Windows 95

The SQL-DMO Hierarchy

What follows is a brief description of the major objects contained in the DMO hierarchy (see Figure 7.2). Later in the chapter we'll dig into the major methods and properties of these objects and look at what you can do with SQL-DMO, but first we'll discuss the major objects we intend to cover. This is not the full set of SQL-DMO objects. For the full set, refer to your "Programming SQL Distributed Management Objects" manual or the online SQL Distributed Management Objects help file.

FIGURE 7.2:

Simplified DMO hierarchy diagram

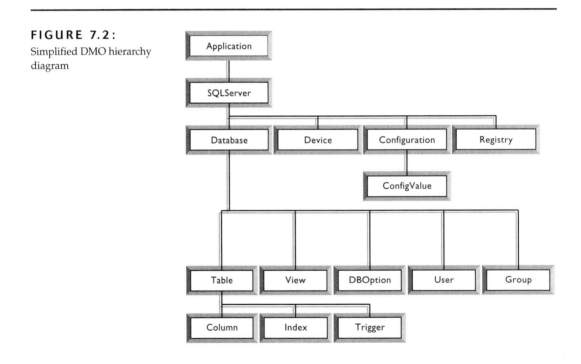

Application

The Application object manages the entire application environment. Its correlate in DAO would be the DBEngine object. There is a subtle difference between this Application and DBEngine, though; Application represents the total SQL-DMO layer, not the underlying SQL Server program itself. Also, you cannot connect directly to the SQLOLE.Application object. Instead, you must connect to a specific SQLServer object and retrieve its Parent property, which points to the Application object. It is the parent of all other objects, and you cannot have more than one active Application object in your code. Like any other object, it has a collection of Properties. It also manages the collection of SQLServer objects, which refer to individual servers. The Application object is mainly useful for checking on the SQL-DMO layer itself. For example, you can retrieve the version of the SQL-DMO library you're currently using, which will be important in the future when Microsoft upgrades this software.

> **NOTE** Although the full set of objects are referred to as SQL-DMO, the type library is called SQLOLE. Thus you'll see individual objects declared in code this way: `Dim New objDatabase As AQLOLE.Database`. Some parts of the SQL Server documentation use the term "SQLOLE layer." We prefer the term SQL-DMO.

SQLServer

The SQLServer object is the top-level object within the Application object, and all other objects are accessed through it. Any initialized SQLServer object contains a single connection to a particular SQL Server, initiated by using the Connect method. This is the only starting point for interactions with SQL-DMO, and you must know the name of your server, as well as a valid user name and password, to connect this SQLServer object to a particular SQL Server. The appropriate named pipe or other connectivity method must already be in place.

Device

A Device represents an SQL Server device—either a database device or a dump device. You can use a Device object to retrieve information concerning the physical storage of data on your server.

Configuration

The Configuration object and its ConfigValues collection can be used to alter the configuration of a running SQL Server. For example, you can change the number of available locks, the number of open databases allowed, or the amount of memory devoted to SQL Server with appropriate changes to these objects.

Registry

A Registry object allows you to retrieve information from the Windows NT Registry that pertains to SQL Server. For example, you can retrieve information on the named pipe and default login from which SQL Server has been started from appropriate Registry objects.

Database

A Database object, as you would expect, is what you use to interact with lower-level objects that contain data. Each SQLServer object has a collection of Database objects which, in turn, can contain such data objects as tables. You can also use the Database object to run queries against an SQL Server database.

User

The User object contains information about a database user. Each user is associated with a single SQL Server login. Users are discussed in Chapter 9.

Group

A Group object contains information about a collection of users. Groups are discussed in Chapter 9.

Table

A Table object contains rows of data in the database. With SQL-DMO you can explore the structure of a table as well as modify it or gather the information necessary to recreate it.

Column

A Column object defines a specific type of information that is maintained in a table.

Index

An Index object is used to speed up access to a table. There are two types of indexes: a clustered index, where data is stored in the same order as the index, and a nonclustered index, where data is unordered and stored separately from the index. A table can have only a single clustered index.

Trigger

A Trigger object contains information about a particular SQL Server trigger—a piece of code that's run whenever a row is added, deleted, or updated in a table. SQL-DMO lets you list existing triggers and add new ones.

View

A View object is logically similar to a table, although data in a view cannot be updated (views are very similar to Access snapshots). The data that a View object represents is defined by a SELECT statement (the Text property) that includes specific columns (either actual or aggregated) from one or more tables in a database.

Other Objects

SQL-DMO has one of the richest object models of any Microsoft application, and we can't cover all of it here. The online help file is an excellent reference for reviewing the other objects. Table 7.1 lists the SQL-DMO objects that we do not explicitly cover in this chapter.

TABLE 7.1: Other SQL-DMO Objects

Object	Parent Object	Description
Backup	Application	The Backup object is used to start a backup of SQL Server data.
Permission	Application	Information on a particular user or group's permissions.
QueryResults	Application	An object that holds the result of various system and user queries.
HistoryFilter	Application	A HistoryFilter object is used to selectively purge the SQL Server event history.
Names	Application	A collection of object names known to this server.

TABLE 7.1 : Other SQL-DMO Objects (continued)

Object	Parent Object	Description
Login	SQLServer	An individual user logged in to a server.
Language	SQLServer	A language in use on a server.
RemoteServer	SQLServer	A remote server that the current server recognizes.
RemoteLogin	RemoteServer	A user logged in to another SQL Server.
Subscriber-Info	RemoteServer	Information on replication subscriptions at a remote server.
Executive	SQLServer	The scheduling engine for SQL Server.
Task	Executive	An individual task scheduled to be executed.
AlertSystem	Executive	Information that controls the processing of SQL Server alerts.
Integrated Security	SQLServer	Information on how SQL Server security is integrated with the host Windows NT security.
Alert	SQLServer	A SQL Server alert.
Operator	SQLServer	A SQL Server operator.
Stored Procedure	Database	A SQL Server stored procedure.
Rule	Database	A SQL Server rule.
Default	Database	A SQL Server default.
Transaction-Log	Database	A SQL Server transaction log.
System-Datatype	Database	A SQL Server system datatype.
UserDefined-Datatype	Database	A user-defined datatype, which is always based on a system datatype.
Publication	Database	A particular replication publication.
Article	Publication	An object included in a replication publication.
Subscription	Article	A subscription to an article.
DRIDefault	Column	A Domain Referential Integrity object.
Key	Table	Information about a particular key on a table.
Check	Table	Information about a check constraint on a table.

Using DMO

The following steps are required to use SQL-DMO objects:

1. Include the DMO type Library.

2. Create an SQLServer object.

3. Connect to a server.

4. Use the SQLServer object.

5. Release the SQLServer object.

Carrying out these steps in Visual Basic is discussed in more detail below.

Include the DMO Type Library

In Access you need to create a reference to the SQL-DMO typelib (SQLOLE32.TLB). You can declare objects as a generic object type without creating the reference, but you will not get the best performance this way. To add a reference, open any module in your database and select Tools ➤ References from the menus. Check the box marked "Microsoft SQLOLE Object Library" to create the reference. This will have two effects. First, it will make the actual SQLServer objects available in your code. Second, it will add the SQLOLE library to the Object Browser. Since this library is fully implemented according to the current library rules, you can retrieve constants, jump directly to its help file, and insert call skeletons directly from the Object Browser, as shown in Figure 7.3.

FIGURE 7.3:

The SQLOLE Library in Access
Object Browser

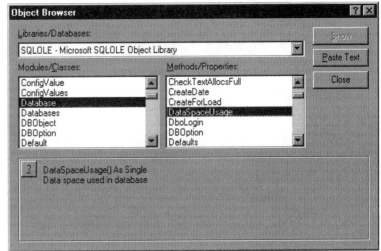

Create an SQLServer Object

The preferred way to create an SQLServer object is to use the Dim
statement with the New keyword:

```
Dim objSQLServer As New SQLOLE.SQLServer
```

Using the New keyword tells Access to both create and initialize the
storage for this object in a single step.

An alternative syntax is to use the CreateObject function and the Set
keyword:

```
Dim objSQLServer As SQLOLE.SQLServer
Set objSQLServer = CreateObject("SQLOLE.SQLServer")
```

The third way is to declare the object as a generic object type:

```
Dim objSQLServer As Object
Set objSQLServer = CreateObject("SQLOLE.SQLServer")
```

This method will not be as efficient as declaring an object variable as a specific SQL-DMO type. However, it can be used in databases which lack a reference to the SQLOLE type library, as long as SQL-DMO is properly installed on the machine.

Connect to the Server

You can connect to the newly created and empty SQLServer object by using the object's Connect method, which takes the parameters of the SQL Server name, Login ID, and Password. If the Connect method succeeds, the SQLServer object is returned with information about the SQL Server to which it is connected, and all objects in the DMO hierarchy are now available. Using one of the SQLServer objects we created above, enter:

```
objSQLServer.Connect "Guppy", "sa", "aquarium"
```

This statement will attempt to connect to the Guppy server, logging in as the system administrator with a password of "aquarium." If the login cannot be completed, the Connect method returns a runtime error. Once connected, SQL-DMO maintains all of the SQL Server information in a cache stored in memory at the client machine (to improve performance). You can use the Refresh method at any time to update the cache with current values without having to reconnect to the server.

Use the SQLServer Object

Once you have used this method to connect to a particular SQL Server, you can retrieve other objects to manage it by following the path down through its collections. One minor annoyance is that there is no way within the library to go out and search for currently running servers. You'll need to use the Connect method to get to each one, based on information that you supply from your program. Our SQL Explorer sample stores information on servers that you have visited in the Registry so that you may get back to them more quickly in the future.

Release the SQLServer Object

When you're done with the server, you can release the SQLServer object by setting the object variable to Nothing:

```
Set objSQLServer = Nothing
```

Visual Basic will automatically release an object when its variable goes out of scope, so normally you don't have to release any local object variables, only the global or module-level ones.

General SQL-DMO Programming Topics

SQL-DMO generally follows the standard VBA practices in dealing with object variables, methods, and properties. There are some subtle differences, particularly in dealing with SQL-DMO collections. If you already understand the basics of using OLE Objects from a type library in your VBA code, the syntax of using SQL-DMO should seem quite natural.

Declaring Additional Object Variables

Although you only need the single object variable pointing to the server, you will probably want to declare further object variables to make your code easier to read and maintain, as well as run faster. You can also declare further DMO-specific object variables to deal with different aspects of DMO, such as the following code snippet to create a DMO database object:

```
Dim objDatabase as SQLOLE.Database
```

or the less-preferred and slower generic object:

```
Dim objDatabase as Object
```

You can then assign a specific SQL database to the object, as shown in the following example, which connects to the pubs database (a sample database which ships with SQL Server). Before running this code, of course, you'll need to be sure that the objSQLServer variable is connected to a running SQL Server.

```
Set objDatabase = objSQLServer.Databases("pubs")
```

Retrieving and Using DMO Properties

You can retrieve property values by setting variables to refer to them. Some properties (but not all) can also be updated. The syntax for dealing with properties is exactly the same as it is with native Access properties. For example, to read the name of the host computer for a server:

```
Dim strHost As String
strHost = objSQLServer.HostName
```

To set a property, in this case the UserData property of a server:

```
objSQLServer.UserData = 2317
```

You can also iterate through the Properties collection of any SQL-DMO object with a For-Each loop:

```
Dim prpProp As SQLOLE.Property
For Each prpProp in objSQLServer.Properties
    Debug.Print prpProp.Name, prpProp.Value
Next prpProp
```

Calling SQL-DMO Methods

An SQL-DMO method is a function that performs an action using an SQL-DMO object, as opposed to a property, which describes the object or the state of an object. Some SQL-DMO methods take input parameters (sometimes these parameters are optional), and some return values.

The three syntax forms are as follows, shown using named arguments. If you do not use named arguments, you must specify the parameters in their required order. The first syntax is appropriate for a method which has no return value or parameters—for example, the Pause method of the SQLServer object:

```
objSQLServer.Pause
```

The second syntax invokes a method with parameters, but without a return value. Note that you can use this syntax even if the method returns a value, if you don't care to look at the return value:

```
objSQLServer.ShutDown Wait:=True
```

The third syntax invokes a method with parameters and a return value. In this case, since we're using a method that returns an object (instead of a simple value) the Set keyword is required.

```
Dim objResults As SQLOLE.QueryResults
Set objResults = objSQLServer.ExecuteWithResults _
    (Command := "SELECT * FROM pubs.dbo.authors")
```

DMO Collections

A collection can contain from zero to many objects, all of the same type, and fits within the hierarchical DMO containment structure. Every object has a corresponding collection. For example, all Database objects are contained in the Databases collection. All collections are contained within the parent object except for Application, which sits at the top of the heap. Both collections and the objects within them have methods and properties, which you refer to through the parent object. For example, you can retrieve the number of databases for a particular server with the Count property of its Databases collection:

```
Dim lngCount As Long
lngCount = objSQLServer.Databases.Count
```

You can refer to individual objects within a collection either by name or ordinal value (1-based), as the example below shows referring to the pubs database within the Databases collection:

```
Set objDatabase = objSQLServer.Databases("pubs")
```

To refer to the first database (whatever that might happen to be) in the Databases collection by its ordinal number, you would use:

```
Set objDatabase = objSQLServer.Databases(1)
```

Each parent object also has a default collection (as in DAO) for which you can use the ! specifier instead of the default collection name. The following example refers to the pubs database of the default Database collection:

```
Set objDatabase = objSQLServer!pubs
```

To use this syntax you have to know what the default objects are for each parent, which are listed in Table 7.2.

TABLE 7.2: Default SQL-DMO Collections

Parent Object	Default Collection
Configuration	ConfigValues
Executive	Tasks
SQLServer	Databases
Database	Tables
Table	Columns

To iterate through a collection, you can use a For Each loop. For example, to list the databases in the SQLServer object:

```
Dim objDatabase As SQLOLE.Database
For Each objDatabase in objSQLServer.Databases
    Debug.Print objDatabase.name
Next objDatabase
```

If you want to add a new DMO object to a collection, you first need to create a new instance of the DMO object that you want to create, set its properties, and then add it to the collection. As with DAO, it is the adding to the collection that actually saves the object. For example, you can add a new Device to a SQLServer object as follows:

```
Dim objNewDevice As New SQLOLE.Device
With objNewDevice
    .Name = "NewDevice"
    .PhysicalLocation = "C:\SQL60\DATA\NEWDEV.DAT"
    .Size = 10
    .Type = SQLOLEDevice_Database
End With
objSQLServer.Devices.Add objNewDevice
```

Removing an object from a collection is much simpler. The Remove method reverses the process and deletes the object:

```
objSQLServer.Devices.Remove "NewDevice"
```

The Refresh Collection Method

The Refresh method in SQL-DMO takes a single parameter, either True or False. If you choose True, then all objects under the collection are reinitialized and current information is retrieved from the server, invalidating any object variables you may have set further down in the collection. If False, then only objects that have been dropped are affected, and variables that refer to nondropped objects do not need to be reinitialized. In the following line of code, the Databases collection would be refreshed and any object variables set to individual databases (such as pubs) would be invalidated:

```
objSQLServer.Databases.Refresh(True)
```

SQL-DMO Lists

Using lists in SQL-DMO is similar to working with collections, except that you cannot use lists to create or delete objects. A List object, like the Collection object, contains a group of specific objects. It uses an index of identifiers to retrieve objects from collections, and, like all other objects, it contains properties and methods. Most lists are returned to

QueryResults objects for easier processing. For example, you can retrieve a list of all processes connected to your SQLServer object:

```
Dim qrsProcesses As SQLOLE.QueryResults
Set qrsProcesses = objSQLServer.EnumProcesses
```

You can also iterate through lists using the familiar For Each statement, as follows:

```
For Each objStoredProcedure In _
    objSQLServer.ListStartupProcedures
        Debug.Print objStoredProcedure.Name
Next objStoredProcedure
```

You can also use the Refresh method with a list, but, unlike collections, it does not release or invalidate object variables.

SQL-DMO Programming Examples

In this section we dig more into the specifics of many of the SQL-DMO objects. This is by no means a complete reference; the SQL Server "Programming SQL Distributed Management Objects" manual takes over 300 pages for an exhaustive listing. Rather, we'll try to cover some of the most important methods and properties that you can use in a client-server setting. Most of the code examples here are taken from SQLDEMO.MDB, the SQL Explorer sample application that's included on the companion disk.

SQL-DMO Sample Application

We've included a sample application which demonstrates some of the power of SQL-DMO. SQL Explorer is a general-purpose interface from

Access to SQL Server, similar in concept to the SQL Enterprise Manager, but with fewer features. We'll use code from this application as a way to demonstrate the use of SQL-DMO. The application is included on the companion CD, and you can use code from it to help build your own server management tools in Access.

SQL Explorer

The SQL Explorer is a general purpose tool to help you learn more about SQL Server from within Access, which may be a more familiar environment. To use it, open SQLDEMO.MDB in Access 95. You will be presented with the form shown in Figure 7.4, which will allow you to enter your server name, login, and password. When you click the Log In button, the form will attempt to establish a connection with the specified server.

FIGURE 7.4:

The SQL Explorer main form

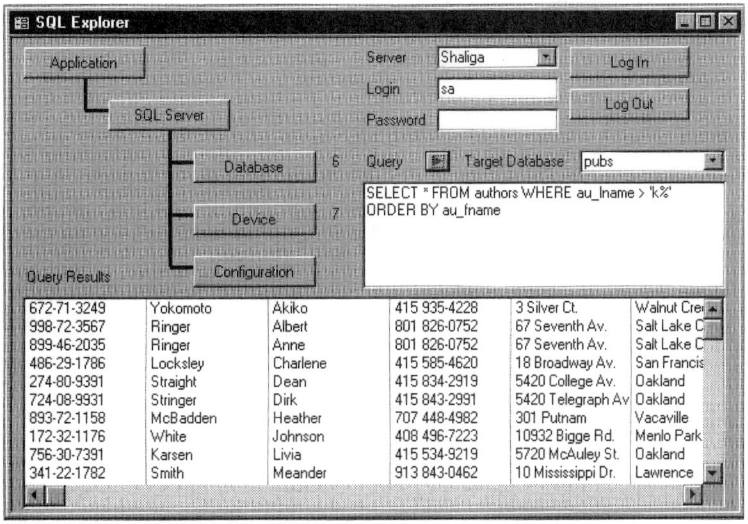

Because we will need a variable to refer to the SQL Server we are managing throughout this application, it's declared globally in basSQLServer:

```
Global gobjSQLServer As New SQLOLE.SQLServer
```

This variable is initialized by the SQLLogin() function. This function uses the .Connect method of the SQLServer object to connect to the particular server specified by the user:

```
Function SQLLogin(strServerName As String, _
    strUID As String, strPWD As String) As Boolean
' Log in to the indicated SQL Server using
' the supplied user id and password
' Sets the global SQLServer object
' Returns True on success, False on any error
On Error GoTo SQLLoginErr
    Const erSQLAlreadyLoggedIn = -2147211004
    SQLLogin = True

    DoCmd.Hourglass True
    gobjSQLServer.Connect strServerName, strUID, _
        strPWD

SQLLoginExit:
    DoCmd.Hourglass False
    Exit Function

SQLLoginErr:
    Select Case Err.Number
        Case erSQLAlreadyLoggedIn
            SQLLogin = True
            Resume Next
        Case Else
        MsgBox "Error " & Err.Number & ": " & _
            Err.Description, vbCritical, "SQLLogin()"
    End Select
    SQLLogin = False
    Resume SQLLoginExit
End Function
```

This is a general-purpose function you can use any time you need to connect to SQL Server via the DMO layer. In the SQL Explorer application, it's called from the Log In button. If the function succeeds, the application goes on to perform some other housekeeping steps:

1. Enable the other controls on the form.

2. Retrieve the number of databases and devices available.

3. Refresh any other loaded forms in the application.

4. Save the name of this server in the Registry.

5. Rebuild the list of databases on the main form.

Using the Registry to Store Information

One thing the SQL-DMO layer does not provide is a way to get the names of all running servers. Since it is an annoyance to enter the same information over and over again, we've provided a mechanism to keep track of servers the user has visited. Use this list to provide suggestions when the SQL Explorer application is started. To store this information, SQL Explorer uses the Windows Registry, a database of information that VBA can read and write directly under Windows NT or Windows 95.

When the user successfully connects to a server, the application uses the VBA SaveSetting statement to make a record of this.

```
SaveSetting "SQLExplorer", "Servers", Me![cboSer-
verName], 1
```

This adds a value to the registry key \\HKEY_CURRENT_USER\ SOFT-WARE\VB and VBA Program Settings\SQL Explorer\Servers. If you connect to a server named CATFISH, for example, it will write a key with the name "CATFISH" and the value 1 to this part of the registry tree.

When you open the SQL Explorer form, it uses the VBA GetAllSettings function to retrieve all values from this part of the registry.

```
Private Function GetServers() As String
' Get a list of known servers from the registry
    Dim varSettings As Variant
    Dim i As Integer
    Dim strServers As String
    varSettings = GetAllSettings("SQLExplorer", _
        "Servers")
    If IsEmpty(varSettings) Then
        GetServers = ""
    Else
        For i = LBound(varSettings, 1) To _
            UBound(varSettings, 1)
            strServers = strServers & _
                varSettings(i, 0) & ";"
        Next i
        GetServers = Left$(strServers, _
            Len(strServers) - 1)
    End If
End Function
```

GetAllSettings returns an array of key names and key values. This function takes advantage of VBA's ability to store an array in a variant, and walks through the returned array, extracting all the server names found. These are built up into a semicolon-delimited list which is used as the source of the Server's combo box on the main SQL Explorer form.

VBA also provides GetSetting and DeleteSetting statements to retrieve or remove individual registry settings.

Application

Clicking on the Application button opens the Application form, which will display the DB-Library Version, SQL-DMO Full Name, SQL-DMO Name, and SQL-DMO Version, as shown in Figure 7.5.

These text boxes are populated by the following procedure, Refresh-Me, which is called from the Open event of the form. Note that the

Application object is declared and that its properties are referenced as sources for the text box controls.

```
Sub RefreshMe()
    Dim objSQLApplication As SQLOLE.Application
    Set objSQLApplication = gobjSQLServer.Application
    With objSQLApplication
        Me![txtDBLibraryVersion] = .DBLibraryVersionString
        Me![txtFullName] = .FullName
        Me![txtName] = .Name
        Me![txtVersion] = CStr(.VersionMajor) & "." _
            & CStr(.VersionMinor)
    End With
End Sub
```

Each of the forms contains a RefreshMe procedure for populating its controls. By splitting this procedure off instead of including it as a part of the form's OnOpen event procedure, it becomes a method of the form and can be called from outside the form. For example, when the main form wants to refresh the Application form, it runs the single line of code:

```
Forms![frmApplication].RefreshMe
```

This ability to treat CBF procedures as methods of a form helps to greatly extend the object model of Access 95 compared to previous versions.

You'll see that there's really not a lot to the Application object in SQL-DMO. Table 7.3 lists properties which are common to all SQL-DMO objects, and Table 7.4 lists the unique properties of the Application object. Table 7.5 lists the single method of this object. Notice the .UserData property, which allows you to add a long integer of your choosing to the Application object. All SQL-DMO objects have a .UserData property, which you may use freely. However, these properties are not persistent—as soon as the object goes out of scope, they are reset to zero.

TABLE 7.3 : Common Object Properties

Property	Type	Write?	Comments
Application	Application	No	The Application object.
Parent	(varies)	No	The parent of the current object. The Application object is its own parent.
TypeOf	SQLOLE_OBJECT_TYPE	No	The type of object.
UserData	Long	Yes	Temporary storage space contained in this object for private use by the application. SQL-DMO does not use this property. User information stored in this property is discarded when the object goes out of scope.

TABLE 7.4 : Properties Unique to the Application Object

Property	Type	Write?	Comments
DBLibrary-VersionString	String	No	The DB-Library version string.
FullName	String	No	The full path and file name of the SQL-DMO component object layer. In SQL Server 6.0, this will be the location of the SQLOLE32.DLL file.
Name	String	No	The name of the SQL-DMO component object layer.
VersionMajor	Long	No	The SQL-DMO component object layer version number to the left of the decimal point.
VersionMinor	Long	No	The SQL-DMO component object layer version number to the right of the decimal point.

TABLE 7.5: The Single Method of the Application Object

Method	Comments
Quit	Closes all open connections made with the current application via SQL-DMO and releases all storage held. Any SQLOLE object variable will go out of scope when the Application.Quit method is executed.

SQL Server

Clicking on the SQL Server button opens the SQL Server form, shown in Figure 7.6, which also has a RefreshMe procedure retrieving the properties of the SQLServer object in order to fill its text boxes:

```
Sub RefreshMe()
    Dim intNetPacketSize As Integer
    Dim intStatus As Integer
    Dim strStatus As String
    With gobjSQLServer
        Me![txtName] = .Name
        Me![txtConnectionID] = .ConnectionID
        Me![txtHostName] = .HostName
        Me![txtLanguage] = .Language
        Me![txtMaxNumericPrecision] = .MaxNumericPrecision
        intNetPacketSize = .NetPacketSize
        ' 0 for Net Packet Size indicates SQL Server
        ' default of 4096 bytes
        If intNetPacketSize = 0 Then
            intNetPacketSize = 4096
        End If
        Me![txtNetPacketSize] = intNetPacketSize
        Me![txtProcessID] = .ProcessID
        Me![txtQueryTimeout] = .QueryTimeout
        intStatus = .Status
        Me![txtStatus] = SQLServerStatus(intStatus)
        Me![txtVersionString] = .VersionString
        With .Registry
            Me!chkAutostartLicensing = .AutostartLicensing
            Me!chkAutostartMail = .AutostartMail
            Me!chkAutostartServer = .AutostartServer
            Me!chkCaseSensitive = .CaseSensitive
            Me!txtErrorLogPath = .ErrorLogPath
```

```
            Me!txtMasterDBPath = .MasterDBPath
            Me!txtPhysicalMemory = CStr(.PhysicalMemory) & " MB"
            Me!txtSortOrder = .SortOrder
        End With
    End With
End Sub
```

The SQL Server form

Note that, depending on which property of the server you wish to re-trieve, you may need a different object to work with. The properties in the second column on the form (Autostart Licensing, Autostart Mail, and so on) are all stored in the Windows NT Registry. SQL-DMO pro-vides a special Registry object, a child of the SQLServer object, to retrieve these settings.

SQLServerStatus() is a general-purpose function to convert the intrinsic constant associated with the Status property of the server to an appro-priate text string that can be displayed to the user. There are many places in the SQL-DMO layer where such enumerated datatypes are used, and if you're going to make use of any of them you should probably come up with similar functions to ease the repetitive processing needed to display this information.

```
Function SQLServerStatus(intStatus As Integer) As String
' Translate the intrinsic server status constants to
' human-readable strings
    Select Case intStatus
        Case SQLOLESvc_Unknown
            SQLServerStatus = "Unknown"
        Case SQLOLESvc_Running
            SQLServerStatus = "Running"
        Case SQLOLESvc_Paused
            SQLServerStatus = "Paused"
        Case SQLOLESvc_Stopped
            SQLServerStatus = "Stopped"
        Case SQLOLESvc_Starting
            SQLServerStatus = "Starting"
        Case SQLOLESvc_Stopping
            SQLServerStatus = "Stopping"
        Case SQLOLESvc_Continuing
            SQLServerStatus = "Continuing"
        Case SQLOLESvc_Pausing
            SQLServerStatus = "Pausing"
        Case Else
            SQLServerStatus = "Unknown"
    End Select
End Function
```

The SQL Server form also has two buttons, Pause and Continue, which will either cause the server to pause or continue by invoking the corresponding methods of the SQLServer object:

```
gobjSQLServer.Pause
gobjSQLServer.Continue
```

We could also have provided buttons to start and stop the server entirely, but these operations are extremely dangerous in a multi-user situation, so we opted not to enable them.

Tables 7.6 and 7.7 show the properties and methods of the SQLServer object.

TABLE 7.6: SQLServer Object Properties

Property	Type	Write?	Comments
Application-Name	String	Before Connect	The name of the application. You can supply whatever string you like here before you actually connect to a particular server.
AutoReConnect	Boolean	Yes	Determines if SQL-DMO will automatically re-establish broken connections.
Command-Terminator	String	Yes	The Transact-SQL command terminator. If you don't set this, it defaults to the word "go."
Configuration	Configuration	No	The Configuration object for this SQL Server.
ConnectionID	Long	No	The SQL-DMO connection ID unique for this SQL-DMO instance.
Distribution-Database	String	No	The replication distribution database for this server (if one exists).
Distribution-Server	String	No	The replication distribution server for this server (if one exists).
Distribution-Working-Directory	String	Yes	The replication distribution working directory for this server (if one exists).
Executive	Executive	No	The Executive object for this SQL Server.
HostName	String	Before Connect	The name of the client computer. Supplied by the application.
Integrated-Security	Integrated-Security	No	The IntegratedSecurity object for this SQL Server.
Language	String	Yes	The language used by the SQL Server.
Login	Identifier	Before Connect	The login ID used to connect to SQL Server. This is the UID parameter you supply when you use the .Connect method to connect to a particular SQL Server.
LoginSecure	Boolean	Before Connect	Determines if a secure connection is requested when the Connect method is called. If True, a secure connection is requested. If False, a normal connection is requested.

TABLE 7.6: SQLServer Object Properties (continued)

Property	Type	Write?	Comments
LoginTimeout	Long	Before Connect	The number of seconds to wait for a connection attempt to succeed. The default is -1, which means 60 seconds. A value of 0 means no timeout.
MaxNumeric-Precision	Long	No	The maximum precision available for exact numeric datatypes, including decimal and numeric.
Name	String	Before Connect	The name of the SQL Server. Supplied by the application before you invoke the .Connect method.
NetPacketSize	Long	Before Connect	The network packet size in bytes. The default is 0, which means 4096 bytes.
NextDevice-Number	Long	No	The next available device number. The maximum device number is 256.
Password	Identifier	Before Connect	The password used to connect to SQL Server. This is the password parameter you supply to the Connect method.
ProcessID	Long	No	The SQL Server process ID of the connection used by the SQLServer object.
QueryTimeout	Long	Yes	The number of seconds to wait for a query execution attempt to begin returning results. Use -1 or 0 to set this to be an infinite wait.
Registry	Registry	No	The Registry object for this SQL Server.
SaLogin	Boolean	No	Indicates if the login used for the connection has system administrator (SA) privilege on the server.
Status	SQLOLE_SVCSTATUS_TYPE	No	The service status of the SQL Server (whether it is running, paused, etc.).
TrueLogin	Identifier	No	The real login used of the connection to SQL Server. This may be different than Login for a secure connection.
TrueName	Identifier	No	The name of the SQL Server stored in @@servername.

TABLE 7.6: SQLServer Object Properties (continued)

Property	Type	Write?	Comments
UserProfile	SQLOLE_ SRVUSERPRO FILE_ TYPE	No	The SQL Server profile information for the currently connected user. This information includes the security status of the user.
VersionMajor	Long	No	The SQL Server version number to the left of the decimal point.
VersionMinor	Long	No	The SQL Server version number to the right of the decimal point.
VersionString	String	No	The version of the SQL Server stored in @@version.

TABLE 7.7: SQLServer Object Methods

Method	Comments
BeginTransaction	Starts a transaction on the server (a group of related activities which will be written to disk as a whole).
Close	Disconnects from the SQL Server.
Command-ShellImmediate	Shells out to the operating system without returning results.
CommandShell-WithResults	Shells out to the operating system and returns any output in a QueryResults object.
Commit-Transaction	Writes an open transaction to disk.
Connect	Connects to a specific SQL Server.
Continue	Continues a paused server.
DisConnect	Disconnects from the current SQL Server.
Execute-Immediate	Executes a Transact-SQL statement on the server without returning results.
Execute-WithResults	Executes a Transact-SQL statement on the server and returns any results in a QueryResults object.
KillDatabase	Removes a damaged database.
KillProcess	Ends a process on the specified server. You can't use KillProcess to end the process that this Server is connected via.
Pause	Pauses a running server.

TABLE 7.7 : SQLServer Object Methods (continued)

Method	Comments
ProcessInput-Buffer	Retrieves the input buffer for a specified process.
ProcessOutput-Buffer	Retrieves the output buffer for a specified process.
PurgeHistory	Removes information from the task history log for this server.
ReadBackup-Header	Retrieves information about backups stored in a particular dump device, and places this information into a QueryResults object.
ReadErrorLog	Reads the error log for this server and places the information into a QueryResults object.
ReConnect	Re-establishes a connection that was closed with DisConnect, as long as you haven't connected to a different server with this SQLServer object since.
RemoveSubscriber-Subscriptions	Terminates the subscriptions of a particular subscriber on this server.
Rollback-Transaction	Discards any open transaction.
SaveTransaction	Sets a savepoint within an open transaction.
Start	Starts an SQL Server.
StatusRefresh-Interval	Controls how often SQL Server information is fetched back to the local cache.
ShutDown	Stops a running SQL Server.
UnloadODSDLL	Unloads an Open Data Services DLL from memory.
VerifyConnection	Checks to make sure that a connected SQLServer object is still valid.

Database

Clicking on the Database button opens the Databases form, which shows a list of the available databases on the server. Selecting a database from the list will populate the controls on the form with information for that particular database, as shown in the Figure 7.7.

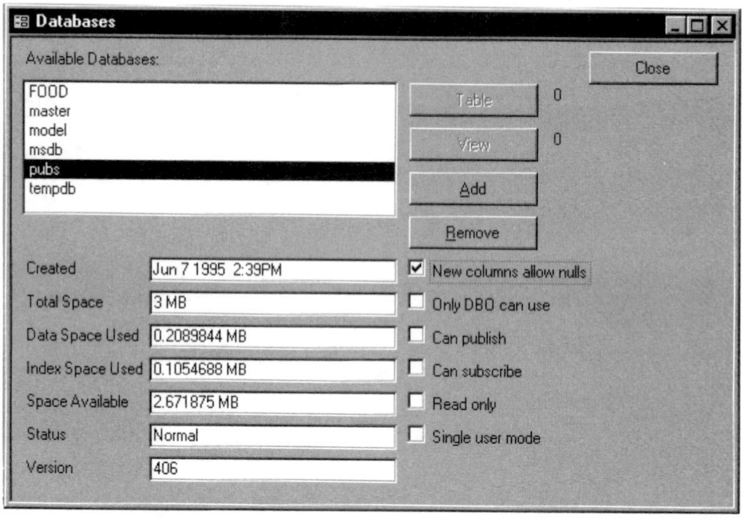

FIGURE 7.7:

The Databases form

For ease of programming, we opted to make the list box on this form a bound list box, relying on a temporary local table. The RefreshMe sub-procedure, which is called by the OnOpen event, flushes and refills this temporary table and then requeries the list box.

```
Sub RefreshMe()
    Dim rstDatabase As Recordset
    Dim objDatabase As SQLOLE.Database

    CurrentDb.Execute "DELETE * FROM tblDatabase"

    Set rstDatabase = CurrentDb.OpenRecordset("tblDatabase")
    With rstDatabase
        For Each objDatabase In gobjSQLServer.Databases
            .AddNew
                ![DatabaseName] = objDatabase.Name
            .Update
        Next objDatabase
    End With
    Me![lboDatabases].Requery
End Sub
```

When the user selects a database in the list box, the properties are retrieved for that particular database (there's no point in retrieving all properties of all databases, since the user might never look at some of them). This is accomplished in the after update event of the list box:

```
Private Sub lboDatabases_AfterUpdate()
' Retrieve properties for indicated database
    Dim intStatus As Integer
    Dim strStatus As String
    DoCmd.Hourglass True
    If Not IsNull(Me![lboDatabases]) Then
        Me![cmdTables].enabled = True
        Me![cmdViews].enabled = True
        ' First get the actual database properties
        With gobjSQLServer.Databases(CStr(Me![lboDatabases]))
            Me![lblTableCount]. _
                caption = .Tables.Count
            Me![lblViewCount]. _
                caption = .Views.Count
            Me![txtCreateDate] = .CreateDate
            Me![txtDataSpaceUsage _
                ] = CStr(.DataSpaceUsage) & " MB"
            Me![txtIndexSpaceUsage _
                ] = CStr(.IndexSpaceUsage) & " MB"
            Me![txtSize] = CStr(.Size) & " MB"
            Me![txtSpaceAvailableInMB _
                ] = CStr(.SpaceAvailableInMB) & " MB"
            intStatus = .Status
            Me![txtStatus] = SQLDatabaseStatus(intStatus)
            Me![txtVersion] = .Version
            ' Now retrieve the DBOption properties
            With .DBOption
                Me![chkColumnsNullByDefault _
                    ] = .ColumnsNullByDefault
                Me![chkDBOUseOnly] = .DBOUseOnly
                Me![chkEnablePublishing _
                    ] = .EnablePublishing
                Me![chkEnableSubscribing _
                    ] = .EnableSubscribing
                Me![chkReadOnly] = .ReadOnly
                Me![chkSingleUser] = .SingleUser
            End With
        End With
```

```
    Else
        ' If no database selected, put defaults everywhere
        Me![cmdTables].enabled = False
        Me![cmdViews].enabled = False
        Me![lblTableCount].caption = 0
        Me![lblViewCount].caption = 0
        Me![txtCreateDate] = ""
        Me![txtDataSpaceUsage] = ""
        Me![txtIndexSpaceUsage] = ""
        Me![txtSize] = ""
        Me![txtSpaceAvailableInMB] = ""
        Me![txtStatus] = ""
        Me![txtVersion] = ""
    End If
    DoCmd.Hourglass False
End Sub
```

Note the Database object is somewhat more complex than the other objects we have looked at so far. In particular, some of its properties are actually assigned to a subsidiary object, the DBOption object. This object has a series of Boolean properties—for example, whether or not the database is in read-only mode. As all of these properties are read/write, we've added code to the AfterUpdate event of each check box to actually update them on the selected database.

```
Private Sub chkSingleUser_AfterUpdate()
    gobjSQLServer.Databases(CStr(Me![ _
        lboDatabases])).DBOption.SingleUser = Me![chkSin-
gleUser]
End Sub
```

The Databases form also gives the user the ability to add and remove databases. Removing a database is simple, since this involves only using the .Remove method of the Databases collection, but because of the danger of this operation, we make sure to put up a warning method first.

```
Private Sub cmdRemove_Click()
    Dim intResponse As Integer
    If Not IsNull(Me![lboDatabases]) Then
        intResponse = MsgBox("Removing this database will " & _
```

```
                    "permanently delete all data in it. Are you SURE?", _
                    vbOKCancel + vbCritical + vbDefaultButton2, _
                    "Remove Device Warning")
            If intResponse = vbOK Then _
                gobjSQLServer.Databases(CStr(Me![lboDatabases])) _
                .Remove
                If SQLIsLoaded("frmSQLExplorerTop") Then
                    Forms![frmSQLExplorerTop]![lblDatabaseCount _
                        ].caption = CStr(SQLGetDatabaseCount())
                End If
                Call RefreshMe
            End If
    End If
End Sub
```

In addition to removing the selected database, this procedure also up-dates the display of the number of available databases on the main form and refreshes the information displayed on the database form.

Adding a database is a bit more difficult, since it requires prompting the user for information. SQL Explorer accomplishes this by opening a separate form, frmAddNewDatabase, as seen in Figure 7.8. This form prompts for necessary information, and then makes the new database in its own CBF. This CBF calls the generic SQLMakeNewDatabase() function, which you can use in your own databases.

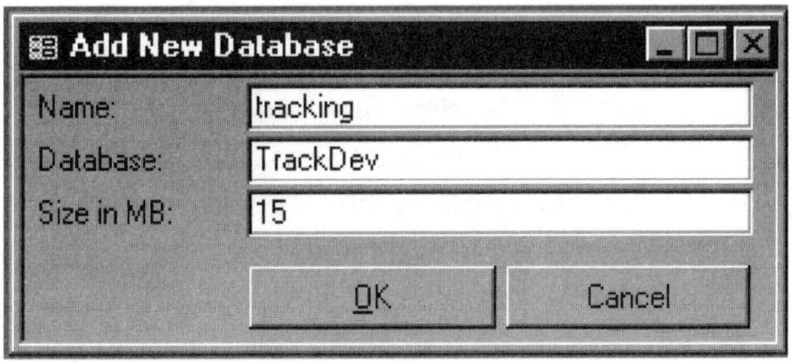

FIGURE 7.8:

Adding a new database

```
Function SQLMakeNewDatabase(strName As String, _
    strDeviceName As String, lngSize As Long)
' Makes a new database for the current SQL Server
On Error GoTo SQLMakeNewDatabaseErr
    SQLMakeNewDatabase = True

    Dim objNewDatabase As New SQLOLE.Database
    If Not gobjSQLServer Is Nothing Then
        DoCmd.Hourglass True
        With objNewDatabase
            .Name = strName
        End With
        ' This will create the database on the default device
        gobjSQLServer.Databases.Add objNewDatabase
        ' Now add extra size on the specified device
        With objNewDatabase
            .ExtendOnDevices (strDeviceName & "=" & _
                CStr(lngSize))
            .Shrink (lngSize)
        End With
    Else
        SQLMakeNewDatabase = False
    End If

SQLMakeNewDatabaseExit:
    DoCmd.Hourglass False
    Exit Function

SQLMakeNewDatabaseErr:
    MsgBox "Error " & Err.Number & ": " & Err.Description, _
        vbCritical, "SQLMakeNewDatabase()"
    SQLMakeNewDatabase = False
    Resume SQLMakeNewDatabaseExit
End Function
```

Note that all new databases are created on the default device, and that we then use methods of the Database object to move as much space as possible to the device specified by the user when calling this function. Tables 7.8 and 7.9 show the properties and methods of the Database object, including some that we don't use in our example.

TABLE 7.8: Database Object Properties

Property	Type	Write?	Comments
CreateDate	String	No	The date and time this database was created.
CreateForLoad	Boolean	Before Add	Determines if this database was created with the FOR LOAD option. A database created with this option is placed in a special state that does not allow modifying the data until the database owner verifies that existing data has been loaded properly.
DataSpaceUsage	Float	No	The space in megabytes (accurate to two decimal places) used to store data.
DBOLogin	Boolean	No	Indicates if the login used for the connection (contained in the SQLServer object) has database owner privilege in this database.
DBOption	DBOption	No	The DBOption object for this database.
IndexSpace-Usage	Float	No	The space in megabytes (accurate to two decimal places) used to store indexes.
ID	Long	No	The database ID.
MinimumSize	Long	No	The minimum size this database can be reduced to with the Shrink method.
Name	Identifier	Yes	The name of this database.
Owner	Identifier	No	The login of the database owner.
Size	Long	No	The total storage space in megabytes allocated for this database. This includes both used and available space.
SpaceAvailable	Long	No	The unused storage space in kilobytes available for new data.
SpaceAvailable-InMB	Float	No	The unused storage space in megabytes (accurate to two decimal places) available for new data.

TABLE 7.8: Database Object Properties (continued)

Property	Type	Write?	Comments
Status	SQLOLE_DBSTATUS_TYPE	No	The status of this database.
SystemObject	Boolean	No	Indicates if this is an SQL Server system database. If True, this is an SQL Server system database. If False, this database was created by a user.
TransactionLog	TransactionLog	No	The TransactionLog object for this database.
UserName	Identifier	Yes	Name of the current database user. The system administrator or database owner can change this property to that of an existing user in this database, thus impersonating the other user.
UserProfile	SQLOLE_DBUSER PROFILE_TYPE	No	The database profile information for the currently connected user.
Version	Long	No	The version of the database as contained in the sysdatabases system table.

TABLE 7.9: Database Object Methods

Method	Comments
CheckAllocations	Performs a DBCC NEW ALLOC on the database.
CheckCatalog	Performs a DBCC CHECKCATALOG on the database.
Checkpoint	Flushes the SQL Server cache for this database, causing all changed pages to be written to disk immediately.
CheckTables	Performs a DBCC CHECKDB and DBCC CHECKTABLE on the database.
CheckText-AllocsFast	Performs a fast check of the consistency of text and image pages in the database.
CheckText-AllocsFull	Performs a full check of the consistency of text and image pages in the database.

TABLE 7.9: Database Object Methods (continued)

Method	Comments
Dump	Backs up the database.
Execute-Immediate	Executes a Transact-SQL statement on the database without returning results.
ExecuteWith-Results	Executes a Transact-SQL statement on the database and returns any results in a QueryResults object.
ExtendOnDevices	Creates additional storage space for the database.
Generate-BackupSQL	Generates a backup script for the database.
GetDatatypeBy-Name	Returns an object of any datatype, including a user-defined datatype.
GetMemoryUsage	Performs a DBCC MEMUSAGE on the database.
GetObjectBy-Name	Returns an object of the specified SQL-DMO type.
Grant	Gives privilege to users or groups.
IsValidKey-Datatype	Checks a datatype as to whether it can be used in a primary key.
Load	Loads a backup into this database.
ManualSync Completed	Tells the database that you have finished a pending replication synchronization.
ManualSync Pending	Tells the database that you are about to start a manual replication synchronization.
RecalcSpace-Usage	Recalculates all the space usage properties of the database.
Remove	Drops the database from the server and closes the Database object.
Revoke	Removes privileges from users or groups.
SetOwner	Changes the ownership of the database to another login.
Shrink	Removes space from a database.
SpaceAllocated-OnDevice	Returns storage allocated for this database on a particular device.

Executing a Query

SQL-DMO provides yet another alternative for retrieving data from SQL Server, with its ExecuteImmediate and ExecuteWithResults methods. In our timings, these methods are as fast as doing queries against attached tables, and faster than passthrough queries for many operations. There are some other factors to keep in mind when choosing this method of querying a server:

- Like passthrough queries, queries done via SQL-DMO are always Snapshots rather than Dynasets. However, you can execute Update and Insert queries to change data on the server.

- In a networked environment, you don't have to do any special setup to make the server visible to the client via SQL-DMO. Compared to keeping ODBC data sources up to date, this is a significant improvement.

- You can only use SQL-DMO querying from 32-bit clients, whereas ODBC can connect 16-bit clients to 32-bit servers.

In the SQL Explorer application, the main form provides an interface for SQL-DMO queries, as shown in Figure 7.9. You can execute a query against either the SQLServer object or an individual Database object by using the appropriate SQL string. For the Server object, you need to specify the database name in the SQL string—for example, "SELECT * FROM pubs.dbo.authors". To query a specific database, you can leave out the database name, for example, "SELECT*FROM dbo.authors". Any valid Transact-SQL statement can be executed against a server this way.

The SQL Explorer main form uses an Access callback function to display the results of SQL-DMO queries. A callback function provides a means to use an arbitrary function to fill a list box or combo box; Access calls it when it wants a specific piece of information—for example, the number of rows in the result set or the data for a particular row and column. The SQLQueryList() function in the SQL Explorer database does the work:

```
Function SQLQueryList(ctl As Control, varID As Variant, _
    lngRow As Long, _
    lngCol As Long, intCode As Integer)
    On Error GoTo SQLQueryListErr
    Static qrs As SQLOLE.QueryResults

    Select Case intCode
        Case acLBInitialize
            If Len(Forms![frmSQLExplorerTop]![cboDatabase] _
                & "") = O Then
                Set qrs = gobjSQLServer.ExecuteWithResults _
                    (Forms![frmSQLExplorerTop]![txtQuery])
            Else
                Set qrs = gobjSQLServer.Data-
bases(CStr(Forms![frmSQLExplorerTop] _
    ![cboDatabase])).ExecuteWithResults(Forms _
    ![frmSQLExplorerTop]![txtQuery])
            End If
```

```
            SQLQueryList = True
        Case acLBOpen
            SQLQueryList = Timer
        Case acLBGetRowCount
            SQLQueryList = qrs.Rows
        Case acLBGetColumnCount
            SQLQueryList = qrs.Columns
        Case acLBGetColumnWidth
            SQLQueryList = 1440
        Case acLBGetValue
            If Not qrs Is Nothing Then
                SQLQueryList = qrs.GetColumnString( _
                    Row:=lngRow + 1, _
                    Column:=lngCol + 1)
            Else
                SQLQueryList = ""
            End If
        Case acLBGetFormat
            SQLQueryList = -1
        Case LB_END
            Set qrs = Nothing
    End Select

SQLQueryListExit:
    Exit Function

SQLQueryListErr:
    MsgBox "Error " & Err.Number & ": " & Err.Description, _
        vbCritical, "SQLQueryList()"
    SQLQueryList = False
    Resume SQLQueryListExit
End Function
```

The two key methods used in this example are the .ExecuteWithResults method and the .GetColumnString method. The .ExecuteWith-Results method sends a query to the SQL Server or database specified, and returns a QueryResults object. This object in turn has a .GetColumn-String method which can return the data from an arbitrary field and row of the result set. The QueryResults object also has .Rows and .Columns properties which specify the size of the result set. Armed with this information, writing the appropriate callback function is easy.

Although a QueryResults object is read-only, you could write some additional code to update the results. This would require retrieving the primary key of the result set and then writing single-row Update queries, which could be executed with the .ExecuteImmediate methods of either the SQLServer or Database objects.

Table

From the Database form, you can select a specific database and click the Table button to drill down to the Tables form, as shown in Figure 7.10. This form actually presents information on the Tables and shows two of the collections of a table when you select it: Columns and Indexes.

FIGURE 7.10:
The SQL Explorer Tables form

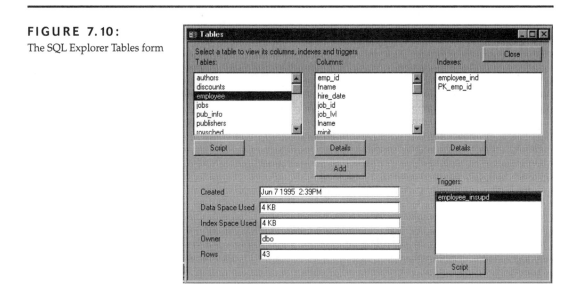

This form uses the same techniques for retrieving data as do the previous ones in the series. The major difference is that the Tables form is designed to show information on the child objects of the table as well as the table itself, so the procedures involved are more complex. For example, when a table is selected from the list box, it must iterate three separate collections to retrieve all the information that it displays.

```
Private Sub lboTables_AfterUpdate()
    Dim rstDatabase As Recordset
    Dim objColumn As SQLOLE.Column
    Dim objIndex As SQLOLE.Index
    Dim objTable As SQLOLE.Table
    Dim objTrigger As SQLOLE.Trigger

    DoCmd.Hourglass True

    Set objTable = mobjDB.Tables(CStr(Me!lboTables))

    CurrentDb.Execute "DELETE * FROM tblColumn"
    CurrentDb.Execute "DELETE * FROM tblIndex"
    CurrentDb.Execute "DELETE * FROM tblTrigger"

    Set rstDatabase = CurrentDb.OpenRecordset("tblColumn")
    For Each objColumn In _
        mobjDB.Tables(CStr(Me!lboTables)).Columns
        rstDatabase.AddNew
            rstDatabase![ColumnName] = objColumn.Name
        rstDatabase.Update
    Next objColumn
    Me![lboColumns].Requery

    Set rstDatabase = CurrentDb.OpenRecordset("tblIndex")
    For Each objIndex In _
        mobjDB.Tables(CStr(Me!lboTables)).Indexes
        rstDatabase.AddNew
            rstDatabase![IndexName] = objIndex.Name
        rstDatabase.Update
    Next objIndex
    Me![lboIndexes].Requery

    Set rstDatabase = CurrentDb.OpenRecordset("tblTrigger")
    For Each objTrigger In _
        mobjDB.Tables(CStr(Me!lboTables)).Triggers
        rstDatabase.AddNew
            rstDatabase![TriggerName] = objTrigger.Name
        rstDatabase.Update
    Next objTrigger
    Me![lboTriggers].Requery
```

```
    Me![txtCreateDate] = objTable.CreateDate
    Me![txtDataSpaceUsage] = objTable.DataSpaceUsed & " KB"
    Me![txtIndexSpaceUsage] = objTable.IndexSpaceUsed & " KB"
    Me![txtOwner] = objTable.Owner
    Me![txtRows] = objTable.Rows

    DoCmd.Hourglass False
End Sub
```

The Script button takes advantage of SQL Server's ability to decompile its own objects—a capability which Access does not have. When you press this button, it invokes the Script method of the selected table:

```
Private Sub cmdScript_Click()
    Dim strScript As String
    If Not IsNull(Me!lboTables) Then
        strScript = mobjDB.Tables(CStr(Me!lboTables)).Script
        DoCmd.OpenForm "frmTableScript"
        Forms!frmTableScript!txtTableScript = strScript
    End If
End Sub
```

The resulting script is displayed on the Table Script form, shown in Figure 7.11. Unfortunately, Access cannot properly display tabs in a text box, but the information is still there and can be saved out to disk. If

FIGURE 7.11:

Script created from a table

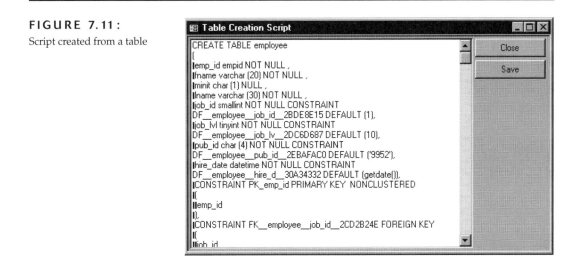

you load the saved script into ISQL or another SQL querying tool and run it, this script will recreate the original table.

Tables 7.10 and 7.11 list the properties and methods of SQL-DMO Table objects.

TABLE 7.10 : SQL-DMO Table Object Properties

Property	Type	Write?	Comments
Attributes	SQLOLE_ TABLEATT_TYPE	No	The attributes of this table. You can use this property to check whether a table is a system object, a replicated table, whether it has a constraint, and so on.
ClusteredIndex	Index	No	The Clustered Index object for this table (if it has one).
CreateDate	String	No	The date and time this table was created.
DataSpaceUsed	Long	No	Storage space in kilobytes used by the rows of this table.
ID	Long	No	The object ID of the table.
Index- SpaceUsed	Long	No	Storage space in kilobytes used by the indexes on this table.
Name	Identifier	Yes	The name of the table.
Owner	Identifier	No	The user who created the table.
PrimaryKey	Key	No	The Primary Key object for this table, if it has one.
Rows	Long	No	The number of rows currently in this table. You may need to execute the table's .Refresh method to update this number.
SystemObject	Boolean	No	Indicates if this is an SQL Server system table. If True, this is an SQL Server system table. If False, this table was created by a user.

TABLE 7.11 : SQL-DMO Table Object Methods

Method	Comments
BeginAlter	Similar to starting a transaction on data, the BeginAlter method tells SQL Server to start saving changes to a table to execute as a unit.
CancelAlter	Discards any changes pending since a BeginAlter method.
CheckTable	Performs a DBCC CHECKTABLE on the table.
CheckText-AllocsFast	Performs a DBCC TEXTALLOC FAST on the table.
CheckText-AllocsFull	Performs a DBCC TEXTALLOC FULL on the table.
DoAlter	Performs any changes pending since a BeginAlter method.
DoAlterWithNo-Check	Performs any changes pending since a BeginAlter method, but does not check existing data in the table for compliance with new constraints.
Grant	Grants privileges to users or groups.
InsertColumn	Adds a new column to the table. Note that new columns can only be added to the end of the table, and existing columns cannot be deleted. To delete a column, you must build a replacement table without the column, transfer the data, delete the original table, and rename the new table.
RecalcSpace-Usage	Updates the properties dealing with disk space usage.
Recompile-References	Marks each stored procedure and trigger that depends on this table to be recompiled the next time it is executed.
Refresh	Updates the table properties with the current information from the server.
Remove	Drops the table from SQL Server and removes its reference.
Revoke	Revokes privileges from users or groups.
Script	Generates a Transact-SQL Script to recreate this table.
TruncateData	Removes all data from the table.
UpdateStatistics	Recalculates all index statistics for this table. These are used by SQL Server to determine the most efficient query plan for queries involving the table.

Column

When you select an individual table on the Tables form, SQL Explorer shows you all of the columns in the table. Double-clicking a column, or selecting a column and clicking the Details button, will bring up a separate form with some of the properties of the column, as shown in Figure 7.12. The code for retrieving the properties of the column is quite simple, and is kept in the RefreshMe procedure of the column form.

```
Sub RefreshMe()
    Dim objColumn As SQLOLE.Column

    Set objColumn = mobjTable.Columns( _
        CStr(Forms![frmTable]![lboColumns]))
    With objColumn
        Me![chkAllowNulls] = .AllowNulls
        Me![txtDatatype] = .Datatype
        Me![txtLength] = .Length
        Me![txtName] = .Name
    End With
End Sub
```

FIGURE 7.12:

Details of a table column

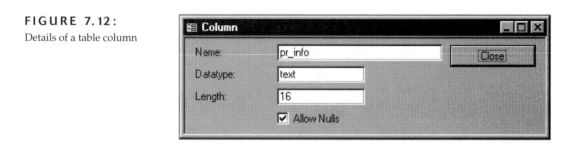

The Tables form also allows you to add a new column to an existing table. This is simply a matter of opening a form to collect information for the column, creating a new Column object, and adding it to the Table's Columns collection:

```
Private Sub cmdOK_Click()
    Dim objColumn As New SQLOLE.Column
    With objColumn
```

```
            .Name = CStr(Me![txtName])
            .Datatype = CStr(Me![cboDataType])
            .Length = CLng(Me![txtLength])
            .AllowNulls = Me![chkAllowNulls]
        End With
        mobjTable.Columns.Add objColumn
End Sub
```

Although adding a column to an existing table is simple, SQL Server does not let you remove a column from a table. You can, of course, simply stop using a column, or even create a new table and copy the contents of all the other columns to the new table. SQL Server also does not allow adding a new column to an existing table unless its AllowNulls property is set to True, so on the Add Column form this is permanently set as a default. (We've left an invisible check box for choosing this value in case you want to use this form in an application of your own that adds Columns to new tables).

Tables 7.12 and 7.13 show the properties and single method of Column objects in SQL-DMO.

TABLE 7.12: SQL-DMO Column Object Properties

Property	Type	Write?	Comments
AllowNulls	Boolean	Before Add	If True, the column allows NULL values.
DataType	Identifier	Before Add	The system or user-defined datatype of the column.
Default	Identifier	Yes	The default bound to the column, if any.
DRIDefault	DRIDefault	No	The DRIDefault object for this column, if any. DRIDefault objects provide information on SQL 6.0's Domain Referential Integrity.
ID	Long	No	The column ID and ordinal number in the table.
Identity	Boolean	Before Add	If True, this is the identity column for this table.

TABLE 7.12: SQL-DMO Column Object Properties (continued)

Property	Type	Write?	Comments
IdentityIncrement	Long	Before Add	The value added to the previous identity value to get the next identity value.
IdentitySeed	Long	Before Add	The value automatically assigned to the identity column of the first row inserted into the table.
InPrimaryKey	Boolean	Before Add	True if this column is part of the primary key for this table.
Length	Long	Before Add	The number of bytes used to store a value in this column.
Name	Identifier	Yes	The column name.
NumericPreci-sion	Long	Before Add	The precision of an exact numeric datatype column.
NumericScale	Long	Before Add	The scale of an exact numeric datatype column.
PhysicalDataType	Identifier	No	The system datatype on which the user-defined datatype is based, if this column is based on a user-defined datatype.
Rule	Identifier	Yes	The rule bound to the column, if any.

TABLE 7.13: SQL-DMO Column Object Method

Method	Comments
Remove	Removes the column from its table. This method can only be used on columns that are part of tables that have not yet been added to the Tables collection.

Index

The Tables form in the SQL Explorer application also shows the indexes for the selected table. Selecting an index and clicking the Detail button brings up the Index form, as shown in Figure 7.13. The properties and methods of index objects are shown in Tables 7.14 and 7.15.

FIGURE 7.13:
Details of an Index object

TABLE 7.14: Index Object Properties

Property	Type	Write?	Comments
FillFactor	Long	Before Add	The percent of each page that SQL Server will fill with index data when creating a new index on a table. Valid values are 0 through 100. Using a smaller fill factor will make operations that rearrange the index more efficient at the cost of extra storage space.
ID	Long	No	The object ID of the index.
Name	Identifier	Yes	The name of the index.
SpaceUsed	Long	No	Storage space in kilobytes used by this index.
Type	SQLOLE_ INDEX_ TYPE	Before Add	The type of index. By evaluating this property you can tell, for example, whether or not an index is clustered.

Trigger

Selecting a trigger and pressing the Script button shows the Transact-SQL for the selected trigger. This script, as shown in Figure 7.14, may be quite lengthy.

The script for a trigger is retrieved with its .Script method. The other most important property for a trigger is the type of trigger it is. This is represented by the Type property of the trigger. However, unlike most other enumerated types, a particular trigger may be more than one of

TABLE 7.15: Index Object Methods

Method	Comments
Generate-CreationSQL	Generates a series of Transact-SQL statements that can be used to generate an index with the same properties on another table.
IndexedColumns	The IndexedColumns method accepts a semicolon-delimited list of columns, and is used when creating a new index to tell it which columns to index.
Rebuild	Drops and recreates the index. Can be useful when you've made a lot of changes and index pages are filling up.
RecalcSpace-Usage	Updates the statistics of space used by this index.
Remove	Removes the index.
Script	Generates a series of Transact-SQL statements to recreate this index.
UpdateStatistics	Causes SQL Server to analyze the index based on its current data to determine its most efficient use in Transact-SQL operations.

FIGURE 7.14:

Script for a trigger

```
/* ************************ employee trigger ************************ */
/*
 Because CHECK constraints can only reference the column(s)
 on which the column- or table-level constraint has
 been defined, any cross-table constraints (in this case,
 business rules) need to be defined as triggers.

 Employee job_lvls (on which salaries are based) should be within
 the range defined for their job. To get the appropriate range,
 the jobs table needs to be referenced. This trigger will be
 invoked for INSERT and UPDATES only. For information about
 triggers, see the Microsoft SQL Server Transact-SQL Reference.
*/
CREATE TRIGGER employee_insupd
ON employee
FOR INSERT, UPDATE
AS
/* Get the range of level for this job type from the jobs table. */
DECLARE @min_lvl tinyint,
    @max_lvl tinyint
```

these types, since a particular trigger may be fired by multiple events. To check the type of a trigger, you need to use the SQL-DMO-supplied constants to evaluate the individual bits in the Type property:

```
Function SQLTriggerType(objTrigger As SQLOLE.Trigger) As
String
    Dim strType As String
    If objTrigger.Type And SQLOLETrig_Insert Then
        strType = strType & "Insert"
    End If
    If objTrigger.Type And SQLOLETrig_Update Then
        strType = strType & ", Update"
    End If
    If objTrigger.Type And SQLOLETrig_Delete Then
        strType = strType & ", Delete"
    End If
    If Left$(strType, 1) = "," Then
        SQLTriggerType = Mid$(strType, 3)
    Else
        SQLTriggerType = strType
    End If
End Function
```

View

The View button on the Database form brings up a list of all views in this database (of the SQL Server default databases, only the pubs database contains any views). This Form is shown in Figure 7.15, displaying "titleview" from the pubs database.

FIGURE 7.15:

The Views form

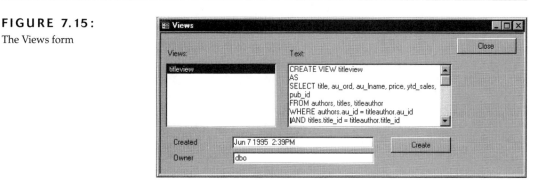

Once again, retrieving the properties of a view is simple:

```
Private Sub lboViews_AfterUpdate()
    Dim objView As SQLOLE.View
    Set objView = mobjDB.Views(CStr(Me!lboViews))

    Me![txtCreateDate] = objView.CreateDate
    Me![txtText] = objView.Text
    Me![txtOwner] = objView.Owner

End Sub
```

The Create button on the Views form allows you to create new views. Creating new views in SQL Server is rather simple via DMO, since the only properties of the View object you need to set are the Text (SQL Statement for the view) and Name properties. The code behind frmCreateView handles this job and provides error trapping for any Transact-SQL or other errors. For example, you cannot have an ORDER BY clause in a view (though you can later run an SQL statement to SELECT from a view and add an ORDER BY at that point).

```
Private Sub cmdCreate_Click()
On Error GoTo cmdCreateErr
    Dim objView As New SQLOLE.View
    If Not IsNull(Me!txtName) And Not IsNull(Me!txtText) Then
        objView.Name = Me!txtName
        objView.Text = Me!txtText
gobjSQLServer.Databases(CStr(Forms!frmDatabase! _
        lboDatabases)). _
    Views.Add objView
    End If
    Forms!frmView.RefreshMe
    DoCmd.Close acForm, Me.Name
CmdCreateExit:
    Exit Sub
cmdCreateErr:
    MsgBox "Error " & Err.Number & ": " & _
        Err.Description, vbCritical, "cmdCreate()"
    Resume CmdCreateExit
End Sub
```

Tables 7.16 and 7.17 list the properties and methods for SQL-DMO View objects.

TABLE 7.16: SQL-DMO View Object Properties

Property	Type	Write?	Comments
CreateDate	String	No	The date and time the view was created.
ID	Long	No	The object ID of the view.
Name	Identifier	Yes	The name of the view.
Owner	Identifier	No	The user who created the view.
SystemObject	Boolean	No	This will be true for system views created by the SQL Server itself, and False for user-created views.
Text	LargeText	Before Add	The original Transact-SQL statement used to create the view.

TABLE 7.17: View Object Methods

Method	Comments
Grant	Grants privileges on the view to users or groups.
Remove	Drops the view and removes the View object.
Revoke	Revokes privileges on the View object from users or groups.
Script	Generates a series of Transact-SQL statements to recreate this view.

Device

SQL Server uses devices to store databases, including their transaction logs. Dump devices are used for backup, and restore devices are used in loading operations. Clicking on the main form's Device button opens the Device form and populates its Device list box with the RefreshMe procedure, which lists the server's available devices:

```
Sub RefreshMe()
    Dim rstDevice As Recordset
    Dim objDevice As SQLOLE.Device

    CurrentDb.Execute "DELETE * FROM tblDevice"
```

```
    Set rstDevice = CurrentDb.OpenRecordset("tblDevice")
    For Each objDevice In gobjSQLServer.Devices
        rstDevice.AddNew
            rstDevice![DeviceName] = objDevice.Name
        rstDevice.Update
    Next objDevice
    Me![lboDevices].Requery
End Sub
```

After selecting a particular device from the list, the additional controls on the form are populated by an AfterUpdate procedure. The populated form is shown in Figure 7.16.

```
Private Sub lboDevices_AfterUpdate()
    DoCmd.Hourglass True
    If Not IsNull(Me![lboDevices]) Then
        With gobjSQLServer.Devices(CStr(Me![lboDevices]))
            Me![txtDeviceNumber] = .DeviceNumber
            Me![txtMirrorName] = .MirrorName
            Me![txtPhysicalLocation] = .PhysicalLocation
```

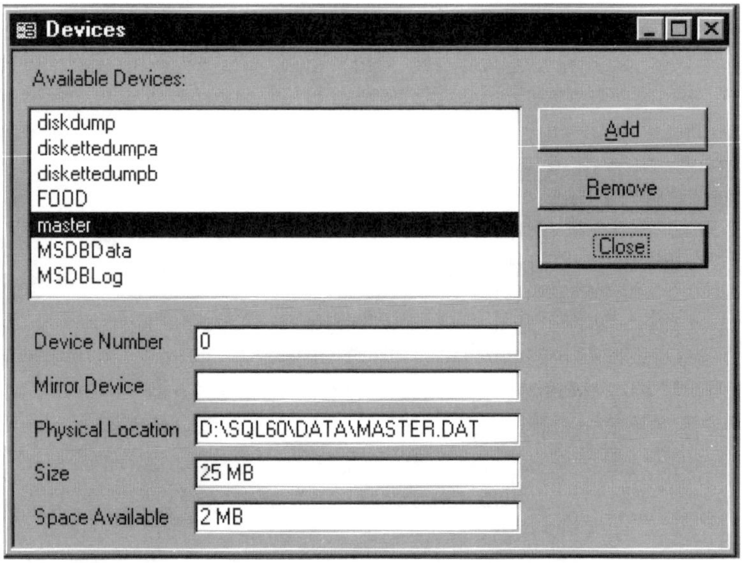

FIGURE 7.16:

The Devices form

```
                    Me![txtSize] = CStr(.Size) & " MB"
                    Me![txtSpaceAvailable] = CStr(.SpaceAvailable) _
                        & " MB"
                End With
            Else
                Me![txtDeviceNumber] = ""
                Me![txtMirrorName] = ""
                Me![txtPhysicalLocation] = ""
                Me![txtSize] = ""
                Me![txtSpaceAvailable] = ""
            End If
            DoCmd.Hourglass False
        End Sub
```

The Add button on the Devices form adds a new device. This calls a function which makes a new SQLOLE.Device object, sets its properties, and appends it to the Devices collection of the current server.

```
Function SQLMakeNewDevice(strName As String, _
    strPhysicalLocation As String, lngSize As Long, _
    intType As Integer) As Boolean
' Makes a new device for the current SQL Server
On Error GoTo SQLMakeNewDeviceErr
    SQLMakeNewDevice = True

    Dim objNewDevice As New SQLOLE.Device
    If Not gobjSQLServer Is Nothing Then
        DoCmd.Hourglass True
        If IsMissing(intType) Then
            intType = SQLOLEDevice_Database
        End If
        If IsMissing(lngSize) Then
            lngSize = 2
        End If
        With objNewDevice
            .Name = strName
            .PhysicalLocation = strPhysicalLocation
            .Size = lngSize
            .Type = intType
        End With
        gobjSQLServer.Devices.Add objNewDevice
    Else
        SQLMakeNewDevice = False
    End If
```

```
SQLMakeNewDeviceExit:
    DoCmd.Hourglass False
    Exit Function

SQLMakeNewDeviceErr:
    MsgBox "Error " & Err.Number & ": " & Err.Description, _
        vbCritical, "SQLMakeNewDevice()"
    SQLMakeNewDevice = False
    Resume SQLMakeNewDeviceExit
End Function
```

Removing a device is simply a matter of removing it from the Devices collection, but since this is such a perilous operation, we make sure to warn the user first.

```
Private Sub cmdRemove_Click()
    Dim intResponse As Integer
    If Not IsNull(Me![lboDevices]) Then
        intResponse = MsgBox("Removing this device " & _
            "will permanently delete all databases on " & _
            "the device. Are you SURE?", _
            vbOKCancel + vbCritical + vbDefaultButton2, _
            "Remove Device Warning")
        If intResponse = vbOK Then
            gobjSQLServer.Devices(CStr(Me![lboDevices])).Remove
            If SQLIsLoaded("frmSQLExplorerTop") Then
Forms![frmSQLExplorerTop]![lblDeviceCount]._
    Caption = CStr(SQLGetDeviceCount())
            End If
            Call RefreshMe
        End If
    End If
End Sub
```

Table 7.18 lists the properties of the Device object, and Table 7.19 lists the methods of this object. Note that you have complete control over device mirroring (causing SQL Server to simultaneously write all database changes to two different physical devices) from SQL-DMO.

TABLE 7.18: Device Object Properties

Property	Type	Write?	Comments
Default	Boolean	Yes	When you create or extend a database, SQL Server uses space from the default device pool. Setting a device's Default property to True causes SQL Server to place the device in this pool.
DeviceNumber	Long	No	The virtual device number.
FirstPage	Long	No	The first virtual page number. This property is -1 for dump devices.
LastPage	Long	No	The last virtual page number. This property is -1 for dump devices.
MirrorName	String	No	The full path and file name of the mirror device, if any.
MirrorState	SQLOLE_ MIRROR_ TYPE	No	The current mirror state of the device.
Name	Identifier	Yes	The name of this device.
Physical Location	String	Before Add	The full path and file name of the device storage space.
Size	Long	Before Add	The size of this device in megabytes.
SkipTapeLabel	Boolean	Yes	Determines if ANSI tape labels are ignored for dump devices.
SpaceAvailable	Long	No	Unused space in megabytes.
Status	Long	The status bitmap	
SystemObject	Boolean	No	If True, this is an SQL Server system device. If False, this device was created by a user.
Type	SQLOLE_ DEVICE_ TYPE	Yes	The type of the database or dump device.

TABLE 7.19: Device Object Properties

Method	Comments
Mirror	Creates a mirror device.
ReadBackupHeader	Creates a QueryResults object with information about the current backup help on a dump device.
ReMirror	Re-establishes mirroring after it has been suspended.
Remove	Drops the device. You can't drop a device while it has databases on it.
SwitchToMirrorDevice	Redirects all reads and writes to the mirror device.
SwitchToMirrorTemp	Redirects all reads and writes to the mirror device, but does not mark it as the new primary device.
UnMirrorDevice	Permanently disables mirroring.
UnMirrorTemp	Temporarily stops writing data to the mirror device.

Configuration

Clicking on the Configuration button opens the Configuration form, shown in Figure 7.17, whose RefreshMe procedure displays the configuration information for this server in a list box. The Configuration object exists only to contain a collection of ConfigValues, each of which has a maximum, minimum, and current setting. These are the operating parameters for the SQL Server. The last column of the list box indicates whether a particular value can be changed "on the fly," or whether you must shutdown and restart the server for any change to take effect.

```
Sub RefreshMe()
    Dim rstConfigValue As Recordset
    Dim objConfigValue As SQLOLE.ConfigValue
    CurrentDB.Execute "DELETE * FROM tblConfigValue"
    Set rstConfigValue = _
        CurrentDb.OpenRecordset("tblConfigValue")
    For Each objConfigValue In _
        gobjSQLServer.Configuration.ConfigValues
        With rstConfigValue
```

FIGURE 7.17:
The Configuration form

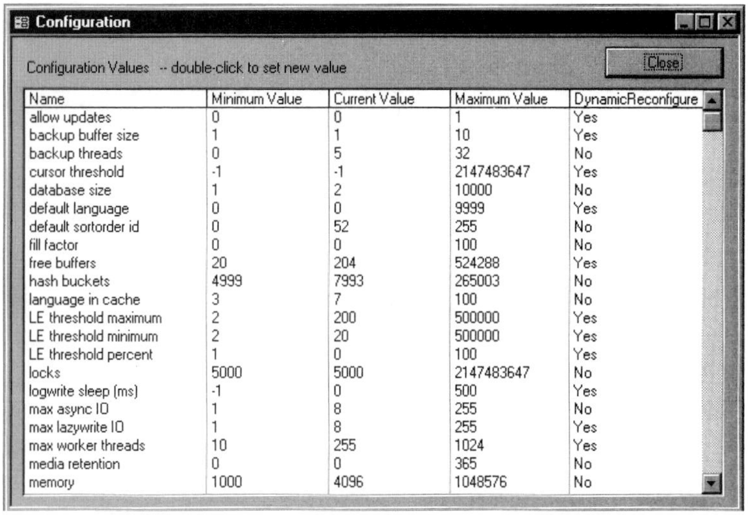

Name	Minimum Value	Current Value	Maximum Value	DynamicReconfigure
allow updates	0	0	1	Yes
backup buffer size	1	1	10	Yes
backup threads	0	5	32	No
cursor threshold	-1	-1	2147483647	Yes
database size	1	2	10000	No
default language	0	0	9999	Yes
default sortorder id	0	52	255	No
fill factor	0	0	100	No
free buffers	20	204	524288	Yes
hash buckets	4999	7993	265003	No
language in cache	3	7	100	No
LE threshold maximum	2	200	500000	Yes
LE threshold minimum	2	20	500000	Yes
LE threshold percent	1	0	100	Yes
locks	5000	5000	2147483647	No
logwrite sleep (ms)	-1	0	500	Yes
max async IO	1	8	255	No
max lazywrite IO	1	8	255	Yes
max worker threads	10	255	1024	Yes
media retention	0	0	365	No
memory	1000	4096	1048576	No

```
            .AddNew
                ![Name] = objConfigValue.Name
                ![MinimumValue] = objConfigValue.MinimumValue
                ![CurrentValue] = objConfigValue.CurrentValue
                ![MaximumValue] = objConfigValue.MaximumValue
                ![DynamicReconfigure] = _
                    objConfigValue. _
                    DynamicReconfigure
            .Update
        End With
    Next objConfigValue
    Me![lboConfigValues].Requery
End Sub
```

Double-clicking on any of the rows in the Configuration list box will open the Reconfigure form, shown in Figure 7.18. When you open this form, it populates itself with the configuration information selected in the Configuration form, using the Column property of the Access list box (not to be confused with an SQL-DMO Column object!):

```
With Forms![frmConfiguration]![lboConfigValues]
        Me![txtName] = .Column(0)
        Me![txtMinimumValue] = .Column(1)
        Me![txtCurrentValue] = .Column(2)
```

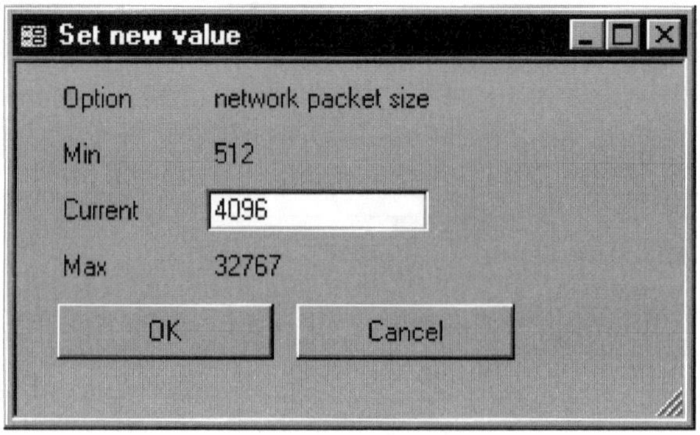

FIGURE 7.18:

The Reconfigure form

```
    Me![txtMaximumValue] = .Column(3)
    Me![txtCurrentValue].ValidationRule = "Between " & _
        .Column(1) & " and " & .Column(3)
End With
```

If you change any of the configuration values from the popup, they will be written back to the server and you will be warned if the settings will not take effect until the server has been restarted:

```
Private Sub cmdOK_Click()
    Dim intResponse As Integer
    DoCmd.Hourglass True
    gobjSQLServer.Configuration.ConfigValues( _
        CStr(Forms![frmConfiguration]![lboConfigValues])) _
        .CurrentValue = Me![txtCurrentValue]
    gobjSQLServer.Configuration.ReconfigureCurrentValues
    If Not gobjSQLServer.Configuration.ConfigValues( _
        CStr(Forms![frmConfiguration]![lboConfigValues])) _
        .DynamicReconfigure Then
        intResponse = MsgBox("You must restart the server " & _
            "for this change to take effect. Restart now?", _
            vbYesNo + vbQuestion + vbDefaultButton2, _
            "Reconfiguration Warning")
        If intResponse = vbYes Then
            gobjSQLServer.Shutdown
            gobjSQLServer.Start
        End If
    End If
```

```
      End If
      DoCmd.Hourglass False
      Forms![frmConfiguration].RefreshMe
      DoCmd.Close acForm, Me.Name
End Sub
```

Summary

As you can see from the sample application, SQL-DMO provides an elegant programming interface for accessing SQLServer objects and does not require an excessive amount of coding. For the Access programmer, it offers a familiar paradigm for thinking about the way SQL Server works. As you become more comfortable with the hierarchy of objects in SQL Server, you'll be better able to understand the server software on its own terms.

In this chapter, we've covered the major objects in the SQL-DMO layer:

- Application
- SQLServer
- Database
- Device
- Configuration
- ConfigValue
- Registry
- Table
- View
- Graph

- DBOption
- User
- Group
- Column
- Index
- Trigger

With these objects as a starting point, you can build complex Access applications that interactively manage SQL Servers across your network.

CHAPTER

EIGHT

Replication in Access and SQL Server

- What is replication?

- Replication in Access

- Replication in SQL Server

- Choosing a replication model

- Using Access and SQL Server replication together

Replication refers to the process of keeping two or more copies of a single database synchronized so that each contains the same data. Both Access and SQL Server support replication in their current releases, though with very different architectures. In this chapter, we'll sort out the differences between the two models and discuss how they can be used in client/server applications.

Consider the growth of a typical client/server application. It might start out as a small SQL Server database used by three or four Access users on a local area network (LAN). As the application is tuned, more and more users are added. Some might be on the LAN; some might be using Microsoft's dial-in solution, Remote Access Services (RAS), over modem lines to connect to the data. People in remote branch offices who find the data useful could connect to the server via a corporate wide area network (WAN) or a third-party remote-node solution. Eventually, the limits of the network and server will be reached. With hundreds of users attempting to query the same database, response time will deteriorate. As the data is used from more far-flung locations, traffic on the network will increase dramatically.

The traditional way to fix these problems is to throw money at them. The server can be upgraded from one 486 to four Pentiums and equipped with a faster drive array and multiple network cards. All the remote sites can be equipped with fast ISDN phone lines, and the corporate network backbone can be upgraded. Since SQL Server scales up to multiple processors, this is a workable, if expensive, approach.

In some situations, replication can provide a cost-attractive alternative to upgrading existing systems. Rather than connect every user to the exact same server, replication can duplicate the data across multiple servers. Each server can be less expensive, since it is supporting fewer users. And since each server can be located close to the users who actually work with it, network traffic and associated costs drop as well.

The tradeoff in this scenario is loss of concurrency. *Concurrency* is a measure of how up-to-date your data is at any given site and time. If everyone is using the same database, concurrency is very high. As you move to more distributed solutions, users may be seeing old (low concurrency) data. Replication is not magic. The data still has to get to each individual user somehow. But by grouping updates together into batches, and sending them at low-traffic times, replication can help keep costs manageable at the price of reduced concurrency.

When properly implemented, replication can assist with reducing the load on your primary server and your network. If your application doesn't need immediate updates to data, replication is an attractive alternative to upgrading hardware. With both SQL Server and Access replication, it's easy to make changes to the replication schema, providing the flexibility to respond to changing user needs.

Common Uses for Replication

Before we discuss the specifics of replication in these two products, let's take a look at some common uses for replication. You might consider using replication in any of these situations:

- Data needs to be shared between multiple offices.
- Data needs to be shared with mobile users, or others only occasionally connected to the network.
- Hot or warm backups of data are required.
- Upgrades to your application need to be distributed.
- Some users need only decision support services.

- Some users need only part of your data.
- Data needs to be redundant to provide additional up time.

We'll discuss each of these uses in the following sections. Some are a good fit for replication in Access or SQL Server (or both), and some are not. Don't make the mistake of thinking that replication is a magic bullet to solve all database problems, no matter how thoroughly it's being evangelized by Microsoft.

Sharing Data between Offices

Data sharing is a classic use of replication. Your headquarters can send its corporate data to each satellite office using replication, where it can be used for day-to-day operations. Alternatively, you can distribute the "ownership" of the data itself to multiple offices. In this scenario, each office would be responsible for entering and maintaining a portion of the data and sending that portion to the other offices. You can also mix replicated and non-replicated tables in your application. For example, the corporate expense code table could be replicated so it would be the same everywhere, but individual offices could maintain their own non-replicated expense account tables.

Sharing Data with Distributed or Occasional Users

The "traveling salesman" scenario is another oft-suggested use for replication. Sales representatives who are on the road can use replication in dial-up mode to synchronize their replica with the most current version of the database located in the main office. New orders can be entered into the main database, and the most recent information from the main database can be updated on the local machine, giving the sales representative the most current version of the database without the overhead of copying the entire database.

This sort of replication is really only practical with a desktop product such as Access, rather than SQL Server, since it's unlikely that your sales representatives would have laptops powerful enough to run SQL Server.

A similar application for replication occurs when some users are only occasionally connected to your network. They might be in a part of the world where phone services are expensive or unreliable, for example. In this case, you can use replication to keep a copy of your data on their end of the unreliable link. While this data might be out of date compared to the corporate central data, it will always be available. When the link is in place, you can update the remote server to show the most recent transactions on the main database.

Keeping Hot and Warm Backups

One of the first ideas that occurs to most people when they run across replication is to use it for hot or warm backups. (A *hot* backup preserves the state of the database as changes are made; a *warm* backup might be hours or days out of date.) With Access replication, this can be a sensible idea, since replication only makes a complete copy of the database when a replica is created and subsequently synchronizes that replica's objects with the original objects only if those objects are changed. Access replication also covers all database objects, not just tables, so using a replica as a backup can preserve a safe copy of the user interface as well as the data. The concurrency of the backup can be controlled by how often you synchronize the backup and the original database.

> **NOTE**
>
> Replication can give you a hot backup of your data only if the replica is on a second computer. For a true hot backup, you must be able to recover almost instantaneously from a complete server failure. Replication to a different drive on the same computer does not fit this definition, since both copies could be made inaccessible if, for example, the motherboard failed.

For SQL Server, replication is less suited to maintaining backups. SQL Server replication only moves data, not other parts of your application such as triggers or stored procedures, to the replica. More to the point, using the DUMP and LOAD statements in Transact-SQL is faster than using SQL Server's transaction-based replication for data backup. For true hot backups on SQL Server, you should investigate using a hardware RAID device, Windows NT's software-based RAID, or SQL Server's native device mirroring, instead of replication.

Access does have one advantage here: A replica being used for backup, unlike a SQL Server dump device, is a full working copy of the database that users can retrieve data from immediately in case of emergency.

Distributing Upgrades

Distributing changes to a user-interface design is another task to which Access replication is well suited. In Access databases, design changes as well as data changes can be replicated. This allows you to propagate updates to multiple copies of an Access database without writing any installation routine or using the Access Developer's Toolkit (ADT) Setup Wizard.

A drawback to using Access replication for distributing design changes in a client/server setting is that there must be some connection between the individual client copies outside of the server. SQL Server won't participate in this sort of replication.

Maintaining Decision-Support Servers

In many applications, there's a clear division of labor between users who maintain information and those who use it to make decisions. You might, for example, have a payroll database with weekly timecard inputs from the payroll department. The information in this database will be used in many corporate decisions, but most of the decision makers will never actually input a timecard. Indeed, they should probably be prevented from modifying the data.

In cases like this, you can use replication to set up a decision-support server. The payroll department would continue to work with the "live" data on the original server. Other users would connect to a second server that runs a replica of the database. This has several advantages. First, the people doing data maintenance are not slowed down by queries from other users. Second, the real data is protected from accidental or malicious damage by users who only need to run queries against it. Finally, you can use selective replication to limit the most sensitive data to only those users who really need to see it.

Partitioning Applications

This is a special case of the multiple-office scenario we discussed above. In a large organization, different sets of users do the same operations with different subsets of a database. For example, a time and billing database for a large law firm might contain records from offices in Chicago, Detroit, Houston, and New York. Each of these offices needs to do the same basic operations with their data, but it would be unlikely for an associate in Chicago to bill hours to a Houston job or vice versa. Yet the managing partners still want to see all of the entries from all offices when making corporate decisions.

This situation can be handled by having each local office running a copy of the database with the same structure as all the others. Rather than replicating information between these copies, though, each office would replicate their own information to some central repository that could later be used for "roll-up" reporting.

Providing Redundancy

You can also use replication to provide an additional level of redundancy in case of emergencies. Suppose you take orders in both Cleveland and Columbus, and use the corporate WAN to move data into one central replica for inventory control. If the communications link between locations went down, you could continue working on individual servers in each office. When normal connections are restored, you can use replication to update the inventory information. Operations do not have to stop at the individual sites while the larger problems are being diagnosed and repaired.

Two Types of Replication

Access and SQL Server use very different paradigms for their individual replication capabilities. Access uses a peer-to-peer model, in which all operations can be distributed between replicas. SQL Server uses a publish-and-subscribe model, in which data is "owned" by particular servers. Neither one is capable of heterogeneous replication—replication between two databases stored in different products (but see the later section "A Glimpse of the Future"). We'll describe both types of replication and discuss how you might choose between them depending on your application. Table 8.1 summarizes the basic conceptual differences between Access and SQL Server replication.

TABLE 8.1: Major Differences between Access and SQL Server Replication

Area	Access	SQL Server
Model	Peer-to-peer; all copies of the database may make changes to the data.	Publish-and-subscribe; data is read-write in publishing database and read-only in subscribing databases.
Scope	All database objects, including tables, queries, forms, reports, macros, and modules.	Data only.
Partitioning	Not supported.	Supports both horizontal (row-wise) and vertical (column-wise) partitioning of replicated data.
Dissimilar databases	Synchronizes the entire database, so replicas must be a duplicate of the original database.	Supports subscribing databases that are not a copy of the publishing database.
Replication frequency	On demand, or programmable by schedule with Replication Manager.	Scheduled or transaction-based.
Schema changes	Replicated.	Not replicated.
Customizable triggers	No. Replicated data must appear exactly as it is in the original.	Yes. Replicated data can call custom update, delete or insert triggers on the subscriber.
Conflict resolution	Built-in or custom.	Not needed, since only one server can change the data.
Heterogeneous replication	Not in Access 95, and no capabilities announced.	Not in SQL Server 6.0, but announced for SQL Server 6.5.

Access Replication Architecture

Access replication allows two or more databases to synchronize their design changes and data at specified intervals, or on demand, without copying every record or every object. One of the databases must function as the Design Master (the only copy in which design changes are allowed to be made), and other copies of the database, called *replica*s, are cloned from the Design Master. The entire group of copies is called a *replica set*. Each member of the replica set contains a common set of replicable objects such as tables, queries, forms, reports, macros, or modules, although each may also contain objects that are not replicable or part of the replica set (local objects). When you synchronize a pair of replicas from a set, they exchange information on both data and object changes. Replicas can be located on different computers or in different physical locations and still remain synchronized.

Design changes to the application can be easily distributed from the Design Master using replication. Changes to database objects and code as well as data are replicable. Because only the incremental changes are transmitted during synchronization, the time and expense of keeping data up-to-date are minimized.

Access replication can be controlled in four different ways:

- With the Windows 95 Briefcase
- From the Tools ➤ Replication menu in Access
- From VBA code within your Access application
- From the Replication Manager, a tool which ships with the Access Developer's Toolkit

For many applications, Briefcase Replication isn't really an option, since it depends on users understanding the interface. You'll most likely find yourself writing code for the bulk of your Access replication activities and using Replication Manager to track more complex replica sets.

Access Replication Components

Access replication is designed to be as automatic as possible after the initial setup. There are four major components involved in the replication process:

- Tracking Layer
- Replication Manager
- Transporter
- Briefcase Reconciler

Tracking Layer

Access includes dedicated tracking services specifically designed to handle replication. Unlike SQL Server, which uses existing log services to manage replication (as we'll explore later in this chapter), Access does not have any native logging ability. Instead, when you're working with a replicated database, the Jet Engine uses a special "tracking layer" set of libraries to write changes to log files within the database itself. This sort of logging is designed specifically for replication, not for secure backup or rollforward/rollback services.

Replication Manager

Replication Manager is a component included in the Access Developer's Toolkit. This component provides a user interface specifically for managing replicas spread across multiple computers, possibly in diverse locations. In addition to management tools, it also includes the ability to generate reports on replication activities after they have taken place. Although you can manage complex replica sets entirely in code, Replication Manager provides a much friendlier interface for many activities. Figure 8.1 shows the Replication Manager interface.

FIGURE 8.1:

Replication Manager showing the communications link between two replicas and a schedule for replication

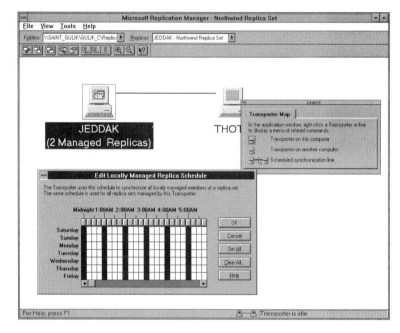

Transporter

The Transporter is another component that ships with the Access Developer's Toolkit. Even without the Transporter, you can instruct Jet to synchronize two members of a replica set. However, the Transporter can also perform indirect replication, leaving changes in a "dropbox" directory for a replica that is not currently online. The Transporter is extremely useful for wide area networks and for laptop replicas that are not always available.

The Transporter runs as a resident program on the computer containing at least one of the replicas being managed. When it's instructed to synchronize, either through code or through the scheduling engine in Replication Manager, the Transporter first tries to directly connect to both replicas and exchange information between them. If this attempt fails, it will leave a message for the Transporter assigned to the target replica at a shared network folder for later pickup.

Briefcase Reconciler

The Briefcase Reconciler is a utility that manages .MDB files left in the Windows 95 Briefcase. By default, the Briefcase does simple file copies of any files stored inside itself. The reconciler modifies this behavior so that Access databases left in the Briefcase are reconciled via replication instead. It also converts any Access database dragged into the Briefcase into a replica.

Replication Using the Briefcase

The simplest way to see the replication capabilities of Access in action is to use the Windows 95 Briefcase. To make an Access database replicable, use the Windows 95 Explorer to locate your master database on the network and simply drag it into the Briefcase folder icon on your local machine. You can synchronize changes on your local replica with changes made to the Design Master on the network by clicking Update All in the Briefcase.

When Briefcase replication is installed, it registers a special class ID (CLSID) for Microsoft Jet 3.0 .MDB files. When a file with the .MDB extension is dragged into Briefcase, the Briefcase Reconciler automatically converts the database into a replicable form. You are also given the opportunity to make a backup copy of the original database file, in case you need to continue using it in its nonreplicable form. (We strongly recommend making such a backup when you're learning about replication.) The Reconciler then converts the database into a replicable form, leaving the Design Master at the source and placing a replica in the Briefcase, or placing a replica at the source and the Design Master in the Briefcase. The Briefcase Merge Reconciler merges changes to the members of your replica set when you choose either Update All or Update Selection from the Briefcase menu. It only does "on demand" replication at the time the command is selected, so if you need the ability to set a schedule, synchronize more than two replicas, or further customize replication, you need to use the Microsoft Replication Manager or write custom VBA code.

Physical Changes to Your Database

Making an Access database replicable adds considerable overhead to it. During the conversion process, additional systems tables and properties are added to the database as well as additional fields in each table. The behavior of some fields is changed (AutoNumber fields are modified from sequential to random numbering), and the physical size of the database increases due to the inclusion of these new tables, fields, and properties.

The fields added are a unique identifier, a generation indicator, and a lineage indicator. The unique identifier, or ReplicationID, is created during the conversion process from any fields using AutoNumber (with a field size of ReplicationID), and its behavior is changed to random from increment. If there is no AutoNumber field, an s_Guid field is added, which stores the ReplicationID AutoNumber that uniquely identifies each record. The ReplicationID AutoNumber for a specific record is identical across all replicas. The generation indicator, or s_Generation field, expedites incremental synchronization by tracking whether a record has been updated since the last synchronization. Whenever a record is modified, its generation is set to 0, which causes it to be synchronized. Once it has synchronized with a database, this number is changed to the current generation number. The lineage indicator, or s_Lineage, which is added to each table in the database, contains a list of nicknames for replicas that have updated the record and the last version created by each of those replicas. This is a binary field that is not readable by users and is incremented when the record is changed.

A replicated Access database also contains a number of new system tables, as shown in Table 8.2. These are the tables that the tracking layer uses to store information on user and design activity in the database.

TABLE 8.2: System Tables Added to Replicated Access Databases

Table Name	Purpose
MSysRepInfo	Stores information about the entire replica set, most notably the identity of the Design Master, the description of the replica set, and the retention period beyond which replicas are considered too old to synchronize. This table will be identical in every member of a replica set.
MSysReplicas	Stores information on all replicas in the replica set. This includes the name and location of each replica, as well as the last date that this replica synchronized with each member of the set.
MSysTableGuids	Assigns a unique number to each table in the database. It also contains information on the order that tables should be updated to avoid referential integrity conflicts.
MSysSchemaProb	Stores errors which occur while synchronizing design changes between members of a replica set.
MSysErrors	Stores errors which occur while synchronizing data changes between members of a replica set.
MSysExchange-Log	Stores information about synchronizations that have taken place between this replica and other members of the replica set.
MSysSidetables	In cases where there has been a conflict between data changes in two replicas, stores information as to which table contains the conflicting records.
MSysSchChange	Stores design changes that have occurred at the Design Master so that they can be distributed to any member of the replica set.
MSysTombstone	Stores information on deleted records. This is necessary in case a deletion cannot be carried out and needs to be rolled back later.
MSysTransp-Address	Stores addressing information for Transporters and defines the set of Transporters known to this replica set.
MSysSchedule	Stores the Transporter schedule for this replica.
MSysGenHistory	Stores information on groups of changes that this replica knows about. In cases when you receive multiple updates at once from a seldom-connected replica, this can be used to minimize update traffic.
MSysOthers-History	Stores a record of groups of changes known to other replicas in this replica set.

The properties added to your database during conversion are Replicable, ReplicaID, and DesignMasterID. The Replicable property indicates that the database is replicable (by setting this property to "T"). The ReplicaID provides the Design Master or replica with a 16-byte identifier, and the DesignMasterID property designates the Design Master for the replica set.

Access Replication Topologies

Since Access replication is basically peer-to-peer, there are many ways to arrange the connections between members of a replica set. Which topology you choose depends on your needs and your network. We'll indicate some of the ways to choose between topologies below, but you'll have to temper this with your own experience.

Appropriate topologies for Access replication include:

- Star
- Ring
- Fully Connected
- Linear

Star

The Star topology consists of a single hub with the replicas at each of the spokes (shown in Figure 8.2). The hub periodically synchronizes with each of its satellites. All data is shared among replicas through the hub. Since all data travels through the hub, data has to travel no more than two "hops" to synchronize with other set members. This works well if small amounts of data are being synchronized. The main drawback of the Star topology is that the first satellite does not receive any new data from the other hub satellites (while the last satellite receives all the new data) unless a second pass is made. Another potential problem is the amount of traffic that must pass through the hub, although this can be partly ameliorated by connecting multiple stars by their hubs. It is not a good idea to locate the Design Master at the hub. Rather, you should place the Design Master at one leg of the star, since this will make it easier to make design changes offline and synchronize it when you're done. If you do this, you don't have to worry about partially tested design changes being propagated to other members of the replica set.

FIGURE 8.2:

Star topology

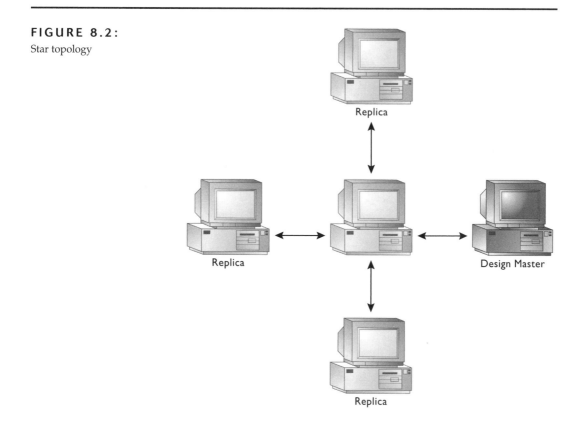

Ring

The Ring topology is configured with each replica in a circle and connected to only one other replica on each side (see Figure 8.3). Synchronization occurs in a circular fashion with A synchronizing with B, B synchronizing with C, and C synchronizing with A to complete the circle. This distributes the load evenly except when the replica at a given computer is used to control synchronization. In a Ring topology, data might have to travel multiple hops before being propagated to every

FIGURE 8.3:

Ring topology

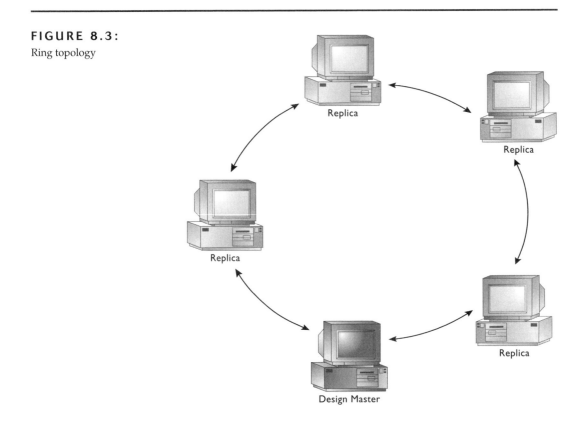

replica in the set. This would work well for a small number of replicas but takes a long time for a larger number. Another bottleneck is that, if any one of the replicas fails or is not available, the chain is broken and data does not propagate, although you can anticipate this and handle it in code by routing synchronization around the failure point. Rings can also be expanded by adding additional rings and connecting them through designated replicas in each ring set.

Fully Connected

Think of the Fully Connected topology as stars in which every replica also functions as a hub. In this configuration, data is sent directly to every other replica without having to indirectly disperse through a series of replicas (see Figure 8.4). The impact of failure of any one replica is minimized since each replica is a controlling replica and initiates synchronization directly. This is a good topology when data changes frequently and is needed in all replicas as quickly as possible. The downside is heavier traffic and more overhead since it involves many more synchronizations than other topologies—the number of synchronizations that occurs with twenty replicas would be (20×19)/2, or 190 separate synchronizations, although this can be partially ameliorated by staggering the synchronization schedules.

Linear

The Linear topology is similar to the Ring topology, with each replica synchronizing with one on either side. However, the circle is never completed because the first and last replicas never synchronize with each other (see Figure 8.5). Each replica must send data in both directions. Although this makes managing the schedule of any particular replica simpler, the problem is that changes made to the data in the last replica may take a substantial amount of time to propagate to the other end of the line.

FIGURE 8.4:

Fully Connected topology

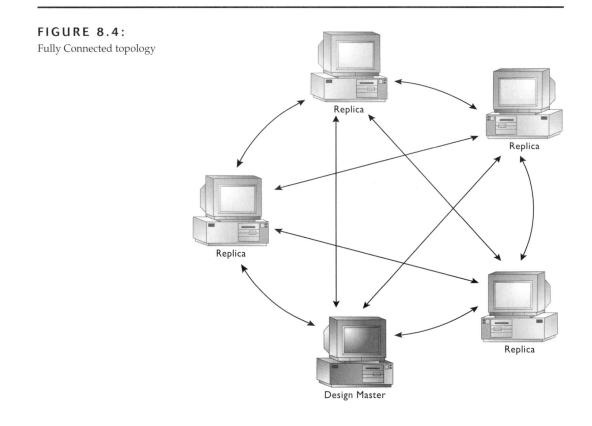

FIGURE 8.5:

Linear topology

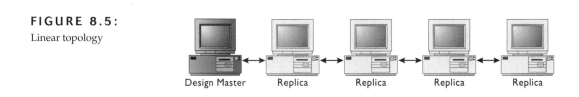

Programming Access Replication

You can use Access, Visual Basic 4.0, or Visual C++ 4.0 to access the Data Access Objects (DAO) programming interface to the Jet database engine, which allows you to make a database replicable, create additional replicas, control the synchronization process, and manipulate the properties of replicable databases. Just about everything that you can do with Replication Manager or the Access menus can also be done by writing code. In addition, code allows you to extend the capabilities of the Replication Manager and the Access user interface. For example, although we won't review the process here, you can write your own custom code to handle any conflicts in synchronizing replicas.

> **NOTE** Custom conflict resolution and other advanced Access replication topics are well covered in the **Access 95 Developer's Handbook**, by Ken Getz and Paul Litwin with Greg Reddick and Mike Gilbert (Sybex, 1996).

Although the Replication Manager provides a quick and painless method for creating and managing a replica set, you may want to consider DAO instead when you need to (1) support event-driven replication or (2) design a simplified replication interface for users who might be lacking in the knowledge necessary to use the Replication Manager interface. Programming replication in DAO gives you the ability to customize your replication system and extend its functionality beyond that provided with the Replication Manager.

You'll need to master four basic methods to program replication:

- Marking objects as non-replicated
- Creating a Design Master
- Creating a replica
- Synchronizing two replicas

Marking Objects as Non-Replicated

Before you convert your database into a replica, you need to identify any objects in the database that you don't want replicated and set their KeepLocal property to the string "T".

> **NOTE** Even though it's logically a Boolean value, KeepLocal is a string property. If you set it to True rather than to "T" you will not get the results that you expect.

Once your database is turned into a replica, you can't change any replicated objects back again and retroactively make them local. To set the KeepLocal property, you must first make sure that it has already been created and appended to a given object, since by default objects don't have this property. For Databases and TableDefs, the KeepLocal property is appended to the object's Properties collection; for forms, reports, macros, and modules, the KeepLocal property is appended to the Properties collection of the Document object.

For example, to set the KeepLocal property of a table, you could use this function:

```
Function KeepTableLocal (strName As String)
    Dim tdf As TableDef
    Dim prp As Property
```

```
    Set tdf = CurrentDB.TableDefs(strName)
    Set prp = tdf.CreateProperty( _
        "KeepLocal", dbText, "T")
    tdf.Properties.Append prp
End Function
```

If you have related tables you wish to keep local, you will have to delete the relationship between them since both tables must be either local or replicable. After you have made both tables local, you can reset the relationship.

Creating a Design Master

Creating a Design Master is also a matter of just defining and setting a property. Setting a database's Replicable property to "T" makes it replicable. Again, since this is not a built-in property, you will have to create it before you can set it. Running this function in any Access database will make it the Design Master of a new replica set:

```
Function MakeDesignMaster()
    Dim prp As Property
    Set prp = CurrentDb.CreateProperty( _
        "Replicable", dbText, "T")
    CurrentDb.Properties.Append prp
End Function
```

Creating a Replica

After you have created your Design Master, you can create additional replicas by using the MakeReplica method. You can use the dbRep-MakeReadOnly constant to control whether or not users are able to make changes to the data in the new replica. The new replica will contain all of the objects from the source replica, except those whose Keep-Local property is set to "T". The function MakeNewReplica shown below takes the file name for a new replica and a constant that should be set to True for a read-write replica and False for a read-only replica.

```
Function MakeNewReplica(strName As String,_
  intReadWrite As Integer
    If intReadWrite Then
        CurrentDb.MakeReplica strName, _
            "Replica of " & CurrentDb.Name
    Else
        CurrentDb.MakeReplica strName, _
            "Replica of " & CurrentDb.Name, _
            dbRepMakeReadOnly
    End If
End Function
```

Additional replicas can be created from either the Design Master or another replica in the set. Make sure that the objects being replicated are not open. If they are locked, the replica cannot be created.

Synchronizing Two Replicas

Synchronization is necessary to communicate between members of the replica set and attempt to make the design and data in all members identical. You can choose to perform one-way or two-way synchronizations by using the Synchronize method of the database object. A one-way synchronization takes changes from one replica and applies them to the other, in one direction only; a two-way synchronization exchanges the design and data changes between the two replicas. To export changes from the current database to another database, you use this syntax:

```
CurrentDB.Synchronize "Other.Mdb", dbRepExportChanges
```

To import changes from the other database without exporting changes from the current database, use the dbRepImportChanges flag instead of dbRepExportChanges. Finally, for a two-way synchronization, use the dbRepImpExpChanges flag.

Partial Synchronization

Partial synchronization is not built into Jet replication, nor can you program it. However, it is possible to achieve the same result by making some clever design changes to your database and creating two separate databases. One database would hold only local data, and it would synchronize one way only—for example, from the satellite office to the main office, sending updates to the central database that are not necessary for other replicas in the set (other satellite offices) to have. The other database, which would consist of tables from the main office containing information applicable to all replicas in the set (lookup tables, global information, and shared data, etc.), would synchronize data back to the satellite office. Obviously this would take advance planning since it would impact the design and normalization of your application.

> **NOTE** Make sure to compact your database before synchronizing, which not only reduces the overhead required for storing changes but also reduces the amount of information sent to the replicas.

Conflicts and Errors

If a record is updated at two different locations, Jet treats this as a synchronization conflict even though different fields in the record may have been affected. It merely chooses one record to be the official change based on the record's version number (s_Lineage, which increases by one every time a change is saved to a record) and writes the other record to a conflict table. In other words, a record with more changes will be chosen over a record with fewer changes. If both records have the same s_Lineage value, the record from the database with the lowest ReplicaID will be selected. The conflict table will be named *table*_Conflict and will be stored in the replica set member that originated the losing update.

Conflict tables need to be edited either manually or using DAO. Each record needs to be either deleted or the data re-entered in the database. You can also develop a custom conflict resolution scheme by assigning a higher priority to changes in one replica over another or on any other criteria that may be applicable in your particular environment.

If you are using Access for replication, the conflict resolver will notify you of conflicts each time you open a replica that has conflicts. The conflict resolver wizard can assist you in reviewing conflicts, or you can elect to replace it with your own conflict resolution code. You would create a ReplicationConflictFunction property and set its value to the name of your conflict resolution function, which must exist in the Design Master and be replicated itself.

SQL Server Replication Architecture

SQL Server replication is based on the notion of transferring a transaction log. That is, transactions are read from the log at one copy of a database and applied to another copy of the database. Several key points immediately follow from this basic architectural premise:

- Changes that are not logged will never be replicated. For example, using UPDATETEXT, WRITETEXT, SELECT INTO, or fast bulk copy (fast BCP) to modify a SQL Server database will result in some changes to the database that do not have corresponding transaction log entries. You can prevent this from happening by executing

```
sp_dboption dbname, "select into/bulkcopy", False
```

on your database.

- Two databases cannot both maintain the same data in a replicated table, since this would result in an infinite loop. When database A replicates changes to database B, those changes are reflected in B's transaction log. If B were set up to replicate back to A as well, the changes would continually bounce back and forth between the two transaction logs.

SQL Server manages this replication by maintaining three different databases: a publication database where changes can be made, a distribution database that is dedicated to holding and processing the transaction queue, and one or more subscribing databases where changes will be applied. We'll discuss each of these components below.

SQL Server maintains its changes in *articles* and *publications*.

- An *article* is the basic unit of SQL Server replication. It can be either an entire table or a horizontal or vertical partition of a table. (A horizontal partition replicates only selected records from a table; a vertical partition replicates only selected fields from a table.) Any vertical partition must include the column or columns that make up the primary key in the table. Otherwise the subscription server would have no way of knowing in what rows to apply individual changes.

- A *publication* is a collection of one or more articles from the same database. The publication is what the publishing database makes available to subscribing databases. A subscribing database may pick and choose individual articles within the publication. However, security is set at the publication level. If you restrict access to a publication, then servers without the proper permission can't view any of the articles within that publication.

Components of SQL Server Replication

SQL Server replication takes place among three logically (though not always physically) distinct servers: the publication server, distribution server, and subscription server. What's published are articles, collected into publications. In this section, we'll look at some of the mechanics of these various components.

It's important to realize that a single SQL Server may participate in replication in multiple roles. It might be the publication and distribution server for some publications, while simultaneously being the subscription server for other publications. The modular architecture of SQL Server allows you to split all these components in cases where performance considerations make it necessary.

Publication Server

A publication server is any server that makes a publication available for replication to other servers. The server does this by sending copies of all changes made to a publication to the distribution server for that publication.

Distribution Server

The distribution server does not contain any user tables. Rather, it is a repository for changes being transmitted from a publication server to one or more subscription servers. Depending on your configuration, the distribution server might actively transmit those changes to the subscription servers or wait for them to be requested.

Normally, the distribution server is the same as the publication server. If the publication server is extremely busy handling real-time queries, though, you might find that distribution activities impose too much delay on its processing. In that case, you'll want to move the distribution server to a second computer on your network, so that the publication server doesn't have to spend any machine time dealing with distribution tasks. Of course, this will come at the expense of increased network traffic, since updates must now be sent over the network to the distribution server. Also, when you move the distribution server to a separate machine, you'll need to purchase an additional SQL Server license.

Subscription Server

A subscription server is any server that subscribes to a publication. You should treat the data in this publication as read-only from the subscription server's point of view. You need to realize, though, that this is a business rule rather than a data integrity rule. If you should happen to mark the subscription server's database as actually a read-only database, it will no longer receive replicated changes.

SQL Server Replication Topologies

Because SQL Server replication uses such a different model from that used by Access replication, a different set of topologies are appropriate for SQL Server installations. These include:

- Central Publisher
- Remote Distributor
- Publishing Subscriber
- Central Subscriber
- Multiple Publishers
- Downloaded Data

Central Publisher

Central Publisher is the simplest of the SQL Server replication scenarios. One server is designated as the publication server, and all of the other servers subscribe to publications from this server (see Figure 8.6). This model is useful whenever you have data maintained at one location that must be available in many locations. This could be corporate-wide lookup tables, summary data from an accounting server, or other relatively static data. Subscription servers treat this data as a given and receive changes to it as necessary.

Remote Distributor

Conceptually, this scheme is identical to having a Central Publisher. Physically, the difference is that the publication server and the distribution server are different machines (see Figure 8.7). There are several

FIGURE 8.6:
Central Publisher topology

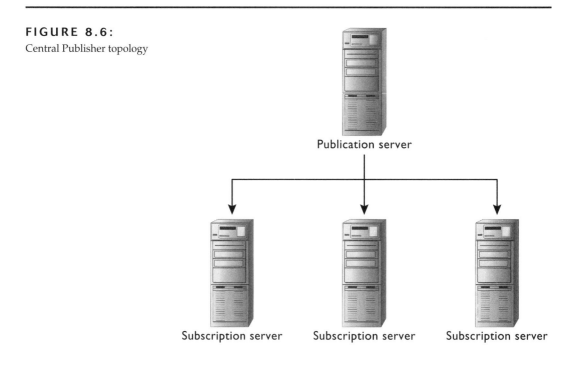

Publication server

Subscription server   Subscription server   Subscription server

FIGURE 8.7:

Remote Distributor topology

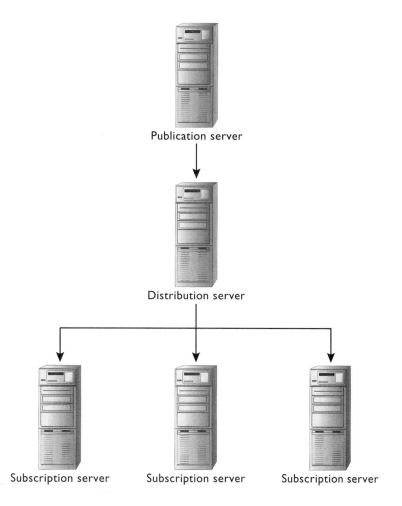

cases in which this is the most reasonable architecture. One is when the publication server is heavily loaded and must not spend the time managing updates. Another is when the publication server is near the capacity of its hardware and you have to offload some processing to another machine. In these cases, it makes sense to physically separate the publication and distribution servers, even when they're on the same local network.

Publishing Subscriber

This variant is useful when there are a number of subscription servers at the far end of a slow or expensive communications link to the original publication server. Here it makes sense to place a second publication server at the far end of the link as well (see Figure 8.8), so that only one set of changes gets distributed across this link. Note that it wouldn't work to place the distribution server at the far end of a slow link from the original publication server, since changes must be transmitted to this server on a frequent basis as transactions occur in the tables.

Central Subscriber

This configuration is essentially the Central Publisher turned inside out. Instead of having one publisher and many subscribers, it revolves around one subscriber and many publishers (see Figure 8.9). This topology is appropriate for applications that involve the "roll-up" of data from multiple branch offices into a single, unified reporting database. Each branch would "own" a horizontal partition of the master database. For example, the roll-up database might contain a sales table with a primary key consisting of order number plus branch name. The Dubuque office would send in all the orders with a branch name of "Dubuque," while Cedar Rapids would do the same with its own branch orders. The Central Subscriber can subscribe to all of these articles with no conflicts, since the same row of data never occurs at two different branches.

FIGURE 8.8:

Publishing Subscriber topology

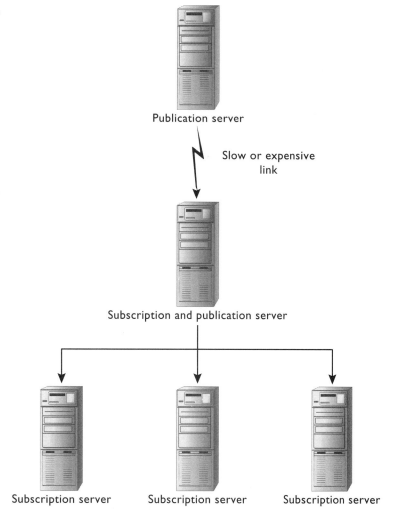

Publication server

Slow or expensive link

Subscription and publication server

Subscription server   Subscription server   Subscription server

Multiple Publishers

If you modify the Central Subscriber topology to include the notion that each office should have all of the orders from the other offices

FIGURE 8.9:

Central Subscriber topology

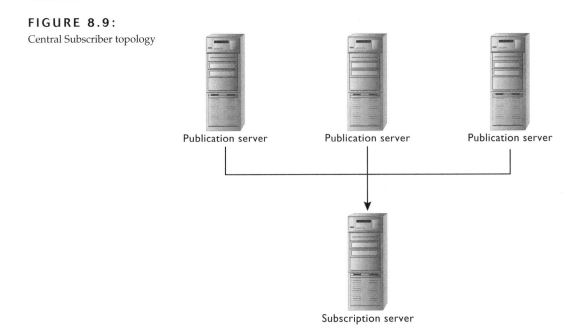

Publication server   Publication server   Publication server

Subscription server

available for analysis, you'll come up with the Multiple Publishers topology (see Figure 8.10). Here each server is a publisher of some part of a table and a subscriber to other parts of the same table. A strict horizontal partition is the key to making this topology work. If there's any overlap in rows between two publishers, you'll end up with an infinite update loop as their transactions are bounced back and forth.

Downloaded Data

The Downloaded Data topology works for a network of SQL Servers that all need access to some bit of external data—typically, data downloaded from a mainframe (see Figure 8.11). If the costs of connecting to the mainframe or converting the data are large, it makes sense to get

FIGURE 8.10:

Multiple Publishers topology

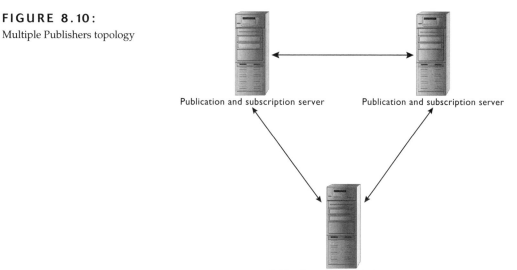

Publication and subscription server   Publication and subscription server

Publication and subscription server

the data onto a single SQL Server and then use replication to move it around. Another scenario where this topology makes sense would be when data comes from a single Access database (perhaps a sales order database on an agent's laptop computer), and its results must be made available to many servers on the network. Here again, it is sensible to only undertake the difficult task of data translation once, rather than once for every server.

Mechanics of SQL Server Replication

Now that we've explained the basic concepts of SQL Server replication, let's look at the actual mechanics of setting replication up between

FIGURE 8.11:

Downloaded Data topology

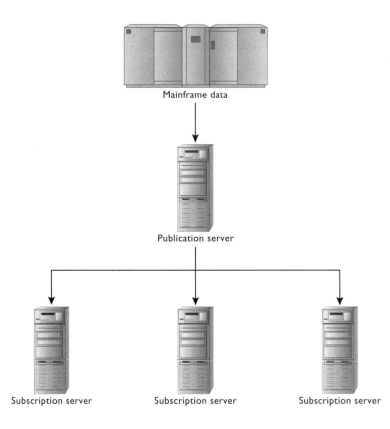

Mainframe data

Publication server

Subscription server · · · Subscription server · · · Subscription server

a pair of servers. We'll work through this on paper rather than trying to include a sample database. Since you need at least two servers to experiment with SQL Server replication, the chances are very good that you'll have a sample database of your own on which to try things.

Prerequisites

Before setting up replication, you should check a number of things on your servers. Refer to the following checklist:

- Any distribution server should have at least 32MB of memory, with at least 16MB assigned to SQL Server itself. You can use SQL Enterprise Manager to check this by selecting the server and then choosing Server ➤ Configurations from the menu.
- All servers participating in replication with one another should use the same character set and the same sort order.
- Your distribution server must be set to use Named Pipes or Multi-Protocol as the default network.
- It's easier to set up replication if you create the publishing and subscription databases before enabling replication.
- Add primary keys to every table that will be published. You can do this with Transact-SQL using the following query:

```
ALTER TABLE [database.[owner.]]table_name
ADD CONSTRAINT constraint_name
PRIMARY KEY [CLUSTERED | NONCLUSTERED]
(column_name [{, column_name}...])
```

Installing the Distribution Database

By default, SQL Server comes without replication installed. This makes sense because there's a certain amount of overhead to tracking and replicating all transactions. To install replication, the first thing you need to do is configure a distribution database. This can be done on your intended publishing server or on a separate server. The easiest way to set up a distribution database is to use the SQL Enterprise Manager. We'll review the steps to set up your publishing server to be its own distribution server. You can find instructions for more complex situations in the SQL Books Online.

1. Select the server in SQL Enterprise Manager.

2. Choose Server ➤ Replication Configuration ➤ Install Publishing from the menus.

3. Fill in the names of the data and log devices you wish to use for replication. You can select "<new>" from the combo boxes on this dialog box to create new devices.

4. Double-check your work. Your screen should resemble Figure 8.12. When you're satisfied, click OK.

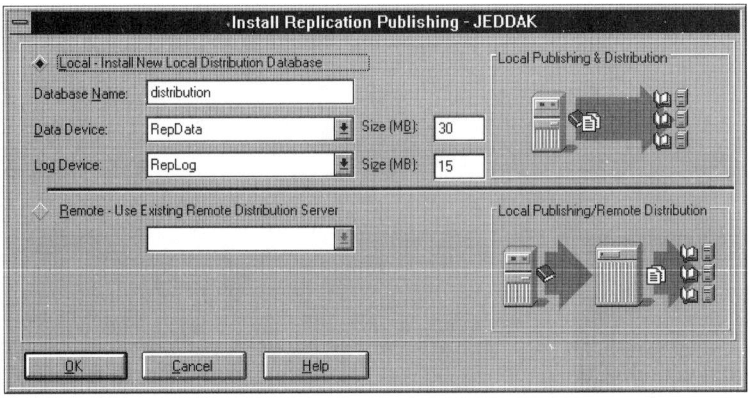

FIGURE 8.12:
Installing a distribution database on a new server. The sizes shown are the minimums that Microsoft suggests for a distribution database.

Setting Publication Options

When you first install replication on a server, you'll be given the options to add publishing databases as soon as the distribution database is created. You can also do this later, by selecting Server ➤ Replication Configuration ➤ Publishing from the SQL Enterprise Manager menus. Either way, you will get a dialog box similar to the one shown in Figure 8.13.

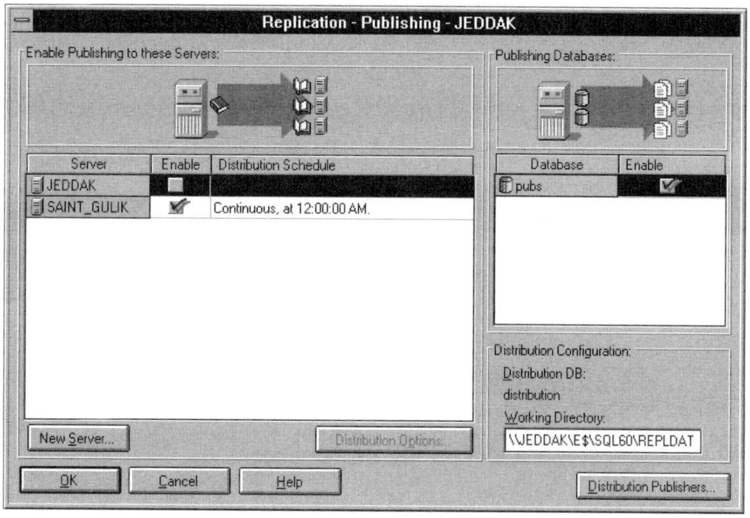

FIGURE 8.13:

Setting publication options on
a server

To complete this dialog box, take the following actions:

1. Click the Enable check box for each server that should be allowed
   to subscribe to publications from this server. (The list will only
   show servers registered with your copy of SQL Enterprise Manager. You can register a new server with the New Server button.)

2. Click Distribution Options for each server and set it for transaction-
   based or scheduled replication. By default, servers will receive transaction-based replication information once every
   100 transactions.

3. Click the Enable check box for each database from which you
   want to publish articles.

4. Click OK to create the necessary tasks and scripts to carry out the
   replication you've chosen.

Setting Subscription Options

Now that you've set up your publication and distribution servers, you can set up your subscription servers. Select each subscription server in SQL Enterprise Manager and select Server ➤ Replication Configuration ➤ Subscribing. SQL Enterprise Manager will display the dialog box shown in Figure 8.14. Select the publishing databases from which this server will receive publications, select the databases on the subscription server that will be updated, and then click OK. Once again, you can use the New Server button in this dialog box to register additional servers with SQL Enterprise Manager.

FIGURE 8.14:

Setting up subscription options

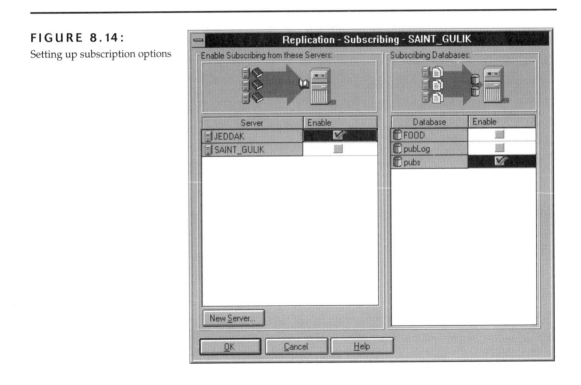

Synchronization

Before data can be replicated between servers, the tables involved must be synchronized. Synchronization is a method of ensuring that the tables at each end of the replication relationship share the same starting schema and data. Until you synchronize a subscribing table with the publishing one, you can't replicate changes between them. You'll set up synchronization as part of setting up publications and subscriptions.

Creating Publications and Articles

After setting up publishing and subscribing servers, the next step is to decide what information to replicate between them. We'll work through the steps to publish changes in the authors table in the sample Pubs database from one server to another.

Start by selecting the publishing server in SQL Enterprise Manager. Then choose Manage ➤ Replication ➤ Publications from the menus. Select the Publishing database and click the New button to see the Edit Publications dialog box. Follow these steps to create a new publication containing a single article:

1. Name the new publication in the Publication Title box. This name must follow the standard SQL Server rules for identifiers. You may also enter an optional description in the Description box.

2. Select either Transaction-Based or Scheduled replication for this publication. If the table you're publishing contains Text or Image columns, you must select Scheduled.

3. Select the Articles tab and choose the tables you wish to include in this publication. The Edit tab will let you set advanced properties, including scripts, to run when a transaction is replicated, as well as horizontal or vertical partitioning.

4. If you want to change the method or schedule used for synchronization, select the Synchronization tab. The defaults here should be suitable for most installations.

5. If you want this publication to be available only to selected subscribing servers, choose the Security tab and check only those servers.

6. Choose the Add button to actually create the publication.

Figure 8.15 shows a new publication with two articles being created.

FIGURE 8.15:

Adding a new publication to a publishing server

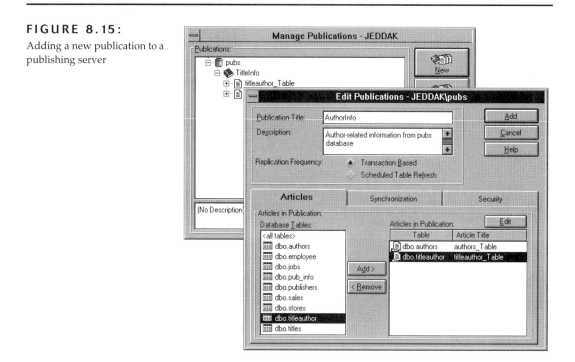

Horizontal and Vertical Partitioning

To create a horizontal or vertical partition of a table, you use the Edit button in the Edit Publications dialog box. This will open the Manage Article dialog box, shown in Figure 8.16.

FIGURE 8.16:

Creating a partitioned article

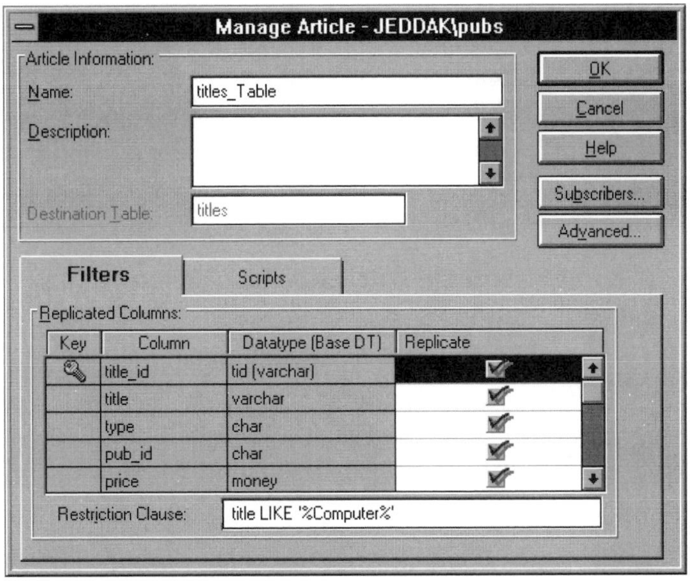

To create a vertical partition (an article containing only selected columns from a table), uncheck the Replicate box for each column you do not wish to replicate.

To create a horizontal partition (an article containing only selected rows from a table), enter a WHERE clause in the Restriction Clause box.

Subscribing to an Article

You can set up subscriptions from either the publishing server (a *push* subscription, because articles are pushed out to other servers) or the subscribing server (a *pull* subscription, because articles are being pulled from the other server). There's no difference between the two once they're set up. Use the following steps to set up a pull subscription:

1. Select the subscribing server in SQL Enterprise Manager and choose Manage ➤ Replication ➤ Subscriptions.

2. The Manage Subscriptions window shows a tree view of every publishing server, publication, and article to which this server is allowed to subscribe. Expand the tree far enough to find the article or publication to which you want to subscribe. Subscribing to a publication subscribes to all articles in that publication.

3. Select the article to which to subscribe and click the Subscribe button.

4. Choose the destination database name and sync method. Ordinarily, you won't need to change either of these options.

5. Click OK to create the subscription. Figure 8.17 shows the subscription process.

At this point, the authors table is replicated from the publishing server to the subscribing server. If you've been following along with a pair of your own servers, you can test this. Open the table on your publishing server and make a number of changes to it. (The number of changes you need to trigger replication is governed by the options you selected when you set up the publishing server.) Then open the table on your subscribing server. You should see the same changes there.

FIGURE 8.17:

Creating a new subscription to
the authors table

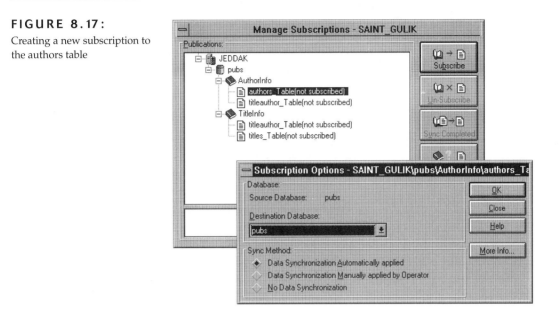

Miscellaneous Limits

There are a few minor "gotchas" that you need to watch out for when
using SQL Server replication. Like any other system, there are some
areas where it doesn't work exactly as you might expect:

- Schema changes are not replicated.
- Identity property is not replicated.
- Timestamps become binary columns.
- Text and Image columns cannot participate in transaction-based
  replication.

Schema Changes Are Not Replicated

Unlike Access, SQL Server has no capability for replicating changes to your data schema. If you change the design of a table in a replicated database, you'll need to drop and recreate the table on every server involved in replication. You'll also need to resynchronize to the publishing server after the schema changes have been made. Alternatively, you can use scheduled rather than transaction-based replication for a table you're expecting to change in schema. Scheduled replication simply overwrites the entire table every time the schedule period occurs.

Identity Property Is Not Replicated

Although you can replicate a table with an Identity column, that column will not have the Identity property on the subscription servers. Since you shouldn't be changing the data on a subscription server, this should not present a problem.

Timestamps Become Binary Columns

A timestamp column on a publishing server will be changed to a binary (8) column on a subscribing server. This means that the timestamp will not be automatically updated if the table is edited on the subscribing server. Once again, this does not present a problem, since tables on subscribing servers should be treated as read-only. However, this is a problem if the table is horizontally partitioned. In this case, you will need to find a replacement for the timestamp column, since only one of the partitions can be correctly updated.

Limits on Replicating Text and Image Columns

Text and Image columns cannot be included in a log-based (transaction-oriented) article. To work around this problem, you'll want to split any replicated Text or Image columns into a separate table, and use a scheduled, rather than log-based, method of replicating this table.

Deciding Which Replication to Use

Now that we've explained the differences between the two types of replication and their mechanics, let's take a look at the choices you'll need to make. Given a particular task, should you use Access or SQL Server replication? Some of the points to consider include:

- Different replication models
- Client software
- Location of data

Differences in Model

As we've discussed in earlier sections of this chapter, there are substantial differences between Access and SQL Server replication. The major difference is that Access is peer-to-peer while SQL Server is publish-and-subscribe. Although you can shoehorn most tasks into either of these models, there are cases where one is clearly superior to the other. In general, the more centralized your work is, the better the SQL Server model will fit and the less the Access model will work.

For most client/server applications, you'll probably find the SQL Server model more appropriate. If the data is important enough that you need to centralize its management, it's probably not data that you want propagated in a decentralized fashion. It's also likely that you have too much data to store in an Access database. If this is the case, you simply won't be able to use the Access replication model with your database.

Accessibility to 16-Bit Clients

The need to have data widely available to a variety of client software can also be a strong factor in favor of SQL Server replication. There are a wide variety of front-end applications that can connect to SQL Server, including a number that run on Windows 3.1 (such as Access 2.0). In contrast, replicated Access data is only available to Access 95, Visual Basic 4.0, and programs written using the latest Microsoft Visual C++. If you've got legacy clients to support in diverse locations, SQL Server replication is probably the best way to get the data to them.

Replicating Front-End versus Back-End Tables

But not every factor argues for SQL Server replication. Since neither SQL Server nor Access supports heterogeneous replication in this release, you may have to use a mix of the two to support your application. Suppose, for example, that you've got a local table of pricing codes in your Access client application. This is an appropriate place for this table, since it is relatively small, does not change often, and needs to be used frequently in places such as combo box rowsources. That table can't be replicated directly by SQL Server replication, since there's no way for SQL Server to reach into your Access database and grab it.

Given this situation, you have two choices for replicating the front-end tables. One is to use Access replication and provide a means of communication among the client programs. The other is to keep the master copy of this table on the server and arrange to periodically download new copies into the front-end database. Given that the latter strategy will keep you from having to manage two sets of replication programming, it might be worth writing the code to manage the downloads instead.

Mixed Replication Scenarios

You can't always make a clear-cut decision to use only one replication model or the other. Although the default rule of thumb is to use SQL replication for client/server applications and Access replication for file/server applications, there are several scenarios in which you should consider a mix of the two. We'll review three of these that we feel are important:

- Data and design replication
- Traveling data sets
- Remote ordering

Data and Design Replication

Just as you use two different products for the client and the server, you should consider using two different methods of replication. Even if all of your data is stored on the server, you've still got the problem of distributing updates to your client application. Without replication, this involves shipping diskettes or disk images to every client site and going through an installation process. After this, the newly updated client application has to be relinked to the server. All in all, this is a slow process that requires lots of man-hours.

Instead of distributing client updates in this fashion, consider using Access replication. There has to be at least an indirect path between each pair of clients to use Access replication to distribute changes—since every client can see at least one of your servers, this path must be there. You can install hub copies of your Access database on each publishing and subscribing server, and take advantage of the Access "dropbox" capability to pass client design updates along the same paths that server data updates take. As long as you're not making frequent changes to the client application, this is not likely to lead to a substantial increase in network traffic.

Figure 8.18 shows schematically what this strategy might look like when combined with a Central Publisher SQL replication topology.

FIGURE 8.18:

Data and design replication

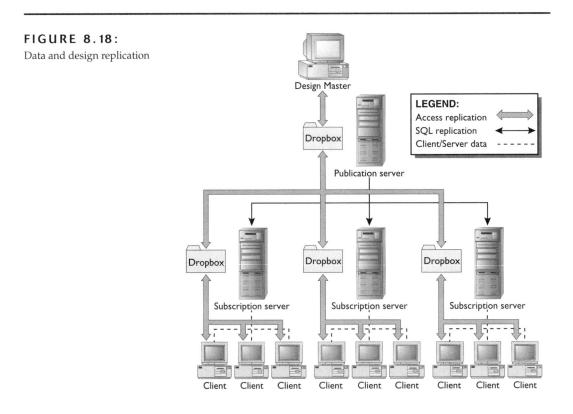

Traveling Data Sets

You may at times need to send subsets of your SQL Server data out on the road. Marketing representatives, for instance, might need a catalog of current part numbers and inventories on their laptops for the week.

The corporation needs to have the inventory history, but the representatives don't. This problem is also amenable to a mixed replication solution, assuming you don't want to buy a topflight laptop for each marketing representative and install SQL Server on it.

The first step is to use SQL replication to get the data to a server local to each marketing representative. A dedicated Access front-end program could perform a series of steps once every week:

1. Delete all rows from a local (Access) copy of the inventory table.

2. Run an append query to insert only the current week's data in the local copy of the inventory table.

3. Repeat these steps for each table the marketing representatives need to have on their laptops.

Rather than download this Access database to their laptops in its entirety, the marketing representatives can simply synchronize a copy on their laptop to a copy on the network. Since all of the data changes are captured in Access tables, they will be synchronized to the laptop replica. This synchronization could even be done over a RAS connection for representatives on the road. Figure 8.19 shows schematically the architecture for this application.

Remote Ordering

This is the inverse of the remote data set scenario. In this case, salespeople in the field take orders with their laptop PCs. The goal is to get all of the orders into a central sales database with a minimum of effort.

In this architecture, orders are taken in a dedicated Access application on the laptop. When the salespeople return to the office, they follow a series of steps:

1. Connect the laptop to the network and synchronize (one-way) to a desktop copy of the database.

FIGURE 8.19:

Traveling data set replication

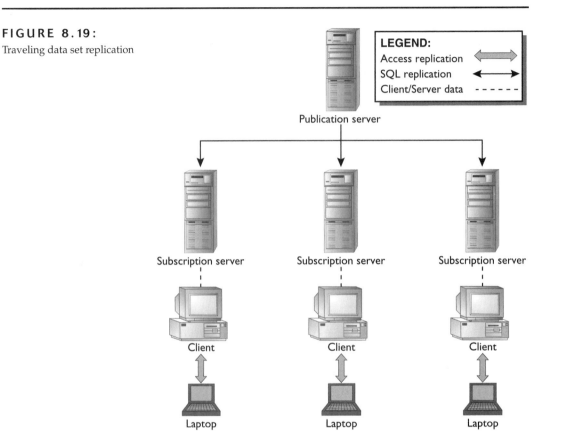

2. Flush all old orders out of the laptop copy, so it will be ready for future sales.

3. Periodically run a maintenance procedure on the desktop copy to INSERT the new orders into a SQL Server database, which can then replicate them to other servers.

This architecture allows for a multitiered collection of data. A number of salespeople could pool their orders into a desktop Access database for their own group. These group databases would in turn put their orders into a regional SQL Server database, and all of the regional databases could push their orders into a Central Subscriber at corporate headquarters. Figure 8.20 shows this architecture.

FIGURE 8.20:

Remote ordering application

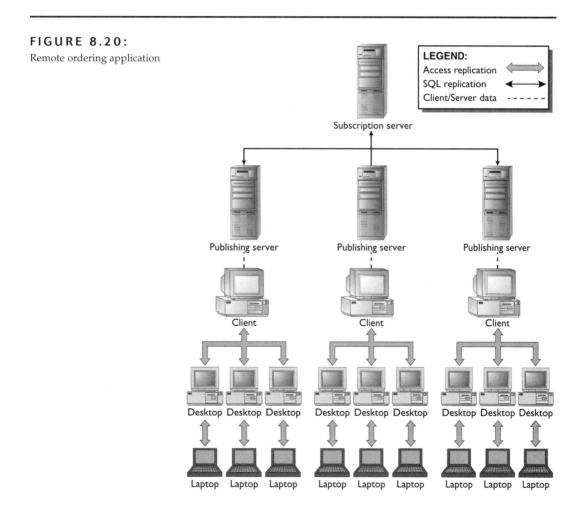

A Glimpse of the Future

This chapter is based on the shipping version of SQL Server at the time of publication, SQL Server 6.0. In late 1995 Microsoft announced a new version, SQL Server 6.5, which is scheduled to be shipped sometime in 1996. One of the most significant improvements to this version will be its support of heterogeneous replication.

Heterogeneous replication refers to a replication scheme in which the two databases being synchronized are not kept on the same type of server. For example, one copy might be a Microsoft Access database, while the other could be a SQL Server database. The initial target platforms for interoperability with SQL Server replication are DB2, Sybase, Oracle, and Access.

Details of this new capability are very sketchy at the time of this writing. Apparently, heterogeneous replication will be accomplished via ODBC, and databases in other products can be either publishers or subscribers. Presumably, some setup procedures will be necessary on these databases to support the appropriate system tables that SQL Server expects to see in a replica.

When this new version ships, database administrators should find their flexibility expanded immensely. For example, you could maintain all of your corporate data in a single SQL Server database and use row-wise partitioning to publish selected portions into laptops running Access. If you're working with Access and SQL Server, you'll want to watch for further news on this enhancement as it becomes available.

Summary

In this chapter we've taken a look at the major aspects of replication in Access and SQL Server:

- Access replication architecture
- Access replication mechanics
- SQL Server replication architecture
- SQL Server replication mechanics
- Strategies for mixed replication

Replication in databases is a relatively new technology that many people are just starting to explore. Access 95 and SQL Server 6.0 are the first versions of these products to include any replication capabilities, so it's unlikely that anyone has figured out the full range of applications for which replication is useful yet. Because this is so clearly a strategic technology for Microsoft, we urge you to experiment with replication in your own applications. As computing power becomes ever more distributed, it's sure to increase in importance.

CHAPTER

NINE

Securing Your
Client/Server Application

- Access security

- SQL Server security

- Windows NT security

Whenever you build a client/server application, you are, at a minimum, making a substantial investment in development and deployment. Such applications provide access to valuable data. Whether the data is essential to daily operations or is historical information that managers analyze to improve the efficiency of operations, you need to understand the tools and techniques available to protect your application and its data.

For an information-processing application such as an order-entry system, you may only need to ensure that only authorized users have access to the system and that no one can insert incorrect data into the system. For an operational application such as a payroll-processing system, you may need to provide discrete access control over parts of the application or the data it processes. This chapter is designed to help you understand the security facilities available in Access, and SQL Server, and Windows NT Server so that you can implement appropriate security measures for your client/server applications.

Microsoft Access Security

Microsoft has designed Access security to be as robust as is possible for a desktop product. However, data and objects in an Access database are more vulnerable than a server database running on a secure server and should not be considered for applications that require absolute data security. Any time someone can make copies of the physical file, perhaps by gaining access to the desktop machine and booting it from their own floppy, you are vulnerable since tools exist to break into anything. If a user has access to the drive an Access database is located on,

Access's security will not prevent it from being copied or hacked. Contrast that with SQL server on a secured NT installation, in which the user cannot actually "see" a discrete physical file in order to copy it. In a client/server environment, you should take advantage of the security features in SQL Server running on a secured installation of Windows NT in order to secure your data.

If you require absolute security on the application side, then you should consider a compiled application programming language such as Visual C/C++. Access security, although robust for a desktop product, has proved vulnerable to several highly-publicized "holes" in both Access 2.0 and Access 95. (See the related discussion later in this chapter for details.) The security holes uncovered so far require that a user have a valid logon ID and password, underscoring the point that it is always necessary to monitor the activity of your users.

Access Security Architecture

As shown in Figure 9.1, the Access security model is made up of users, groups, objects, and permissions. It's important to understand that Access stores its security infomation in two separate locations. Access records user and group profiles (and the specific option settings for each user) in the workgroup file. The default name for the workgroup file in Access 95 is SYSTEM.MDW. Access stores the permissions to the objects themselves in the database file that contains the objects.

Access security is always active, even if on the surface this does not appear to be the case. The only default user account, Admin, is installed by default on every Access installation and cannot be removed. The user Admin belongs by default to a special group called Admins that has irrevocable administrative privileges over any Access database. The internal ID for the user Admin is the same for every workgroup information file created during the Access installation process, although unlike the Admins group, the Admin user account has no intrinsic privileges. The internal ID for the workgroup itself (actually, the ID of

FIGURE 9.1:

The Microsoft Access security architecture

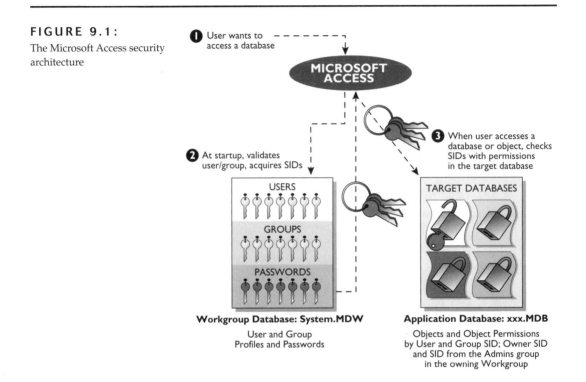

the group Admins) is unique and is based on information you supply when you install Access or create a new workgroup information file. (See the related discussion later in this chapter for the procedure to create a new workgroup information file.) The other default group in Access is the Users group, to which every user account (including the Admin user account) must belong. By default, the Users group is granted full access to any new object you create. The internal ID for the Users group is the same in all workgroup information files.

NOTE   Access 2.0 also included a default user named Guest and a default group named Guests. You won't see these in Access 95 unless you're using a converted workgroup information file.

Access security won't be active until you assign a password to the Admin user, forcing a logon screen when Access is activated. (If the Admin account's password is blank, Access does not prompt for a password.) The user ID and password is validated by the workgroup information file—if a user does not supply a valid ID and password, Access will not start. If the Admin account password is cleared (set to an empty string), the logon dialog box is bypassed and the user is automatically logged on as the Admin account without being prompted. As you can see, the combination of an Admin user without a password, and all objects open to the default Users group, make the Access security subsystem completely transparent when it's not implemented.

Users and Groups

In Access, you can create any number of users and assign a unique password to each one. Users may be members of one or more groups. As you'll see a bit later, creating groups makes it easy to assign permissions on objects to many users at once rather than assigning specific permissions to each user.

The Built-in Users and Groups

Access has several built-in user and group accounts that you should be aware of. None of them can be deleted and they each have special properties that you need to understand:

Admins Group The Admins group has permissions to administer your database that cannot be removed even though the Access interface may sometimes mislead you into thinking that you have done so. Members of Admins can grant and revoke permissions, create and delete user and group accounts, and change or clear passwords for other users. If you remove object permissions from a member of Admins, that member can always grant the permission back to themselves.

Members of Admins can even remove other members from the Admins group. Membership in this group, therefore, should be restricted to the absolute minimum required for effective administration.

Users Group   The Users group includes every user listed in your workgroup information file. When you create a new user account using the Access Security UI, they are automatically listed in the Users group. If they were not in the Users group, they would not be able to launch Access because they would not have the necessary permissions to the Access system files that are granted to the Users group. Because all users in all installations of Access must be members of the Users group and, by default, the Users group has full permission to all objects, you must remove the permissions of the Users group from all objects. This is an absolutely critical step in your security implementation plan.

Admin User   The Admin user is the default account in every Access installation, and is identical to every other Access Admin account in all workgroup databases. By default, the Admin user is a member of the Admins group, so a crucial step in securing an application involves removing the Admin user from the Admins group and removing all explicit permissions from the Admin user. Otherwise, the Admin user will have the sweeping permissions that any member of the Admins group will always have. At this stage the Admin user will be a member of the Users group only, which should also have restricted permissions.

Guests Group and Guest User   The Guests group and a Guest User exist in Access 2.0, but have been phased out in Access 95. By default neither the Guests group nor the Guest user had permissions on anything. If you see either of these accounts listed in the Security dialog boxes, it is a good indication that an Access 2.0 workgroup information file is being used.

Be aware that any permissions assigned to the Admin user or the Users group are in effect assigned to every user of any copy of Microsoft Access, as these are identical across every installation of Access. However, the Admins group is unique to each installation. By using the Workgroup Administrator to create a new workgroup file before you start, you ensure that only members of your Admins group have administrative privileges for the databases you create in that workgroup.

Custom Groups

In a multi-level secured application, you should not use the built-in accounts as these will not be secure. You should instead create your own custom groups and users in order to guarantee that the appropriate level of permissions have been assigned for each group and user combination and that users do not inherit unintended permissions by membership in one of the default groups. Usually it makes sense to organize your groups according to the tasks that have to be performed. In a large application you will most likely have many objects and many users, so you will never want to assign direct permissions to any user, as administration would quickly become a nightmare.

For example, in an orders database you might have two groups, Clerks (who do data entry only) and Supervisors (who can approve orders, accept payments, and have access to other sensitive information). You create a user named Susie, and make her a member of the Clerks group. Susie has no permissions directly assigned to her, but she inherits all of the permissions of the Clerks group. If Susie gets promoted to supervisor, all you have to do to augment her permissions is make her a member of the Supervisors group as well. Susie will then have all of the permissions of the Supervisors group plus the limited permissions she possesses as a member of Clerks. This is called the *least restrictive rule*. That is, a user's permissions on an object are the least restrictive of their own directly-assigned permissions combined with the permissions of all the groups of which they are a member.

Objects and Permissions

Permissions are properties of objects which are assigned to a specific user or group. As illustrated in Figure 9.2, permissions to objects can either be assigned to users directly (called *explicit* permissions) or users can inherit permissions assigned to a group they belong to (called *implicit* permissions).

FIGURE 9.2:

Explicit and implicit permissions for users and groups

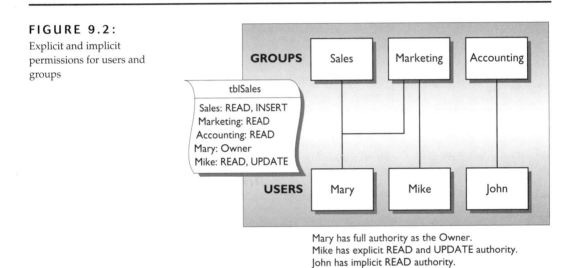

Mary has full authority as the Owner.
Mike has explicit READ and UPDATE authority.
John has implicit READ authority.

Permissions are properties of Access objects that are assigned to specific User and Group objects. You can assign different permissions to users and groups for each object in a database through the user interface or in code through referencing the intrinsic security constants which manipulate the actual bits set for the permissions on each object.

You can also assign default permissions for new objects to your groups and users. A default permission applies to all objects not yet created and is assigned to the container, not an individual object. For example, by assigning default permissions on the Forms container to a specific group, you ensure that any new forms created will default to those permissions for that group.

Another feature of the Access security model is that the person who creates an object is the Owner of that object. An object's owner has irrevocable administrative rights over that object, and can grant and revoke permissions to that object. Only the object's owner or a member of the Admins group can transfer ownership of an object to another user or group.

Securing Your Database

Access 95 comes with a built-in Security Wizard to help with a lot of the drudgery in securing a database, but the Security Wizard won't do everything for you and is no substitute for a clear understanding of the concepts involved. Leave out one step, and the whole process fails and you might as well not have bothered.

Steps to Take before Running the Wizard

You must take some discrete steps in securing your database, and they must be performed in the correct order for your database to be adequately secured. We will walk through the process here:

1. Create a new workgroup information file by using the Workgroup Administrator, which is installed as a separate application on your Desktop. As you are creating the file, the program will prompt you to provide Name, Organization, and Workgroup ID strings, as shown in Figure 9.3. You need to type in a distinct Workgroup ID because Access uses all three pieces of information to create a unique workgroup ID for the Admins group. Anyone who can access your machine can determine your default name and organization name to recreate the default SYSTEM.MDW file created during setup since those strings are displayed in the

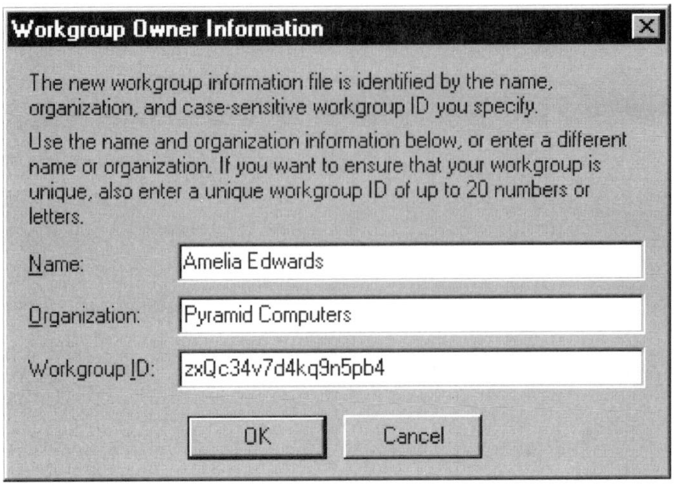

FIGURE 9.3:

Provide name, organization, and unique workgroup ID information to the Access Workgroup Administrator.

Workgroup Owner Information

The new workgroup information file is identified by the name, organization, and case-sensitive workgroup ID you specify.

Use the name and organization information below, or enter a different name or organization. If you want to ensure that your workgroup is unique, also enter a unique workgroup ID of up to 20 numbers or letters.

Name: Amelia Edwards

Organization: Pyramid Computers

Workgroup ID: zxQc34v7d4kq9n5pb4

[OK]   [Cancel]

Help ➤ About window. The workgroup ID string you input here will not be displayed by the system anywhere, so you need to write these strings down and store them in a safe place in case your workgroup information file ever becomes lost or corrupted. The only way you will be able to get back into your secured database is if you recreate your workgroup information file from scratch or restore it from a backup. Creating the new workgroup information file will automatically cause Access to use it the next time you start Access.

2. Open Access, create a new user account and add it to the Admins group. Choose Tools ➤ Security ➤ User and Group Accounts to see the dialog box shown in Figure 9.4. Click New under the Users tab to create a new user, then add the new user to the Admins group. You will be prompted to provide a name and Personal ID, or PID, which is another unique string that you create. Record these settings for the same reason that you wrote down workgroup information. Access combines the PID and the name to create a Security Identifier (SID), a machine-generated, non-readable binary string that uniquely identifies each user and group.

FIGURE 9.4:

Creating a new user in the
User and Group Accounts
dialog box

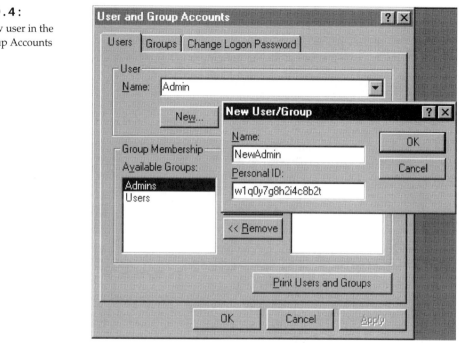

3. Remove the Admin user from the Admins group. (The Access
user interface allows you to remove the Admin user only if there
is at least one other user in the Admins group.) To do so, in the
User and Group accounts dialog box (shown in Figure 9.5),
choose Admin in the Name combo box, click on Admins in the
Member of box, then click Remove.

4. You are still logged on as Admin, so you can set a password for
the Admin user. This will cause Access to provide a logon dialog
box the next time you start Access. Choose the Change Logon
Password tab in the User and Group Accounts dialog box and
then enter and verify the new password.

5. Exit Access and restart it. Log on using the account you just created. Since you have not yet set a password for this account, don't type anything in the box provided for a password. The PID you entered for this account is not the password.

6. Once you are logged on, set a password for your new account.

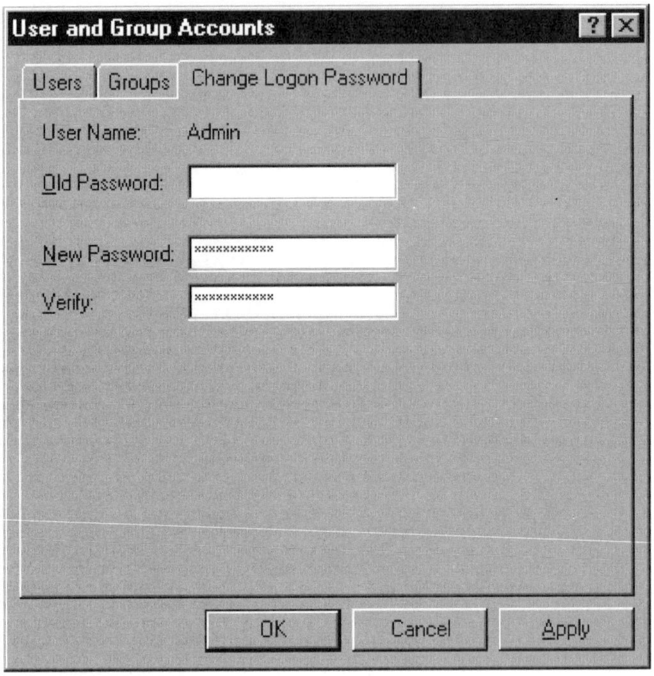

FIGURE 9.5:

The User and Group Accounts dialog box

Using the Security Wizard

Once you have completed the above steps, you are ready to run the Security Wizard. Open the database that you want to secure, and choose Tools ➤ Security ➤ User-level Security Wizard. You will see a verification dialog box. Select the objects you want to secure (it's a good idea to choose all of them). When you click OK, the Wizard will prompt you for the name and location to create a new, encrypted, database with all the objects and relationships from the original database.

After the Wizard creates the encrypted database, permissions to all objects will be revoked for the Admin user and the Users group. The new account you created in the previous section will be the owner of all objects, and the Admins group will be granted full permissions on all objects. As a new database has been created, you can delete or archive the old one, which hasn't been changed in any way. You can now close the old database and open up the new one to continue the process of securing it.

Steps to Take after Running the Wizard

As permissions have been removed from the Users group and allowing users to be members of Admins jeopardizes security, you need to create your own groups and assign them appropriate permissions for the objects in your database. Once your groups are created, create user profiles in Access and assign the users to the appropriate groups according to the level of permissions you want them to have.

Encryption

Encryption on its own is meaningless without implementing security, as anyone with a copy of Access can open an unsecured database by logging on as the Admin user (Access will interpret the encrypted data correctly). Encrypting a database prevents someone unable to log on to Access legitimately from using a file or disk editor to get at data in secured Access databases. Without encryption, string data can be easily retrieved directly from a file using a low-level text editor, bypassing Access entirely. Only the creator of the database or a member of the Admins group of the workgroup information file in use when the database was created has permission to encrypt or decrypt a database.

Access encrypts databases at the page level, with the Jet Engine reading and writing one page (2048 bytes) of the file at a time using RSA Data Security's RC4 algorithm. Data, tables, modules, indexes, and so on are all encrypted in 2KB segments without regard to what is being encrypted. This process creates a certain amount of overhead as Jet writes and reads the pages, so there is consequently a performance hit of approximately 10-15% for encrypted databases. Compression programs such as PKZip or DoubleSpace will be unable to reduce the size of an encrypted database as they will not find the data redundancy that the compression algorithms require to operate effectively.

Common Security Mistakes

Most complaints that Access security doesn't work turn out to be cases of improper implementation. Here are a few of the most common errors:

- **Failure to remove the Admin user from the Admins group before securing your database.** Whoever is in the Admins group of the workgroup that is active when the database is created has the right to assign permissions on the objects in that database. The Wizard warns you if you're running it while logged on as the Admin user, because Admin will become the owner of the database, and anyone's Admin can get in and administer the database. Just because Admin is a member of Admins when you create the database grants no explicit authority to Admin. But if you don't remove Admin from your Admins group, then Admin can grant itself full rights later.

- **Forgetting to remove permissions from the Users group.** This error leaves the database open to all Access users, because all workgroups have a Users group and the internal SID for Users is the same in all workgroups. If you use the Security Wizard, the Wizard takes care of this for you. But if you have implemented security by hand, don't forget the least-restrictive rule: any permissions granted to Users are granted to *all* users.

- **Implementing security on the default workgroup file created when you installed Access.** Anyone can rebuild your original workgroup database from the settings in the Help ➤ About dialog box. For example, your original workgroup can be recreated merely by reinstalling Access or by using the Workgroup Administrator to create a new workgroup database using those settings.

- **Forgetting that the Admin user owns the database or objects in the database**. The creator of an object owns that object. Ownership in Access security means that the owner has irrevocable administrative permissions on that object. It may appear that you can revoke the owner's explicit permissions on that object, but in fact they can reassign themselves permissions any time they choose. Members of the Admins group in the workgroup used to create the database can change ownership of that object. You can't prevent users from creating new forms, reports, macros, or modules, although you can use Visual Basic to prevent them from creating new tables and queries by removing permissions on the container object. The code in the following example removes permissions from the Users group to create tables and queries.

```
Dim db as Database
Dim con as Container
Set db = ws.OpenDatabase(CurrentDb().Name)
Set con = db.containers("Tables")
con.username = "Users"
con.permissions = con.permissions And Not dbSecCreate
```

Security Holes in Access

It is important to remember that Microsoft does not guarantee Access security. Generally speaking, security holes found in one version of the product are fixed in the next version, but so far there has been only one patch released for a security hole found in an existing version. As of this writing, no verifiable security holes have been found in either Access 2.0 or Access 95 that will expose the data in your encrypted application to hackers who do not have access to a valid logon and password combination in your workgroup information file.

- Access 2.0 has a security hole that allowed hackers to decrypt the workgroup database in order to read and write password strings and so promote themselves to a higher level of security. Microsoft issued a patch for Access 2.0 and this problem does not exist in Access 95.

- A security hole in the user interface of Access 2.0 allows users to copy secured application objects (forms, reports, macros, and modules), thus transferring ownership to themselves. Tables can still be secured if no Read Data permissions are granted and queries with the Run Permissions set to Owners are used to access the tables. The danger to data security with this bug arises when you have embedded a valid Admins ID and password in module code in order to perform security functions. This can be read and used to log on and secure access to the data.

- Both Access 2.0 and Access 95 have another security hole that makes data vulnerable to hackers armed with a logon ID and password and with enough knowledge to exploit the Access systems tables. As of this writing, there is no workaround for this hole other than monitoring the activities of your users and controlling who has access to the database.

Access Security and NT

It would be nice if you could integrate Access security with NT security, but integrated security does not yet exist between the two products. Access needs to allow every user read/write access to any .MDB share in order to write the .LDB file in that directory. If a user who has read-only permissions on the database opens the file first, subsequent users logging on to Access are also logged on with read-only permissions. If a user with read/write opens the database first, then those users who only have read-only permissions can also write to it. The bottom line is that you have to depend on Access security to control access to the database.

SQL Server Security

If you are familiar with Access security, you will find many similarities with SQL Server security. You can assign permissions directly to users or groups; permissions are granted for each object, and ownership of objects confers special privileges. That being said, there are enough differences to make the transition challenging. SQL Server security controls who can log on to the server, which databases and objects users have access to, and the administrative tasks each user is allowed to perform.

Like Access security, SQL Server security comprises users and groups, but the functionality of the built-in accounts is quite different. Also like Access security, SQL Server security assigns permissions for objects to groups and users, but the way in which those permissions are granted and revoked is completely different from the way Access does it. For one thing, there is no such thing as the least restrictive rule in SQL Server—the order in which permissions are assigned determines the controlling permissions.

SQL Server security comes in three flavors: Integrated, Standard, and Mixed. Integrated security synthesizes SQL Server security with NT security, allowing a user to log in to SQL Server without supplying a user ID and password a second time if their ID has already been validated through logging in to NT. Standard security uses SQL Server's login validation and requires a user to enter a valid login ID and password, which is separate from the NT logon ID and password. Mixed security allows logins to be validated using either Integrated or Standard. Once a user logs in using mixed security, a username or alias (discussed shortly) must be assigned for them in each database they need to use.

Login IDs, Users, and Groups

SQL Server users and groups function quite differently from Access ones as well. The concept of a user is actually split into two parts: a database user and the login ID with which a user logs into SQL Server. A login ID can be mapped to a user ID as defined in a database, or multiple login IDs can be mapped to the same user ID in a database, which is known as *aliasing*. Aliasing allows you to assign permissions to the user ID, and all the login IDs that alias to that user ID will share those permissions. This can be used in place of group memberships as users are only allowed to be a member of one group.

To create a login ID, open the SQL Enterprise Manager and either double-click the Logins folder or choose Manage ➤ Users... from the menu. Figure 9.6 shows the dialog box for aliasing user Ratbert to user Twinky, a member of the Clerical group in the NWindSQL database. This will allow Ratbert, who is not a defined user in NWindSQL, to access the database with the permissions granted to user Twinky and the Clerical group. Ratbert will then shadow the Twinky account and any permissions granted to it, immediately or in the future. You can only alias a login ID to one user account per database. A person can have a valid login ID and not be able to open any databases unless you have also mapped their login ID to a user ID for them in each database, as the login ID by itself is meaningless in a database unless it is mapped to a user ID either directly or through an alias.

You can also define groups in SQL server, but these are not quite the same as groups in Access as they are database-specific and not global.

FIGURE 9.6:

Creating an alias

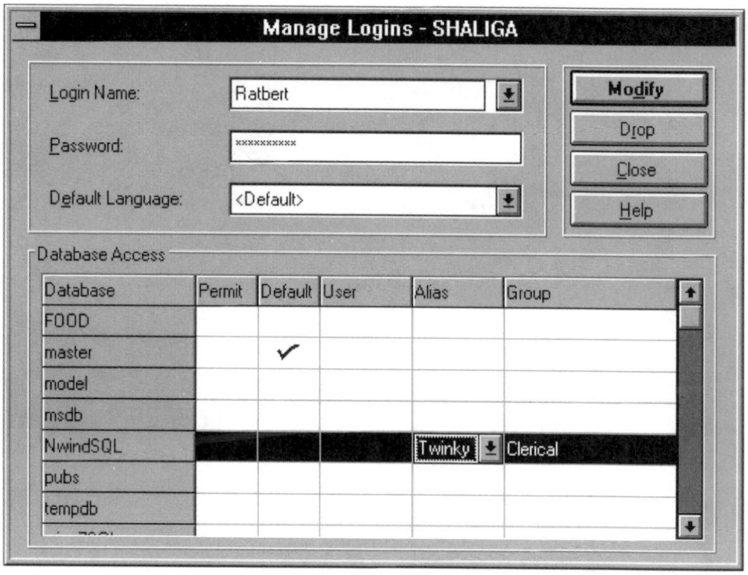

In other words, a NewUsers group in one SQL Server database will have no relation to a NewUsers group in another database as that information is not saved globally, but with the database itself. If you are using integrated security with Windows NT, NT groups cannot be linked to SQL Server database groups. To create a group for a database, select the database in the SQL Enterprise window in the Databases folder and then choose Manage ➤ Groups…. Select <New Group> from the Group drop-down list and type the name of the group. Figure 9.7 shows user Binky being added to the Managers group.

You should grant permissions to groups and then assign users to the appropriate group. Unlike Access, which permits users to be members of many groups and employs the least restrictive rule, users in SQL Server are allowed to be members of only one group at a time besides the built-in public group.

The built-in users and accounts in SQL Server cannot be deleted and they have special properties, as described below.

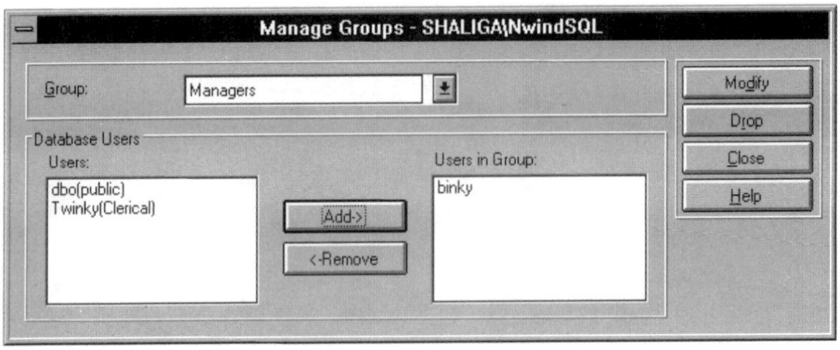

FIGURE 9.7:

Adding a user to a group

SA or System Administrator The System Administrator (SA) in SQL Server is analogous in functionality to the Admins group in Access. The SA has full, irrevocable rights over everything in SQL Server and is responsible for setup and maintenance of the SQL server itself, as well as for creating users and assigning permissions. A SQL Server SA need not be a Windows NT Administrator, but you may find it convenient to make them one. The SA account is global across all databases.

Database Owner (DBO) A DataBase Owner (DBO) is the user who creates a database. The DBO has full privileges inside of that database and administers the security rights of other users. You can alias multiple login IDs to one DBO or make the SA account the DBO by logging on using the SA account to create databases.

Probe A special ID used for internal administrative tasks such as retrieving performance information for the Windows NT Performance Monitor utility. Unlike the SA account, probe is not intended to be used as a login ID.

The public group The public group is automatically built into every database and is analogous to the Users group in Access. Every user is a permanent member of public.

The guest user   If you create a user named "guest" in a database, then anyone with a valid login ID can access the database, even if they do not possess an assigned user name for that database. This allows you to provide access to the database without explicitly mapping users to usernames in a database. The default permissions for the guest user are the same as for the public group, but you can adjust the rights to fit your needs.

repl_publisher   Used when a server is configured for replication and set as a subscription server subscribing to replicated data from a publication database. This ID is not intended to be used as a login ID, but is aliased to DBO on the destination database when that database is marked for subscription.

repl_subscriber   Also used for replication to allow execution of stored procedures on the publication server. Like repl_publisher, repl_subscriber is not intended to be used as a user login.

You can also create your own custom groups and assign permissions to these groups. Users in the groups inherit permissions granted to the group.

Permissions

SQL Server uses permissions to enforce security. You can set permissions on groups or users defined in your database, but not on login IDs. (Remember, though, that within a database, many login IDs can map to one user ID.) There are two different types of permissions: object permissions and statement permissions. Object permissions apply to database objects such as tables and views. You use the GRANT or REVOKE statements to set permissions for both objects and statements. Statement permissions can only be assigned by the SA or the database owner and are not object-related. They include actions such as CREATE DATABASE, CREATE TABLE, DUMP DATABASE, and so on.

SA Permissions

The SA has absolute control over permissions in SQL Server. There are no restrictions on what SAs can do and there are many statements that only the SA can execute—they are not transferable to any other user. These include server-specific functions such as DISK INIT, DISK REFIT, DISK REINIT, DISK MIRROR, DISK REMIRROR, DISK UNMIRROR, KILL, RECONFIGURE, and SHUTDOWN. These tasks are maintenance functions for the server as a whole and not related to a specific database. DISK INIT, for example, is the SQL statement that can create an entirely new device. Only the SA can permit users to create databases.

Owner Permissions

There are two types of owners in SQL Server: the database owner (DBO) and database object owners. The DBO is the creator of a database and has full privileges inside of that database, including the ability to grant permissions to other users to create objects and execute commands within the database. The Database Owner owns exclusive rights to the following commands: CHECKPOINT, DBCC, DROP DATABASE, GRANT and REVOKE, LOAD DATABASE, LOAD TRANSACTION, and SETUSER, and can grant permission to others to execute the following database-specific tasks: CREATE DEFAULT, CREATE PROCEDURE, CREATE RULE, CREATE TABLE, CREATE VIEW, DUMP DATABASE, and DUMP TRANSACTION.

A database *object* owner is the creator of an object, whether it's a table, index, view, default, trigger, rule, or procedure. The object owner automatically has full permissions on that object, and must explicitly grant other users permissions to it as, by default, they are automatically denied all permissions. Specifically, the owner of a table object has exclusive rights (and cannot reassign these rights) to the following commands: ALTER TABLE, CREATE INDEX, DROP INDEX, CREATE TRIGGER, DROP TRIGGER, DROP TABLE, TRUNCATE TABLE, and UPDATE STATISTICS.

It is important to remember that ownership in SQL Server cannot be changed without dropping (deleting) the object and re-creating it under a new owner. You also can't delete a user from a database if that user owns any objects in it. However, you can log on as the SA or DBO, impersonate the owner of an object, and thus use the SETUSER statement to modify permissions on objects that are owned by others.

Setting Permissions

You can grant and revoke permissions to both groups and users by using the Enterprise Manger or by the SQL statements GRANT and RE-VOKE. If you grant permissions to a group, you do not also need to grant permissions to a user who is a member of that group. You must, however, explicitly grant permissions to the objects in your database to those whom you want to use them as, by default, only the owner can access objects.

To assign permissions, choose Object ➤ Permissions from the SQL Enterprise Manager, and then click on the By User tab. Figure 9.8 shows the Object Permissions dialog box with permissions selected for the Clerical group. By using the SQL Enterprise Manager you are able to grant and revoke permissions without having to write code to do so.

You can also set permissions by object, which allows you to see a list of all of your users and groups so you can assign permissions to that object all at one time. Figure 9.9 shows setting permissions for the Employees table for the Managers group. Note that the public group has no permissions to the table object nor do any of the individual users. This view allows you to clearly see the relative levels of access to a given object for all groups and users at the same time.

The order in which you grant and revoke permissions matters in SQL Server. Granting or revoking permissions first to a user and then to a group will have a different result than reversing the procedure. If you set a user's permissions first and then the group's permissions, the

FIGURE 9.8:

Setting permissions by group

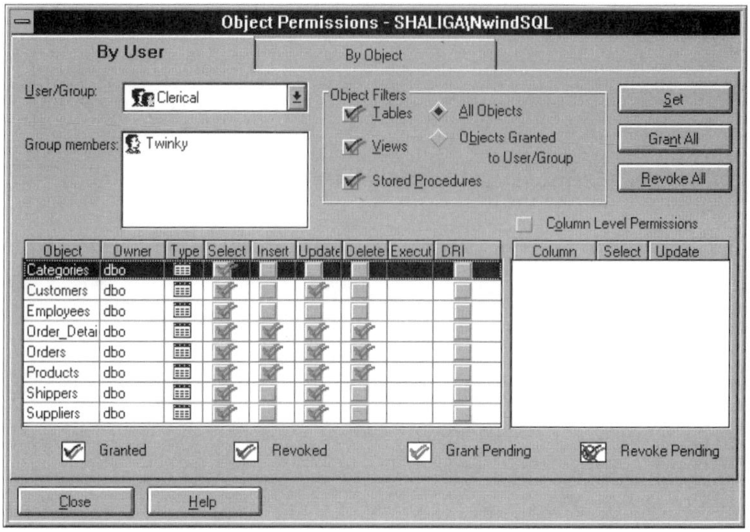

FIGURE 9.9:

Setting permissions by object

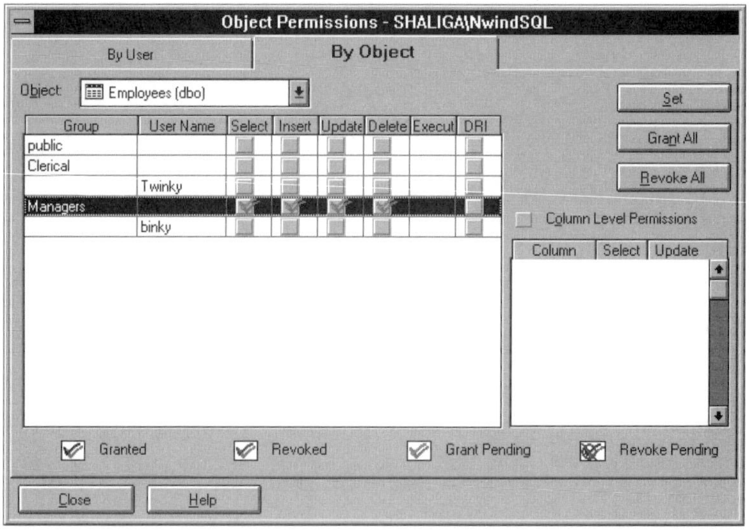

user's permissions will be overwritten. Conversely, by setting the group's permissions first and then the user's, the user's permissions will be differentiated from the group's. For example, if you grant all permissions on an object to a group (say the public group) you can then revoke permissions for a specific user. Everyone in public except for that particular user will have full permissions on the object. To standardize or reset permissions among members of a group who have had individual permissions granted or revoked, set the permissions for the group as a whole and all the individual permissions will be reset to that of the group. In other words, setting group permissions after you have set individual permissions wipes out the individual ones.

You can grant users permissions on views and stored procedures without giving them any permissions on the underlying objects. For example, you can define views on a table which restrict data access based on either columns or rows without granting permissions on the entire table.

Integrating SQL and Access Security

If you use integrated security in SQL Server and use NT logon IDs for user IDs in Access, then you can make it look relatively transparent. The user will still get prompted for a password when they start Access, but it will normally default to their current NT logon ID. They shouldn't get prompted again when they open an SQL Server resource. Microsoft is promising better integration with Access and NT security down the road—in other words, you won't have to log on twice.

Monitoring SQL Server Activity

The NT operating system monitors SQL Server activity. You can use SQL Setup or the Enterprise Manager to set an alert and write a failed logon attempt to the NT application log by. We will cover this subject more fully in the following section on NT security.

NT Network Security

Windows NT Server's security conforms to the U.S. government C-2 evaluation requirements for operating systems. C-2 requires individual authentication, discretionary access control, auditing, and security assurances via controls such as zeroing memory and configurable rights. NT implements this by means of a user account database which authenticates users and allows centralized security management.

Security in NT is assigned per user and validated at logon, and applies equally to the local computer as well as to network resources. Users can be permitted or denied access to NT resources and actions.

NT's basic unit of security and centralized administration is the *domain*, or a network of computers with a common security accounts database. The four types of computers involved in domain security are called *primary domain controllers* (PDCs), *backup domain controllers* (BDCs), *servers*, and *workstations*.

The PDC maintains the security accounts database for a domain, which can have many BDCs. Each BDC has a copy of the PDC's security accounts database, enabling it to assist in authenticating domain logins. If the PDC goes off-line, the BDCs will continue to authenticate logins until it returns.

The members of a domain are other computers running Windows NT (workstation or server version), which participate in domain security by maintaining a local security accounts database to authenticate local logins. In addition, machines that are not technically part of the domain (such as Windows 95 computers) can access the domain by supplying a valid domain user name and password.

Users and Groups

Group accounts are used to simplify administration, so that allocation of resources does not have to be made on a user-by-user basis. A user in a group inherits all access rights and privileges of that group.

NT recognizes two types of groups: *local groups* which grant access to resources within the domain, and *global groups* which grant access across domains. Local groups can contain local users, global groups, and individual users from other domains. A global group may only contain individual local user accounts. Global groups are used mainly in multi-domain networks as a means of providing all user accounts with access to resources that exist in another domain.

To create new user accounts, activate the User Manager for Domains found in the Administrative Tools group. Figure 9.10 shows the user accounts created, and below them a list of the built-in groups with a description of each.

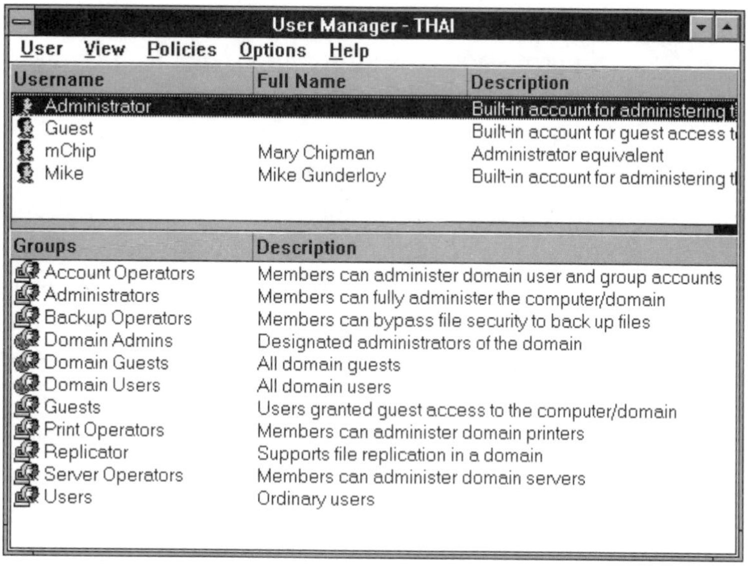

FIGURE 9.10:

The User Manager for Domains in NT Server

```
═                        User Manager - THAI                    ▼ ▲
User   View   Policies   Options   Help

Username                  Full Name           Description
  Administrator                               Built-in account for administering t
  Guest                                       Built-in account for guest access t
  mChip                   Mary Chipman        Administrator equivalent
  Mike                    Mike Gunderloy      Built-in account for administering t


Groups                    Description
  Account Operators       Members can administer domain user and group accounts
  Administrators          Members can fully administer the computer/domain
  Backup Operators        Members can bypass file security to back up files
  Domain Admins           Designated administrators of the domain
  Domain Guests           All domain guests
  Domain Users            All domain users
  Guests                  Users granted guest access to the computer/domain
  Print Operators         Members can administer domain printers
  Replicator              Supports file replication in a domain
  Server Operators        Members can administer domain servers
  Users                   Ordinary users
```

Trust Relationships

To enable user accounts and global groups from one domain to use resources in another, you must set up *trust relationships* between the domains. Trust relationships permit the domains to share account information and validate the permissions of the users and groups residing in the trusted domain as though the domains were a single administrative unit. There are several different models of trusted domain configuration; the one you choose depends on your security needs and the size, location and number of your domains.

To establish a trust relationship, you first must enable one domain to permit a second domain to trust it, and then set the second domain to trust the first. In the User Manager for Domains, choose Policies ➤ Trust Relationships to establish trust relationships. Figure 9.11 shows the Trust Relationships/Add Trusted Domain dialog boxes. The Add button in the Trust Relationships dialog opens the Trusted Domain dialog box.

Permissions

Permissions in NT are covered by Security Policies, so the terminology for permissions is slightly different: user permissions are referred to as *rights*. That is, what SQL Server or Access call permissions, NT calls rights; NT permissions relate to files instead of users. Group and user accounts are covered by the User Rights policy, which basically means that you grant a user the right to perform a certain action on the system, such as connecting to a specific computer on the network. The easiest way to manage rights in NT is to add a user to the built-in group that already possesses these rights. There are no restrictions on how many groups a given user can belong to. To create a new user, choose User ➤ New User... from the User Manager menu. Figure 9.12 shows the New User dialog, where you can set password options, the expiration date for the account, the workstations a user is able to log on to, the hours of the day they are allowed to log on, and a home directory.

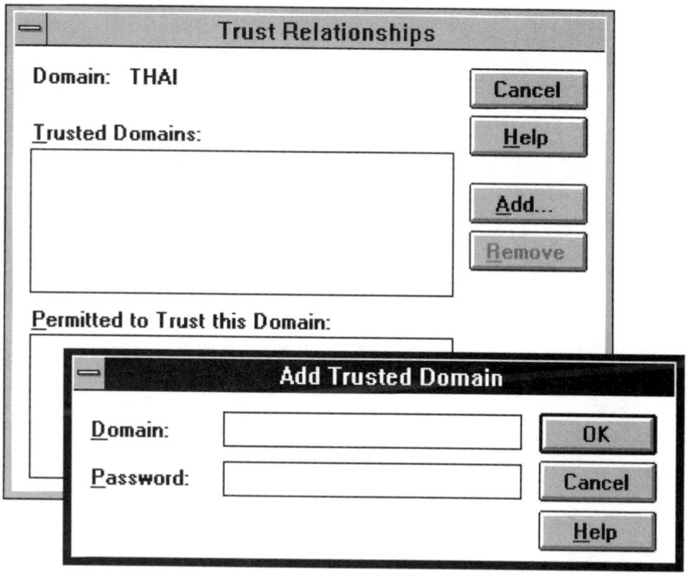

FIGURE 9.11:

Adding a trusted domain

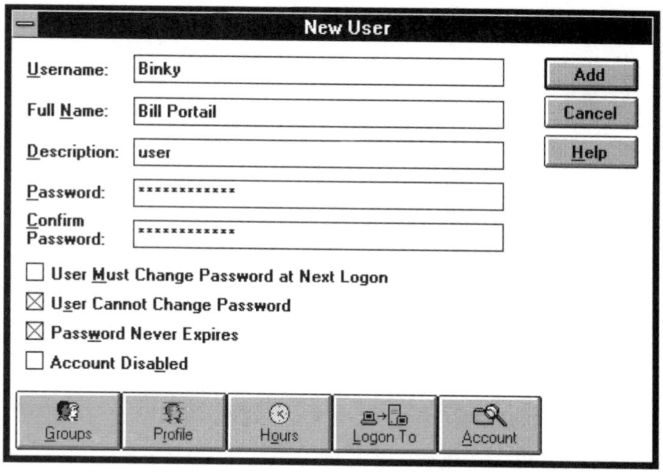

Trust Relationships

Domain: THAI

Cancel

Trusted Domains:

Help

Add...

Remove

Permitted to Trust this Domain:

Add Trusted Domain

Domain: [   ]   OK

Password: [   ]   Cancel

Help

FIGURE 9.12:

Creating a new user account

New User

Username: Binky   Add

Full Name: Bill Portail   Cancel

Description: user   Help

Password: ***********

Confirm
Password: ***********

☐ User Must Change Password at Next Logon

☒ User Cannot Change Password

☒ Password Never Expires

☐ Account Disabled

Groups   Profile   Hours   Logon To   Account

To add a user to the appropriate groups, click the Groups button in this dialog box and select groups to which to add the user, as shown in Figure 9.13.

If you need additional flexibility with user rights above and beyond that available from the built-in groups, you can create your own group and define the rights of that group by choosing User – New Global Group or User ➤ New Local Group. To grant rights to the new group, choose Policies ➤ User Rights Policy. The rights are assigned to groups on a right-by-right basis, so you need to select each right in the top drop-down list and then add the group that you want to have the right. Figure 9.14 shows the dialog box used for adding rights to a new group called Clerical. You can also remove rights from groups by the same process.

FIGURE 9.13:

Adding a new user to groups

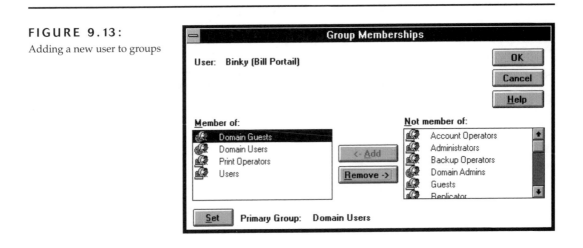

Integrating NT Security and SQL Security

You can integrate NT security with SQL security so that users only have to log on once and so only have to maintain one login ID and

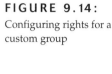

FIGURE 9.14:
Configuring rights for a custom group

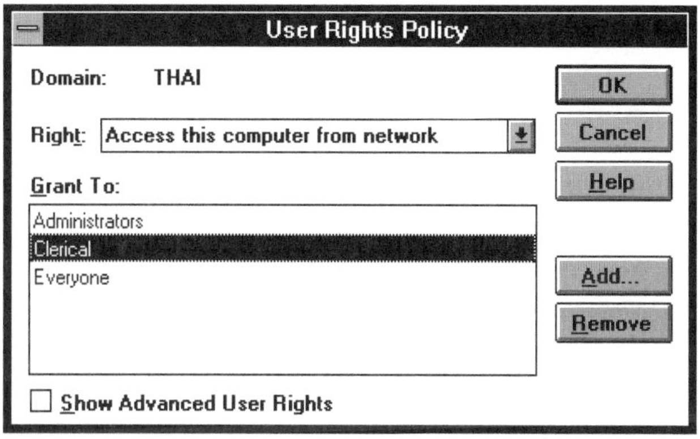

password. SQL Server uses the identity established when a user logs in to Windows NT to validate each user account. This validation is achieved through network protocols called *trusted connections*. Once a user is validated, then SQL Server security operates as usual through permissions granted within individual SQL Server databases.

The recommended way to implement integration is to create two groups in NT, one to define user privileges and one which is mapped to the SA login ID. By doing this, you can control who has SA privileges over your databases with minimal effort. Within SQL Server, you can add the login IDs to the appropriate groups.

With integrated security, the nuts and bolts of database security still falls under the SQL Server aegis and permissions continue to be managed by the database owner. Nothing changes—it is still necessary to create your own database groups and users in SQL Server, and you'll assign permissions to objects and statements as described earlier.

Monitoring NT Security

Monitoring NT Security is also configured through the User Manager for Domains. You need to set up an Audit Policy to track the various events you are interested in; to do so, choose Policies ➤ Audit. Figure 9.15 shows setting up an Audit Policy to track system logon and logoff and file and object access. This will monitor SQL Server logon and logoff as well.

In addition to configuring your Audit Policy, you have to think about how you are going to manage your security log, as it is limited in size. To configure your security log, activate the Event Viewer in the Administrative Tools group and choose Log ➤ Log Settings. There are three logs available: System, Security, and Application. The System log displays events logged by NT system components, the Security log records security events, and the Application log shows events logged by applications. Figure 9.16 shows setting a maximum log size of 512KB and Overwriting Events as Needed. This allows the log to flush itself if it reaches the 512KB threshold. You can also select to either overwrite events by their age or to not overwrite events at all and clear the log manually. If you do not clear the log manually and it becomes too full, you will receive error messages directly on the server console as errors occur, possibly interrupting server operations, and these messages will not be saved in the log. You will want to configure your log for all three log types.

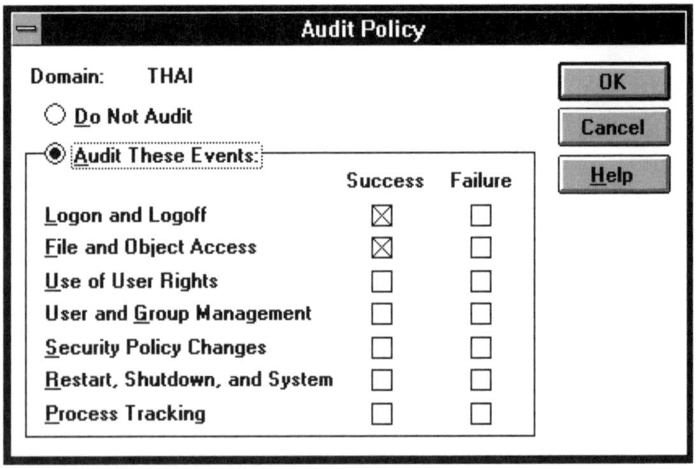

FIGURE 9.15:

Configuring your audit policy

410

FIGURE 9.16:
Configuring the Event Log

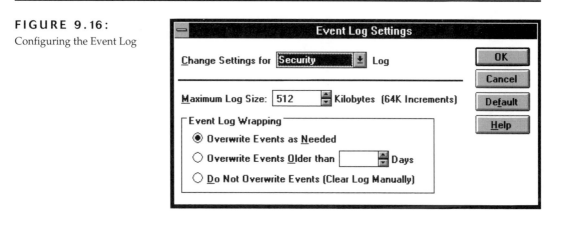

The Event Viewer also gives you the capability for filtering events that you want to view, choosing the order in which the events are displayed, and drilling down into detail on event error messages by double-clicking on any individual event, thus opening a dialog box with more detailed information. The System log will track events for NT, the Security log will record access to NT objects, and the Application log will record SQL Server events (as well as those posted by other applications).

Summary

In this chapter, we've given you an overview of security in Access, SQL Server and NT. We've discussed the strengths and weaknesses of all three and shown you how to take advantage of their various capabilities. It is to be hoped that future releases of all three products will bring tighter integration of security features. In Chapter 10, we'll discuss some administrative tools that are not related to security.

CHAPTER

TEN

Installation and Management of Client/Server Applications

- Installing SQL Server

- Licensing issues

- Distributing application updates

- SQL Server backups

- Server-based help

- Transaction log management

Most of this book has been concerned with the mechanics of storing and retrieving data using the combination of Access and SQL Server. These are the topics of most concern to the application developer. But there is another group of concerns that belongs largely to the database administrator, the person who is responsible for keeping a server running from day to day. There's no way to draw a firm line between the duties of the developer and the administrator. While this book is not intended to make you a database administrator, a variety of these borderline topics are important enough for most developers to get acquainted with. In this chapter, we'll cover some of these topics, including installation and licensing issues, upgrading applications, server backups, help for applications, and transaction log management. We certainly could have picked other topics for this chapter. If you'd like a wider view of the duties of the database administrator, you should browse through the *Microsoft SQL Server Administrator's Companion*, located in SQL Books Online.

Installing SQL Server

If you're upsizing your skills from a desktop product such as Access, it may seem more than a bit odd to wait until the last chapter of the book to tell you how to install SQL Server. But when you're dealing with software such as SQL Server, it's quite usual for the person who installs and manages the database to be different from the person who writes applications to use the database. If you're in a large organization, you may never even get to see the machine where SQL Server is actually running. As long as you can make network connections to it, this shouldn't get in the way of doing client/server development, since tools such as SQL Enterprise Manager make it easy to manage servers remotely.

However, if you're in a small organization (perhaps you're even a one-programmer shop), you'll need to know how to install SQL Server. Even in larger companies, this knowledge can help you understand the choices involved during installation. You should also be aware of some pitfalls along the way.

Installing the Server

As with just about every other Microsoft product, you start installing SQL Server by running the SETUP.EXE program from the CD-ROM. However, you won't find this program in the root directory. Since SQL Server runs on four different hardware platforms (Alpha, MIPS, PowerPC, and Intel), you have to pick the setup program from the appropriate subdirectory.

The first few dialog boxes verify that you really want to run this program, and then prompt for your name, organization, and product ID. You'll find the product ID sticker on the jewel case in which the SQL Server CD-ROM was shipped.

WARNING   **Don't lose your product ID!** If you ever have to call for technical support, you'll need this to prove that you're a legitimate owner of the product. Some people prefer to use a felt tip marker to write the product ID directly on the label side of the CD-ROM. Others, worried that this may hurt the CD-ROM, just keep very careful track of the original packaging.

Figure 10.1 shows the installation options dialog box. The first time through, you'll want to select Install SQL Server and Utilities. Later, you can change many of the options you've selected by rerunning Setup. Some options cannot be changed without a great deal of trouble, though, so you should take your time with the setup process and look up anything that you don't understand.

FIGURE 10.1:

SQL Server setup options

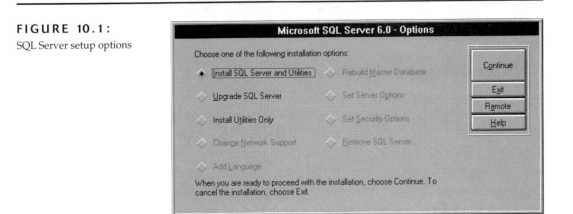

The next dialog box asks you to pick, and then confirm, a licensing mode, either Per Server or Per Seat. We'll discuss licensing issues in more detail later. If you're not sure which licensing mode makes sense for your needs, choose Per Server. You can legally convert a Per Server license to a Per Seat license at a later date, but you cannot convert a Per Seat license to a Per Server license.

The next dialog box asks you to choose a drive and path for installation. The 43MB required space this dialog box shows is the minimum that SQL Server installation will take—this does not leave any room for your data. You'll want to pick a drive with plenty of extra space. If your experience is with Access databases, estimate that your SQL Server databases will take between one-and-a-half and two times the disk space of the corresponding Access databases (primarily because the SQL Server databases will save a transaction log).

The next dialog box asks how much space you want for your *master* database device. This device holds several databases:

- The master database, where system tables are stored
- The model database, which is the template for each new database you create
- The tempdb database, where temporary objects are stored
- The (optional) pubs database, which contains some sample SQL Server objects with which to experiment

The 25MB suggested space for this device is usually adequate for a new SQL Server installation. You may eventually want more space on this device, particularly if you save many custom objects in the *model* database. You can use the DISK RESIZE command to increase the size of this device at a later time.

The next dialog box lets you choose where to install the online documentation. If no one is going to be working directly at this server, you should choose Do Not Install on this dialog box to conserve disk space. Later, you can use the client install to place copies of the online documentation on individual developers' workstations.

The next dialog box, shown in Figure 10.2, lets you select various other installation options. Table 10.1 lists these options and your choices.

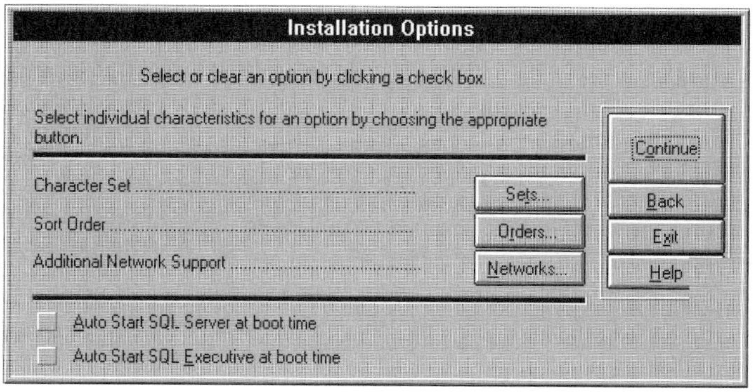

FIGURE 10.2:
SQL Server installation options

TABLE 10.1: SQL Server Installation Options

Option	Explanation
Character set	The default character set for SQL Server is the ISO 8859-1 character set, also called the ANSI Windows or Latin 1 character set. This is the native character set of Windows NT, and should be chosen unless you have a good reason to change it. The Multilingual and US English character sets provide two other general purpose sets. The others listed differ in the selection of accented characters they offer. If you select the wrong character set, changing it later will be an enormous nuisance, since you'll need to dump and rebuild every database on your server.
Sort order	The default sort order is case-insensitive dictionary order. That is, *a* and *A* sort together, with no preference given to either one in sorts. You can choose from a variety of other sort orders, including Binary (where *Z* sorts before *a* because it has a lower ASCII value) and case-sensitive, with either upper or lower case letters having the sort preference. As with character set, changing this later is difficult. You should leave it set to the default unless you have a good reason for changing it.
Additional network support	By default SQL Server is installed to communicate over the Named Pipes network protocol. This works well if your client machines are all running some variation of Windows (Windows 3.1, Windows 95, or Windows NT). You can also install support for additional network types. Do *not* deselect Named Pipes, since the setup program itself depends on using this interface. Also note that the Multi-Protocol library has provisions to encrypt passwords, which are otherwise sent across the network in plain text.
Auto start SQL Server at boot time	If you select this option, SQL Server will be started by Windows NT whenever the computer is booted, whether anyone logs in or not. For most dedicated servers, you should select this option. This provides additional robustness and security, since the server will come back up automatically after a power failure but no one ever needs to log on to it.
Auto start SQL Executive at boot time	If you select this option, the SQL Server Executive service will be started by Windows NT whenever the server is booted, whether anyone logs in or not.

The next dialog box asks you to supply an account name and password for the SQL Executive service to use when starting. You should choose an account that is a member of the Administrators local group and that has been granted the Log On As a Service right. It's also a good idea to set this account to Password Never Expires. Don't select the Install to Log On As Local System Account check box. If you do this, you won't be able to set up replication tasks on this server.

SQL Executive is the scheduling engine for SQL Server, responsible for running such tasks as alerts and backups at the intervals you specify.

These are all the choices you need to make to set up SQL Server. If you've been following along, now would be a good time to get a cup of coffee. The full install process, including setting up the new databases, takes around 15 to 25 minutes on most computers. Although the onscreen prompt will tell you that you can continue with another task, don't bother; unless you have a computer with multiple processors, the second task will be slowed to a crawl by the demands of the server install.

Post-Install Checklist

There are also some tasks you need to do after installing SQL Server. These may include installing the ODBC Driver, setting up Data Source Names, preparing for replication, installing scripts on older servers, and setting up clients.

Although SQL Server setup installs the SQL Server 6.0 ODBC driver by default, this install might fail unexpectedly. This can happen if some other program you've run on the server before the SQL Server setup has loaded one of the ODBC DLLs into memory. If this happens, it's not a big deal. Just reboot the machine and run the ODBC setup by itself. You'll find this in the ODBC subdirectory of the directory from which you originally ran the SQL Server setup.

For this server to be visible to client machines, you'll need to configure ODBC on those computers with an appropriate Data Source Name

(DSN). We discussed setting up DSNs, using ODBC Administrator or custom code, in Chapter 5.

If this server is going to be either a publication server or a subscription server in a replication relationship, you'll have to set up replication for the server. Instructions for setting up replication are in Chapter 8.

If this is the first version 6.0 server on a network that also contains version 4.21 servers, you'll need to install the SQLOLE42.SQL script on the older servers. Instructions for running this script are in Chapter 7.

You will also want to install SQL Server tools on the workstations your developers are using. To install the client tools on Windows 95 or Windows NT (your developers, if they're using Access 95, must be running one of those two operating systems), run the same SETUP.EXE program that you used to install the server. Choose the Install Client Utilities option when asked what action to take. This will install the following utilities on the computer:

- ISQL/W, the Interactive SQL execution tool
- The SQL Client Configuration Utility, which lets you choose which network protocol to run from this computer
- SQL Enterprise Manager
- SQL Help, which has basic Transact-SQL syntax in it
- SQL Security Manager, a tool for managing users and groups
- SQL Books Online, which contains the entire SQL Server documentation set

For developers who frequently work with the server, you will probably want to install the entire Books Online set on the hard drive. This will consume about 15MB, but will make it possible to quickly look things up without locating the original CD-ROM or paper manuals. The rest of the tools take up about 10MB of drive space.

Licensing Issues

As with any other piece of software, SQL Server requires that you buy a license before you use the software. However, the situation is more complicated with SQL Server than it is with Access or another desktop product. SQL Server licensing is based on a two-part model: Both the client and the server must have valid licenses before they can use the software. SQL Server has two different modes of licensing: Per Seat and Per Server.

- With Per Seat licensing, every client that uses data from the server must have its own Client Access License. The server in this model is limited only by network traffic in how many clients it can support at one time.
- With Per Server licensing, the server owns a "pool" of Client Access Licenses that can be used by any client. The server in this model has a maximum number of simultaneous legal connections.

If you install your server with Per Server licensing, you can later opt to change it to Per Seat licensing. You cannot legally change a server from Per Seat to Per Server licensing.

Per Seat Licensing

With Per Seat licensing, licenses are allocated to the individual workstations on your network. You must purchase one license from Microsoft for each computer that's going to connect to any of your SQL Servers. (Microsoft does offer bulk pricing for these licenses; see "License Economics" later in this chapter for some examples.) It doesn't matter how you get the data to the client: Whether the connection is direct from Access through linked tables, via RDO, or via SQL pass-through, the moment you touch the server you need a license to retrieve data from it.

Per Seat licensing is usually the most economical model when your organization has multiple SQL Servers. In this model, one Client Access License covers the computer for access to *all* of the servers on your entire network. This applies no matter how many applications you have running. If you're retrieving data from two servers with an Access application, and from a third server with a copy of Visual Basic, you still only need one Client Access License for that computer.

When your server is running in Per Seat mode, you can use the Windows NT License Manager application (you'll find this in the Network Administration group in the Program Manager) to keep track of licenses. This application, shown in Figure 10.3, will track usage and licenses for you. You should keep a central record of which computers have had licenses assigned to them, and be prepared to produce this data in case your software use is ever audited.

FIGURE 10.3:

Managing licenses for server software

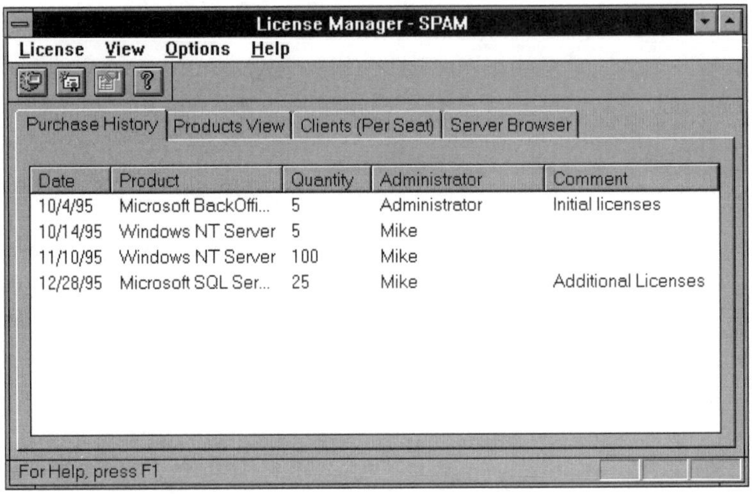

Per Server Licensing

By contrast, Per Server licenses are allocated to the servers instead of the clients. You still need to purchase the individual Client Access Licenses, but you install them on the server. When your server is running in Per Server mode, you enter the number of Client Access Licenses you purchased at the time you installed the server. If you add additional licenses later, you can use the Licensing applet in the Windows NT Control Panel to notify the server that it should allow more simultaneous users. Figure 10.4 shows the process of changing the number of users for a SQL Server.

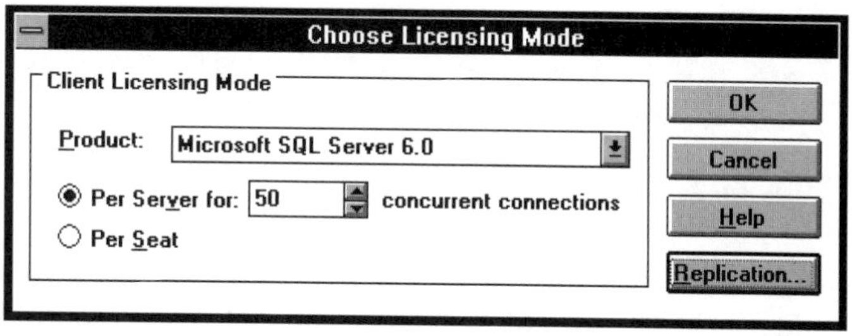

FIGURE 10.4:

Setting the number of simultaneous users for a Per Server license

If only a few of the users on your network are using client/server applications at any given time, you may find Per Server licensing to be the most economical alternative. Remember, though, that if those users are retrieving data from more than one server, there must be a license available for their use on every server.

License Economics

Pricing SQL Server licenses can be quite complicated. The cost of the Server and Client Access Licenses is only a part of the story. In addition, you may need to purchase Windows NT licenses for each client as well. Windows NT is licensed on a Per Seat basis similar to that previously discussed for SQL Server. However, if you're not using the NT server for basic network services, you don't need Windows NT Client Access Licenses. That is, if you're running a Novell Netware or other competitive network for your basic file and print services, and you are only using a Windows NT server to host SQL Server, you don't need Windows NT Client Access Licenses for your client machines.

Microsoft offers a variety of discount plans. Some involve committing to a minimum purchase. Others involve purchasing licenses for the entire BackOffice suite (Windows NT, SQL Server, Mail, SMS Server, and SNA Server) at the same time. To help cut through the confusion, Microsoft has released a freeware BackOffice Pricing Tool, which is included on the companion CD for this book. It includes a wizard to work you through choosing the most economical pricing for any given group of BackOffice clients and servers. Figure 10.5 shows the results of running the wizard for one hypothetical network:

- 4 Windows NT servers
- 3 SQL Servers
- 250 clients, all logged on to at least one of the Windows NT servers continuously
- A maximum of 75 simultaneous users on each SQL Server

The selected configuration would cost $31,703 to install from scratch (counting both client and server licenses) and $14,909 in annual maintenance (to be ensured of upgrades to new releases). This is using the official Microsoft pricing. Of course, for any purchase of this magnitude you should shop around for a reseller who's willing to discount the purchase.

FIGURE 10.5:

Pricing for a hypothetical network

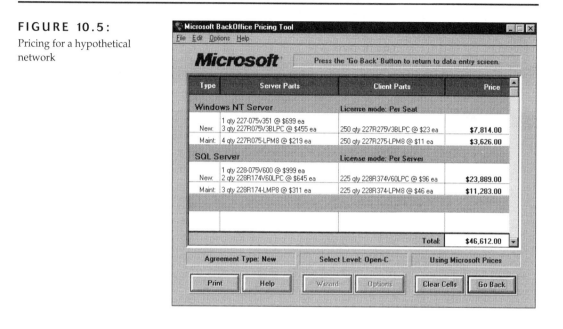

Keeping Versions Current

Applications naturally grow and change, and client/server applications are no exception to this rule. In most cases, you won't need to worry about changes to the server side of the application, since it will only be running in one place. But you might have fifty or a hundred copies of your client application scattered across your network. How can you handle distributing changes to all of these copies without going crazy in the process? The answer is that you need to take advantage of the programmability of Access to help automate the changes. You can either do this with disk-based changes or with Access replication.

Distributing Access Changes via Disk

Probably the simplest way to handle changes is to distribute a new .MDB file when you've got a new version ready. This file could be sent through electronic mail to each user, or you could place it in a central directory on your network and use electronic mail to notify users that it was ready for copying. As long as you don't have to change the arguments used to connect with your server or link to any additional tables, your users can just copy a new version over the old one and expect it to work.

For a slightly more sophisticated approach, you might want to construct a message-passing mechanism that works within the application, rather than through electronic mail. This way, users will see your status messages when they log into your application, whether they do so directly across the network or through a RAS connection, and whether they check their mail or not.

CH10.MDB contains an example of this technique. To test this database, you'll need to create a table named tblMessages on your server with two fields: MessageNumber (smallint) and Message (varchar 255). Give the table a clustered unique index on MessageNumber and link it to CH10.MDB. Rename the attachment from dbo_tblMessages back to tblMessages. Open the table and put several messages into it, starting with number 1. Figure 10.6 shows what the table should look like after you've stocked it.

Now run the macro mcrGetMessages. (Ordinarily, you would incorporate this macro into your AutoExec processing.) You should see a message box for each entry you made in the tblMessages table.

This example works by storing the last-read message number as a property of the database. User-defined properties on Database objects

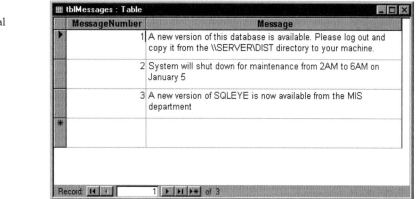

tblMessages with several waiting messages

are a new feature of Access 95, and they're very useful for storing information related directly to the database. We could have used the SaveSetting and GetSetting Registry functions to store information, but this way the information travels with the database. SetLastMessage is a function that sets this property to a new high-water mark. It creates the property if it doesn't already exist.

```
Function SetLastMessage(intMessage As Integer) As Boolean
' Set the last message number read by this database
' Returns true on success, false on any failure
On Error GoTo SetLastMessageErr
    Dim prp As Property
    SetLastMessage = True

    CurrentDb.Properties("LastMessage") = intMessage
SetLastMessageExit:
    Exit Function
SetLastMessageErr:
    Select Case Err.Number
        Case errPropertyNotFound
            Set prp = CurrentDb.CreateProperty("LastMessage", _
                dbInteger, intMessage)
            CurrentDb.Properties.Append prp
            Resume SetLastMessageExit
```

```
        Case Else
            MsgBox Err.Number & ": " & Err.Description, _
                vbCritical, "SetLastMessage"
    End Select
    SetLastMessage = False
    Resume SetLastMessageExit
End Function
```

The inverse of SetLastMessage is GetLastMessage, which reads the current number from this property. If it can't find the property, it assumes that no messages have been read:

```
Function GetLastMessage() As Integer
' Returns the current last message number
' Or zero if this cannot be determined
On Error GoTo GetLastMessageErr
    GetLastMessage = CurrentDb.Properties("LastMessage")
GetLastMessageExit:
    Exit Function
GetLastMessageErr:
    Select Case Err.Number
        Case errPropertyNotFound
        Case Else
            MsgBox Err.Number & ": " & Err.Description, _
                vbCritical, "GetLastMessage"
    End Select
    GetLastMessage = 0
    Resume GetLastMessageExit
End Function
```

The ShowNewMessages function is the one that the AutoExec macro calls. It opens a recordset on the server messages table. If it can't find the table, it assumes there are no messages and quietly exits. Otherwise, it puts each message onscreen and then resets the high-water mark property so that these same messages don't get shown the next time the database is opened.

```
Function ShowNewMessages()
' Show all new messages from the server
On Error GoTo ShowNewMessagesErr
    Dim intLast As Integer
    Dim intRet As Integer
    Dim rstMessages As Recordset
    intLast = GetLastMessage
```

```
    Set rstMessages = CurrentDb.OpenRecordset( _
        "SELECT * FROM tblMessages WHERE " & _
        " MessageNumber > " & intLast & " ORDER " & _
        "BY MessageNumber", dbOpenDynaset)
    With rstMessages
        Do Until .EOF
            MsgBox !Message
            intRet = SetLastMessage(!MessageNumber)
            .MoveNext
        Loop
        .Close
    End With
ShowNewMessagesExit:
    Exit Function
ShowNewMessagesErr:
    Select Case Err.Number
        Case errNoSuchTable
            ' Error message table doesn't exist
            Resume ShowNewMessagesExit
        Case Else
            MsgBox Err.Number & ": " & Err.Description, _
                vbCritical, "ShowNewMessages"
    End Select
    Resume ShowNewMessagesExit
End Function
```

This example demonstrates an easy way for you to pass information to the users of your database without needing to directly address it to them. If they use the database, sooner or later they'll see your messages. With a little extra effort, you could add a second related table to the server to record who read each message and when.

Distributing Access Changes via Replication

As we discussed in Chapter 8, you can also use Access replication to distribute changes to your client database. If the overhead imposed by replication is not enough to hurt your application, and all users of the database are on one network, replication is the simplest way to distribute changes. We recommend using the Star topology for your Access replication, with the hub on the same server as your main SQL Server database and the Access Design Master on a spoke that is not automatically synchronized.

When you're at the point of being ready to release a new version of your client software, you would synchronize the Design Master with the hub replica. Then, as the hub synchronizes with other copies of the database, changes are automatically propagated.

Using Microsoft Tools

Anyone working on a network has figured out that Microsoft is packing a lot into operating systems and applications software these days. In this section we'll review a couple of Microsoft tools that are applicable to client/server applications with which you may not yet have extensive experience: the Access Developer's Toolkit and the various alternatives for taking a backup of your databases.

The Access Developer's Toolkit

The Access Developer's Toolkit—more commonly referred to as the ADT—contains a grab bag of tools for the Access developer:

- The Setup Wizard (discussed in more detail below) for creating royalty-free distribution disks for your Access applications
- The Access Developer Sampler CD-ROM, with technical support and training information on Access
- Replication Manager and Transporter, to help manage replicated databases (see Chapter 8)
- The Access Language Reference and Data Access Reference manuals in printed form

- A selection of OLE custom controls for more flexible user interfaces in Access

- Microsoft Help Workshop, for creating help files

- The Win32 API Viewer, a tool to help declare Windows API functions in Access VBA code

- A guide to using OLE Automation objects in Office

For our purposes, the most significant of these components is the Setup Wizard. This tool allows you to create distribution disks for Access applications. Although you need to have a Client Access License for every computer that will use SQL Server, you do *not* need to have a copy of Access for every computer that will run your client program. Instead, you can use the ADT Setup Wizard to create installable copies of your application and use those everywhere. This can add up to a substantial savings for users who do not need to have Access to create new databases.

Setup Wizard

The Setup Wizard works by installing a special "runtime" copy of Access on target machines. Actually, this is the exact same Access executable that comes in the main product, but it is launched with a special switch. If you'd like to see the runtime version in action without buying the ADT, you can just create a shortcut using this switch:

```
msaccess.exe /runtime YourDB.MDB
```

If you launch Access in this fashion, you'll notice that it becomes crippled so as not to allow the design of new objects. The design views of all objects are permanently invisible if you use the /runtime switch (although they still exist—you can, for example, open a form in design view and make changes to it under code control). In addition, certain keystrokes such as F11 and Ctrl-Break are ignored when Access is in runtime mode. The net effect is to produce a version of Access that runs your client programs perfectly, while not allowing the user to build new applications.

To create a distribution set for your clients, follow these steps:

1. Use the Windows 95 Start menu or the Windows NT Program Manager to launch the Setup Wizard program.

2. On the first screen, tell the wizard you want to create a new set of setup options. (You can save these options to reuse in subsequent runs of the wizard.)

3. On the next screen, use the Add button to add your .MDB file to the setup set. Specify that it should install in $(AppPath) and set it as your application's main file.

4. On the next screen, create a shortcut with the name of your application. You can also specify an icon file to represent the application. This shortcut will be the way that your users launch your client database.

5. You can skip the next screen on Registry values unless some part of your application requires use of the Registry. Use this screen to add the appropriate keys to the Registry to register an ODBC data source, as we discussed in Chapter 8.

6. On the optional components screen, select Microsoft Access Run-Time Version and ODBC Support with SQL Server.

7. If you're not using Access security, accept the prompt that warns you that the Setup Wizard will create a workgroup file for you. (If you are using security, you should include your workgroup file in step 3.)

8. Use the next screen to mark all of the components as required.

9. On the next screen, fill in the name and default installation directory for your application.

10. Skip the next screen, unless you have a separate program you want to launch when setup is finished (for example, a readme file can be shown with Notepad at this point).

11. On the next screen, select the type of setup to create. While you're developing, you should always create an uncompressed network setup, because the compression step is quite time-consuming. If you have geographically dispersed users to whom you want to send diskettes, you should do a final run to create diskettes after you are sure everything is working properly.

12. Click Finish to actually create the setup files. The Setup Wizard will prompt you to save your choices. If you're intending to re-fine this setup, it's a good idea to do so.

The directory you specified for disk images will contain everything you need to set up the runtime version of Access along with your client application on any computer running Windows 95 or Windows NT. As shown in Figure 10.7, the setup is very similar to those used by Microsoft for its own applications.

FIGURE 10.7:

Running a custom setup program created with the ADT

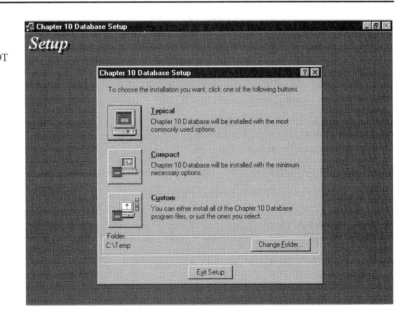

Editing the STF File

As you can see in Figure 10.7, the ADT Setup Wizard gives your users Typical, Complete, and Custom install choices by default. If you're trying to make sure everyone on a network has the same setup, you probably don't want this flexibility. There's a relatively simple (but undocumented) change you can make to the setup files to restrict your users to a Typical setup.

WARNING   The documented way to achieve this functionality is to instruct your users to run "setup /q", which automatically does only a typical setup. In our opinion, this is not enough to keep most users out of trouble.

To restrict your users to a Typical setup, follow these steps:

1. Locate the file SETUP.STF in the directory where you created setup disk images. Make a backup copy of this file, since as soon as you start editing it you lose your support from Microsoft.

2. Use Microsoft Excel to open the SETUP.STF file. This file is tab-delimited text, and Excel will preserve the file format. If you edit the file with a regular text editor, it will cease working.

3. Starting on row 23, you'll find a section of the file headed "Install Types."

4. Look at column F in this section. You should see a series of entries that look like this:

    40 45 50 :1100

5. Edit each of these entries so that they read:

    40 : 1100

6. Save the file and test the setup.

If you've properly followed these directions, setup will now give your users *only* Typical as an installation type, no matter how they attempt to run the setup.

Backup

If a database is important enough to justify the expense and trouble of setting up an SQL Server, it's important enough to back up. Though SQL Server is very reliable software, neither it nor the hardware it runs on is perfect. One way or another, you need to have copies of your SQL Server database stored safely where they can be used to quickly restore data in times of emergency.

Windows NT Backup

At first glance, it might seem that the backup built into Windows NT would be adequate. After all, it works for all your other files. For the most part, though, this is *not* the case.

WARNING   It's far too easy to get lulled into a false sense of security when using file-based backup to save copies of databases. Because SQL Server opens files in shared mode, it will let your backup software copy those files. But if the server writes to the file while it's being backed up, the backup will be corrupted. The same applies to Access databases stored on your server.

If you can arrange to do backups only at times when there are no users in the database, then regular server backup programs are adequate. However, if your database gets round-the-clock use you'll need to learn how to use SQL Server's own tools for backup instead.

Hot Backup: Mirroring

SQL Server has a built-in mirroring facility to allow you to keep a redundant copy of your data. *Mirroring* is the process of writing all changes to the database to two separate copies of the database. In this fashion, if anything happens to the primary copy, the mirrored copy is waiting to take over.

To implement mirroring in SQL Server, use SQL Enterprise Manager to display the devices on the server with which you're working. Right-click the device you wish to mirror, and enter the name of the mirror file in the dialog box shown in Figure 10.8. When you click the Mirror button, SQL Server will create the mirror device. From that point on, all changes written to any database on the original device will also be written directly to the mirror device.

FIGURE 10.8:

Mirroring a SQL Server drive

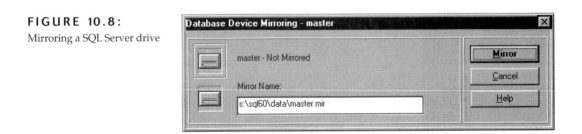

You can control the operation of a mirrored device by right-clicking on it in SQL Enterprise Manager. This gives you a choice of four operations:

- *Switch to Mirror Device – Retain*: This option causes the mirror device to become the one to which users connect but retains the original device for possible repair.

- *Switch to Mirror Device – Replace*: This option causes the mirror device to become the one to which users connect and drops the original device.

- *Turn Off Mirroring – Retain Mirror Device*: This option disables mirroring but preserves both copies of the data.
- *Turn Off Mirroring – Remove Mirror Device*: This option disables mirroring and drops the mirror device.

All mirroring must take place on local drives that are actually physically present in the server. You can't mirror an SQL Server device to a network drive.

If your drive space is limited, you might consider mirroring just the device holding the transaction log. If you do this, and take periodic backups of the main database, you'll still have enough information to recover operations should something go wrong with the main database.

NOTE   There are two other levels at which you can mirror things in Windows NT. First, Windows NT has built-in drive mirroring, which allows two different hard drives to mirror writes from one another. Second, Windows NT can use hardware RAID devices for mirroring that don't depend on software at all. Either of these is more expensive than the built-in SQL Server mirroring, but they may be preferable because they won't impose as much of a performance hit on the server.

Warm Backup: Replication

As we discussed in Chapter 8, you can also use replication to back up important parts of a database. Replication may be preferable to mirroring for absolutely critical information, because it can back up information to network drives and remote servers. By using transaction-based replication, you can also strike a balance between network traffic and concurrency in your data.

On the other hand, replication requires at least two SQL Servers to do anything at all. Unless you're already running multiple servers on your network, replication may not provide a cost-effective way to back up your data.

Also bear in mind that you must back up more than just your own database to be sure to recover from a disaster. You must arrange backups of the following:

- All databases
- All transaction logs
- The master database
- The msdb database
- The distribution database (on distribution servers)

Since you can't use replication to back up system tables, you won't be able to build a complete backup solution using replication.

Cold Backup: Dump and Restore

SQL Server also includes its own integrated backup capabilities. If you're not mirroring or replicating your databases, this is the backup you should use for all of your server databases. SQL Server's built-in backup capabilities explicitly allow for backing up a database that is in use. You're guaranteed that the backup represents the database as it was at the time you initiated it with the SQL Server DUMP command. Transactions executed while the database is being backed up will not corrupt the backup.

It doesn't do much good to back up a corrupted database. Before doing any backups, Microsoft recommends that you run these three Transact-SQL statements, using ISQL/W, passthrough queries, or SQL Enterprise Manager:

```
DBCC CHECKDB (database_name)
DBCC NEWALLOC (database_name)
DBCC CHECKCATALOG (database_name)
```

If any of these statements returns error messages, you should diagnose and fix the problems before doing a backup.

NOTE You may get spurious errors from DBCC NEWALLOC if the database is in active use. If this occurs, you should set the server to single-user mode and read-only and rerun the command. Unfortunately, this may not be practical on production servers.

Although you can back up a database solely through the use of SQL statements, it's easier to use SQL Enterprise Manager. Start by selecting the database you want to back up, right-click on it, and select Backup/Restore from the shortcut menu. Select the backup device you want to use and click the Add button to place it in the Backup Destination box. Figure 10.9 shows an example of setting up a backup from within SQL Enterprise Manager.

FIGURE 10.9:
Creating a backup in SQL Enterprise Manager

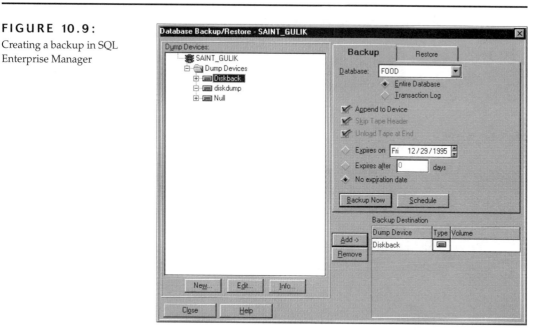

You can either execute the backup immediately or schedule it. More likely you'll want to set up some sort of recurring schedule. As Figure 10.10 shows, the scheduling options are quite flexible. If you desire, you can back up a database at 4 a.m. on the first Sunday of every month. On the other end of the spectrum, it's possible to run your backups once an hour every day, which might be prudent for extremely critical databases running on fast servers. While you're scheduling a backup, you can also set options for recording success or failure. When a backup succeeds or fails, SQL Server will write a message to the Windows NT Event Log, send an e-mail message to a specified operator, or both, depending on the options you choose.

FIGURE 10.10:

Backup scheduling options

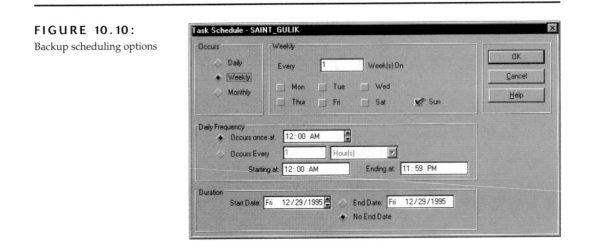

After you've created a backup, you can use the LOAD statement from a query or SQL Enterprise Manager to restore it should it ever become necessary. You can also save time doing backups by backing up the database infrequently and the transaction log more frequently. If you ever need to restore in this situation, you'll need to LOAD the database first and then LOAD each subsequent transaction log DUMP in order.

For more information on these and other advanced backup topics, see the *SQL Server Administrator's Companion*.

Getting Help

Any professional application these days requires a help file. Users expect to be able to press F1 and receive context-sensitive help. Fortunately, this type of help is getting easier and easier to supply. Microsoft ships the Microsoft Help Workshop with the Access Developer's Toolkit. There are also many third-party programs that make creating help for your applications even easier. We'll quickly review the basics of creating help files, and then look at a technique that will let you store some of your help topics on the server instead of the individual client machines.

Creating Help Files

Access allows you to supply custom help whenever your user presses F1 and the current object is a form. Each form has a HelpFile property that specifies the name of a help file (in Windows .HLP format) and a HelpContextID property that specifies which topic in the file goes with this form. In addition, individual controls can have HelpContextID properties that specify a topic number to be displayed if the user presses F1 while the focus is on that control.

Though the Help Workshop is a new component, the basics of creating a Help file haven't changed much since Access 2.0. Help topics are written as a series of Rich Text Format (.RTF) files and are combined with a Help Project (.HPJ) file to create the final help file. The HCW.EXE help compiler does the actual work of creating the help file. To learn the correct format for the source files, you need to read through the help for the Help Workshop itself.

Third-Party Help Tools

Though, with patience, a help file can be constructed by following these "official" instructions, it's rare for developers to do so. Instead, most developers use a "front-end" help precompiler. There are a variety of programs that will create .RTF files in the format that the HCW.EXE compiler expects, but which have a more reasonable user interface. Microsoft makes two unsupported tools, WHAT and HULK, available through its TechNet CD-ROM subscription series. Other programs, including Visual Help, ForeHelp, RoboHelp, and Doc-to-Help, are widely advertised. If you have access to CompuServe, most of the major players in this market have trial versions or publicity available on the WINSDK forum, where the help compiler is supported.

Storing Help on the Server

While client-side help is widely used, you may never have considered any server-side help. Suppose, though, you have an SQL Server that is used by many users from many different client front-end programs. How do you deliver effective help on the defaults for a particular field or the use of a particular table? Wouldn't it be nice to have help topics related to fields on the server, and available from any client application?

An example in CH10.MDB, on the companion disk, shows you how to move in this direction. This sample assigns a special range of HelpContextID properties to the server and displays messages from the server when Help is invoked with one of these IDs. Though you'll still have to set up the mapping between fields, controls, and HelpContextIDs yourself, this sample demonstrates a way to reuse help topics in multiple applications with minimal effort.

Setting Up the Sample

There are three setup steps you need to take before you can use this sample:

1. Link the authors table from the SQL Server pubs sample database to CH10.MDB. The name of the linked table should be dbo_authors.

2. Run the HELPMSG.SQL query file on your server. You can load this file into either ISQL/W or the Query Analyzer window of SQL Enterprise Manager.

3. Open the basMessages module in CH10.MDB and modify the sqlConnectString constant. The string that's stored here is:

```
Const sqlConnectString = _
 "odbc;dsn=SGPubs;uid=sa;pwd=;database=pubs;"
```

   You need to put the DSN, user ID, and password for your own SQL Server into this string.

After these setup steps, you're ready to try the sample. Open the form frmAuthors, place the cursor in any of the data entry fields, and hit the F1 key. You'll receive a message similar to the one in Figure 10.11. This message comes from the server, not from a local help file or any part of the client program.

Adding Server Messages

The messages used in this example are stored on the server when you run the HELPMSG.SQL file. This file consists of a series of SQL statements similar to this one:

```
sp_addmessage 150004, 1, →
'Enter the phone of the author in this field'
```

FIGURE 10.11:

Displaying help from the server

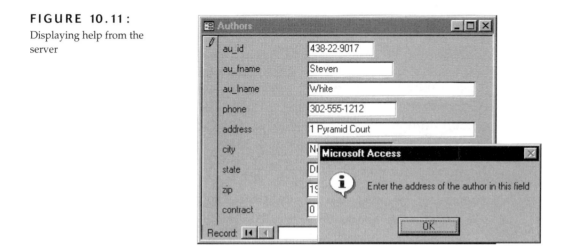

The built-in sp_addmessage stored procedure in SQL Server 6.0 adds new messages to the internal table of error messages used by SQL Server. It takes three arguments: a message number, a severity level (with 1 being the mildest possible warning), and the message itself. We've arbitrarily chosen 150,000 as the lowest number to use for our custom messages in this application. You can use any message number from 50,001 up to the maximum for a long integer.

As soon as the stored procedure shown here is run, SQL Server understands that there is a new error message with the number 150004. You can invoke this message directly by running SQL from ISQL/W:

```
RAISERROR (150004, 1, -1)
```

The RAISERROR statement triggers an error condition on the server. This is similar to using the Err.Raise method in VBA. As part of its response, RAISERROR returns an information message with the text of this error. As we'll see, getting this message into an Access message box requires some work, but it can be done.

Intercepting F1

To subvert the regular help process, you need to intercept the F1 keystroke when the focus is on the form. In previous versions of Access, this was very difficult, because it required writing code for every single control on the form. In Access 95, though, it's simple. All you need to do is set the KeyPreview property of the form to True, and then write a single event procedure to react to the form's KeyDown event:

```
Private Sub Form_KeyDown(KeyCode As Integer, Shift As Integer)
    Dim varRet As Variant
    If KeyCode = vbKeyF1 Then
        If Screen.ActiveControl.Tag = "SQLHELP" Then
            varRet = MsgBox(GetSQLMessage _
                (Screen.ActiveControl.HelpContextId), _
                vbInformation)
            KeyCode = 0
        End If
    End If
End Sub
```

You also need to do two things for each control on the form that should return a server-based help message:

1. Set the HelpContextID property to the number of the message stored with the sp_addmessage procedure.

2. Set the Tag property to "SQLHELP".

Whenever the user hits F1, the code in the KeyDown event checks the Tag property. If it's "SQLHELP", it calls the GetSQLMessage procedure, discussed in a moment, and then sets the KeyCode to zero. This causes Access to disregard the default processing of this key.

On the other hand, if the Tag property is set to anything but "SQLHELP", or if any key other than F1 is pressed, then the keystroke is passed through to Access unchanged.

Retrieving Server-Based Help

The core of this technique is the GetSQLHelp procedure, which is stored in basMessages. To understand this procedure, you need to know how Jet handles information messages from SQL Server. The only way to retrieve these messages is to use a SQL passthrough query whose LogMessages property is set to True. This will cause Jet to build a local table, named after the current user, containing any messages returned by the server. This applies to messages only—not recordsets, which are handled in an entirely different way.

The function starts out by looking for a local table with the appropriate name to be a message table, and deleting the table if it finds one:

```
Set dbCurrent = CurrentDb()
' See if there's already a message table for
' the current user, and if there is, get rid
' of it
strMsgTable = CurrentUser() & " - 00"
On Error Resume Next
strTemp = dbCurrent.TableDefs(strMsgTable).Name
If Err = 0 Then
    dbCurrent.TableDefs.Delete strMsgTable
End If
On Error GoTo GetSQLMessageErr
```

The next step is to build the query we'll execute. Here lngMessage is the message number, which is passed into the function. Ordinarily, we'd use a temporary querydef for this purpose, for faster processing, but that's not possible in this case. LogMessages is a user-defined property, not a default one, and it's impossible to store a user-defined property on a temporary querydef. Instead we need to delete any existing query by this name and create a new permanent one:

```
' We have to use a permanent query, because you
' can't add a user-defined property to a temporary
' one. So get rid of it if it already exists.
```

```
On Error Resume Next
dbCurrent.QueryDefs.Delete "qryHelpQuery"
On Error GoTo GetSQLMessageErr
' Create and execute a pass-through query to run
' the stored procedure on the server
Set qdfTemp = dbCurrent.CreateQueryDef("qryHelpQuery")
qdfTemp.Connect = "odbc;dsn=SGPubs;uid=sa;database=pubs;"
qdfTemp.SQL = "RAISERROR (" & CStr(lngMessage) & ", 1, -1)"
qdfTemp.ReturnsRecords = False
Set prp = qdfTemp.CreateProperty("LogMessages", _
    dbBoolean, True)
qdfTemp.Properties.Append prp
```

Executing the query will create the messages table, but this still doesn't give us the message. To get this, we have to actually open the table and read out the first record. In addition, the function strips off some preamble characters that the ODBC driver places on the front of the original message:

```
qdfTemp.Execute
' Now the returned message is in the table.
' So go fetch it.
Set rstMessage = dbCurrent.OpenRecordset(strMsgTable)
If Not rstMessage.EOF Then
    strTemp = rstMessage!ODBC
    ' Strip off the junk
    intFlag = InStr(1, strTemp, "[SQL Server]")
    strTemp = Mid$(strTemp, intFlag + 13)
Else
    strTemp = ""
End If
GetSQLMessageExit:
    GetSQLMessage = strTemp
```

Even with the speed hit of creating both a query and a table, this function still runs in a second or two. Certainly when compared with the delay in starting up the new version of Windows Help, this is completely acceptable.

Transaction Log Management

One of the areas of SQL Server administration that frequently trips up beginning developers is the whole notion of a transaction log. If you just install SQL Server, forget about it, and begin working with data, sooner or later things will grind to a halt, and you'll get a message that the transaction log is full. To avoid this condition, you must understand what a transaction log is and how you should manage it. Too often beginning developers view the transaction log as a nuisance rather than as an essential part of the SQL Server strategy for protecting your data.

How the Transaction Log Works

Every SQL Server database has a transaction log dedicated to it. As you change data in the database, SQL Server keeps a record of these changes in the transaction log. You can think of the transaction log as a tape recording of all of your database operations and their consequences. If you update a row of data, for example, the transaction log might contain a record of numerous operations. These would include the deletion of the original row, the insertion of the new row, and corresponding changes to all of the indexes on the table.

Transaction logs should be kept on a separate SQL Server device from the databases they are logging. Preferably, this should be on a separate physical device as well. By separating the log and the data in this way, you gain performance, since the disk writes are distributed to more than one hard drive. More importantly, though, you gain robustness.

Suppose you back up your database Monday night and the hard drive containing the database explodes Tuesday evening, before you have backed it up again. Tuesday's work isn't lost. You can install a new hard drive, restore Monday night's backup, and then "play back" the Tuesday transaction log to that copy of the database. When you're done, the database will be in exactly the same state that it was before the unfortunate disaster.

Disabling the Transaction Log

Naturally, the transaction log takes up space. Since it's recording every database operation, it will take up more and more space until you truncate it. A transaction log is automatically truncated, removing old transactions, whenever it's backed up to a disk or tape device. It can also be truncated in case of emergency (for example, if the log fills up and there is no more space on the device) by issuing the DUMP TRANSACTION WITH TRUNCATE ONLY statement through SQL Enterprise Manager or ISQL/W.

There are times you will want to disable the transaction log temporarily so that you can perform a large operation without filling the log. Some examples of this might include:

- Mass updates to large tables
- Importing large amounts of data via bulk copy (BCP)
- Deleting large tables
- Using large insert queries

In these cases, you can temporarily disable the transaction log using SQL Enterprise Manager. Select the database on which you're performing the operation, right-click, and choose Edit. Click the Options tab and select Truncate Log on Checkpoint, as shown in Figure 10.12.

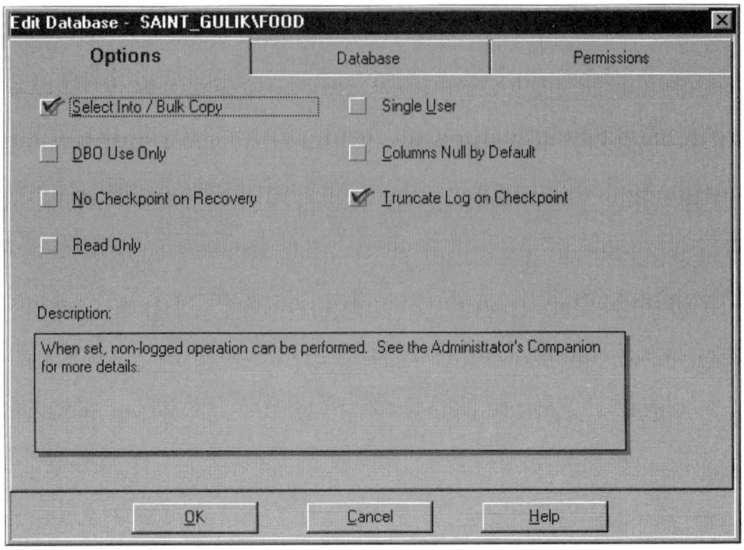

FIGURE 10.12:

Disabling transaction logging
on a database

You can also use the Select Into/Bulk Copy check box to specify that these two operations should always be unlogged.

WARNING It's important to understand that disabling transaction logging also disables your ability to recover from disaster! Always turn the transaction log back on again as soon as the unlogged operation is finished. You must also execute a DUMP DATABASE command (or use SQL Enterprise Manager to do a full backup of the database) to put things back at a known starting point. Until you do this, you will not be able to dump the transaction log.

Dumping the Transaction Log

You can dump the transaction log by executing a DUMP TRANSAC-TION statement (for example, from ISQL/W) or through SQL Server's timed backup facility. Since the transaction log is your lifeline, it's imperative that you do this often enough to keep it from filling up. In planning a transaction log strategy, you also need to consider how much trouble you're willing to go through to recover from disaster. Suppose you back up the database once a week and dump the transaction log twice a day in between. Since each dump of the log only records transactions committed since the last dump, you'll need to have all these dumps handy in case of disaster. If the drive fails just before a full backup, you might have to apply a dozen transaction logs to the original backup to bring the database back up to date.

As an alternative to timed transaction log dumps, you can set up Windows NT Performance Monitor to dump the transaction log whenever necessary. For example, to set up the server to automatically dump the transaction log from the pubs database whenever it is 80% full, follow these steps:

1. Create an SQL command file that will do the actual dump. This is just a text file of SQL commands. In this case we only need one command in the file:

   ```
   DUMP TRANSACTION Food TO Tape01 WITH NOUNLOAD, NOINIT,
   NOSKIP
   ```

   This instructs the server to dump the transaction log for the Food database to the Tape01 tape device. We'll call this command file FOODTRAN.SQL and save it in the C:\SQL60\SCRIPTS directory.

2. Make sure the SQL Server is running.

3. Start Windows NT Performance Monitor.

4. Select View ➤ Alert from the Performance Monitor menu.

5. Select Edit ➤ Add to Alert to create a new alert.

6. Choose SQL Server - Log as the object to monitor.

7. Choose Log Space Used (%) as the counter to monitor.

8. Choose Food as the instance to monitor.

9. Enter **80** in the Alert If Over box.

10. Enter a command to run ISQL (the command-line version of ISQL/W) when the alert happens. In this case, the command is:

```
isql -Sservername -Uusername -Ppassword
    -ic:\sql60\scripts\foodtran.sql
```

11. Click the Add button to create the alert. Figure 10.13 shows the completed Add to Alert dialog box.

FIGURE 10.13:

Creating an alert to dump the transaction log

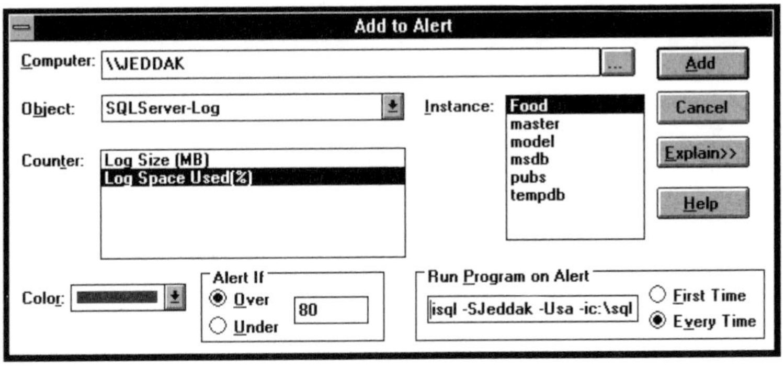

You should also use the File ➤ Save As command in Performance Monitor to save this alert once you're satisfied that it is working correctly. Then you can add a Performance Monitor icon to your Startup group with this saved alert so that it is automatically in place whenever you load Windows NT.

Summary

In this chapter we've covered some of the tasks you'll need to perform to keep a client/server installation running smoothly. These include installing servers, distributing application updates, and providing server-based help. We also looked at backing up servers and keeping their transaction logs under control. These maintenance tasks are essential if you want to keep your data available at all times. It makes sense to plan for them early, rather than be forced to suddenly learn these aspects of application management when an emergency occurs.

APPENDIX

A

SQL Server Basics

- SQL Server concepts

- Installing ODBC

- Moving data

This appendix is intended primarily for developers who are moving from Access to SQL Server. We'll look at the key concepts from SQL Server that we covered in this book, and then show you how to move existing Access data to SQL Server. Some of this material may be familiar to you from working with Access, but you'll want to pay particularly close attention to ideas that have the same name in SQL Server as they do in Access. There are some subtle (and not-so-subtle) differences lurking to trap the unwary.

SQL Server Concepts

SQL Server includes a rich set of objects, with design-time properties that can be manipulated by SQL-DMO (see Chapter 7). Rather than try to cover all of these objects, we'll just look at the ones that are most important to the Access developer. Your best references for more information on these and other objects are the *Database Developer's Companion* and *Transact-SQL Reference* that ship with SQL Server. You should be sure to review these references for changes when you install a new version of SQL Server.

In this appendix, we'll look at the core SQL Server objects:

- Devices
- Databases
- Tables
- Defaults
- Views

- Rules
- Users and Groups
- Stored Procedures
- Triggers

Devices

There's no direct Access analog for a SQL Server device. Although it sounds like something physical, a device is really nothing more than a disk file. For example, the device MSDBData, which SQL Server creates by default when it's installed, maps to the disk file MSDB.DAT. Devices must reside on a local hard drive on the server. When you create a new device, SQL Server automatically creates and initializes a new disk file to hold the contents of that device. However, when you drop (delete) a device using SQL Enterprise Manager, SQL Enterprise Manager does not delete the matching disk file. You'll need to use File Manager in this case to remove it from your hard drive yourself.

A device can hold one or more databases and one or more database logs. Generally speaking, for robustness you'll want to have the database and its log in separate devices on different physical hard drives. You can also spread a database across multiple devices if it grows too large for a single device. See the SQL Server documentation on the sp_extendsegment stored procedure to learn how to do this.

SQL Server also recognizes a special object called a *dump device* (SQL Enterprise Manager calls dump devices Backup Devices). A dump device is designed to hold database backups. Unlike regular devices, a dump device may be a file on a remote network drive; it may also be a tape drive or a floppy disk drive, although floppy disk drive dump devices are only supported for compatibility with earlier versions of SQL Server. SQL Enterprise Manager, for example, cannot initiate a dump to a floppy disk dump device.

When you install SQL Server, it automatically creates a special dump device named "diskdump." Do *not* back up to this dump device! Disk-dump is a shortcut to the NULL device. It provides a fast way to get rid of databases or transaction logs that you no longer require, but you cannot restore a backup from the diskdump device.

When you're first setting up SQL Server, your primary concern should be to ensure that each database is assigned two devices: one for the database and one for its log. You may also wish to designate a particular dump device for the database, perhaps a third hard drive located in a different computer on your network.

Databases

Just as in Access, a SQL Server database is a collection of tables and other objects that reside on one or more devices. Unlike Access databases, SQL Server databases always have a transaction log containing a record of every operation that SQL Server performs within the database (unless logging is explicitly turned off for a particular operation). In case of disaster, the transaction log can be used in conjunction with a backup of the database to restore the database.

If you're using SQL Server 6.0, the easiest way to create a new database is to use SQL Enterprise Manager—just right-click on the Databases entry and choose New Database from the context menu. You can also use the CREATE DATABASE Transact-SQL statement to create a new database; this is the method that the Access Upsizing Wizard uses. (See Chapter 6 for more information on the Access Upsizing Tools.)

Whenever you create a new database, it starts as a copy of the model database, which SQL Server installs when you first set up the server. If there's some object you want to have appear in every database you create, such as a custom stored procedure that implements business rules, simply place that object in the model database.

It's important to realize that SQL Server databases need periodic maintenance to prevent them from filling up their devices. If you should ever fill up the log device, you can expect error messages from any attempt to change the database until you correct the situation. See Chapter 10 for more information on backing up (dumping) SQL Server databases and transaction logs.

Tables

Just as in Access, a SQL Server table is a collection of information about one particular entity. What Access calls "fields," SQL Server calls "columns." SQL Enterprise Manager includes a table designer which is fairly similar to the Access table design view. If you're an Access developer, though, you'll probably find it easier to continue creating your tables in Access and exporting them to SQL Server. You can also create tables by using the CREATE TABLE Transact-SQL statement.

One important distinction between Access and SQL Server tables is that you can't delete columns or change datatypes in a SQL Server table. Instead, you can use the SELECT INTO statement to create a new table with the necessary changes. SELECT INTO is a non-logged statement: that is, it has no impact on the transaction log. Because not logging is dangerous, you must explicitly enable SELECT INTO for any database in which you want to use it. You can do this by running the sp_dboption stored procedure on the master database with the appropriate options, including the name of the database in which you want to allow non-logged operations:

```
sp_dboption 'pubs', 'select into', TRUE
```

Once you've turned on this option, you can use the INTO clause of the SELECT statement. To create a new table named "aunames" which only contains three columns from the authors table, execute this SQL statement:

```
SELECT au_id, au_fname, au_lname
INTO aunames
FROM authors
```

You could then drop the old authors table and rename the new table to "authors," thus effectively dropping all of the other columns from authors. You can use a similar procedure to change the datatype of a column, by using a calculation to create the column in the list used by SELECT INTO.

SQL Server also supports temporary tables, which do not exist in Access. A *temporary table* is a table which only exists in memory and which is dropped as soon as you disconnect from the server. To create a temporary table, just start the table name with a pound sign (#). For example, this SQL statement creates a temporary table called "#aunames" in pubs:

```
SELECT au_id, au_fname, au_lname
INTO #aunames
FROM authors
```

Defaults

In Access, all the parts of a table are parts of one object. SQL Server has a somewhat more distributed view of table design. A default value for a column (called just a *default* in SQL Server) is a separate object from the table that holds it. This allows you to reuse default objects across multiple tables. To take advantage of this ability, you need to first create reusable defaults and then bind them to particular columns. As with other SQL Server design operations, you can use Transact-SQL to perform these steps.

To create a default, use the CREATE DEFAULT statement. The following statement creates a new default named lastnamedefault:

```
CREATE DEFAULT lastnamedefault
AS 'Smith'
```

Once a default has been created, you can bind it to as many columns as you like by using the sp_bindefault stored procedure. To attach this default to the au_lname field of the aunames table created in the example above, you'd use this SQL statement:

```
sp_bindefault lastnamedefault,
'aunames.au_lname'
```

Now, whenever you insert a new record in the aunames table, the last name will be set to "Smith" if you don't supply a name in the INSERT statement.

NOTE By using the DEFAULT keyword in the CREATE TABLE statement in SQL Server 6.0, you can also specify a default when you create a table. These defaults are not implemented as default objects and cannot be reused across tables. If you're dealing with a column shared among multiple tables, you should still consider creating a default object and binding it to all the instances of the column. This makes it easier to make changes to the default should the business rules in your application ever change.

Views

You can think of a view as the SQL Server equivalent of an Access query, although SQL Server has stricter rules than Access on allowing columns in a view to be updated (see Chapter 3 for more information on updating views). In SQL Server documentation, you will sometimes find a reference to a *query*. This term refers to the SQL statement used to create a view, not to the data in the view itself.

SQL Server treats views as virtual tables—anywhere that you could use a table in Transact-SQL you can substitute a view. But the data in a view is never stored; it's always created when you open the view. As with Access, you can use views to enforce row-level and column-level security on your data. You can also use views to partition a table for replication among multiple servers (see Chapter 8).

To create a view, you use the CREATE VIEW Transact-SQL statement. For example, we could look at only the authors whose last names begin with the letters K through Z in our hypothetical table with this statement:

```
CREATE VIEW some_aunames
AS
SELECT *
FROM aunames
WHERE au_lname > 'k'
```

Rules

Rules are the SQL Server equivalent of Access's Validation Rules. Like a SQL Server default, however, a *rule* is a separate object that can be bound to multiple columns within your database. As with defaults, you can take advantage of this independence to encapsulate business rules on your server and share them among tables without having future maintenance problems.

To create a rule, use the CREATE RULE statement as follows:

```
CREATE RULE markup_allowed
AS
@value >= 0 AND @value < .5
```

Here, "@value" refers to the value inserted in the column. You can use any name for this value, as long as it starts with the "@" sign. Once you've created the rule, you can bind it to a particular column with the sp_bindrule stored procedure, as shown here:

```
sp_bindrule markup_allowed, 'inventory.markup'
```

Users and Groups

Users and groups on SQL Server can be confusing to developers migrating from Access. In some respects they behave like the objects of the same names in Access; in others, they are very different.

A SQL Server *user* is a user of a database, but it does not have to be a unique network user. You can map a single SQL Server user to multiple network users, or use integrated security with your SQL Server to have your network users automatically become SQL Server users (see Chapter 9 for a discussion of the ins and outs of SQL Server security).

A *group* is a collection of SQL Server users. However, in SQL Server a user can only belong to a single custom group. By default all users are in a group named public, in addition to their custom group membership (if any).

Just as in Access, you can assign permissions to users or to groups. In SQL Server, you use the GRANT and REVOKE Transact-SQL statements, or SQL Enterprise Manager, to assign permissions or take them away.

Stored Procedures

Stored procedures are similar to SQL Server views in that they are a series of SQL statements. However, as their name implies, stored procedures are permanently stored on the server. They are also parsed the first time they are run to create an execution plan. This allows the server to skip many of the optimization steps when it runs the stored procedure again in the future, resulting in very fast execution.

As shown here, you can create a stored procedure using the CREATE PROCEDURE statement:

```
CREATE PROCEDURE aufirst
AS
SELECT au_fname
FROM aunames
```

After it's been created, you can invoke a stored procedure simply by submitting its name to the server through whatever query interface you are using (for example, ISQL/W, pass-through queries, or SQL Enterprise Manager) like this:

```
au_fnames
```

The stored procedure will return a result set just as if you had run the original query.

Stored procedures can also contain *input arguments* (similar to the arguments used with an Access parameter query) and *output arguments* (a return value). For more details on using arguments with stored procedures, see the *Transact-SQL Reference* under CREATE PROCEDURE.

SQL Server also installs a large number of *system stored procedures* when you create a new server. These are stored procedures that you can invoke to perform particular tasks—for example, the sp_bindefault stored procedure that binds a default to a particular column. A few of the more useful system stored procedures are listed in Table A.1; the full list varies depending on which version of SQL Server you are running. See the Transact-SQL documentation for a full list of stored procedures.

TABLE A.1: Some System Stored Procedures

Name	Use
sp_addalias	Maps a new user to an existing user
sp_addmessage	Adds a new error message to the sysmessages table
sp_adduser	Adds a new user
sp_configure	Displays or change SQL Server configuration options
sp_depends	Displays a list of which objects depend on which other objects
sp_extend segment	Extends a database to a new device
sp_help	Returns help about a database object
sp_helpdb	Returns summary information about a database
sp_helpsql	Returns syntax information on Transact-SQL statements
sp_lock	Returns information on locks in the database
sp_monitor	Displays global statistics about a server
sp_who	Displays information about current users and processes for a server

NOTE   Stored procedures are optimized when they are first executed. If you make substantial changes to your database (for example, by adding many rows or several indexes to a table), you'll want to re-optimize the stored procedures. You can do this by invoking the sp_recompile system stored procedure with the name of a table, as follows:

```
sp_recompile authors
```

This will cause all of the stored procedures that depend either directly or indirectly on the authors table to be re-optimized the next time that they are run.

Triggers

Triggers do not exist in Access; the closest Access analog to a trigger is an event procedure on a form. However, in SQL Server triggers are generated from tables rather than forms, making them completely independent of the user interface. Once you define a trigger, it is executed no matter how the data in the table is changed, whether from a user interface such as an Access form or directly through a SQL query.

In SQL Server, each table can have up to three triggers, defined from the three basic data events:

- Insert
- Update
- Delete

Because of their universal scope, triggers are often used to enforce business rules. The Access Upsizing Tools, for example, create triggers to enforce referential integrity between tables on a SQL 4.21 server (which does not include the ability to use Declarative Referential Integrity when creating tables). A trigger and the statement that triggers it are treated as a single transaction by SQL Server, and you can cancel the entire transaction from within the trigger. This allows you to validate data and accept or reject it before the changes are actually made to the table.

You create triggers with the CREATE TRIGGER statement. Unlike CREATE RULE or CREATE DEFAULT, CREATE TRIGGER specifies the table to which the trigger applies. For example, this trigger would print a warning message whenever someone tried to delete a row from the aunames table:

```
CREATE TRIGGER warndelete
ON aunames
FOR DELETE
AS RAISERROR (50001)
```

If you also included ROLLBACK TRANSASCTION in the AS clause of the trigger, it would completely prevent deletions of data from this table.

Moving Access Data to SQL Server

As an Access developer, you probably already have a great deal of data stored in Access tables. In fact, Access developers turning to SQL Server tend to have more data in Access tables than other developers do, as one common reason for upsizing is that a database has become too large and slow to handle in Access any longer. Fortunately, it's relatively easy to move a table from Access to SQL Server. You'll need to follow a four-step process:

1. Install ODBC.

2. Export tables.

3. Set indexes.

4. Link tables.

We'll consider each of these steps in turn.

Installing ODBC

Before you can move any data from Access to SQL Server, you'll need to install some Open Database Connectivity (ODBC) components on your client computer (the one running Access). The ODBC Administrator and ODBC Manager are installed automatically when you do a full install of Access. You'll also need to install a SQL Server ODBC Driver.

SQL Server ODBC drivers have shipped with each version of Access and SQL Server. Generally, you should use the most recent driver that you have available. At the time we're writing this book, that's the version that ships with Access 95. However, a new version with additional enhancements should ship with SQL Server 6.5 when that version is released. You can install an ODBC driver by running Setup from the directory that contains the driver—on the SQL Server CD-ROM, this will be something like \i386\odbc.

In addition to installing the appropriate driver, you'll need to create a database and a data source before you can move tables to a SQL Server. Creating a database can be done with either SQL Enterprise Manager or the CREATE DATABASE Transact-SQL statement, as discussed above. Setting up an ODBC data source is discussed in Chapter 5.

Exporting Tables

Once you have the database and data source in place, exporting tables from Access to SQL Server is simple. Just follow these steps:

1. Open Access and load your database.

2. In the Database Explorer, select the table that you wish to export.

3. Choose File ➤ Save As/Export ➤ To an external File or Database.

4. Select "ODBC Databases" in the "Save as Type" combo box.

5. Choose a name for the exported table.

6. Choose a data source to which to export the table.

This will create a copy of the table on your server and move all of the data from your Access table to your new SQL Server table.

Setting an Index

Exporting an Access table to SQL Server (or any other ODBC database) does not export all of the design information from the Access table. Column names and data types (and the data itself) are exported, but nothing else is. In particular, indexes are not exported. Since the Jet Engine treats any linked table without an index as a read-only table, this presents a problem if you want to continue using these exported tables from your Access database.

To create an index for the exported table, follow these steps:

1. Start SQL Enterprise Manager.

2. Expand the Databases portion of the tree and locate the database containing your table.

3. Expand the Objects and Tables portions of the tree and locate the table you just exported.

4. Right-click on the table and choose Indexes from the context menu.

5. Name the index and choose the columns to be indexed. Click the Add button after selecting each column to include in the index.

6. Check the Unique Keys box in the Index Attributes section

7. Click on the Build button.

This will create a unique index on the specified columns. When you link a SQL Server table to an Access database, Access chooses a primary key for the table by looking at the indexes in a specified order. If the table includes a clustered unique index, Access uses this index as the primary key. Otherwise, Access retrieves the names of all the indexes and uses the alphabetically first index as the primary key.

NOTE If you're using SQL Server 4.21, you won't have SQL Enterprise Manager available to create an index—you'll need to use the CREATE INDEX Transact-SQL statement instead. You can run this statement either directly from ISQL/W or from an Access passthrough query.

Linking Tables

Finally, to use a SQL Server table in Access, you need to link to it. To link to a SQL Server table, follow these steps:

1. Right-click in the Tables tab of Database Explorer in your Access database and choose Link Tables.

2. Select ODBC Databases in the Files of Type combo box.

3. Choose a data source.

4. Log on to the server.

5. Choose the table to which you want to link.

When Access links to a SQL Server table, it includes the name of the database owner (by default, DBO) as a part of the table name. For example, the authors table in the pubs database will be named dbo_authors when you link it. You can change the name seen by the client to anything you want by renaming the table in Access. This will have no effect on its actual name in SQL Server.

Summary

Because all database programs have the same purpose—to store and protect your data—it's not surprising that there are many similarities between Access and SQL Server. However, don't let these similarities fool you, as there are also substantial differences between the two products. In addition to the object differences listed above, there are also differences in SQL Server SQL compared to Jet SQL. You can find further information on these differences in Chapter 4 of this book and in the *Transact-SQL Reference*.

APPENDIX

B

The Companion CD-ROM

The companion CD-ROM contains all of the examples used in this book. It's organized by chapter, with one folder for each chapter that includes samples (not every chapter includes a sample database). This appendix includes instructions for installing the samples on your own computer.

Before you can load the SQL Server samples, you will need to install SQL Server itself. Chapter 10 includes instructions for installing SQL Server 6.0—you cannot open the sample databases under earlier versions.

> **NOTE**   All of the files on the CD-ROM have been saved using the old short file names. When a database is referred to with a different name in the chapters, we've noted that in parentheses after the name used on the CD-ROM.

Chapter 2 Samples: Designing Databases for Client/Server

PS.MDB (Parts and Services.MDB) contains the normalization examples for Chapter 2. This is an Access-only version of this database, and does not involve SQL Server at all.

SQLT.MDB (SQLTransfer.MDB) includes a general-purpose function for moving Access data to SQL Server.

Chapter 3 Samples: Designing Applications for Client/Server

PS2.MDB (Parts and Services.mdb) is the client-server version of the Parts and Services database.

PSDUMP.DAT is a backup of the SQL Server data for the Parts and Services database.

To use these files, you will have to load the PartsAndServices database to your SQL Server, and then relink the tables to the Access database.

To load the PartsAndServices database to your SQL Server:

1. Copy PSDUMP.DAT from the CH03 folder on the CD-ROM to your SQL Server's data directory (by default \SQL60\DATA).

2. Start SQL Enterprise Manager.

3. Right-click on "Dump Devices" in the treeview and select New Dump Device.

4. Name the new dump device "PSDump." Make sure the Disk option button is selected, and click OK.

5. PSDump should appear in the main SQL Enterprise Manager window. If you click on it, you should see a single volume already in it.

6. Right-click on "Database Devices" in the treeview and select New Device.

7. Name the new device PartsAndServices. Choose a drive and path for the new device, make the device 10MB in size, and then click OK to create it.

8. Right-click on Databases and select New Database.

9. Name the new database PartsAndServices, place it on the Parts-AndServices device, and Click OK.

10. Right-click on the PSDump device and select Restore.

11. Expand the PSDump device in the tree and select the Volume 1 backup. Click the Add button to add it to the Restore Locations list, selecting the PartsAndServices database as the destination for the restore. Figure B.1 shows the completed restore dialog.

12. Click Restore.

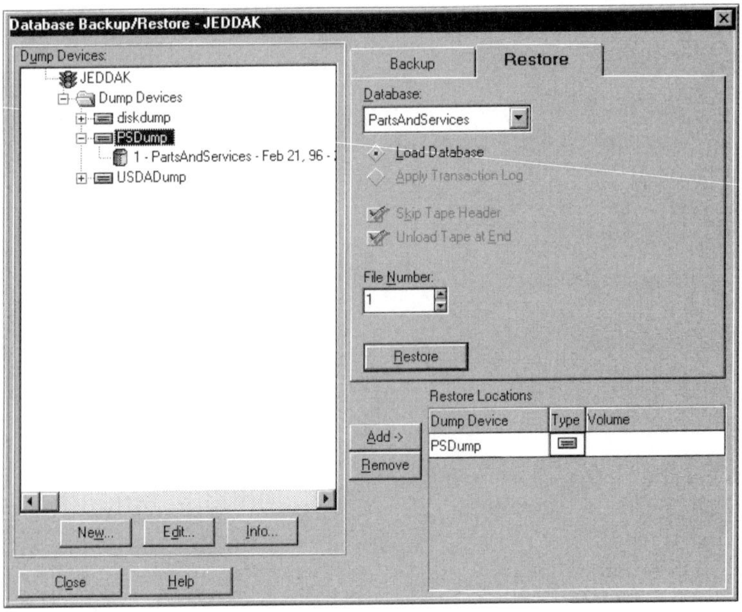

FIGURE B.1:

Restoring the PartsAndServices database

To relink the tables to the Access database:

1. Copy PS2.MDB to your hard drive.

2. Launch Access and load PS2.MDB.

3. Select Tools ➤ Add-Ins ➤ Linked Table Manager.

4. Click Select All to select all of the linked tables, and then click OK.

5. Click Cancel to cancel the default login (this default will point to the development server we used while writing the book). You will have to repeat the Cancel for every table in the database.

6. When you have canceled all of the default logins, you'll see the SQL Data Sources dialog box. Click New to create a new ODBC data source.

7. Select SQL Server as the type of data source to create.

8. Name the new data source Parts and Services, and type the name of your server into the Server combo box.

9. Click the Options button, enter PartsAndServices as the database name, and click OK to create the data source.

10. Select the new data source in the Data Sources dialog and click OK.

11. Enter the login ID and password for your SQL Server administrator account and click OK.

12. The Linked Table Manager will refresh the links when you log in to your server. Close the Linked Table Manager after the tables have been refreshed.

Chapter 5 Samples: Using the ODBC API

CH5ODBC.MDB contains all of the ODBC examples from the chapter.

RDOFORMS.MDB contains the RDO examples from the chapter.

USDADUMP.DAT is a backup of the USDA sample SQL Server database.

To use CH5ODBC.MDB, you will have to load the USDA database to your SQL Server and then relink the tables to the Access database.

To load the USDA database to your SQL Server:

1. Copy USDADUMP.DAT from the CH05 folder on the CD-ROM to your SQL Server's data directory (by default \SQL60\DATA).

2. Start SQL Enterprise Manager.

3. Right-click on "Dump Devices" in the treeview and select New Dump Device.

4. Name the new dump device "USDADump," make sure that the Disk option button is selected, and click OK.

5. USDADump should appear in the main SQL Enterprise Manager window; if you click on it, you should see a single volume already in it.

6. Right-click on "Database Devices" in the treeview and select New Device.

7. Name the new device "USDA." Choose a drive and path for the new device, make the device 15MB in size, and click OK to create the device.

8. Right-click on Databases and select New Database.

9. Name the new database USDA and place it on the USDA device. Click OK.

10. Right-click on the USDADump device and select Restore.

11. Expand the USDADump device in the tree and select the Volume 1 backup. Click the Add button to add it to the Restore Locations list, selecting the USDA database as the destination for the restore.

12. Click Restore.

To relink the tables to the Access database:

1. Copy CH5ODBC.MDB to your hard drive.

2. Launch Access and load CH5ODBC.MDB.

3. Select Tools ➤ Add-Ins ➤ Linked Table Manager.

4. Click Select All to select all of the linked tables, and then click OK.

5. Click Cancel to cancel the default login (this default will point to the development server we used while writing the book). You will have to repeat the Cancel for every table in the database.

6. When you have canceled all of the default logins, you'll see the SQL Data Sources dialog box. Click New to create a new ODBC data source.

7. Select SQL Server as the type of data source to create.

8. Name the new data source "USDA," and type the name of your server into the Server combo box.

9. Click the Options button and enter USDA as the database name. Click OK to create the data source.

10. Select the new USDA data source and click OK.

11. Enter the login ID and password for your SQL Server administrator account and click OK.

12. Close the Linked Table Manager after the tables have been refreshed.

To use the RDOFORMS.MDB sample database, you'll need to refresh the single link to the authors table from the pubs database. You can either follow the instructions above to use the Linked Table Manager to refresh the link, or just delete the existing link and use File ➤ Get External Data ➤ Import to link to your own pubs database.

Chapter 7 Samples: Managing SQL Server with DMO

SQLDEMO.MDB is the SQL Explorer sample application discussed in Chapter 7. SQL Explorer is a tool that uses SQL Distributed Management objects to manage objects of any SQL Server.

Chapter 10 Samples: Installation and Management of Client/Server Applications

CH10.MDB is the sample file of administrative tools discussed in Chapter 10. The chapter contains instructions on using this sample.

HELPMSG.SQL is the SQL Server script to create the user-defined messages used by CH10.MDB.

PRICTOOL.EXE is the Microsoft BackOffice freeware pricing tool. To use it, first copy PRICTOOL.EXE to a new folder on your hard drive, then run PRICTOOL.EXE. It will expand into several files, including SETUP.EXE. Run SETUP.EXE and it will finish setting up the file.

INDEX

Note to the Reader: Throughout this index **boldfaced** page numbers indicate primary discussions of a topic. *Italicized* page numbers indicate illustrations.

D

E

F

G

I

J

K

N

O

P

T

V

W

Workgroup Owner Information dialog
box, 387, *388*

workstations, 404

wrapper functions, **172–178**, 212

wraptest function, **176–177**

wSize value, 141

X

X-Windows system, 9

xBASE products, 18

y

Yes/No datatype, 141

z

zip codes in lookup tables, 49

What's on the Companion CD-ROM

The Companion CD-ROM includes sample files for both Access and SQL Server that demonstrate the programming techniques we cover in the book. These include:

- The Parts and Services database used to demonstrate basic concepts of data normalization and client/server application design (Chapters 2 and 3).
- Examples of ODBC API programming and simulating bound forms with the new Remote Data Objects (Chapter 5).
- SQL Explorer, a tool that uses SQL Distributed Management Objects to manage objects on any SQL Server (Chapter 7).
- Sample code for administering help messages on a SQL Server (Chapter 10).
- The SQL Server pricing tool that helps you pick the most cost-effective licensing scheme for your installation (Chapter 10).
- Several large SQL Server databases to provide test data.

For more information on installing the files from the Companion CD-ROM, see Appendix B.